CORNELL STUDIES IN CLASSICAL PHILOLOGY

EDITED BY
FREDERICK M. AHL * KEVIN C. CLINTON
JOHN E. COLEMAN * W. R. JOHNSON
G. M. KIRKWOOD * GORDON M. MESSING
PIETRO PUCCI

VOLUME XL

From Myth to Icon:
Reflections of Greek Ethical Doctrine in Literature and Art

———————

Lucan: An Introduction
by Frederick M. Ahl

Poetry and Poetics from
Ancient Greece to the Renaissance:
Studies in Honor of James Hutton
edited by G. M. Kirkwood

Early Greek Monody
by G. M. Kirkwood

Temperance adjusting a clock, illustration from *Epître d'Othée* by Christine de Pisan (1450). Oxford, Bodleian Library, MS Laud Misc. 570, fol. 28ᵛ.

FROM MYTH
TO ICON

*Reflections of Greek Ethical
Doctrine in Literature and Art*

HELEN F. NORTH

CORNELL UNIVERSITY PRESS

ITHACA AND LONDON

This book has been published with the aid of a grant from the
Charles Beebe Martin Classical Lectures Fund of Oberlin College.

First published 1979 by Cornell University Press.
Published in the United Kingdom by Cornell University Press Ltd.,
2-4 Brook Street, London W1Y 1AA.

International Standard Book Number 0-8014-1135-1
Library of Congress Catalog Card Number 79-9205
Printed in the United States of America
*Librarians: Library of Congress cataloging information appears
on the last page of the book.*

TO HARRY CAPLAN

...tibi numquam eloquentiae maiorem
tribui laudem quam humanitatis.

Cicero, *De Oratore* 1. 106

Contents

	Preface	11
	Abbreviations	17
1	The Mythology of Sophrosyne	23
2	Politics and Education	87
3	Eloquence	135
4	The Iconography of Sophrosyne	177
	Appendix: Unusual Attributes of Temperantia	265
	Index	269

Plates

Temperance adjusting a clock, manuscript (1450)   *Frontispiece*
  I. *Triumph of Chastity,* painting by Jacopo del Sellaio
     (second half of fifteenth century)   25
 II. *St. Francis in Ecstasy,* painting by Sassetta (ca.
     1440-1444)   43
III. Fortitude and Temperance with representative
     heroes (Samson and Scipio Africanus?), detail of *The
     Seven Virtues,* on a cassone by Francesco Pesellino (ca.
     1460)   85
 IV. Modestia triumphant over Ebrietas, relief, Church
     of St. Peter, Southrop, Gloucestershire (twelfth
     century)   195
  V. Paradise under a mystical form, illustration from
     Speculum Virginum (first half of thirteenth century)   209
 VI. Temperance with sheathed sword by Andrea
     Pisano, detail of south door of Florentine Baptistery
     (1333)   219
VII. Temperance with bridle and compass, sculpture by
     Giovanni Caccini (1583-1584)   224
VIII. Temperance with clock and bridle, detail of tomb of
     François de Lannoy, Folleville (Somme)
     (mid-sixteenth century)   235
 IX. Allegory of Temperance by Domenico Zampiero
     (Domenichino), detail of pendentive of cupola, San
     Carlo ai Catinari, Rome (1628)   247
  X. Illustration from Petrarch's *Triumph of Chastity,* by
     Master of the Vatican Homer (ca. 1480)   251

XI. Initial page, Petrarch's *Triumph of Chastity*, by Master
of the Vatican Homer (ca. 1480)   252

XII. Allegory of Temperance, detail of ceiling by Luca
Giordano, Palazzo Medici-Riccardi, Florence
(1682–1683)   256

XIII. Emblem of Temperance, painting by Jan Simonsz
Torrentius (1614)   261

Preface

When my book *Sophrosyne: Self-Knowledge and Self-Restraint in Greek Literature* was published in 1966, no one except the author, I am sure, suspected that this volume was itself the product of prodigious self-restraint, but such indeed was the case, so many were the subjects excluded from consideration, so inviting were the paths not taken. The temptation to follow at least some of those paths ultimately proved irresistible, and the present volume offers the results of my forays into some areas which, while touched upon in the earlier book, still seemed to me to justify further exploration, this time from a point of view more topical than chronological and with greater attention to contexts in which sophrosyne was but one of several related and interacting moral values.

An invitation to deliver the Charles Beebe Martin Classical Lectures at Oberlin College in 1972 supplied the impetus for renewed study of sophrosyne and other cardinal virtues in a variety of periods and social situations, as they were affected by important trends—moral, political, religious, educational, and iconographic. The resulting lectures, disparate though they may at first glance appear, are unified not only by their preoccupation with one central concept, but also by their common historical framework and the many links that bind their subjects together. Thus the book moves from the archaic Greek myths of Chapter 1 through the political and rhetorical adaptations of the concept of sophrosyne in classical Athens and Rome, treated in the two central chapters, and in the fourth progresses in time through the

Middle Ages and the Renaissance. This last chapter returns for its theme to some of the early myths and exemplary figures and shows how they, together with allegories and symbols popularized in the postclassical period, persisted in religious and secular art down to the close of the eighteenth century. Many of the same figures, whether mythical or historical, recur throughout the book. Like the indestructible, yet ever-changing, concept of sophrosyne iteslf, they remind us of the perennial vitality and capacity for renewal that mark the fundamental insights expressed by the earliest poets and artists of the Greek world.

I have been emboldened to venture into regions remote from those in which a philologist may safely stake a claim by the current and growing interest in interdisciplinary approaches to classical culture and by the need for fresh perspectives that will allow us to examine the achievements of Greece and Rome from a vantage point beyond the familiar chronological frontiers. Since my observations on iconography in Chapter 4 may well remind some readers of the audacious voyages undertaken by those *impiae rates*—impudent little skiffs—whose leap across forbidden shoals Horace in *Odes* 1. 3 pretends to deplore, some apology is due for such a conspicuous act of *hybris,* doubly perverse in a book devoted to sophrosyne.

In my earlier book on the subject, I listed in a brief appendix the principal types of imagery devised by ancient authors to dramatize the concept, mentioning also a few obviously related ways of portraying the derived virtue of *temperantia* in mediaeval and Renaissance art and expressing the intention of someday pursuing this study in greater detail. Such was the genesis of Chapter 4. But the iconography of the cardinal virtues, the Platonic canon to which sophrosyne belongs, scarely begins to be important before the Carolingian era, and any study of the ways in which *temperantia* and other virtues rooted in sophrosyne were portrayed in art must look not only backward to the imagery and allegory of late antiquity, but forward from the Vivian Bible all the way to the emblem books of Alciati and Ripa. There is, in fact, no natural stopping place for one who mines this lode, until the vein itself, at certain periods so rich and various, peters out in the arid stretches of the eighteenth-century reaction against baroque exuberance and the enthusiasms of the Counter Reformation.

The significance of an iconographical study of the virtues and vices, both for its own sake and as a clue to changing attitudes toward the traditional system of values derived in the main from Plato and the Stoics, is self-evident, yet we have had no comprehensive survey for the entire period—more than a millennium—stretching from the *Psychomachia* to the emblem books. There have indeed been notable studies of particular periods, places, and problems: in art history the indispensable works of Emile Mâle, Raimond van Marle, Karl Künstle, and above all Adolf Katzenellenbogen; in literature the magisterial writings of Rosemond Tuve, Samuel Chew, and Lynn White, Jr. To all these I am deeply and obviously indebted. But I have tried to provide something nowhere else available, so far as I know: a kind of Ariadne's thread to serve as a guide through the labyrinthine iconography of sophrosyne/*temperantia* all the way from its beginnings in the coins and sarcophagi of late antiquity to its end in such specimens as the Reynolds window for the Ante Chapel of New College, Oxford, and Canova's tomb for Pope Clement XIV in Rome, both of them dating from the very same time (1785–1787). My study emphasizes the literary sources that inspired new modes of representing the virtues and vices, rather than the strictly formal aspects of their portrayal, and it is offered primarily to philologists and other amateurs of art history, for whom such a survey of sources may, I hope, prove helpful.

The illustrations have been chosen for their relevance both to the iconography of the virtues and to the topics treated in other chapters, especially the first, since the myths related to sophrosyne and *hybris* in ancient times not only become a source of allegory in mediaeval and Renaissance poetry, but often provide a clue to the understanding of pictorial symbolism in painting and sculpture, as when Sassetta in *St. Francis in Ecstasy* uses Alexander the Great as a type of pride, and the illustrators of Petrarch's *Triumph of Chastity* people the procession with such figures as Hippolytus, Lucretia, Verginia, Tuccia, and Scipio Africanus the Elder. I have sought to provide, as often as possible, unhackneyed examples of the iconography of temperance, while referring the reader to easily accessible standard works in which may be found the more familiar illustrations from the *Psychomachia* manuscripts, the Carolingian Bibles, the Romanesque churches, and the baroque tombs.

As was the practice in my earlier book, the noun sophrosyne has been treated as if it were an English word and has normally been transliterated without italics, unless it occurs as part of a Greek sentence or phrase. Related words are italicized and the long vowels indicated by a circumflex. In the adjective, gender and number are distinguished: masculine and feminine singular, *sôphrôn*, plural, *sôphrones;* neuter singular, *sôphron,* plural *sôphrona*. So that the reader will not be distracted by innumerable italicized words, the names of personified virtues and vices in both Greek and Latin, especially when referred to as characters in works of literature or in art, have normally been set in roman type.

Each of these four chapters is based, however remotely, on my doctoral dissertation, written at Cornell in 1945, and I am exceptionally fortunate in having been able to turn again and again for advice and criticism to its two supervisors. To Harry Caplan, who read all four chapters, and to Friedrich Solmsen, whose criticism of Chapter 3 enabled me to remove many questionable judgments and outright errors, I offer my thanks for yet another evidence of magisterial concern and friendship that go back, in my case, over thirty years. My colleague Martin Ostwald read the entire manuscript at an early stage and is responsible for significant improvements in the present version. I acknowledge with gratitude many illuminating discussions in which John F. Callahan has helped me with the interpretation of philosophical texts, the translation of obscure passages in several languages, and the solution of iconographical problems. He, too, has read all four chapters and pointed out errors and infelicities. None of these scholars is to blame for the defects that remain, some doubtless because I failed to heed their *sôphronizôn logos*.

My warm thanks go also to the anonymous readers for the Press, who made perceptive suggestions about organization and continuity, as well as calling attention to sources that I had overlooked and passages that I had misinterpreted. I am particularly indebted to them for helping me to clarify sections of the manuscript that had become increasingly obscure through many revisions.

In a work some parts of which have been in progress for many years it is impossible to acknowledge scrupulously all the help I have received at various stages (and I am uneasily conscious of my failure to name many scholars, especially art historians at the American Academy in Rome, who in the generous spirit characteristic of that institution have answered innumerable questions and advised me about bibliography), but even the briefest litany of praise cannot omit the friends who spent precious time locating, photographing, sketching, and otherwise capturing for me rare and elusive specimens of Temperantia and other virtues: Virginia Babcock, Hilde D. Cohn, Barbara Colbron, Sarah L. Lippincott, Helen M. McCann, Lucy McDiarmid, and Susan B. Snyder.

I wish also to name with grateful affection the two typists who patiently typed and retyped so many drafts of these chapters: my mother, the late Catherine D. North, and my former secretary, Frances W. Slaugh. To my sister, Mary Carol North, I owe unique and special thinks for all manner of help, ranging from typing and photography to those intricate life-support systems on which scholars depend for survival.

I am deeply obliged to the members of the Martin Classical Lecture Committee at Oberlin College—Charles T. Murphy, Nathan Greenberg, and James Helm—who honored me with the invitation to participate in this distinguished series and who have been patient enough to allow me all the time I needed, amid urgent professional obligations, to reshape the original lectures into this book.

Trudie Calvert, as copy editor, bestowed meticulous attention upon the manuscript, which owes much to her care.

I acknowledge also the generous support of the National Endowment for the Humanities, the American Council of Learned Societies, and Swarthmore College during two leaves of absence from teaching (1967–1968 and 1971–1972), when most of the research for the Martin Lectures was done, and additional assistance from the American Council of Learned Societies and Swarthmore College during the summers of 1973 and 1974, when the book was written. Final revisions were made in the summer months of 1977 and 1978, with support from the research fund attached to the William R. Kenan, Jr., Chair at Swarthmore.

Mention of Swarthmore College reminds me of still another debt, harder to define, but never to be forgotten, one that in common with all who served on the faculty in the fifties and sixties I owe to the late Courtney C. Smith and the late Susan P. Cobbs, former president and dean, respectively. As I bring to a conclusion a book begun with their support, it is fitting to express my appreciation for the unfailing encouragement that they gave to scholarly projects such as this one, and for all that they did to make Swarthmore what it was in those halcyon years.

And finally, the dedication of this book betokens the gratitude and affection that I, together with generations of other Cornell classicists and rhetoricians, owe to Harry Caplan.

HELEN F. NORTH

Swarthmore, Pennsylvania

Abbreviations

Books

Bartsch
Adam Bartsch, *Le peintre graveur* (Vienna, 1803–1821), 21 vols.

Burgess
Theodore C. Burgess, "Epideictic Literature," *University of Chicago Studies in Classical Philology* 3 (1902) 82–261.

Chew
Samuel C. Chew, *The Pilgrimage of Life* (New Haven and London, 1962).

D-K
Hermann Diels, *Die Fragmente der Vorsokratiker*, 10th edition, with index, by Walther Kranz (Berlin, 1960–1961).

Evans, *Cluniac Art*
Joan Evans, *Cluniac Art of the Romanesque Period* (Cambridge, Eng., 1950).

Evans, *Mediaeval*
Joan Evans, *Art in Mediaeval France, 987–1498* (Oxford, 1948).

Kaibel
Georg Kaibel, *Epigrammata graeca ex lapidibus conlecta* (Berlin, 1878).

Katzenellenbogen
Adolf Katzenellenbogen, *Allegories of the Virtues and Vices in Mediaeval Art from Early Christian Times to the Thirteenth Century*, trans. Alan J. P. Crick (New York, 1964).

Katzenellenbogen, *Chartres*
Adolf Katzenellenbogen, *The Sculptural Programs of Chartres Cathedral* (New York, 1964).

Kennedy, I	George Kennedy, *The Art of Persuasion in Greece* (Princeton, 1963).
Kennedy, II	George Kennedy, *The Art of Rhetoric in the Roman World, 300 B.C.–A.D. 300* (Princeton, 1972).
Künstle	Karl Künstle, *Ikonographie der christlichen Kunst,* vol. I (Freiburg, 1928).
Mâle, I	Emile Mâle, *Religious Art in France. The Twelfth Century: A Study of the Origins of Medieval Iconography.* Bollingen Series XC. 1 (Princeton, 1978), ed. Henry Bober, trans. Marthiel Matthews.
Mâle, II	Emile Mâle, *L'art religieux du XIIIᵉ siècle en France* (Paris, 1923).
Mâle, III	Emile Mâle, *L'art religieux de la fin du moyen âge en France* (Paris, 1931).
Mâle, IV	Emile Mâle, *L'art religieux après le Concile de Trent* (Paris, 1932).
Meiss	Millard Meiss, ed., *De artibus opuscula XL: Essays in Honor of Erwin Panofsky* (New York, 1961), 2 vols.
Molsdorf	Wilhelm Molsdorf, *Christliche Symbolik der mittelalterlichen Kunst* (Graz, 1968).
Nauck	August Nauck, *Tragicorum Graecorum Fragmenta.* With supplement by Bruno Snell (Hildesheim, 1964).
North	Helen North, *Sophrosyne: Self-Knowledge and Self-Restraint in Greek Literature* (Ithaca, N.Y., 1966).
North, "Temperance"	Helen F. North, "Temperance (Sōphrosynē), and the Canon of the Cardinal Virtues," *Dictionary of the History of Ideas* (New York, 1973), IV, 365–378.
Panofsky, *Studies*	Erwin Panofsky, *Studies in Iconology* (Oxford, 1939).
Panofsky, *Titian*	Erwin Panofsky, *Problems in Titian, Mostly Iconographic* (New York, 1969).

Panofsky, *Tomb Sculpture*	Erwin Panofsky, *Tomb Sculpture: Four Lectures on Its Changing Aspects from Ancient Egypt to Bernini* (New York, 1964).
P.G.	Jacques Paul Migne, *Patrologiae cursus completus: Series graeca* (Paris, 1857–1912).
P.L.	Jacques Paul Migne, *Patrologiae cursus completus: Series latina* (Paris, 1844–1890).
Pope-Hennessy, I	John Pope-Hennessy, *Italian Gothic Sculpture*, rev. ed. (New York, 1972).
Pope-Hennessy, II	John Pope-Hennessy, *Italian Renaissance Sculpture* (London, 1958).
Pope-Hennessy, III	John Pope-Hennessy, *Italian High Renaissance and Baroque Sculpture* (London, 1963).
Porter	Arthur Kingsley Porter, *Lombard Architecture*, vols. I–IV (New Haven, 1915–1917).
PW	Pauly-Wissowa-Kroll, *Real-Encyclopädie der classichen Altertumswissenschaft* (Stuttgart, 1893–).
Réau	Louis Réau, *Iconographie de l'art chrétien*, vols. I–III (Paris, 1955–1959).
Saxl	Fritz Saxl, *Lectures*, vols. I–II (London, 1957).
Schiller	Gertrud Schiller, *Iconography of Christian Art*, vols. I–II, trans. Janet Seligman (New York, 1972).
Schubring	Paul Schubring, *Cassoni: Truhen und Truhenbilder der italienischen Frührenaissance* (Leipzig, 1915).
Seznec	Jean Seznec, *The Survival of the Pagan Gods*, trans. Barbara Sessions (New York, 1953).
s'Jacob	Henriette s'Jacob, *Idealism and Realism: A Study in Sepulchral Symbolism* (Leiden, 1954).
SVF	Johannes von Arnim, *Stoicorum Veterum Fragmenta* (Stuttgart, 1964), 4 vols.
Tervarent	Guy de Tervarent, *Attributs et symboles dans l'art profane 1450–1600: Dictionnaire d'un langage perdu* (Geneva, 1958).

Tuve, *Allegorical Imagery*	Rosemond Tuve, *Allegorical Imagery: Some Mediaeval Books and Their Posterity* (Princeton, 1966).
Tuve, "Virtues" I, II	Rosemond Tuve, "Notes on the Virtues and Vices," Part I, *Journal of the Warburg and Courtauld Institutes* 26 (1963) 264–303; Part II, ibid. 27 (1964) 42–72.
Van Marle	Raimond van Marle, *Iconographie de l'art profane au moyen âge et à la renaissance, et la décoration des demeures*, vols. I–II (New York, 1971).
Wind	Edgar Wind, *Pagan Mysteries in the Renaissance* (London, 1967).

Periodicals

A.J.A.	American Journal of Archaeology
A.J.P.	American Journal of Philology
C.P.	Classical Philology
C.Q.	Classical Quarterly
G.R.B.S.	Greek, Roman, and Byzantine Studies
H.S.C.P.	Harvard Studies in Classical Philology
J.H.S.	Journal of Hellenic Studies
J.R.S.	Journal of Roman Studies
J.W.C.I.	Journal of the Warburg and Courtauld Institutes
Mus. Hel.	Museum Helveticum
P.M.L.A.	Publications of the Modern Language Association
T.A.P.A.	Transactions of the American Philological Association
W.S.	Wiener Studien
Y.C.S.	Yale Classical Studies

FROM MYTH
TO ICON

1

The Mythology
of Sophrosyne

ὁ μάντις 'Αμφιάραος, οὐ σημεῖ' ἔχων
ὑβρισμέν', ἀλλὰ σωφρόνως ἄσημ' ὅπλα

(The seer, Amphiaraus, having no arrogant device,
but a shield modestly unblazoned)
—Euripides, *Phoenissae*, 1111–1112

Petrarch's *Triumph of Chastity*—the second of his six *Trionfi*—
describes the aftermath of a *psychomachia* between Amore and
Pudicizia, a procession in which the triumphant virtue is accompanied not only by a host of allegorical figures representing qualities closely allied with herself, but also by a group of men and
women, some mythological in origin, some biblical, some historical, whose connection lies in their common devotion to chastity.
The triumphal procession, after leaving Cyprus, the island sacred
to Venus, where Chastity has vanquished Love, arrives in Italy at
Baiae, near the ancient home of the Cumaean Sibyl, and makes its
way, first to Liternum in Campania, the place of retirement chosen by Scipio Africanus the Elder, then to Rome, to the temple of
Venus Verticordia (Turner-of-hearts-to-chastity), and finally to
the shrine of Pudicitia Patricia, where Hippolytus and Joseph
guard the door. The attendants of Pudicizia include Penelope, the
perennial ideal of the faithful wife, Lucretia and Verginia, the
most illustrious Roman exemplars of chastity, and Judith, the
biblical type of *sobrietas* and *castitas*. Others who share the triumph
are Dido (according to the legend that made her faithful to

Sychaeus), the Vestal Tuccia, the Sabine Queen Hersilia, Hippo of Crete, who cast herself into the sea to escape from Minos, and the Teutonic women, who, when captured by Marius, preferred death to slavery.

Artists inspired by this popular theme added details freely to the scene described by Petrarch. Most important among the later additions is the triumphal chariot drawn by unicorns (which are not mentioned by Petrarch; only in the case of the first triumphator, Amore, does he prescribe a chariot), but also included are significant new figures connected with *pudicitia* in legend or history. Plate I, a painting on a cassone by Jacopo del Sellaio (1442–1493), shows on the triumphal car not only the victorious Pudicizia herself and the fettered Amore, but also Temperantia (on the right) who proclaims her identity by pouring water into a vessel of wine.[1] Pudicizia herself is portrayed as Petrarch's Laura; her attendants are engaged in some of the traditional activities of Amore's foes—breaking his bow and plucking feathers from his wings, as well as binding his hands behind his back. A sixteenth-century engraving by George Pencz puts a sphinx beside Pudicizia's throne.[2] (In the original poem the only symbolic animal linked with Chastity is the ermine on her banner.) An early sixteenth-century Flemish tapestry shows the procession passing an elaborate shrine that contains a statue of Diana, goddess of chastity, flanked by two worshipers, presumably Hippolytus and Joseph.[3]

The range of figures included in such pictures and the varied sources from which they come suggest the scope of the mythology that grew up around the concept of sophrosyne, the Greek original of Petrarch's *pudicizia*. Patterns of myth and mythical figures illustrating the principal aspects of this virtue add to our knowledge of the ways in which it was interpreted at various times and by authors working in different literary genres. The purpose of

[1]See Van Marle, II, 111 ff., and cf. Schubring, No. 373. The iconography of the Triumph of Chastity is further discussed in Chapter 4. See also D. D. Carnicelli, *Lord Morley's Tryumphes of Fraunces Petrarcke* (Cambridge, Mass., 1971) 38–46.

[2]Van Marle, II, Fig. 134. For the sphinx as a symbol of restraint associated with *Temperantia,* see Chapter 4.

[3]Ibid., 128.

Plate I. Triumph of Chastity by Jacopo del Sellaio (second half of fifteenth century), Museo Bandini, Fiesole. Alinari/Editorial Photocolor Archives.

this chapter is, first, to identify the principal categories of myths concerned with sophrosyne and offer some examples, then to examine the principal figures, human or divine, who represent important facets of the virtue. Certain of the human figures are historical rather than genuinely mythical, and for that reason all the more interesting, since they demonstrate the ease with which fact passes into legend. The Elder Scipio will serve as an example. A few figures are ambiguous in that they exemplify sophrosyne in some of their actions, while in others they are types of *hybris* or another antithetical vice. Bellerophon and Alexander the Great are notable in this respect. To afford an idea of the way mythical figures might change in the course of centuries, we shall look at that notoriously protean figure, Odysseus. Some characteristic ways in which myths related to sophrosyne were employed by certain authors will be noticed, and we shall also observe how philosophers created new myths out of old materials to dramatize their ethical doctrines.

The myths fall into four broad categories: (1) the punishment of *hybris*, (2) the *sôphrôn* hero, (3) the *sôphrôn* heroine, and (4) philosophical myth. Within the limited scope of this chapter it will not be possible to list every myth in each category, nor to trace individual myths to their ultimate origin. In most cases the origin of a mythical figure or pattern is of less consequence for our purposes than its interpretation at a particular period or by a particular author. Our focus will not be on the myth for its own sake, but on its capacity to enlarge our understanding of sophrosyne.

THE PUNISHMENT OF *HYBRIS*

It is tempting to begin with still another category, order out of chaos. This might be justified by the relation established as early as the fifth century B.C. between sophrosyne and such concepts as *kosmos* (order) and *taxis* (regularity), illustrated in tragedy by the regular procession of the seasons and the alternation of opposites, both of which were offered as a model for human behavior by the tragic poets (Sophocles, *Ajax* 670–677, Euripides, *Phoenissae* 541–544). The great speech of deception in which Ajax describes the inexorable process of mutability in nature concludes with the admission that "We" (Ajax and all mankind) must learn *sôphronein* (to accept limits), while Jocasta in the *Phoenissae*, after explaining to Eteocles the operation of *isotês* (equality) and regular alternation in human life and in the heavens, warns him against injustice and *pleonexia* (overreaching), adding that sufficiency is enough for the *sôphrones* (the modest or moderate ones). In each case the poet reminds us of the example of the natural order only to have the tragic character—Ajax, Eteocles—violate it.

Plato actually identified sophrosyne with the principle of order that holds together heaven and earth, gods and men (*Gorgias* 506C–508C). The possibilities inherent in such myths as the warfare of the gods and Titans, or the gods and Giants, even before the philosophers took them up, are suggested by what Pindar does in the *First Pythian*, when he equates the victory of Zeus over Typhon with that of the Greeks over the Persians, the Carthaginians, and the Etruscans, hence of civilization over barbarism, and ultimately harmony over discord, order over chaos. The sculptors of archaic and classical times expressed the same insight at Selinus, Delphi, Athens, Olympia, Bassae, and many other temple sites, using the Centauromachy and comparable stories. But the principal myths that belong to this category—the Titanomachy, Gigantomachy, and Centauromachy, plus the warfare of the Greeks against the Amazons—can be brought under the rubric of the punishment of *hybris* (wantonness, arrogance, defiance of the gods, contempt for the rights of others), and there the principle of economy makes it preferable to leave them, though with the reminder that myths in which a cosmic battle banishes forces that are in some way violent, primitive, or chaotic and establishes the supremacy of order and civilization are far older than Homer, common to the Greeks and many other peoples in the Mediterranean and regions to the East,[4] and obviously antedate the development of such quintessentially Hellenic concepts as *hybris* and sophrosyne.

The interpretation of the Gigantomachy and related myths to

[4]See Joseph Fontenrose, *Python: A Study of Delphic Myth and Its Origins* (Berkeley and Los Angeles, 1959), for an analysis of this type of myth and an attempt to link the slaying of the Python with a number of other stories, Greek and non-Greek, that reflect the struggle between chaos and *kosmos*.

mean the defeat of *hybris* becomes a commonplace in the poetry of
Bacchylides and Pindar in the early fifth century; presumably
their implication is the same in contemporary vase painting and
relief sculpture. In the fifteenth *Ode* of Bacchylides, Menelaus,
after praising the Hesiodic trinity of Justice (Dikê), Good Order
(Eunomia), and Peace (Eirênê), tells the Trojans that *hybris* destroyed the Giants, the sons of Earth (59–63), and Pindar in the
Eighth Pythian cites Porphyrion, King of the Giants, as one
punished for *hybris* (12–20). The poet of the *Odyssey* had already
characterized the Giants as a violent race (*laon atasthalon*, 7.
60), but the earliest specific reference to the Gigantomachy in literature seems to be Pindar, *Nemean* 1. 67 f. (probably 476 B.C.).[5]

The Titans and the Giants, often confused even in antiquity,
are alike in representing forces more brutish, violent, and un-
civilized than the Olympian gods who overcame them. The Centaurs in an obvious way symbolize the bestial elements that mingle
with the human in mankind. The Amazons come to represent
hybris for reasons that grow out of the role considered proper for
women in Greek society; hence their defeat by the Greeks under Theseus is just as much a victory for sophrosyne as is the
triumph of the Lapiths over the drunken and lustful Centaurs.[6]
When Phidias adorned his statue of Athena Parthenos with scenes
from the Centauromachy, the Amazonomachy, and the Gigantomachy, and when the Parthenon metopes were made to show
the Gigantomachy on the east, the Centauromachy on the south,
the Amazonomachy on the west, and the Trojan War on the
north, observers read a moral and political significance highly
flattering to Athens.[7] But other cities and other shrines used the

[5]See Francis Vian, *La guerre des géants* (Paris, 1952), for evidence in literature
and art. No true Gigantomachy in art is recognized before the second quarter of
the sixth century B.C. For an example at the other end of antiquity, consult
Wladimiro Dorigo, *Late Roman Painting* (New York and Washington, 1971) Plates
108, 109: the Giants struck by lightning, Piazza Armerina.

[6]See below for the contrast drawn by the Emperor Julian between the *sôphrôn*
Penelope and the Amazons (*Or.* 3. 127C–128B). On the continuing significance of
Theseus' victory over the Amazons as a symbol of the victory of virtue over vice,
wisdom over appetite, consult D. W. Robertson, *A Preface to Chaucer* (Princeton,
1962) 265.

[7]The significance of the Parthenon metopes is discussed by C. J. Herington,
Athena Parthenos and Athena Polias (Manchester, 1955) 60–62; for the Phidian re-

same myths, for the moral content, if not the political, was universal. Such myths as these provided the Greeks with their first common artistic idiom where the virtues were concerned.

Nor should we forget, in considering this type of myth, the many individual heroes who achieve in single combat with some monster the equivalent of a Centauromachy; sometimes, as in the case of Heracles' victory over Nessus, it indeed is a Centauromachy. Bellerophon and the Chimaera, Perseus and the Gorgon, Theseus and the Minotaur, whatever their divergent origins, ultimately conveyed the same meaning, and in the later history of allegory the individual heroes become more significant than groups of combatants in symbolizing the victory of virtue over vice, since this war is one that every soul must wage alone. The Neoplatonists understood this concept clearly, and Iamblichus cites Bellerophon as an exemplar of sophrosyne, not because he rejected the advances of Stheneboea, but because he slew the Chimaera and thus did away with a whole tribe of wild, bestial, untamed elements. So, too, Perseus, guided by Athena, cut off the head of the Gorgon and according to Iamblichus reached the very summit of sophrosyne.[8]

One further aspect of the Gigantomachy is important for interpreting the mythology of sophrosyne, and this is the fact that each of the Olympian gods who fights on the side of Zeus thereby becomes a *sôphronistês*—a castigator—even such unlikely deities as Dionysus and Aphrodite. Athena is the most prominent, after Zeus himself, and naturally her victory over Pallas and Enceladus is celebrated incessantly in Athenian art, but not only there. The metopes at Selinus and Delphi show that the meaning of her victory over the Giants was appreciated far beyond the boundaries of Attica.

The second mythical pattern illustrating the punishment of *hybris* overlaps at certain points the first. In this type a lesser being

---

liefs on the sandals and shield of the goddess, see p. 65. Richard Brilliant, *Arts of the Ancient Greeks* (New York, 1973) 170, contrasts the Centauromachies of the Parthenon and Olympia with respect to the ability of the Centaurs to profit by their experience (that is, to learn sophrosyne). See pp. 196–197 for the south and west metopes of the Parthenon as symbolizing the victory of sophrosyne.

[8]τὸ ἀκρότατον ... τῆς σωφροσύνης ἀγαθόν, Iamblichus, *Letter to Arete on Sophrosyne* (Stobaeus 5. 46, 47) vol. III Hense.

(usually a mortal) offends a god by claiming to be his superior in some respect or by trying to steal his special gift or prerogative. Some of the most famous examples are Niobe, Asclepius, Salmoneus, Marsyas, Thamyris, and Arachne. Although some such figures make a relatively late appearance in literature (Arachne, for example[9]), others are well known to Homer, who freely alters still earlier versions to suit his own needs and thus becomes the first poet known to use mythology for the purpose of exemplification.[10] Niobe and Bellerophon figure in such manipulations of more ancient tradition.[11] All the sinners being punished in *Odyssey* 11. 576–600 (Tityus, Tantalus, and Sisyphus) have committed some offense against the gods that is later interpreted as *hybris*. Yet the *akmê* of their exemplary value comes, not in the epic period, but in the sixth and fifth centuries, for reasons that led at the same time to the heightened influence of Apollo, the popularity of the sayings of the Seven Wise Men, and the wide circulation of the Delphic maxims "Know thyself" and "Nothing in excess."[12]

Closely related is a third mythical pattern in which a mortal seeks to bridge the abyss that separates men from gods. This form of *hybris*, which defies the Apolline injunction to think mortal thoughts, is often expressed in terms of seeking to marry a goddess or scale the brazen heavens, or both. The warning against marriage to a goddess, which may have originated with Pittacus, one of the Seven Wise Men,[13] is first encountered in the seventh

[9]Known chiefly from Ovid, *Metam.* 6. 5–145, and rarely portrayed in ancient art. Exceptions include a Corinthian aryballos of ca. 600 B.C. and the frieze of the Forum of Nerva in Rome. Consult Gladys D. Weinberg and Saul Weinberg, *The Aegean and the Near East: Studies Presented to Hetty Goldman* (Locust Valley, N.Y., 1956) 262–267.

[10]Homer's manipulation of myth is discussed by M. M. Willcock, *C.Q.* 14 (1964) 141–154, and B. K. Braswell, *C.Q.* 21 (1971) 16–26.

[11]On Niobe in *Iliad* 24 see Willcock. T. B. L. Webster, *From Mycenae to Homer* (London, 1958) 186, suggests that the story of Bellerophon, as told in *Iliad* 5, comes from an earlier catalogue poem in which he, with Peleus and Lycurgus, was an entry in a list illustrating the mutability of human fortune. See also Julia H. Gaisser, *T.A.P.A.* 100 (1969) 175.

[12]For some possible reasons, consult E. R. Dodds, *The Greeks and the Irrational* (Berkeley, 1951) 75, and A. R. Burn, *The Lyric Age of Greece* (New York, 1967) 207–209, 217.

[13]The suggestion is made by A. E. Raubitschek, *W. S.* 71 (1958) 170–172; the proverb does not occur in any of the fragments ascribed to Pittacus. Consult J. T.

century B.C. in the poetry of Alcman (1. 16–18 Page); it occurs in
the fifth century in Pindar (*Pyth.* 2. 21–48) with specific reference
to Ixion, one of the paradigmatic sinners punished in Hades,
though not mentioned in *Odyssey* 11. Ixion attempted to rape
Hera, was deluded by Zeus into making love to a cloud shaped
like the goddess, and thus begot the race of Centaurs. Pindar
emphasizes the exemplary function of this and similar myths.
Ixion, whirling on the wheel, "gives this lesson to mankind," and
"he received a message common to all."[14] Such cautionary *exempla*
are not mere embroidery; they are integral to the Pindaric epini-
cian, whose moral affinity for the Apolline code consistently
reveals itself in stories related to self-knowledge and "mortal
thoughts."

Scaling the brazen heavens is separated from marrying a goddess in the myth of Bellerophon. His effort to reach the realm of
the gods on the back of Pegasus is the most literal example of this
form of *hybris* and the one that surpassed all other myths of its
type in the impression it made on posterity. The winged horse is
among the earliest orientalizing motives to enter Greek art in the
eighth century, but only in Greece is the winged horse bridled and
mounted, thanks to Athena Chalinitis, who gave to Bellerophon
the means of mastering and guiding Pegasus.[15]

Since the tragic impulse of the fifth century often springs directly from the myth of *hybris* and its consequences, it is not surprising that many tragedies were based on stories of the type we
are considering, which dealt with the catastrophic results of over-
stepping limits, whether human or divine. Aeschylus makes this

---

Sheppard, *The Oedipus Tyrannus of Sophocles* (Cambridge, Eng., 1920) lxv–lxvi, on
the relation of the *topos* to sophrosyne and see Euripides, *I.A.* 543–545 and Frg.
503 Nauck.

[14]Cf. *Pyth.* 3. 61–62, where the punishment of Asclepius inspires the poet to
warn his own *psychê* not to seek the *bios athanatos*, immortal life.

[15]See J. J. Dunbabin, *Studies Presented to David Moore Robinson* II (St. Louis, 1953)
1164–1184, on the myth of Pegasus, who appears on Corinthian coins long before
Bellerophon and the Chimaera, and Marcel Détienne, *History of Religions* 11
(1971) 161–184, on the cult of Athena Chalinitis, known in Corinth in the seventh
century. The great popularity of the Bellerophon story in vase painting is due to
Euripides' tragedies, *Bellerophon* and *Stheneboea*, although the earliest illustrations
of the myth go back to the seventh century. See M. L. Schmitt, *A.J.A.* 70 (1966)
341–347.

type of *hybris* myth more central than does any other tragic poet whose works survive, but Sophocles, too, wrote a *Niobe* and a *Thamyris* (close to the date of his *Ajax,* in which he emphasizes that hero's offense against Athena through the hybristic boast that he will conquer without the help of the gods). Euripides wrote not only a *Bellerophon,* but also an *Ixion* and a *Phaethon,* all of them based on the *hybris* myth, and at the very end of his life he made the story of Pentheus, in the *Bacchae,* conform closely to this pattern.

In all these myths the effect of the story is to demonstrate the folly of *hybris* and the wisdom of self-restraint; the paradigm serves the purpose later described by the orators with the phrase *sôphronizein tous allous*[16]—to "sophronize," instill sophrosyne in everyone else. Homer had already ascribed this function to Apollo in *Iliad* 5, when the god warns Diomedes against continuing to attack him, because "never alike are the tribe of immortal gods and men who move on the ground" (440–442). The sophrosyne instilled by such warnings and examples is the kind that teaches men to "think mortal thoughts." Every god when offended becomes a *sôphronistês,* and it is not part of the pattern that the *sôphronistês* himself be *sôphrôn.* More often than not, the offended god is cruel and excessive, like Zeus in the *Prometheus Bound,* Apollo in the myth of Marsyas, Athena in punishing Arachne. In the mind of a poet interested in theology such a situation could arouse bold speculation on the mystery of divinity; some results are Aeschylus' treatment of Zeus in the Prometheus trilogy and Euripides' ambiguous picture of Dionysus in the *Bacchae.* The cruel Athena of Sophocles' *Ajax* is not given an extended treatment, but the contrast between the vengeful goddess and the *sôphrôn* Odysseus in the Prologue cannot have escaped many who saw or read the play.

Under the rubric of the *hybris* myth we may subsume still another pattern, this one especially fruitful in Sophoclean tragedy, that of the hero at odds with society. This type of myth is a secondary development, possible only after the growth of the city-state (although foreshadowed in certain important ways by

[16]See below, p. 163.

Achilles). The high-minded (*gennaios*) hero in Sophoclean tragedy, willing to sacrifice everything else to preserve whatever in his view makes life worth living, is indeed heroic in contrast to his conventionally moralizing counselors, the representatives of society, the *polis*, but he typically goes to some extreme of individualism in pursuit of his own *aretê*, incompatible with the apparent interest of the community, and suffers a catastrophe in which delusion is blended with excess.[17]

THE *SÔPHRÔN* HERO

This category of myth has numerous subdivisions that are helpful in separating the different strands in the closely woven fabric of sophrosyne. The chronological order in which they achieve prominence in literature and art is itself a clue to the historical changes in the concept.

The first and most widespread myth of masculine sophrosyne—found all over the world, not just in Greece—is that of the chaste young man who repels the amorous advances of an older, married woman. This story, best known in the episode of Joseph and Potiphar's wife, actually belongs to folklore; its ubiquity is indicated by the many variants recorded by Stith Thompson[18] and others. In the Greek tradition Bellerophon, Hippolytus, and Peleus all enact the role of Joseph in Egypt, and each version of the myth is marked by certain elements that are specifically Greek, in addition to the core that is worldwide. The Greek element is usually some ironic counterbalance that cancels the hero's achievement and nullifies his glory.

Bellerophon, as suggested above, was an ambiguous figure even in Homer. When Glaucus narrates to Diomedes how his ancestor rejected the wife of his host (Anteia or Stheneboea in different versions) and enumerates his subsequent exploits, including the conquest of the Chimaera, he omits certain elements

---

[17]On this Sophoclean theme, see North, 51 ff.

[18]*Motif-Index of Folk-Literature* (Bloomington, 1955–1958) IV, 474. See also John D. Yohannan, *Joseph and Potiphar's Wife in World Literature* (New York, 1968), and Myles Dillon, *Irish Sagas* (Cork, 1968) 162–175. For folklore elements in the Bellerophon myth consult Rheinhold Stromberg, *Classica et Mediaevalia* 22 (1961) 1–15.

that might reflect discredit on Bellerophon and never mentions Pegasus,[19] perhaps because the winged horse was too vivid a reminder of the *hybris* that caused Bellerophon's disaster. Pindar, when praising Bellerophon's exploits—as a compliment to Corinth—in the thirteenth *Olympian Ode* (91), refers only cryptically to the hero's fate, but elsewhere tells it, as a cautionary tale, in the *Seventh Isthmian,* which honors a Theban athlete.[20] Euripides, who found this myth singularly congenial to his iconoclastic temperament, wrote both a *Stheneboea* and a *Bellerophon,* the first evidently emphasizing the sophrosyne (chastity) of the hero, the second his *hybris.* A fragment of the *Stheneboea* (672 Nauck) is a prayer for the *sôphrôn erôs* that leads to excellence; references to Stheneboea herself, along with Phaedra, in Old Comedy, leave little doubt that the emphasis in this play was like that in the first *Hippolytus.* A fragment from the *Bellerophon* (285 Nauck) speaks of the former prosperity of the hero, in contrast to his present woe; presumably the emphasis in this play was on the hero's downfall.[21]

Bellerophon appears often on vase paintings, especially under the stimulus of Euripides' *Stheneboea,* and also enjoyed a tremendous vogue in mosaics. The earliest figure mosaic with a mythological scene—a pebble mosaic from Olynthus, around 400 B.C.—shows Bellerophon on Pegasus, killing the Chimaera.[22] In the later, philosophical tradition, as we have noted, Bellerophon became a symbol of sophrosyne, not because of his repulse of

---

[19]See Gaisser, *art. cit.,* for omitted details and possible reasons.

[20]Horace, too, separates the key elements in the Bellerophon myth. In *Odes* 4. 11. 25-29 he links Phaethon and Bellerophon as warnings *ut te digna sequare* and says that winged Pegasus *exemplum grave praebet.* In *Odes* 3. 7. 13-20 he links Bellerophon and Peleus as exemplars of chastity; the one is *nimis castus* (14-15), the other *abstinens* (18). See Juvenal 10. 325, where Hippolytus and Bellerophon exemplify chastity.

[21]See T. B. L. Webster, *The Tragedies of Euripides* (London, 1967) 80-84, 109-111, for reconstructions of the plots of the two plays.

[22]See D. M. Robinson, *A.J.A.* 36 (1932) 12-24. The same scene occupies the central zone of the dining room of the late fourth-century Roman villa at Lullingstone, Kent; see Dorigo (above, note 5), Plate 206. The moral implications of this myth in its appearances in mosaics are discussed by Jacques Aymard, *Gallia* 11 (1953) 249-271.

Stheneboea, but because of his conquest of the Chimaera, which had come to be identified with the passions.[23]

The myth of Hippolytus is known in literature only from the fifth century B.C., and it seems likely that the ironic treatment of the hero, as a *sôphrôn hybristês*—*sôphrôn* in his fanatical chastity, hybristic in his fanatical intolerance—is Euripides' own contribution. But the cult—as distinguished from the myth—existed in Trozen from pre-Dorian times, its most prominent aspect being the ceremony in which girls about to be married offered their newly cut hair at the hero's tomb. W. S. Barrett suggests that the folktale of Potiphar's wife was linked with the hero cult to explain these symbolic offerings, which at other shrines in the Greek world are made to virgins who died before marriage.[24]

The myth of Peleus, selected to wed Thetis because he was the most chaste of all men, as he had proved by his rejection of Astydamia, the wife of Acastus, also provided the subject for a lost play by Euripides. The irony in his myth is of a different kind from that in the stories of Bellerophon and Hippolytus. In his case it is rather that his incomparable happiness (marriage to a goddess, the Nereid, Thetis, with full consent of the gods, most of whom attended his wedding) was nullified by the tragic fate of their son, Achilles. Pindar links Peleus with Cadmus (husband of Harmonia, father of Semele, grandfather of Pentheus) in the *Third Pythian* (86–103) because of the likeness both of their glorious weddings and of their tragic offspring. Euripides' play, how-

[23]The popularity of the bridle as a symbol of restraint guaranteed that Bellerophon would flourish in the emblem books; see, for example, Cesare Ripa, *Iconologia* (Venice, 1645) 671–673. For a seventeenth-century instance of the slaying of the Chimaera used as a moral *exemplum* in the Palazzo Barberini, Rome, according to a program supplied by Pope Urban VIII, see Jennifer Montagu, *J.W.C.I.* 34 (1971) 366–372.

[24]W. S. Barrett, *Euripides, Hippolytos* (Oxford, 1964); see pages 3–6 on the cult, 6–15 on the legend. The importance of virginity (or at least celibacy), whether perpetual or periodic, for the efficacy of certain rituals is well attested. Consult E. Fehrle, *Die kultische Keuschheit im Altertum* (Giessen, 1910) 95. Kenneth J. Reckford, *T.A.P.A.* 103 (1972) 415–421, suggests that Hippolytus may have been, in earlier times, an attendant on Aphrodite, even the Dying God, and that he came to symbolize the loss of innocence, the sadness, and the separation inevitable in marriage.

ever, is likely to have concentrated on the episode of the wife of
Acastus, and it is as a type of chastity that Peleus is celebrated,
most notoriously in Aristophanes' *Clouds,* where—after the Just
Argument has praised him as the model of sophrosyne—the Unjust Argument pokes fun at him and represents Thetis' desertion
of her husband as a reproach to his excessive virtue (1063 ff.).[25]

Of the three heroes, Hippolytus survived in literature and art as
the preeminent type of the *sôphrôn* youth, probably because in the
case of Bellerophon the story of Pegasus and the Chimaera was
more memorable, while in Peleus' case it was the marriage with
Thetis, rather than the earlier episode of Astydamia, that caught
the imagination. On Roman sarcophagi Hippolytus is a favorite
subject.[26] Often the scene of attempted seduction by Phaedra is
balanced by a hunting scene, which may symbolize the conquest of
the passions; such, at least, is the effect ascribed to the presence of
this *sôphrôn* huntsman in the neighborhood of wild-beast hunts on
late Roman mosaics.[27] In Latin literature, both classical and
mediaeval, the mention of Hippolytus evokes a whole train of
associations. Thus Horace in *Odes* 4. 7. 25–28:

> Infernis neque enim tenebris Diana pudicum
> liberat Hippolytum

[25]In Pindar, *Isth.* 8, the Aeacids as a family are credited with the cardinal virtues,
and Peleus is specifically commended for his piety (*eusebeia*). In *Nem.* 5. 32 ff., as
Jacob Stern observes, *C.P.* 66 (1971) 169–173, Peleus is unlike Hippolytus: he
repels Astydamia, not because her seductive address fails to arouse him, but because he fears Zeus Xenius, the protector of hospitality.

[26]Consult Carl Robert, *Die antiken Sarkophag-Reliefs* III (Berlin, 1904) 169–219.
Only the virtue, not the *hybris,* of Hippolytus is commemorated on these reliefs.
The episode in which he was restored to life by Asclepius seems not to be repre-
sented.

[27]See Xenophon, *Cynegeticus* 1. 11, for Hippolytus as an exemplar of sophrosyne
in a treatise exalting the chase. For the mosaics consult Doro Levi, *Antioch Mosaic
Pavements* (Princeton, 1947) I, 340. See Fig. 136, for the *Megalopsychia* mosaic (ca.
A.D. 450), which shows six male figures fighting wild animals. All have mythological names, and Hippolytus is among them. See also Vol. II, Plate LXXVIII c. For
another Antioch mosaic, showing Phaedra and Hippolytus, in which she is portrayed in the attitude of a *Pudicitia*-figure, see Vol. II, Plate XI b. Kurt Weitzman,
Dumbarton Oaks Papers 14 (1960) 43–68, discusses the portrayal of Hippolytus and
Phaedra in ancient, Byzantine, and mediaeval art, showing how this myth and that
of Joseph and Potiphar's wife contaminated each other in iconography.

nec Lethaea valet Theseus abrumpere caro
vincula Perithoo.[28]

The final stanza of the *Ode* brings together two examples of dead heroes, Hippolytus and Perithous, who would surely be restored to life, if such a thing were possible. They are subtly contrasted: Hippolytus is chaste (*pudicus*), Perithous (elsewhere in Horace *amatorem . . . Pirithoum, Odes* 3. 4. 79–80) is *carus*, beloved. Since he is in Hades because he attempted to carry off Persephone, the adjective *pudicus* could not be applied to him. But Hippolytus is in Hades precisely because he was *pudicus*. The two dead youths are polar opposites; hence the application of death's inexorable law to both assures us that there can be no exceptions.[29]

Much simpler is the allusion to Hippolytus in the twelfth-century Confession of the Archpoet, where the mere use of his name, without a qualifying adjective, is sufficient to demonstrate the wickedness of the university town, Pavia:

Si ponas Hippolytum hodie Papiae,
non erit Hippolytus in sequenti die.[30]

Although the type of chaste hero represented by Hippolytus existed before the time of Homer (as we know from his use of the myth of Bellerophon), such a youth could not have been called *sôphrôn* until that word began to be applied to the restraint of the appetites, a development that is not complete, where men are concerned, until the late fifth century. (It designates feminine

---

[28]"For neither does Diana free from the shades of Hell chaste Hippolytus, Nor can Theseus tear Lethaean chains away from his dear Pirithous."

[29]Cf. the implications of *saophrôn* in the epitaph for Eubulus by Leonidas of Tarentum, *Anth. Pal.* 7. 452: "Remember sober [*saophrôn*] Eubulus, you who pass by, and let us drink, for common to all is the harbor of Hades."

[30]"If you put Hippolytus in Pavia today, tomorrow he will not be Hippolytus" (F. J. E. Raby, *The Oxford Book of Mediaeval Latin Verse* [Oxford, 1959] 264). For additional twelfth-century instances of Hippolytus as an exemplar of chastity, see the *Architrenius* of Jean of Hanville (ed. Thomas Wright, *Anglo-Latin Satirical Poets* [London, 1872] I, 387) and the *Anticlaudianus* of Alain de Lille (ed. Robert Bossuat [Paris, 1955] VII, 115–116), where Ypolitus and Joseph (together with Helyas=Elias) represent *Pudor*.

virtue much earlier, even in the archaic age.) But the second type of *sôphrôn* hero illustrates what might be called the etymological meaning of the word sophrosyne, the fundamental soundness of mind, good sense, or even shrewdness implied by the word in Homer. Mythical figures who represent this "prudential" type of sophrosyne naturally come early. The first exemplar in Greek literature is Rhadamanthys of Crete (best known as one of the judges in the Underworld), whom Theognis, the elegiac poet of Megara in the sixth century B.C., celebrates for his sophrosyne,[31] together with two other figures always noted for shrewdness combined with persuasive powers: Sisyphus and Nestor (699–718).[32]

By the time of Plato, Nestor has also become an exemplar of sophrosyne, principally because the virtue is so often linked with the wisdom of age, and he is the oldest and wisest of the heroes at Troy. Furthermore, he becomes the prototype of the *sôphrôn* adviser, the *sôphronistês* who plays a part in Graeco-Roman political theory.[33]

The intellectual *aretê* of sophrosyne is a virtue appropriate for teachers. In the fifth century it is ascribed to the teacher of heroes, Chiron the Centaur, whom Pindar in one *Ode* terms *sôphrôn* (*Pyth*. 3. 63), in another *bathymêtis* (deep-thinking, *Nem*. 3. 53).[34] Socrates, the embodiment of the Delphic *Gnôthi sauton*, was a type of sophrosyne in the intellectual as well as in the moral sense. It could not be otherwise, given the origin of Platonic ethical doctrine in the Socratic equation of *aretê* and *epistêmê*. Socrates

[31]Rhadamanthys later appears in Pindar as a type of wisdom; in *Pyth*. 2. 74 he is said to have won for his part the blameless fruit of wisdom (*phrenes*), and in *Ol*. 2. 75–76 he is counselor to the great father (Cronus) in the Isles of the Blessed. In *Od*. 7. 323 ff. the Phaeacians take him to visit Tityus in Euboea, an unexplained mission which Eustathius decided was intended to "sophronize" Tityus (*Commentarii ad Homeri Odysseam* [Hildesheim and New York, 1970] I., 1581).

[32]Theognis emphasizes the eloquence of Sisyphus in persuading Persephone (704); Nestor, too, is introduced as a type of eloquence, so effective as to make false things seem true (713; cf. the boast of the Muses in Hesiod, *Theogony* 27).

[33]See *Laws* 710A-711E and below, p. 116. For sophrosyne as the virtue of old age, see North, 20, note 67. On Nestor's sophrosyne, consult Werner Jaeger, *Paideia*, I. 48 (trans. Gilbert Highet [New York, 1945]).

[34]For a long list of heroes taught by Chiron and the virtues ascribed to each, see Xenophon, *Cyneg*. 1. 1–16.

as the exemplar of sophrosyne in the intellectual sense appears in the *Charmides,* where, however, the profound moral and even political implications of the word are already apparent.

The example of Socrates demonstrates how difficult it is to distinguish sharply between the intellectual and the moral. The distinction is artificial at best, because the two aspects are inextricably mingled in sophrosyne, as in *phronêsis,* and when either of these concepts acquired new meaning, it did not thereby give up the old. Yet the time came, probably in the early classical period (we begin to notice the new emphasis in Aeschylus), when certain mythical heroes were considered *sôphrones* chiefly for moral reasons, namely, their ability to restrain their passions—anger, lust, drunkenness, ambition, cruelty, pride, and the like. Such men were intelligent also; they won distinction because in them reason ruled appetite and passion. But it was their power of restraint, more than their shrewdness or intellectual capacity, that made them famous, and we therefore need still a third category, close to the second, but not identical with it, and quite separate from the first (that of Joseph in Egypt which, as we have noted, is not even specifically Greek). Among mythological heroes the earliest to be termed *sôphrôn* for his powers of restraint is Amphiaraus, the seer whom Aeschylus calls *sôphronestatos* in the *Seven against Thebes* (568) and shortly thereafter credits with four cardinal virtues (610). Although his sophrosyne is by no means devoid of intelligence (he is, after all, a seer, and we note that the Theban hero chosen to confront him must be "of mature mind," γέροντα τὸν νοῦν, 622), it is even more an exemplary form of self-restraint, contrasted with the insufferable arrogance of the other Six, each of whom demonstrates *hybris* in the special form of boasting and bears a shield with a notably hybristic device.[35]

Amphiaraus' sophrosyne is modesty, specifically—in this context—the refusal to indulge in boasts or threats. His shield, in contrast to those of the other Six, carries no blazon. Aeschylus

---

[35]See North, 40–41. For discussions of the shields of the Seven and varying views of their significance consult Helen Bacon, *Arion* 3, no. 3 (1964) 27–38, H. D. Cameron, *T.A.P.A.* 101 (1970) 106, and Thomas Rosenmeyer, *The Masks of Tragedy* (Austin, 1963). On actual Greek shield-devices consult G. H. Chase, *H.S.C.P.* 13 (1902) 61–127.

interprets the blank shield as proof that Amphiaraus wishes to be, not just to seem, *aristos* (most excellent, 591–592), and the shield without a blazon caught the fancy of certain later writers, for whom it became a symbol of sophrosyne. Euripides explicates it thus in the *Phoenissae*, where it is said that the seer Amphiaraus has no hybristic device on his shield, but modestly (*sôphronôs*) carries a shield without a blazon (1111–1112).[36] The contrast between seeming and being, appearance and reality, summed up by Aeschylus in the figure of Amphiaraus, is related to sophrosyne by way of self-knowledge, the Apolline *Gnôthi sauton*, which sees beneath the deceptive surface of things to the underlying reality. Hence the significance of the mosaic in the Terme Museum in Rome, which illustrates the Delphic maxim with a skeleton, the traditional *memento mori*.

Amphiaraus must have been prominent in the lost epics dealing with the story of Thebes, but only from the time of Aeschylus do we find him as a type of modesty or restraint. Whatever his qualities in earlier poetry, he would not have been called *sôphrôn* in this sense in heroic or even archaic verse, since, as noted above, this semantic development belongs to the fifth century. Similarly, Odysseus, that paradigmatic combination of shrewdness and self-restraint, is never called *sôphrôn* in the *Odyssey*. The words for him are *polymêtis*, "of many plans" (for the intellectual *aretê*) and *echephrôn*, "controlling his *phrenes*, restraining himself" (for the moral). By the fifth century, however, the scope of the word sophrosyne has widened to such an extent that Sophocles can present Odysseus as an exemplar of this virtue in the *Ajax* (132) because of his self-restraint and his insight into the human condition. Even the hostile portrait of the unscrupulous Odysseus in the *Philoctetes* preserves one ironic reference to his sophrosyne (equating it with excessive caution or cowardice, 1259–1260). But it is really the philosophers, especially the Cynics and Stoics in the Hellenistic period and the allegorical interpreters of Homer early

[36]Even in driving his chariot-horses, Amphiaraus is notably *sôphrôn* (*Phoen.* 177–178). Euripides' *Hypsipyle*, probably part of the trilogy that includes the *Phoenissae*, also emphasizes the sophrosyne of Amphiaraus; see Chapter 3 for its relation to his persuasive ethos. On the *sôphrôn* shield without a blazon see also Julian, *Letter to a Priest* 303D. Statius, *Thebais* 4. 222, gives Amphiaraus a significant blazon, the conquered Python, emblematic of Apollo. For "bisshop Amphiorax" see Chaucer, *Troilus and Criseyde* 2. 104–105.

and late, who make Odysseus the supreme exemplar of the self-restrained hero, principally because of his resistance to the Sirens and to Circe. The story of Odysseus and Circe with its moral exegesis probably had more influence in the Renaissance than any other myth connected with sophrosyne.[37] Heracles, too, undergoes a like process of moralization, promoted chiefly by the Cynics and Stoics,[38] and some of his labors came to be interpreted as allegories of the conquest of passion, a theme particularly fruitful in Renaissance art, where the two heroes, Odysseus and Heracles, are often connected.

From the fourth century onward (in the wake of Plato) several other models of sophrosyne are such by reason of their restraint. Thus Rhadamanthys, the wise man of Theognis, is an exemplar of sexual morality when he is cited in the *Eroticus* of Ps.-Demosthenes (30); here the gods are said to have loved both Aeacus and Rhadamanthys for their sophrosyne, Heracles, Castor, and Polydeuces for their *andreia,* Ganymede and Adonis for their beauty. Achilles and Patroclus are models of sophrosyne in Aeschines, *Oration against Timarchus* (141–150), where their celebrated friendship, now interpreted in an erotic context, contributes to the *topos* of the *sôphrôn erôs* popular in tragedy, oratory, and philosophy in the fifth and fourth centuries.

Especially curious is the alternation of views about Alexander the Great, who of all historical figures was subjected to the most persistent and diverse mythologizing, even before the growth of the Mediaeval Romance. Depending on the source, Alexander may be a hero of virtue or a monster of vice. Although the notion of a consistently hostile philosophical tradition—Peripatetic, Cynic, Stoic—has now been dispelled,[39] individual members of each school, at various periods, and writers influenced by rhe-

[37]See below, p. 80.

[38]On this process consult Ragnar Höistad, *Cynic Hero and Cynic King* (Lund, 1948), and Felix Buffière, *Les mythes d'Homère et la pensée grecque* (Paris, 1956). A curious minor development is the process by which, as early as Pindar, *Ol.* 3. 43-44, the Pillars of Hercules became a symbol of restraint and prudence, later to be associated with the proverb *Non plus ultra*. On this motto and the Columnar device of the Emperor Charles V, see Earl Rosenthal, *J.W.C.I.* 34 (1971) 204-228, and 37 (1974) 198-230.

[39]See J. R. Hamilton, *Plutarch, Alexander: A Commentary* (Oxford, 1969) lxi. For a critical survey of opinions about the philosophical tradition consult J. Rufus Fears, *Philologus* 118 (1974) 113-130.

torical or nationalistic motives frequently viewed Alexander as an
exemplum malum. Theophrastus (*ap.* Cicero, *Tusc. Disp.* 3. 10. 21)
described him as one who did not know how to use success, and
this became a standard accusation. According to Cicero, Alexander, after he became king, was haughty, cruel, and lacking in
restraint (*Att.* 13. 28. 3); Livy charged that he could not endure *res
secundae* (9. 18. 1), and elsewhere he is accused of being drunken,
wrathful, and subject to uncontrolled passions.[40] In the Middle
Ages the aerial journey of Alexander became an example of arrogance, and Sassetta's painting of the triumph of St. Francis over
the three vices opposed to the Franciscan virtues shows the pros-
trate Alexander as the representative of *superbia* (Plate II).

On the other hand, some rhetorical writers and those influenced by them (especially Plutarch) are inclined to make Alexander an exemplar of the kingly virtues, among which sophrosyne is
prominent because of his honorable treatment of the wives of
Darius—an episode once as well known as the taming of
Bucephalus or the interview with Diogenes. A comparison of
Plutarch's use of the episode of the Persian captives in his early,
extremely rhetorical treatise "On the Fortune of Alexander" with
that in the *Life* shows that the later account is in general more
sober, yet Alexander's sophrosyne emerges from it virtually unchanged.[41]

The other aspect of sophrosyne emphasized in Plutarch's *Life* is
endurance of hardship. An illustrative episode is supplied for
Alexander (refusal of water, 42. 7–10), evidently because Plutarch
needs parallels with the *Life* of Caesar, whose disregard of hardship was famous (for example, ch. 17). Caesar is not represented
as *sôphrôn* in a sexual context.

In Plutarch's rhetorical eulogy, but not in the *Life,* Alexander is
shown to be superior to various philosophers, including Aristotle,
because he accomplished in fact what they merely advocated in

[40]For example, Seneca, *Ep.* 113. 29, *Ep.* 83. 19, 23, and *Ben.* 2. 16. 2.

[41]Plutarch uses two variants of the same commonplace in the two accounts. In
De Fortuna 338D he maintains that Alexander was as far superior to the Persian
women in sophrosyne as to the men in *andreia,* while in the *Life* 30 he has Darius
say that Alexander showed greater sophrosyne to the women than *andreia* to the
men—evidence that sophrosyne is inescapably associated with feminine virtue,
even when practiced by the greatest of generals.

Plate II. St. Francis in Ecstasy by Sassetta (ca. 1440–1444). Fototeca Berenson, Villa I Tatti, Florence.

theory. It is even asserted that in his conquests he was actuated by
a concern for the cardinal virtues (326E). His true equipment for
the journey to the East, Plutarch says, consisted of philosophical
doctrine and teachings concerning fearlessness (*aphobia*), courage
(*andreia*), self-restraint (sophrosyne), and greatness of soul
(*megalopsychia*).

This sweeping statement ascribes to Alexander a kind of *aretê
politikê* (political excellence), and thus we come to the fourth category of masculine sophrosyne—that of the stateman who governs
with moderation, restraint, or shrewdness in the interest of his
people, or who instills sophrosyne in his subjects either by showing them a model in his own life or by making laws that guide
them in the ways of virtue. Here again there is naturally some
overlap with other categories, since the *sôphrôn* ruler is both prudent and self-restrained, but it is possible to distinguish in the
fifth and fourth centuries a type of *sôphrôn* hero whose *aretê* is
exercised primarily in statesmanship. Such a development is conceivable, of course, only when sophrosyne has itself become a civic
virtue, and because this does not happen until the age of the *polis*,
its exemplars are for the most part historical figures, however
much romanticized, rather than gods or mythical heroes. It also
follows that the content of the *aretê politikê* called sophrosyne will
vary according to the state whose values are thus epitomized and
the period of its history involved. Just as the collective sophrosyne
idealized in romantic histories of Sparta differs from Athenian
sophrosyne, so, too, the *aretê politikê* of Lycurgus, the legendary
Spartan lawgiver, is not identical with that of Solon, nor are Pericles, Evagoras—the fourth-century king of Cypriote Salamis—
and the Emperor Julian all *sôphrones* in the same political sense.
What is generally present in any *sôphrôn* statesman is a certain
personal austerity combined with the ability to control the irrational impulses of the citizens.

We encounter Athenian models of political sophrosyne very
often in oratory, history, and biography: Solon, Cleisthenes, Aristides, Themistocles, above all Pericles.[42] The only significant
mythical exemplar of Attic sophrosyne in political life is Theseus,

---

[42]See North, 10-11, 15, 139, with note 54. The Seven Wise Men—statesmen
all—were models of sophrosyne; see chapter 2 on Solon, Pittacus, and Myson.

not the distracted father of Hippolytus, as in Euripides' tragedy, nor the adventurer trapped in Hades with Perithous, but the *sôphrôn* ruler in Euripides' *Suppliants*. Isocrates, in his early sophistic eulogy of Helen, praises Theseus as the possessor of four cardinal virtues, but only to sophrosyne is a political function assigned.[43] Theseus displayed this quality in his *dioikêsis*, his management, of the city—an indication that Isocrates interprets sophrosyne as shrewdness in directing affairs in the interest of the *polis*, rather than as moderation or restraint, which is his tendency in such later treatises as the *Areopagiticus* and the *Panegyricus*. He makes lavish use of exemplars of political sophrosyne, and because of the tremendous influence of his eulogy of Evagoras, which set the style for the *basilikos logos* until the late Renaissance, a treatment of all four cardinal virtues became essential to speeches in praise of a ruler, as well as to the closely related treatises on kingship. One of the requirements for such orations is the *synkrisis*, comparison of the person eulogized to models of the virtues under discussion, and in the Graeco-Roman period Alexander is the exemplar most often cited for every one of the kingly virtues, including sophrosyne.[44]

The exemplars from Roman history illuminate the differences between the sophrosyne of Greek political thought and the *temperantia, moderatio,* or *frugalitas* of the Roman Republic and the *clementia* and *pudicitia* of the imperial models. Cicero, who sets the pattern for many later historians, especially Livy, emphasizes the restraint needed in public life and sets a high value on incorruptibility in office. He idealizes the early Republic and holds up for imitation exemplars drawn from that period, among whom the two Scipios, Cato the Elder, Cincinnatus, Fabricius, and Piso Frugi are models of *abstinentia* and *modestia*.[45] After Julius Caesar became master of Rome, Cicero began to emphasize a new aspect of *temperantia,* namely *clementia,* and from this point onward, throughout the imperial age, instances of mercy on the part of absolute rulers are prominent in orations and treatises on king-

[43] 10. 31. *Andreia, epistêmê, eusebeia* are the other virtues mentioned.

[44] See Burgess, 128-129, note 1, on Alexander as the model king in Julian, Themistius, and Libanius.

[45] Michel Rambaud, *Cicéron et l'histoire romaine* (Paris, 1953) 27-35.

ship and require models from legend or history, if only to be surpassed. Thus Seneca in *De Clementia,* addressed to Nero, eulogizes Nero's own *clementia* and contrasts it with the *crudelitas* of Alexander and Phalaris (1. 25. 1; 2. 3. 3). Thus, too, Julian in his two Orations in praise of Constantius commends his sophrosyne (here forbearance, clemency) and proclaims him superior to Cyrus and Alexander in their treatment of members of their own families.[46] *Synkrisis* with Homeric heroes dominates Julian's second oration. In both speeches Constantius is superior to Nestor and Odysseus, representing strategy and eloquence (1. 32B, 2. 75A ff.). In the second, Magnentius, the usurper, is compared to three exemplars of *hybris:* Typhon in the *Theogony,* Kakia in Prodicus' *Apologue,* and Capaneus in Aeschylus' *Septem* (2. 56D-57A). What is interesting here is the selection of paradigms from three different strands in the fabric of mythology, the progeny of Earth from Hesiod, the allegorical personification of evil from the Sophistic period, and the arrogant attacker of Thebes from Attic tragedy. Petrarch employs a similar method of selection and combination in assembling his heterogeneous groups of attendants in the *Triumphs.*

Finally, a minor but not insignificant aspect of the use of mythical exemplars in ancient treatises on political philosophy may be seen in the topic of the *sôphronistês,* the wise, usually elderly adviser who helps the ruler (often conceived of as an impetuous young man) to become a philosopher-king. Nestor is the mythical prototype to which historical philosophers are made to correspond. As Nestor is to Agamemnon and Achilles, so is Anaxagoras to Pericles, Plato to Dionysius, Aristotle to Alexander, and so would Dio Chrysostom have liked to be to Trajan.[47] While the term *sôphronistês* originally signified a corrector, in Latin, *castigator,* it came to have broader implications, and the virtue instilled did not have to be sophrosyne.

One further set of masculine categories deserves notice: the *sôphrôn* youth and the *sôphrôn* old man. They represent two very different aspects of the virtue, in the first case good conduct, orderliness, quietness (Charmides in Plato's dialogue), in the sec-

[46]1. 41C, 45C-46D.
[47]See Dio, *On Kingship, Or.* 1-4. On the *sôphronistês,* see chapter 2.

ond the calmness that comes when passion is spent and the time is at hand for what Theognis in the sixth century called the *ergmata sôphrosynês*, the works of wisdom (1325–1326). Since both categories figure in rhetorical literature, it was expedient that models be found, and for old age one was readily available—again, Nestor. The young man might be Telemachus, who is twice credited with sophrosyne (modesty, good sense) in the *Odyssey*. But in fact there is a much greater tendency to exemplify this kind of sophrosyne with anonymous groups, such as the youth of Sparta after the reforms of Lycurgus, than with any individual hero. Aristotle points out that sophrosyne is the virtue most needed but most lacking in the young.[48]

THE *SÔPHRÔN* HEROINE

The sophrosyne desirable in the young male—orderly behavior, submission to authority—is always required of women, young and old alike, as Aristotle makes clear in the *Politics*, when he groups together the categories that share the kind of sophrosyne appropriate to those who are ruled—women, children, and slaves (1260a9–11). In addition, feminine sophrosyne includes chastity. The very existence of a distinction between masculine and feminine sophrosyne sheds light on one whole facet of ancient society. In moral treatises, epitaphs, and casual references from the archaic age to the end of antiquity, if only one virtue is ascribed to, or expected of, a woman, it will generally be sophrosyne. If there are others, too, sophrosyne will be the most prominent. In the *Rhetoric*, Aristotle states as a matter of course that the *aretê* of women consists of sophrosyne and *philergia aneu aneleutherias*, industriousness without slavishness.[49]

The *sôphrôn* woman exists as a category of myth, but as such she exhibits less variety than the *sôphrôn* hero and much less development from the Homeric poems to the end of antiquity. The prin-

---

[48]See *Rhet.* 1361a3-4 and 1390b4-6, and cf. *Problems* 28. 4. According to one theory about the origin of the cardinal virtues, they arose from age divisions in primitive society, in which sophrosyne (as obedience) was the virtue required of the young. See F. M. Cornford, *C.Q.* 6 (1912) 246–265.

[49]1361a5-7. These are the *aretai psychês;* the excellences of the body are *kallos* (beauty) and *megethos* (stature). The relation between sophrosyne and feminine industry is discussed in my article in *Illinois Classical Studies* 2 (1977) 35-48.

cipal differences within the category derive from marital status. There is the *sôphrôn* maiden, in the mythical pattern of Daphne, Britomart, or the Danaids, whose efforts are directed to preserving their virginity. There is the *sôphrôn* wife—Penelope, Andromache, Alcestis—whose virtue consists in fidelity, chastity, obedience, self-sacrifice. And even in antiquity there is the *sôphrôn* widow (Evadne, Laodameia). In Christian times these gradations become the three degrees of purity (*hagneia, castimonia*), each with a biblical exemplar: the virgin martyr Thecla or the Blessed Virgin herself for the first, Susanna for chastity in marriage, Anna for the widowed state. When *hagneia (castimonia)* is the general heading, sophrosyne (*pudicitia*) is the subhead proper to matrimony.[50] But the virtue itself is essentially the same in all three conditions and in both pagan and Christian times. It is denoted by the verb *sôphronein,* corresponding to the noun sophrosyne, as early as the seventh century B.C. in the iambics of the misogynist, Semonides of Amorgos, where the verb describes the conduct of a good wife.[51] The admired type—chaste, faithful, obedient, not talkative, a competent housekeeper—is already defined in Homer, who supplies the two primary exemplars for later times, Penelope and Andromache, although neither is called *sôphrôn* in the Homeric poems (and each is much more than a stereotype). The third member of the exemplary triad is Alcestis, who also appears in rhetorical comparisons and in feminine epitaphs down to the end of antiquity.[52] It is significant that all three are married women; perpetual virginity is not admired by the Greeks (except in the case of certain goddesses). Yet premarital chastity is highly valued in most Greek societies that we know anything about, for reasons that originally have nothing to do with morality or religion, but rather with social and economic motives.

The origins of the *sôphrôn* heroine are quite distinct from those of the *sôphrôn* hero in any of his several manifestations. When the

[50]See North, 359, 364.

[51]7. 108-110 Diehl[3]; cf. Epicharmus, Frg. 286 Kaibel.

[52]See Richmond Lattimore, *Themes in Greek and Latin Epitaphs* (Urbana, 1962) 290-301, 335 ff. Cf. Hyginus 256 (*Quae castissimae fuerunt*): Penelope, Evadne, Laodamia, Hecuba, Theonoe, Alcestis, Lucretia. The word *sôphrôn,* applied to the feminine exemplars, becomes common in the fifth century; see Euripides, *Alc.* 182, 615, *Troad.* 645-656, *Andr.* 235, and Aristophanes, *Thes.* 548.

mythical patterns were developing, there was, of course, no conception of a single standard of morality, and save for such philosophers as the Platonic Socrates, Plato himself, and the Stoics, few Greeks ever did believe that virtue was the same for men and women, any more than for gods and men. The feminine virtue of sophrosyne originated in social sanctions designed to maintain behavior desirable from the point of view of husbands and fathers, preserve the purity of the family, and safeguard property rights. Religious sanctions developed later in both Greece and Rome, and such goddesses as Artemis/Diana and Vesta came to be linked with the preservation or exaltation of sophrosyne/*pudicitia.*

The most widespread type of myth involving the *sôphrôn* heroine is that in which a maiden tries so desperately to preserve her virginity from attack by an unwelcome suitor that she prefers death to dishonor. Sometimes she undergoes a metamorphosis that saves her virtue, but at the cost of her human identity (Daphne, Syrinx); sometimes even this expedient fails (Arethusa). And sometimes she takes matters into her own hands and kills the unwelcome suitor (forty-nine of the Danaids). This conduct is considered worthy of eternal, exemplary punishment in Hades.[53]

Virtuous girls such as these often belong to the train of Artemis/Diana (or, like the Danaids in the *Suppliants* of Aeschylus, invoke her as their protector). Some of them are considered by mythologists to be aspects of the virgin goddess herself, like Dictynna or Britomart, who leaped into the sea to avoid the attentions of Minos. Callisto is an interesting variant. Belonging to the troop of nymphs attendant on Artemis, she is raped by Zeus and according to the most common version of the myth—the one that inspired innumerable painters of the Renaissance—she is punished by Artemis when her pregnancy is discovered. Thus Callisto is similar to other mythological figures who unwittingly offend Artemis or another deity and are punished for something that is no fault of theirs. Actaeon is the most famous example,

[53]For a study of the origins of the Danaid myth consult A. F. Garvie, *Aeschylus' Supplices: Play and Trilogy* (Cambridge, Eng., 1969), especially 173–177. Eva Keuls, *The Water Carriers in Hades* (Amsterdam, 1974), discusses the process by which these figures are identified with the Danaids.

turned into a stag and brought down by his own hounds after he accidentally beholds Artemis at the bath. The story of Teiresias, in the *Bath of Pallas,* a doublet of the Actaeon myth, suggests that one of the requirements for this mythical pattern is that the goddess offended by the violation of her privacy be one of the virgin goddesses. Both stories therefore bear a certain resemblance to the "punishment of *hybris*" myth in that a prerogative of a particular god is assailed.

The story of Coronis is more complex. Pregnant by Apollo, she takes a mortal lover and is killed by Artemis at the request of Apollo, who nevertheless preserves their son Asclepius. Such, at least, is the version of Pindar, who always represents Apollo in the best possible light.[54] In origin the story of Coronis seems like an ironic reversal of the "think mortal thoughts" cautionary tale. Herself mortal, she is punished by a god for preferring another mortal to himself, the reverse of the sin—seeking to marry a goddess—for which Ixion, Tityus, and Otus are punished. Yet Pindar emphasizes that the sin of Coronis lay in preferring a lover from far away (an Arcadian, while she was a Thessalian and had Apollo close at hand), hence scorning what was nearby and seeking things afar (*Pyth.* 3. 20–23). As R. W. B. Burton demonstrates, this interpretation supports the theme of *Gnôthi sauton* that runs through the entire *Third Pythian* and is further illustrated by the myth of Asclepius, the son of Coronis and Apollo, who committed *hybris* in another form, by bringing to life the dead Hippolytus. The ode culminates characteristically in advice to Hieron of Syracuse to bear his suffering with courage and understanding of man's destiny—that is, with sophrosyne.[55]

The *exempla horribilia,* the wicked women, naturally attract more interest than the chaste heroines, and some of the principal feminine figures in tragedy are violators of sophrosyne—Clytemnestra, Medea, Phaedra, Helen (in the *Troades,* not the *Helen*), and Stheneboea in the lost play of Euripides. The very qualities that render women unfit to be stereotypes of

[54]For a perceptive analysis of this ode (*Pyth.* 3) consult R. W. B. Burton, *Pindar's Pythian Odes: Essays in Interpretation* (Oxford, 1962) 78–90.

[55]Coronis belongs to one of the most hybristic families in Greek mythology; she is a sister of Ixion, as well as the mother of Asclepius.

sophrosyne—violence, self-will, unchastity, argumentativeness, insistence on their rights—equip them for tragedy. Choral odes, such as the first stasimon of the *Choephoroe,* with its allusions to the "all-daring passions" of Althaea, Scylla, and the Lemnian women (585–652), make effective use of negative paradigms, and the comic poets often refer to them, for misogyny is a primary theme of Old Comedy, whose earliest surviving fragment is Susarion's assertion that woman is *kakon,* a bad thing. Eubulus, in a fragment preserved by Athenaeus, professes to run out of good women long before his list of bad ones is exhausted.[56] The only ones he can think of are Penelope and Alcestis. We remember the complaint of the women against Euripides in the *Thesmophoriazusae:* he portrays Melanippes and Phaedras, but never a Penelope, precisely because she seemed to be a *sôphrôn* woman (ὅτι γυνὴ σώφρων ἔδοξεν εἶναι, 548).

An important function of the mythical models of sophrosyne is to provide material for rhetorical *synkrisis,* as when Julian, in his Eulogy of the Empress Eusebeia, says that her mother surpassed Evadne and Laodameia in sophrosyne, because, whereas they took their own lives when widowed, she devoted herself to bringing up her children and won such a reputation for chastity that no suitor dared to approach her. Hence she was superior also to Penelope, who was notoriously unable to discourage suitors.[57] Later in the address, however, Julian praises Penelope and offers her as a parallel to Eusebeia. Unlike Semiramis and several other ladies who played men's roles, Penelope never led an army nor indulged in public speaking. Rather, she practiced sophrosyne and *philandria* (love of her husband), veiled herself in the presence of men, and spoke in a soft voice (3. 127C-D). Yet from her, and not from the Amazons, much good came to men (128B). Here we get a crossbearing on the myth of the Amazonomachy and see why the Amazons are the moral equivalent of the Centaurs, Titans, and Giants.

[56]Athenaeus 13. 559C. Cf. *Frogs* 1043 (Phaedras and Stheneboeas portrayed by Euripides) and Juvenal 10. 325 (Stheneboea and Phaedra). Propertius 4. 7. 55 ff. contrasts Clytemnestra and Phaedra with Andromeda and Hypermnestra.

[57]Cf. Libanius *Or.* 1. 7 on the sophrosyne of his widowed mother, who drove myriads of suitors from her door.

The other great function of mythical models, as we have already noted, is to enhance the praise of dead women on their tombstones. The range of such heroines is surprisingly narrow. Penelope and Alcestis have the field almost to themselves, with an occasional intrusion by Arete, the mother of Nausicaa (probably because of her suggestive name, even though it is not in fact identical with the word meaning "virtue," and certainly because of her honored position in the Palace of Alcinous).[58]

The Roman heroines of *pudicitia* are almost all supposed to be historical figures, at least by the Roman historians.[59] Supreme among them is Lucretia, whom Valerius Maximus calls *dux Romanae pudicitiae*. (He goes on to make the patronizing observation that her *virilis animus, maligno errore fortunae, muliebre corpus sortitus est:* "her manlike spirit, by a cruel mistake on the part of fortune, was allotted to a woman's body").[60] Dionysius of Halicarnassus calls Lucretia *kallistên . . . kai sôphronestatên,* most beautiful and most chaste (4. 64. 4), and she is so celebrated in this role that there is no need to list the sources or survey the endless *Fortleben.* A recent commentator on Livy 1. 57–59 accepts the basic story as historical, however much elaborated under the influence of the drama. (The picture of Lucretia and her servants hard at work at the significant task of woolworking—ever the mark of the chaste matron—is, R. M. Ogilvie comments, straight out of New Comedy.)[61] The other great heroine of *pudicitia* is less fortunate. Verginia, whose very name is suspicious, is an aetiological myth con-

---

[58]Lattimore, *op. cit.* 293 ff. The name of the Phaeacian queen is Arêtê (prayed to). Dionysius of Syracuse had two daughters, Aretê and Sophrosyne (Plutarch, *Dion.* 6).

[59]Camilla is an exception (*Aen.* 7. 803–817, 11. 581–584). In her exclusive devotion to chastity she is as ambiguous a figure as Hippolytus, at once attractive and pathetic.

[60]6 (*De pudicitia*). Cf. the inscription on Bernini's monument for the Countess Matilda of Tuscany in St. Peter's Basilica, which praises her as a *virilis animi femina,* and note the identical phrase on the urn of Agrippina the Elder in the Conservatori Museum, Rome.

[61]R. M. Ogilvie, *A Commentary on Livy, Books 1–5* (Oxford, 1965) 222, on 1. 57. 9. For Lucretia in Renaissance art, consult Wolfgang Stechow, *Essays in Honor of Georg Swarzenski* (Chicago, 1951) 114–124. Cardinal Giovanni Medici (later Pope Leo X), a grandson of Lucrezia Tornabuoni, wrote a poem *In Lucretiae Statuam* and fostered a cult of Lucretia.

nected with the cult of Venus Cloacina, goddess of the stream Cloaca that runs through the Forum and gives its name to the great sewer, the Cloaca Maxima. This cult had to do with purification, and "it was Cloacina's capacity as a purifier, above all from the taint implicit in *stuprum*, that made her shrine the natural setting for Verginia's death."[62] The early Roman chroniclers evidently felt a strong impulse to make the fall of the tyrannical *decemvir* parallel to the fall of the Tarquins; hence Verginia was modeled on Lucretia and given a significant name.[63]

The two other best-known heroines of Roman *pudicitia*, both of whom are often depicted in Renaissance art, especially on marriage cassoni, are Claudia Quinta[64] and Tuccia.[65] Claudia Quinta, through whose agency the barge carrying the image of Cybele was miraculously moved up the Tiber, was a Roman matron, later thought to be a Vestal Virgin. In either case, by her wondrous achievement she refuted slurs upon her virtue. Tuccia, the Vestal who vindicated her chastity by carrying water in a sieve from the Tiber to the Temple of Vesta, is always identifiable by her attribute, the sieve, which ultimately became an independent symbol in iconography, clasped in the hand of Elizabeth I, for example, in pictures meant to praise her virtue.[66] Normally the attribute that marks a heroine as *pudica* is the spindle ($\dot{\eta}\lambda\alpha\varkappa\dot{\alpha}\tau\eta$, *colus*).

[62]Ogilvie, *op. cit.* 487 (on 3. 48. 5).

[63]A myth about still another chaste Verginia explained the cult of *Pudicitia Plebeia* (Livy 10. 23. 4–11; cf. Ogilvie). Robert E. A. Palmer, *Rivista Storica dell' Antichità* 4 (1974) 113–159, solves many of the mysteries connected with the two cults of Pudicitia and the Roman *matronae* who celebrated them. See chapter 2, on Roman efforts to influence the behavior of women.

[64]On Claudia Quinta consult Livy 29. 14. 12; Propertius 4. 11. 52; Ovid, *Fasti* 4. 290–348; Pliny, *H.N.* 7. 35; Silius Italicus, *Pun.* 17. 20–47, and see the paintings by Garofalo (Barberini Gallery, Rome) and Neroccio de'Landi (National Gallery, Washington, D.C.). Less famous is Sulpicia, chosen as *pudicissima femina* to dedicate a statue of Venus Verticordia (Turner-of-hearts-to-chastity) in 215 B.C., according to Pliny, *H.N.* 7. 35. For Dido as an exemplar of chastity consult Mary Louise Lord, *Harvard Library Bulletin* 17 (1969) 22–44, 216–232.

[65]Tuccia: Valerius Maximus 8. 1. 5; Pliny, *H.N.* 28. 2. 12; Dion. Hal., *Ant. Rom.* 2. 69.

[66]For the association of the sieve motif with virginity in nonclassical cultures, see E. R. Dodds, on *Gorgias* 492D1–493D4. On the "sieve portraits" of Elizabeth I see Frances A. Yates, *J.W.C.I.* 10 (1947) 27 ff., and Roy C. Strong, *Portraits of Queen Elizabeth I* (Oxford, 1963) 22, 66, and Plate X.

Lanificium and *pudicitia* are inseparable in Roman thought, as many inscriptions remind us: *domum servavit, lanam fecit.*[67]

Richmond Lattimore observes that the ideal of the housewife is even more prominent on Roman than on Greek epitaphs,[68] and Gordon Williams in his study of Roman marriage ceremonies and ideals has concluded that wifely obedience is seen as a positive virtue by the Romans much more than by the Greeks.[69] Certainly the ideal is not lacking in Greek attitudes, however, and the work-basket (*talaros*) that appears on some tombstones for Greek women is the equivalent of the *lanificium-topos* on the Roman epitaphs. A stele of the first century B.C. from Sardis which has a *talaros* as a symbol of the "well-ordered virtue" of the dead woman (Menophila) probably deserves a place near the head of the list in the sepulchral iconography of sophrosyne.[70]

PHILOSOPHICAL MYTH

The final category is the most difficult to define because its content is infinitely variable; only its function can be generalized. It is the kind of myth shaped by philosophers in order to illustrate ethical and religious doctrines, to render memorable various concepts arrived at by dialectical processes, or to express in a likely story (as Plato says)[71] what is inaccessible to reason. In almost all cases, such myths build on elements familiar from earlier stages of

---

[67]See Ogilvie on Livy 1. 57. 9 for the woolmaking *topos* with citations of many epigraphic and literary sources. The "Orphic" *katabasis* preserved in the Bologna papyrus characterizes the *sôphrones* heroines in the Underworld by referring to their spindles (Pap. I, vv. 3–4 of folio III, recto). See Reinhold Merkelbach, *Mus. Hel.* 8 (1951) 1–11 and Max Treu, *Hermes* 82 (1954) 24–51.

[68]*Op. cit.* 296.

[69]*J.R.S.* 48 (1958) 16–29.

[70]See *Anatolian Studies Presented to Sir William Mitchell Ramsey,* ed. W. H. Buckler and W. M. Calder (Manchester, 1923) 345–353. The stele is adorned with symbols of the qualities ascribed to Menophila, plus an inscription explaining their significance. A bundle of papyrus scrolls indicates her *sophia* and the *talaros* her orderliness. See page 352, note 1, for other tombs with comparable symbols. Attic grave reliefs sometimes include a mirror, which Christoph W. Clairmont, *Gravestone and Epigram* (Mainz, 1970) 78, suggests may characterize the dead as unmarried. One such (Clairmont, 13) refers to the *aretê* and sophrosyne of the dead girl. Consult Donna C. Kurtz and John Boardman, *Greek Burial Customs* (Ithaca, N.Y., 1971) 138, for baskets, mirrors, spindles, and other household objects on classical reliefs, and 263 for the Sardis stele.

[71]*Timaeus* 29D.

mythology, and if they appeal to the popular imagination they in turn generate a vast series of imitations. Two examples stand out, both so famous as to need no explication. The Apologue of Heracles at the Crossroads, invented by Prodicus the Sophist, but known to us through Xenophon's *Memorabilia* (2. 1. 22), goes back to the Hesiodic theme of the two roads, one long, steep, and difficult, the other short, smooth, and easy, which lead respectively to Aretê and Kakia (Virtue and Vice, *Erga* 287-292). In most exemplars based on this prototype, the choice embodied in the *krisis tou biou peri* (decision about life) is between virtue in a form close to sophrosyne and vice in the guise of one of her regular antitheses, usually *hêdonê* (pleasure).[72] In Xenophon's description of Aretê great emphasis is laid on the fact that she is adorned with *aidôs* and sophrosyne; Kakia is overdressed and plastered with makeup. From this detail develops the *topos* dear to the Cynic-Stoic preachers and their successors among the Church Fathers, according to which the only suitable adornment for a good woman is sophrosyne, the *kosmos akosmos* (adornment unadorned).[73] The seductive enchantress may be called, not Vice (as in Prodicus) or Pleasure (as in Philo Judaeus), but Tyranny, in contrast to true Kingship (as in Dio Chrysostom's first *Oration on Kingship*). In the *Tabula* of Cebes the contestants are True Paideia (Culture) and False. Essentially the Choice of Heracles is a literary expression of the idea that gave rise in sepulchral iconography to the so-called Pythagorean Y-stele from Philadelphia, representing the choice between self-restraint and indulgence in the appetites as decisive for the afterlife.[74]

A second philosophical myth that in an obvious way built on

[72]For a partial list of important imitations of the Apologue of Prodicus consult M. C. Waites, *H.S.C.P.* 23 (1912) 1-46. A Patristic variant is the vision of Gregory of Nazianzus, in which he is addressed by two personifications, Sophrosyne and Hagneia (Purity), both of whom urge him toward the same goal (*P.G.* 37, *Car.* 45). See also A. R. Anderson, *H.S.C.P.* 39 (1928) 7-58.

[73]See North, 340.

[74]For the "Pythagorean" stele and its reliefs suggesting sophrosyne and *akolasia* consult Panofsky, *Tomb Sculpture*, 33. A. D. Nock, *H.S.C.P* 33 (1940) 312, and *A.J.A.* 50 (1946) 146, denies that the Philadelphia relief is actually Pythagorean. For the iconographic development of the Choice of Hercules, consult Panofsky, *Hercules am Scheidewege* (Leipzig and Berlin, 1930), and for some of its literary progeny, to the time of Petrarch, see T. E. Mommsen, *Medieval and Renaissance Studies*, ed. Eugene F. Rice (Ithaca, N.Y., 1959) 175-176.

popular elements in genuine mythology and inspired a host of
imitators, pagan and Christian, is that of Plato's charioteer in the
Phaedrus. No reader of Plato needs to be reminded that he is one
of the great myth makers of the Greek world and that some of his
most successful and memorable myths draw upon the same
primordial associations as the combats with fabulous monsters in
the myths of Perseus, Bellerophon, and like heroes. What Plato
does is to internalize the combat. As Socrates hints in the *Phaedrus*
(230A), he may have within himself a beast more complex and
passionate than Typhon. In the myth of the *Phaedrus*, appetite
and passion, the two inferior faculties of the tripartite soul of the
Republic, are embodied in the two horses, one ugly, wild, and
unruly, the other handsome, gentle, and obedient, and reason is
the charioteer.

The wild beast symbolic of the passions and appetites rears his
ugly heads often in Plato's dialogues—the great beast of public
opinion, whose moods and appetites are studied by the Sophists
(*Rep.* 493A ff.), the variegated and many-headed beast that is
called an image of the soul (*eikôn psychês*) in *Republic* 9 (588B-C),
the erotic beast of *Charmides* 155D—but in the *Phaedrus* a significant change occurs, one that must have had a great deal to do with
the popularity of this myth in later times: the "beast" is now pictured as a team of horses, one of which is endowed with the
admirable traits that all the Greeks must have been familiar with
from the chariot races at the Games, not to mention the spirited
little steeds of the Parthenon frieze. Diogenes Laertius remarks,
without elaborating, that Plato always praised horses (6. 7). Certainly he knew them well, and the great ride of the charioteer to
the region above the heavens, where dwell the Forms of Wisdom,
Justice, Sophrosyne, and the like, impressed itself indelibly on the
imagination of its readers. The conflation of this myth with the
four living creatures of Ezechiel and other scriptural references to
chariots or yokes or winged creatures is too long a story to repeat
here,[75] but it demonstrates the enormous appeal of the mythical
archetype (used by Parmenides before Plato and perhaps by

[75]For the myth of the *Phaedrus* in Patristic literature see Herbert Musurillo, S.J.,
Traditio 12 (1956) 1–64.

heavenly travelers in the shamanistic tradition even before Parmenides).[76]

Other Platonic adaptations of familiar mythical elements could be cited—among them the echo of the Titanomachy heard by F. M. Cornford in the *Timaeus*, where an orderly universe results from the victory of reasonable persuasion over necessity[77] and the capture of the acropolis of the young man's soul, in *Republic* 8, whereupon Sophrosyne and Aidôs are expelled and the young man lives with Lotus-Eaters,[78] but Plato's sovereign mastery of every element in earlier Greek myth and poetry scarcely needs to be demonstrated.

When we turn from types of myth to specific mythological figures, we find that the gods who have a close connection with sophrosyne—Zeus, Apollo, Artemis, Athena—and those who have an occasional, paradoxical link—Aphrodite and Dionysus—reflect such totally different aspects as to give further insight into the complexity of the concept.

Zeus

The moralization of the Indo-European sky-god, who controlled the weather and hurled the thunderbolt on the just and unjust alike, was undertaken as early in Greek thought as *Odyssey* 1. The story has often been told of how he was converted, not without difficulty, into a god of justice, as justice was understood at various times subsequent to the *Iliad*.[79] It took much longer to make him a god of sophrosyne, and this task was even more formidable. To conceive of a *sôphrôn* Zeus was not easy for the Greeks, if for no other reason than the prevalence of myths that represented him as the ravisher of women. These stories began to trouble thoughtful persons as soon as the process that might be

[76]See Alexander Mourelatos, *The Route of Parmenides* (New Haven and London, 1970) 42-45. Cf. Maximus of Tyre 41. 5, p. 483 Hobein, for the charioteering of the soul.

[77]See F. M. Cornford, *Plato's Cosmology* (London, 1937) 361-364, and Helmut Kuhn, *H.S.C.P* 52 (1941) 1-40.

[78]See especially 560B-C.

[79]Consult Friedrich Solmsen, *Hesiod and Aeschylus* (Ithaca, N.Y., 1949), especially 92 ff. For an entirely different point of view, see Hugh Lloyd-Jones, *The Justice of Zeus* (Berkeley, 1971).

called ὁμοίωσις βροτῷ (assimilation to mankind or to human standards) began to incline them to require that their gods abide by a standard of morality not inferior to that of man. Ironically, it was the concept of what "befits" (ἐπιπρέπει) the divine nature, first advanced by Xenophanes, that showed the way to the moral purification of the traditional gods, although Xenophanes himself insists that the one god, greatest among gods and men, is not similar (ὁμοίιος) to men in body or thought.[80] Even in the wake of Xenophanes, little interest was felt in establishing Zeus as *sôphrôn* in any erotic context.[81] Expurgators of myth were content to condemn adultery in general terms, as they did quarreling and deception in the Homeric and Hesiodic accounts of the life of the gods. As long as the anthropomorphic Zeus was uppermost in men's minds, he was inseparable from the stories of his love affairs. But eventually the attention of religious thinkers and philosophers shifted from these stories to other aspects of the divine nature, while the stories themselves were interpreted allegorically and thus rendered innocuous.

Plato in the *Republic* makes it clear that the Zeus of the old immoral stories will not do. A demand for sophrosyne is served on all the gods and heroes in *Republic* 2 and 3, where Socrates insists that only models of moral perfection be presented for the young to imitate (for example, 378E). He is particularly anxious that the models exhibit self-restraint: they must not indulge in undignified laments, abandon themselves to excessive laughter, give in to sexual passion, or be swayed by bribes and persuasion, but in all matters they must demonstrate the rule of reason over appetite.[82] Zeus is not named as an offender in this passage, but certain episodes in the *Iliad* must have occurred to every reader. Plato is content to make his point in this way. Thereafter he looks

---

[80]See Werner Jaeger, *The Theology of the Early Greek Philosophers*, trans. E. S. Robinson (Oxford, 1947) 38–54, on the influence of Xenophanes' conception of the *theoprepes*.

[81]In Euripides, *H.F.*, Amphitryon reproaches Zeus for seducing and abandoning Alcmene (339–347), but the tendency of this poet is to reject the god, rather than to expurgate the myth.

[82]For a contrast to the point of view rooted in Christian morality, it is instructive to note that in the list of activities here deplored, sexual misconduct is given no more emphasis than undue lamentation or susceptibility to bribes.

to those aspects of Zeus's traditional nature that are more capable of being transformed to suit the concept of the *theoprepes,* "that which befits god," in the formulation of Xenophanes. The most promising elements in the mythology of Zeus were those that could be understood as making him the protector of the moral and social order[83] and the divine regulator of the cosmos (what might later be called a *kosmêtês* or *temperator*). Both concepts derive from the same source, Zeus the castigator of *hybris,* the divine *sôphronistês.*

One of the ways in which Zeus protects the moral and social order is by crushing anyone, god, man, or Titan, who threatens to overthrow it through violence, injustice, or other manifestation of *hybris.* In the *Iliad* there is but a faint trace of explicit recognition that this is indeed a function of Zeus,[84] but about the *Odyssey* there can be no question, from the Council of the gods in Book 1 to the speech of Athena at the close of Book 24, in which she accepts as proof of the continuing reign of the Olympian gods the punishment of the suitors for their *atasthalos hybris,* their violent arrogance (351–352).[85] To establish the position of Zeus as father of Dikê (Justice), hence avenger of slights and insults offered to her, is a primary aim of Hesiod, and in the world of lyric and tragic poetry it is accepted without argument that Zeus punishes Ixion, Capaneus, and Prometheus, just as he has overthrown the Titans and the Giants, and for the same reason.

By the time of Aeschylus such concepts as sophrosyne and *eunomia* had begun to appear as antitheses to *hybris* and *atasthalia* in the language of the poets; now the castigator of *hybris,* the protector of Dikê, became the champion of sophrosyne also. Already in the sixth century Theognis had reproached Zeus for not

---

[83]This is number five in the list of seven functions assigned to Zeus in preclassical and classical thought according to Louis Séchan and Pierre Lévèque, *Les grandes divinités de la Grèce* (Paris, 1966) 85.

[84]In the famous simile of 16. 386, sometimes explained as an intrusion from the world of Homer himself (see Dodds, above, note 12, page 32, and consult Pierre Chantraine in *La notion du divin depuis Homère jusqu'à Platon* [Vandoeuvres and Geneva, 1952] 75–76). Lloyd-Jones (above, note 79) 6, pronounces the simile consistent with the theology of the *Iliad* as a whole.

[85]Those who reject *Od.* 24 are referred by Chantraine (above, note 84) 77 to *Od.* 14. 81 ff. (the gods detest injustice).

distinguishing in *moira* (fate, allotment) between the *sôphrôn* and
the hybristic (377–380). One of the aims of Aeschylus is to show
that Zeus does make such a distinction, however long it may take
moira to manifest herself. The great choral ode of the *Agamemnon*,
which expresses the doctrine of *pathei mathos*, maintains that the
consequence of the suffering inflicted by Zeus is sophrosyne
(176–183). In the *Prometheus* we see the first stage in a process that
some scholars believe must have applied the same doctrine to
Zeus himself.[86] The outcome of the trilogy is and doubtless always
will be a source of profound disagreement, but if the final play
did indeed bring about a reconciliation between the tyrant and
the rebel, it could have been achieved only if both learned to
accept the limitations implicit in their relation to each other—
limitations imposed by Prometheus' knowledge and Zeus's power.
Such acceptance would in each case require sophrosyne. Since
the myth is cast in political terms, it would have to be a political
sophrosyne, such as Athena brings about at the close of the
Eumenides, where she emerges as the final representative of her
father, the spokeswoman for *charis* (grace) and sophrosyne, the
Mean between anarchy and tyranny (696–697).

The cosmic aspect of Zeus's reign has left abundant traces.
Among the most impressive are Pindar's association of the harmony of Zeus with the tranquillity of the world order (for example, *Pyth.* 1 and 8), Plato's frequent allusions to the role of Zeus in
bringing about the triumph of order over chaos, and the un-
forgettable vision, in the myth of the *Phaedrus*, of Zeus leading the
procession of the gods through the heavens, ordering all things
and caring for them (διακοσμῶν πάντα καὶ ἐπιμελούμενος, 246E).
From this sublime conception it was but a step to the divine *kosmêtês*, who in Cleanthes' *Hymn* knows how to set in order what is
without order (*kosmein takosma*).[87] That Zeus, far removed from
the ethos reflected in the early tales of lust and violence, became

---

[86]For some of the evidence, see North, 43 and notes 22–24.

[87]Cleanthes does not use the word *kosmêtês*, however. For the survival of the
Platonic and Stoic concept of Zeus as the source of order, see, in Roman poetry,
Horace *Odes* 3. 4. 45–48 (recalling the victories over the Titans, the Giants, and the
Aloidae) and 1. 12. 13–16 (asserting the rule of Zeus over both moral and physical
affairs). Both passages employ the verb *temperare*.

at last a model of moral virtue is evident from the influential passage in the *Laws* that names sophrosyne specifically as the virtue that men must practice if they are to be like God and therefore dear to him (716C-D)[88]—a passage important for the doctrine of ὁμοίωσις θεῷ (likeness to God) in Neoplatonic and Patristic thought, important also for sophrosyne, since it marks the abandonment of the archaic prohibition against trying to be like the gods (the primary form of *hybris* in lyric poetry). Such a reversal of deep-seated, age-old doctrine could occur only when the aspect of the divine nature that man aspired to share ceased to be its superior power or exemption from death and became instead the perfection of moral virtue, in which justice and sophrosyne are united.

Apollo

To the average Greek in classical times it is probable that the god most intimately linked with sophrosyne would have been Apollo, without any close competitor (unless, that is, he was thinking about feminine *aretê*, in which case he would have had a difficult choice between Artemis and Athena). The usual reservations must, of course, be made. Like Zeus and every other male divinity, Apollo is devoid of sophrosyne in a sexual context.[89] Mythology knows many tales of his pursuit of women and boys. That they may be unwilling (like Daphne, Castalia, Cassandra, Marpessa) does not deter him. The *Homeric Hymn* to Apollo records the prediction at his birth that he will be *atasthalos*, violent, and so he is in many of his myths,[90] although so devout an ad-

[88]With *Laws* 716C-D cf. *Theaetetus* 176A, the other most influential passage concerned with *homoiôsis*. (It is *homoiôsis theôi*, to be sure, "assimilation to god," not to Zeus, but the substitution of *theos* for Zeus need not be interpreted as a rejection of the god of mythology, who is the god referred to in the "ancient story" of *Laws* 715E8, the one whose side Dikê never leaves.) A late inscription from Miletus refers to Zeus with an unusual adjective *perisôphrôn* (very wise?); see Thomas Drew-Bear and W. D. Lebek, *G.R.B.S.* 14 (1973) 65-73.

[89]Masculine chastity was never inspired by devotion to Apollo. It is Artemis whom Hippolytus worships; Peleus is in awe of Zeus Xenius, and Bellerophon's motive is doubtless the same. Amphiaraus regards his service to Apollo as obliging him to be truthful (*Hypsipyle*, Frg. 60, 58-59 Bond). He does not relate to the god his famous sophrosyne.

[90]Consult Séchan and Lévèque, *op. cit.*, 203-204.

mirer as Pindar does his best to disguise the fact, as in his version
of the story of Coronis. Ovid, unconstrained by genuine belief in
the mythological gods, tells the story of Daphne in the first book
of the *Metamorphoses* as an instance of Apollo's *superbia* (454), even
playing ironically on his association with the ideal of moderation.[91]

Secondly, like every god who takes part with Zeus in the Gigantomachy, Apollo is a *sôphronistês*, but not, for that reason, *sôphrôn*.
He figures in several notable myths of the type in which a god
punishes transgressions against his own dignity or prerogatives.
The killing of the Niobids and the vengeance on Tityus belong in
this category,[92] when Apollo and Artemis protect the honor of
their mother Leto. Apollo defends his own prerogatives in the
myths of Pan and Marsyas, the second of which shows the god in a
singularly unpleasant light, however ingeniously the story was
endowed with allegorical significance by the Florentine Neoplatonists, who made it a symbol of reality emerging from the surface disguise of appearance, as the skin of the satyr is stripped
from his flesh.[93]

It may seem that Apollo, as he appears in both literature and
art, at least until the end of the classical period, is always more
sôphronistês than *sôphrôn*. The god who stands between the Lapiths
and the Centaurs on the relief from the west pediment of the
temple of Zeus at Olympia, stilling their combat with his outstretched arm, is the most stunning *sôphronistês* imaginable. But in
his personal aura of restraint and austerity, his remoteness from
the struggle, he also embodies an authentic sophrosyne, the kind
that caused him, in *Iliad* 21. 462–464, to decline to fight with
Poseidon "for the sake of wretched mortals." On that occasion he

[91]See, for example, 1. 510–511 (Apollo to Daphne): *Moderatius, oro/ curre fugam-
que inhibe, moderatius insequar ipse* ("Flee more moderately, I beg, and curb your
flight; I myself shall pursue at a more moderate pace"). For Coronis, Pindar, *Pyth.*
3, see above, p. 50. Pindar's characterization of Apollo in his affair with Cyrene, as
a young man guided by *aidôs* (modesty), is discussed by Leonard Woodbury,
T.A.P.A. 103 (1972) 561–573.

[92]Horace, *Odes* 4. 6. 1–3: *Dive quem proles Niobea magnae/ Vindicem linguae Tityus-
que raptor/ Sensit* ("O god, whom the children of Niobe came to know as the avenger
of a boastful tongue, as did the ravisher Tityus").

[93]See Wind, 171–176.

based his refusal on his concept of himself as *saophrôn* (the only time the adjective is applied to a god in the Homeric poems and the only time it is used at all in the *Iliad*), thus affording us a rare opportunity to contemplate the concept of self-knowledge from the point of view of the gods. Apollo thinks immortal thoughts and by implication rebukes Poseidon, who is behaving as if there were no impassable boundary between gods and men. His warning to Diomedes in *Iliad* 5. 440–442[94] proceeds from the same perception of this boundary; the complex of ideas adumbrated by these two passages issues, in the archaic age, in the Delphic code with all its implications for morality, religion, and politics, and the Delphic maxims, especially *Gnôthi sauton* (Know thyself) and *Mêden agan* (Nothing in excess).

When Apollo bids the worshiper approaching the Alcmaeonid temple *Gnôthi sauton*, he is, according to Critias in Plato's *Charmides* (164D), saying in effect, *Sôphronei! Be sôphrôn!* In offering this advice he is still the *sôphronistês*, to be sure, but the accumulated responses of the oracle over the centuries create a strong impression of sophrosyne on the part of the god himself. This impression proceeds above all from the reputation of the Pythia for giving responses that emphasize the worthlessness of human life, the preference of the god for humble rather than ostentatious offerings, and his paradoxical choice of some obscure person as the happiest or wisest of men.[95] A strong preference for reality over appearance pervades these utterances, which constitute an important theme in Herodotus and in tragedy, especially that of Sophocles.[96]

Beyond this evidence of the god's own nature, as it was perceived in the archaic and classical periods, is the effect that Delphi had on certain aspects of Greek law and religion, softening the rigor of ancient institutions and recognizing motive and circumstance, as well as the deed itself, in the judgment of crime. The

[94]See above, p. 32.

[95]See H. W. Parke and D. E. W. Wormell, *The Delphic Oracle* (Oxford, 1956) I, 378–392 for a discussion of such responses and II, nos. 140, 238, 239, 240, 244, 424 for examples.

[96]Cf. the response of Solon to Croesus in Herodotus 1. 31 and see Parke and Wormell, I, 379. On the theme of the misunderstood oracle in Sophocles, see North, 51.

prominent role of Apollo as purifer of homicide,[97] part of his more general function as the god of *katharsis,* is an example of this tempering influence. It was this that Ephorus referred to when he said, in the fourth century, that Apollo in the Delphic oracle summoned men to gentleness (*hêmerotês*) and taught them sophrosyne (ἐσωφρόνιζε).[98]

Among his many other concerns, Apollo's responsibility for healing and for music (with both of which he is identified in the preclassical period)[99] holds rich possibilities for sophrosyne. The parallels between health of body and health of soul (the basic meaning of sophrosyne) were obvious long before Plato exploited them in the *Charmides,* as were the implications of harmony, not only for the individual personality, but for social ethics and politics as well. Pindar combines these ideas in the *Fifth Pythian* (64–67), where he lists among the gifts of Apollo to mankind healing, the lyre, and the Muses, who bring orderly civic life without warfare (*apolemos eunomia,* equivalent in this context to the harmonious tranquillity—*symphônos hêsychia*—of the *First Pythian,* 70). Burton points out that Pindar in general associates *mousikê* with peace and good government and regards all three as characteristic of aristocratic societies.[100] Certainly the *aretê politikê* idealized by Pindar and Bacchylides for the benefit of their royal or tyrannical patrons was the Dorian type of sophrosyne, rather than the Athenian quality, personified among the gods by Athena herself. The prominence of Apollo in Plato's *Laws* is a clue to the kind of civic virtue proposed for the new Cretan city. How smoothly this ideal could be adapted to the needs of the Roman autocracy we see from Horace's celebration of the role of Apollo in the Gigantomachy, the mythical analogue to the victory of Octavian near Apollo's shrine at Actium (*Odes* 3. 4. 60–64).

Among the many myths linking Apollo with music, the lyre, and the Muses, with all that his post as *Musagetes* implies, none has been more influential in art than the story of Marsyas, especially as it was interpreted by the Neoplatonists of the Renaissance. The

[97]See Séchan and Lévêque, *op. cit.,* 213.

[98]Strabo 9. 3. 11, cited by Glenn Morrow, *Plato's Cretan City* (Princeton, 1960) 411.

[99]See Edouard Des Places, S.J., *La religion grecque* (Paris, 1969) 40.

[100]*Op. cit.,* 145–146.

myth is enlightening, not only because it reveals Apollo in his capacity as castigator of *hybris,* but also, incidentally, because it demonstrates the profound distinction felt by the Greeks between stringed and wind instruments and the ethical associations of the different types.[101] The *aulos,* invented by Athena to reproduce the sinister lament of the Gorgons, when she had helped Perseus to slay Medusa (Pindar, *Pyth.* 12. 10–11, 18–21), is linked with licentiousness and uncontrolled passion, while the music of the lyre has a calming, civilizing effect. Both Plato and Aristotle, accepting Damon's doctrine about the ethical influence of the musical modes, held that the music of the lyre instills sophrosyne, that of the *aulos* its opposite.[102]

That the Greeks from early times were aware of the ambivalence of Apollo is proved by the colossal archaic statue erected on Delos by the Naxians, which showed the god holding images of the Graces in his right hand, the bow and arrows in his left.[103] As Macrobius observes, he is depicted thus *quod ad noxam sit pigrior et salutem manus promptior largiatur,* because, that is, he is quicker to bestow what the Graces represent than what the weapons promise.[104] Horace, without alluding to the Naxian statue, nevertheless employs the symbolism of the lyre and the bow in much the same way:

> . . . non, si male nunc, et olim
> sic erit; quondam cithara tacentem
> suscitat Musam neque semper arcum
>   tendit Apollo. [*Odes* 2. 10. 17–20][105]

[101]See Emanuel Winternitz, *Musical Instruments and Their Symbolism in Western Art* (London, 1967) 150–165, and consult Wind, 171–176, for interpretations of the Marsyas myth by Neoplatonists in antiquity and the Renaissance. According to Christoph Clairmont, *Y.C.S.* 15 (1957) 161–178, the incident of the flaying is not depicted until Hellenistic and Roman times; not until the Renaissance does the god himself do the flaying.

[102]See Plato, *Rep.* 399D-E and Aristotle, *Politics* 1341a37–39 and consult Warren D. Anderson, *Ethos and Education in Greek Music* (Cambridge, Mass., 1966), especially 64–81, 136–138.

[103]See Rudolf Pfeiffer, *J.W.C.I.* 15 (1952) 20–32.

[104]Macrobius, *Sat.* 1. 17. 13. Literally, "because he is slower to do damage, and his readier hand bestows well-being." Cf. Callimachus, Frg. 114 Pfeiffer.

[105]". . . if misfortune comes now, it will not always be so. Sometimes Apollo with his lyre awakens the silent Muse. He does not always stretch his bow." Contrast the picture of Apollo in the Gigantomachy, *Odes* 3. 4. 60: *numquam umeris positurus arcum* ("destined never to lay aside the bow from his shoulders").

Artemis

The sophrosyne of Artemis is entirely different from that of
her brother, except in those myths that represent her, like Apollo,
as the avenger of the insults offered to their mother Leto by
Niobe, Otus, or Tityus, or of assaults upon her own person by
Orion.[106] Both Apollo and Artemis exemplify purity, freedom,
and remoteness, but in different ways, for these qualities in
Apollo are spiritual, while in Artemis they belong to a physical
plane. Hence her sophrosyne is that of the flesh—maidenhood,
not moderation—and Aeschylus and Euripides made no mistake
when they portrayed her single-minded worshipers, the Danaids
and Hippolytus, as guilty of excesses so great as to nullify their
virtue. There is no moderation in the character of Artemis, no
sophrosyne in this sense of the word, but rather a merciless austerity, a devotion to purity that is wild and fierce and may be
cruel. It is no accident that many of the hunters and huntresses
who figure in the myths of Artemis come to a violent end, often
through the agency of the goddess herself.[107]

Artemis' special attribute, physical aloofness, causes her to
haunt wild forests and remote peaks. Although in origin she was
evidently a goddess of fertility, like Cybele in being mistress of
wild things because she was in fact their mother, Artemis became
a virgin-goddess, yet retained her connection with the wild wood-
lands and their inhabitants.[108] The *Homeric Hymn to Aphrodite*
knows Artemis as one of the three goddesses impervious to love,
and the most typical of her myths center on her protection of
herself and her devotees from sexual contamination or her
punishment of those who, even unwillingly, violate her modesty.

---

[106]Pindar's interpretation of the myth of Tityus (*Pyth.* 4. 90–92) is parallel to his
comment on the punishment of Ixion for his assault on Hera: one should strive
for loves within one's power.

[107]Walter F. Otto, *The Homeric Gods*, trans. Moses Hadas (New York, 1954) 89.

[108]Consult Séchan and Lévèque, *op. cit.*, 359, and W. K. C. Guthrie, *The Greeks
and Their Gods* (Boston, 1955) 99–101, on the origins of Artemis. Greek and
Roman poetry often link being a hunter with living a life of purity and freedom
(Hippolytus, Atalanta, Camilla), but the theme of the erotic hunt is also common
(for example, Virgil, *Aen.* 4. 130–168, Ovid, *Metam.* passim). The theme is popular
in Roman mosaics, such as those at Halicarnassus, which portray Dido and Aeneas,
Atalanta and Meleager.

The death of Adonis is an extension of her passion for vengeance, since Euripides appears to interpret it as retaliation for the death of her favorite, Hippolytus, the victim of Aphrodite.[109]

However narrow and specialized her sophrosyne may have been, Artemis has much more influence on the iconography of the virtue than does Apollo. Her various attributes—the bow and arrows, the quiver, the crescent moon, the stag, even the hunting dogs—serve as symbols of chastity in the shorthand notation of artists as early as Etruscan and Roman times.[110] In the proliferation of allegorical figures on Renaissance tombs, Temperantia may be represented as a classical Diana[111] (whereas Fortitudo borrows the armor of Minerva). A particularly vivid example of the symbolic use of Diana to enrich the concept of *temperantia* amid the entire quartet of cardinal virtues may be seen in the Apotheosis of the Medici by Luca Giordano, in the Medici-Riccardi Palace, Florence, where the death of Adonis takes place in close proximity to the personified Temperance with her multitude of attendants, and the huntress Diana lurks nearby with her fatal bow.

It is unusual in antiquity for Artemis to assume civic responsibilities, although when she is invoked in the *Oedipus Tyrannus* (with Athena and Apollo) to ward off the plague from Thebes, she is said to have a throne in the middle of the agora (161). She does indeed share a cult in Athens with such political abstractions as Themis and Eunomia, and also with Nemesis,[112] but the city is not her normal place of habitation. Exactly the opposite is true of Athena, whose identification with her city is complete and whose sophrosyne, although it takes several distinct forms, is in one of them conspicuously urban.

Athena

Athena is a more complex goddess of sophrosyne than Artemis. She, too, symbolizes chastity, being the first of the three goddesses

[109]Euripides, *Hippolytus* 1420-1422, and see Barrett.
[110]Panofsky, *Tomb Sculpture*, 31.
[111]See below, chapter 4, note 90.
[112]See Karl Hoener, *Artemis* (Zurich, 1946) 91-92. In the *Homeric Hymn to Aphrodite* (5) Artemis is said to love a city of just men (20); cf. Anacreon, Frg. 348 Page, where she rejoices, looking down on a city of bold-hearted (θρασυκαρδίων) men.

described as impervious to Aphrodite in the *Homeric Hymn*,[113] but she is also something quintessentially Greek, heroic intelligence guided by restraint, and, above all, she is the divine manifestation of the *aretê politikê* of Athens. When the Homeric poems were first interpreted in an allegorical spirit,[114] Athena was equated with *phronêsis* (wisdom), but she is at least as persuasive an embodiment of sophrosyne because in the most influential of her myths she guides the heroes to the effective use of their heroic powers through self-restraint. Unlike Artemis, who haunts the mountaintops in company with nymphs and wild beasts, Athena is ever the comrade of heroes, the divine adviser of Odysseus, Achilles, Heracles, Jason, and Telemachus. And in contrast to the way in which the most celebrated masculine follower of Artemis— Hippolytus—comes to grief, deriving cold comfort from her sponsorship, Athena's protegés without exception find her patronage beneficent.

Like Artemis, however, Athena goes back to diverse antecedents that leave their mark on her character and mythology. In origin the palace divinity of the Minoan and Mycenaean kings, she has two primary functions—to protect the king and to instill the household arts. The sophrosyne myths involving her reflect but do not stop with those functions. Athena appears as a goddess of sophrosyne in four principal categories of myth. In the first, she defends her special prerogatives. As goddess of household arts—of which weaving is the most important—she appears in the myth of Arachne, where she takes a pitiless vengeance on Arachne's *hybris*. Like almost every other divine *sôphronistês,* Athena herself is far from *sôphrôn.* (She is equally ruthless in the myth about the blinding of Teiresias, in which another special prerogative of the goddess, her modesty, is offended, when Teiresias accidentally beholds her at the bath.)

---

[113]7–32. Hestia is the third. Lucian (*Dialogues of the Gods* 23), when listing the goddesses who are impervious to Eros, omits Hestia but adds the Muses, because of their *semnotês* (holiness), a quality often paired with sophrosyne in sepulchral and honorary inscriptions. See the Miletus inscription cited in note 88 above.

[114]By Theagenes of Rhegium in the late sixth century B.C. Consult Buffière, *op. cit.* (above, note 38), 103–105. In Sophocles' satyr-play on the judgment of Paris, Athena represented *Aretê* and Aphrodite *Hêdonê.*

In the second type of myth, Athena is the warrior goddess and the patron of heroes, to whom she teaches moderation. She first appears in such a role in *Iliad* 1, where she prevents Achilles from yielding to his passion for instant revenge, and, in the *Odyssey*, she guides Odysseus to his victory over the suitors, made possible by self-restraint, endurance, and guile. Striking testimony to popular belief in Athena's "sophronizing" power is the tradition about the stone with which she stunned Heracles and thus prevented him from murdering Amphitryon (Euripides, *H.F.* 1002–1006). According to Pausanias (9. 11. 2) it was called the *sôphronistêr lithos*. Still another memorable expression of her influence, with its combination of restraining and inspiring qualities, is the story of her gift of the bridle to Bellerophon, as he slept in her temple at Corinth. With this device he is able to control Pegasus and slay the Chimaera.[115]

Thirdly, Athena plays a prominent part in the Gigantomachy, where she is next to Zeus in importance. As noted above, her defeat of Enceladus and Pallas is a favorite theme in archaic and classical art, not just in Athens, but throughout the Greek world, and everywhere it implies the victory of order over chaos.[116] In the fourth kind of myth, however—where she symbolizes Athenian *aretê politikê*—Athena displays a kind of sophrosyne belonging to her alone among the gods. From the time of Solon she is linked with that sense of measure that Athenian poets and other artists sought to represent as characteristic of their city's social and legal institutions. The most celebrated example is, of course, her role in the *Eumenides* of Aeschylus, where, by her powers of persuasion (backed by the hint of force), she brings about the exemplary compromise between the old and the new that transforms the Furies into Well-wishers and secures for Athens the Mean between tyranny and anarchy. It is perhaps worth recalling the difference among the three gods who are associated with sophrosyne as a political concept: Zeus, who establishes order in

[115]See Pausanias 2. 4. 1 and L. R. Farnell, *Cults of the Greek States* (Oxford, 1869–1909) I, 408 n.95, on Athena Chalinitis. The bridle represents Athena's patronage of craftsmanship at the same time as it symbolizes her power of controlling passion. Consult Détienne, *art. cit.* (above, note 15).

[116]See Vian, *op. cit.* (above, note 5) 56–68.

the heavens and on earth, Apollo, the ideal of the Dorian aristocracy, and Athena, the personification of Athenian democracy, particularly in its idealized, mid-fifth-century form.

The portrayal on ancient reliefs or in vase paintings of an episode from a myth of Athena, unmistakable in her unique dress, with Corinthian helmet, aegis, and gorgoneion, triumphant over a Giant, could easily be interpreted as a celebration of sophrosyne victorious over *hybris,* but this was only the beginning of her influence in Western art. As the symbol of victory over the passions she appears in many allegorical scenes and contexts that have no precedent in classical myth, such as Mantegna's painting (now in the Louvre) in which both Minerva and Diana put to flight Venus, who rides a Centaur and leads a flock of repulsive figures representing her vicious attendants.[117] Botticelli's Minerva and the Centaur depicts the same victory as a peaceful one. This is a particularly interesting example of the combination of two familiar classical figures to make a scene unknown in ancient art, where the conquest of the Centaurs is the task of the Lapiths or of individual heroes like Heracles, and is always violent.

Aphrodite

Another nonclassical development, based on late classical sources, is the union of Minerva and Venus,[118] or (more frequently) Venus and Mars, to suggest a *discordia concors.* "The idea of Venus as a goddess of moderation may seem mythologically odd," Edgar Wind truly observes, after describing the enthusiasm of the Florentine Neoplatonists for the representation of harmony born of Venus and Mars.[119] Yet he points out that when Pico della Mirandola advanced this notion he was following a lead offered by Plutarch, *On Isis and Osiris* (48), and there is indeed a good deal of discussion in late antiquity of the moderating power of Aphrodite/Venus and the union of love and strife. But in the classical period this notion is rare, and only in Platonic conceptions of the *sôphrôn erôs* or the Uranian Aphrodite is much attention paid to such a paradoxical combination of what are usually

---

[117]See Van Marle, II, Fig. 6.
[118]See Rudolf Wittkower, *J.W.C.I.* 2 (1938) 200.
[119]Wind, 119.

violent antitheses. The disguise of Venus as a huntress in *Aeneid* 1—suggesting a combination of her nature with that of Diana— stimulates Renaissance artists, but is not typical of classical thought. In general, antiquity accepted both the Homeric picture of Athena and Aphrodite as being on opposite sides in the Trojan War and Euripides' portrayal of Aphrodite and Artemis, in the *Hippolytus*, as bitter foes. Epitaphs and epigrams of the Graeco-Roman period afford evidence that these assumptions were widespread.[120]

Dionysus

In spite of Oliver Gogarty's reminder that "Virgil made an austere Venus Muse of his song,"[121] the goddess herself makes no claim to be *sôphrôn*, but Dionysus, who appears to be just as much the antithesis of Apollo as Venus is of Artemis or Athena, does make such a claim, and in fact the sophrosyne of Dionysus forms one of the most fascinating paradoxes in ancient literature. This god, who occupies the Delphic temple when its usual tenant is absent during the three winter months, contrasts with Apollo in almost every conceivable way. In opposition to the Delphic instructions—Know thyself, Nothing in excess, Think mortal thoughts—he invites his worshipers to forget themselves, indulge in excess, become one with the god. Bacchus himself is drunken, amorous, unrestrained, yet not only does he claim (in Euripides' *Bacchae* 504, 641) to be *sôphrôn*, but so austere a philosopher as Plato can (in *Laws* 1 and 2) recommend employing him and his symposia as part of the necessary process of testing and training the young in sophrosyne.

Because he takes part in the Gigantomachy, Dionysus has a share in the process of bringing order out of chaos, although he in some ways resembles the Giants more than the Olympians. The Giants are, at least in postclassical representations, serpent-

---

[120]For example Kaibel, 560 (Italy, first century), on Athena as the source of sophrosyne, Cypris of beauty. Cf. 874 and see *Anth. Pal.* 5. 272, 293, 6. 283, 285. Hadrian's inscription at Thespiae, in gratitude to *saophrôn* Eros for the killing of a bear, refers to the Uranian Aphrodite (Kaibel, 811); the Platonic reminiscence suggests a connection with Antinous.

[121]Oliver Gogarty, "Dedication," *Oxford Book of Modern Verse, 1892–1935*. Chosen by W. B. Yeats (New York, 1936) 185.

footed, and Dionysus is accompanied by various beasts that seem to represent his own transformations.[122] Again, like the other gods, he is a *sôphronistês* in punishing offenses against his godhead. The so-called resistance myths all involve this pattern. As his cult is introduced into various cities, the rulers resist and are punished in dreadful ways. We know the story best from the *Bacchae,* where Euripides constructs the plot in such a way that the well-intentioned and conventionally *sôphrôn* young king Pentheus works out the formal pattern of the *contemptor divum* (he despises Aphrodite, too) and receives the punishment reserved for *hybris.* Dionysus as *sôphronistês* appears as early as the *Homeric Hymn* (VII) in his honor, where the story of the Etruscan pirates is told. It is significant that the helmsman, the only member of the crew who tried to spare the captive god, is credited with a *saophrôn* spirit (49). Dionysus, after turning the other pirates into dolphins, renders the helmsman *panolbios*—in every way happy (54). At the end of the *Bacchae* he says to the family of Cadmus (what is left of it), "If you had known how to be wise [*sôphronein*] when you did not wish to be, you would be happy [*eudaimoneite*] and have the son of Zeus as your champion" (1341–1343).[123]

Not only does *eudaimoneite* have special implications derived from the unique *eudaimonia* revealed in this play as the gift of Dionysus, but *sôphronein* must also be read in the light of the ironic treatment of sophrosyne (true and false, conventional and paradoxical) that is one of the themes of the *Bacchae.* The concept has grown beyond the sense in which the adjective *saophrôn* was used in the *Homeric Hymn,* in the sixth century, yet in both the *Hymn* and the *Bacchae* sophrosyne implies the kind of wisdom that enables a human being to distinguish between appearance and reality and thus recognize a god, even in disguise.

The central paradox of Dionysus' sophrosyne is his relation to the tragic drama. The rituals performed in honor of this turbulent god somehow gave rise to the drama that served Athens and

___

[122]See Vian, *op. cit.,* 206–207. Horace refers to him as equipped with the claws and dreadful jaw of a lion (*Odes* 2. 19. 23–24).

[123]Another similarity is the sinister smile on the face of the god in both the *Hymn* and the *Bacchae,* as he effortlessly frustrates the attempts of his captors to bind him. Cf. *Hymn* 13–15 with *Bacchae* 604 ff.

ultimately the world as a source of catharsis and self-knowledge. The Apolline *Gnôthi sauton,* uttered in stone at Delphi as the individual pilgrim approached the temple, was enjoined upon the entire audience in the Theatre of Dionysus, where their crowded proximity doubtless contributed to the effectiveness of the lesson, just as the majestic scene of cliff and gorge and circling eagles at Delphi reinforced the Apolline sense of remoteness and austerity. As a poet of the *Anthology* observed, "Dionysus, though drunken [ὁ μεθύων] taught sobriety [ἐσωφρόνισεν] to the townspeople" (11.32).

None of this went unnoticed by Plato. Dionysus the *sôphronistês* moves from the Theatre to the state-controlled symposium of the *Laws,* where he is to test in the young their power to resist temptation, while training them in self-restraint. In the old he is to implant the power to cast aside the inhibitions of advancing years, so that they will not scruple to sing and dance in public (from purer motives than do the old men, Cadmus and Teiresias, in the *Bacchae*).[124]

Earlier even than the *Laws,* Plato's *Phaedrus* had borne witness to the beneficial results of divine madness—*theia mania.* While the madness chiefly celebrated in Socrates' second speech is that of Eros, other kinds of mania are also praised, including the poetic. Ecstatic poetry is the province of Dionysus, but even ecstasy must be controlled if the result is to be sublime. Hence the development of the concept of *sôphrôn mania (sobria ebrietas)* in rhetoric and poetics, a concept proceeding indirectly from Plato's *theia mania.*[125] In *sôphrôn mania,* controlled inspiration, the two schools of Hellenistic poetry are reconciled, the water-drinkers, devoted to Apollo, and the wine-drinkers, worshipers of Dionysus. Horace is squarely in this tradition when he uses Bacchus as a symbol of the union of poetry and order.[126] His paradoxical references to *modicus Liber* (*Odes* 1. 18. 7) and *verecundus Bacchus* (*Odes* 1. 27. 3) are more than merely examples of *callida iunctura.* They express in mythical terms the *sôphrôn mania* that Horace identified as the source of authentic inspiration.

[124]Cf. *Laws* 666A-C with *Bacchae* 170 ff.
[125]See North, *C.P.* 43 (1948) 1–17.
[126]As noted by Steele Commager, *The Odes of Horace* (Bloomington, 1967) 337.

Odysseus

Odysseus offers the most instructive example imaginable of the
variations in an important exemplar of sophrosyne over the centuries from Homer to the Renaissance (and indeed to modern
times). Since the progress of this *polytropos* figure has been traced
in detail by W. B. Stanford,[127] we need only observe the stages by
which he gains a reputation for sophrosyne.

In the Homeric poems, as we have noted, he is never credited
with this virtue. Telemachus is *saophrôn*, but not his father (nor
even his mother, who afterward becomes the archetype of
feminine sophrosyne). Yet even in the *Iliad* there are evident
qualities in Odysseus that will later be recognized as facets of
sophrosyne: his intellectual gifts and his power to restrain himself
and others.[128] In the *Odyssey*, of course, the signs are much more
evident, and by his powers of self-restraint and endurance the
hero approximates later concepts of the *sôphrôn anêr*.[129] His
tlêmosynê (endurance) commends him to the fourth-century
philosophers, who regard this quality as equivalent to *karteria*
(hardiness) and thus a part, now of *andreia*, now of sophrosyne.
His overcoming of various obstacles encountered in his wanderings and, above all, his behavior toward Calypso and Circe lead to
his being considered *sôphrôn* by the moralists and allegorists, Stoic
and Neoplatonic, but in the *Odyssey* itself there is no hint whatsoever that the hero who is Calypso's lover for seven years and
Circe's for one is displaying sophrosyne of any kind. A revolution
in both morality and semantics has occurred between Homer and
the Stoics.

The career of Odysseus as an exemplar of sophrosyne proceeds
in three distinct stages: tragedy, Hellenistic philosophy, and Renaissance poetry, accurately reflecting the moral climate of the

[127]W. B. Stanford, *The Ulysses Theme* (Oxford, 1954).

[128]See ibid., 15–17, for instances of modesty and restraint on the part of Odysseus in the *Iliad*, especially in the episode of Dolon (Book 10) and the Funeral
Games (Book 23).

[129]Ibid., 34–35, discusses the implications of the three adjectives with which
Athena describes Odysseus in *Od.* 13. 332. *Echephrôn*—controlling one's *phrenes*
(emotions, impulses)—comes closest to the later meaning of *sôphrôn*. See also
Agathe Thornton, *People and Themes in Homer's Odyssey* (London and Dunedin,
1970) 81–92, on Odysseus' capacity for "control," especially as symbolized by the
image of fetters, 20. 23.

periods concerned. In the fifth century the lyric and tragic poets develop hints found in the epic cycle about the character of Odysseus and present him in a diversity of ways, both good and bad. His rivalry with Ajax over the arms of Achilles (an episode of the *Ilias Parva*) was a popular theme that led to varying assessments of his character, depending on the personal preference of the poet and, to some extent, on his political views.[130] Pindar denounced the cunning and guile with which Odysseus had, in his opinion, cheated Ajax of the arms he merited as the greatest Greek warrior after Achilles. Sophocles, on the other hand, chose the story as a vehicle for contrasting the noble, but outmoded, type of heroism represented by Ajax with a form of *arete* more suited to post-Homeric society, and it was in the course of developing this contrast that he portrayed Odysseus as a *sôphrôn anêr*, a kind of prototype of the Athenian ideal in the mid-fifth century.

Odysseus' sophrosyne is brought out in the Prologue when Athena—to whom he behaves with much more formal piety than in the *Odyssey*—describes the attitude of the gods to the *kakoi* and the *sôphrones* and indicates that Ajax and Odysseus represent these two antitheses. In his reaction, first to Ajax's attempt to torture him, then to Ajax's death and to the efforts of the Atridae to deny him burial, Odysseus displays a kind of sophrosyne that has much in common with the Delphic maxims and the archaic injunction to think mortal thoughts, but also resembles the magnanimous sophrosyne that Athenian poets like to think typical of their city—the *arete* ascribed to Athenian kings by Sophocles and Euripides.[131]

Part of Odysseus' characterization in the Prologue involves a degree of caution that many commentators have found excessive. This attribute is magnified into a vice and derided in Sophocles' late tragedy, *Philoctetes*, which presents a contemptible, sophistic Odysseus, contrasted unfavorably with the old hero Philoctetes and with Neoptolemus, the young son of Achilles. This excessive caution is equated with sophrosyne in an ironic speech when

---

[130]Cf. Norman Brown, *T.A.P.A.* 82 (1951) 1–28, for a political interpretation of Pindar's preference for Ajax in *Nem.* 8 and *Pyth.* 8.

[131]For example, Theseus in *Oedipus at Colonus* and the *Suppliants* and Demophon in the *Heracleidae*.

Neoptolemus taunts Odysseus because he has begun to draw his sword and then thought better of it, threatening instead to report Neoptolemus to the Greek army. ἐσωφρόνησας! replies Neoptolemus, "You have begun to be sensible, and if you are of the same mind for the rest of the time perhaps you might keep out of trouble" (1259–1260). For those who remembered Achilles' impulse to attack Agamemnon in *Iliad* 1, only to be restrained by Athena, the contrast must have been arresting. There is no Athena now to save the hero's face.[132]

Excessive caution and excessive cunning are the chief vices with which Odysseus is charged by his critics in the fifth and fourth centuries. The Platonic Socrates implicitly criticizes Odysseus, when in the *Apology* he mentions both Ajax and Palamedes as martyrs unjustly put to death, with whom he would gladly converse in Hades (41B), but he does not actually charge Odysseus with responsibility for their unjust death and elsewhere is not hostile to him. In *Republic* 390D, for example, he quotes Odysseus' address to his *thymos* ("Endure, my heart, even worse have you endured before," *Od.* 20. 18) as an example of *karteria,* here equivalent to sophrosyne.[133] Moreover, in spite of Plato's refusal to allow Homer to be admitted to the ideal state, there to play his traditional role as teacher (*Rep.* 607A), the Myth of Er at the end of the *Republic* uses Odysseus as a moral exemplar. His shade chooses a private (*apragmôn*) lot for its next incarnation, having profited by the example of its own earlier existence and learned the folly of ambition (*philotimia,* 620C-D).

The systematic exploitation of Odysseus as a model of virtue by the Cynics has other notable precedents in fourth-century literature. In Xenophon's *Memorabilia,* Socrates cites the story of Circe as a warning against gluttony and maintains that Odysseus avoided being turned into a pig not just because of Hermes' aid (in the form of the herb moly), but because of his own self-restraint (*enkrateia*). Although this comment is made in jest (1. 3. 7), it anticipates the serious use of such an interpretation by the Cynics and their imitators. Traces of this approach to the ethos of

---

[132]See North, *T.A.P.A.* 78 (1947) 8, for this scene as evidence for hostility to sophrosyne.

[133]Cf. Xenophon, *Mem.* 1. 6. 1–6, where *karteria* is a facet of sophrosyne.

Odysseus may already be seen in Antisthenes' two model speeches, one for Ajax, the other for Odysseus. The second presents Odysseus in terms that later became key concepts of the Cynic ideal of the hero, with emphasis on his service to humanity, his endurance, and his self-reliance.[134]

There is no hint of allegory in Antisthenes' interpretation of the myth of Odysseus, and in spite of the attraction of allegory from the sixth century B.C. onward, the purely moral exegesis, which made Odysseus the model of sophrosyne and related virtues, continued far into the Christian period. According to this fashion, the episodes involving the Sirens and Circe (less often Calypso) were proofs of the hero's ability to resist temptation, usually that of the flesh, although as early as the time of Cicero the Sirens were thought to symbolize concupiscence of the spirit, an interpretation that had a famous outcome in the *Purgatorio* of Dante.[135] A classic statement of the moral exegesis is made by Horace in *Epistles* 1. 2. 17-18, where he maintains that he has learned from Ulysses, that *utile exemplar,* what virtue and wisdom can accomplish. After a free rendering of the opening lines of the *Odyssey,* Horace goes on to say:

> Sirenum voces et Circae pocula nosti:
> quae si cum sociis stultus cupidusque bibisset
> sub domina meretrice fuisset turpis et excors,
> vixisset canis immundus vel amica luto sus. [23-26]

> (You know the songs of the Sirens and the goblets of Circe.
> If, foolish and greedy, he had drunk them with his companions,
> he would have been subject—base and stupid—to a harlot,
> and would have lived like a filthy dog or mud-loving sow.)

Among innumerable allusions to the moral symbolism of the Circe story, the most amusing occurs in Plutarch's dialogue *That Brute Beasts Use Reason,* where Gryllus, a Greek changed into a pig,

---

[134]Consult Höistad, *op. cit.* (above, note 38) 97-100.

[135]Cicero, *Fin.* 5. 18. 49. See Dante, *Purgatorio* 19. 7-33. The Barberini sequences referred to above (note 23) include *Ulysses . . . integer* in the episode of the Sirens. The poem on which the picture was based puts more emphasis on Circe's *pocula.* Odysseus figured as a type of conjugal fidelity in Neopythagorean writings (for example, Iamblichus, *Vit. Pyth.* 57).

declines to be restored to human shape, maintaining that animals are innately superior to men in respect to all the virtues. Referring to Odysseus' belief that he has proved his sophrosyne by scorning the charms of Circe, Gryllus insists that actually the hero is in no way superior to brute beasts, since they do not seek to consort with their betters, but mate only with their own kind and, furthermore, indulge only in natural appetites, avoiding all the perversions and unnecessary desires to which men are subject (988F-991D).

Cleanthes the Stoic in the third century B.C. was apparently the first to interpret the myth of Circe allegorically, when he taught that moly stood for the *logos* (*SVF* 1. 526). After this, many key episodes in the Wanderings were endowed with a nonliteral significance, as when Odysseus leaving Calypso to return to Penelope was taken (by Eustathius, in the twelfth century) to mean that the soul turns from science to philosophy, because Calypso, the daughter of Atlas, represents astronomy, while Penelope, the weaver of the web, represents logic, whose premises are combined to obtain conclusions and thus weave the tissue of the syllogism.[136] The Neoplatonists, both pagan and Christian, found in the myth of Odysseus a symbolic account of the adventures of the soul struggling to rid itself of contamination by the body. Thus Plotinus adapts the Wanderings to his doctrine of the soul's return and in *Ennead* 1. 6. 8 advises the reader to set forth as did Odysseus, when he fled from the witch Circe, not content to stay where the delights of the eyes were all about him. This passage in Plotinus inspired St. Augustine, who, however, substitutes for Odysseus the Prodigal Son, as Gregory of Nyssa had done before him. But just as Plotinus makes sophrosyne the mark of the purified soul, so, too, Augustine emphasizes *temperantia* as essential for the soul's flight to God.[137] For whatever reason—

---

[136]Buffière, 388–389; see 292 on moly. Consult also Franz Cumont, *Recherches sur le symbolisme funéraire des Romains* (Paris, 1942) 23–24, on the Sirens and Circe.

[137]See John F. Callahan, *Augustine and the Greek Philosophers* (Villanova, 1967) 47–74, for this theme in Plotinus and Gregory and its modification by Augustine. For *temperantia* as essential for the flight to God, see Augustine, *Solil.* 1. 14. 24–25 and *Against the Academics* 2. 9. 22. On a supposedly Neopythagorean use of Odysseus to symbolize the flight, in the stuccoes of the Underground Basilica of the Porta Maggiore, Rome, consult Marcel Détienne, *Latomus* 17 (1958) 270–286.

whether as a covert allusion to some doctrine implying salvation or merely as a decorative reminder of a popular myth—the episode of Odysseus and the Sirens appears on sarcophagi of the third century of our era (ten of which have been identified by Pierre Courcelle[138]) and on mosaics of Roman imperial times. Its persistence into the Middle Ages is exemplified by an illustration employing this theme in Herrad of Landsberg's twelfth-century encyclopedia, the *Hortus Deliciarum,* where it symbolizes resistance to the perils of this world.[139]

The moral and allegorical interpretation of the *Odyssey* had profound consequences in Renaissance literature.[140] To cite only two examples, Spenser and Milton, Book II of the *Faerie Queene* (the Book of Temperaunce) adapts both Circe and the Sirens to the adventure of the Knight Guyon, while *Comus* is a Puritan version of the episode of Circe. Spenser's Acrasia in her Bowre of Bliss combines elements of Circe, Calypso, and Venus, but Circe dominates the mixture because of the transformation of the cast-off lovers into beasts and the emphasis on the magic potion that accomplishes their metamorphosis (2, Canto 1. 51–61; Canto 12. 30–87). In the course of the voyage by which Guyon and the Palmer approach Acrasia's island they pass the Sirens (here called Mermayds and five in number, rather than two, as in Homer, or three, as in the popular tradition). Their promise now is "rest from troublous toyle, The worldes sweet IN from paine and wearisome turmoyle" (Canto 12. 32). Spenser's use of the myths and allegories generated by classical and mediaeval conceptions of sophrosyne or *temperantia* goes far beyond these reminiscences of the *Odyssey,* but a close study of the Book of Temperaunce and of the relation of "goodly Temperance in garments clene" to Mercilla in Book 5 (9. 31) would unduly prolong this chapter. Some iconographic observations will be made in Chapter 4.

Milton's Comus is the son of Circe and Bacchus: "much like his

[138]Pierre Courcelle, *Revue des études anciennes* 46 (1944) 65–93 (cited by Callahan, *op. cit.,* pages 107–108, note 87).

[139]*Hortus Deliciarum (Garden of Delights),* ed. and trans. Aristide D. Caratzos (New Rochelle, N.Y., 1977) Plate LVIII.

[140]For moly as a symbol of chastity see Merritt Hughes, *P.M.L.A.* 44 (1929) 696–704, and for Milton's use of the myth of Circe, consult Douglas Bush, *Mythology and the Renaissance Tradition in English Poetry* (New York, 1957) 264–268.

father, but his mother more." Indeed, he "excels his mother at her mighty art." The wizard mentions his mother Circe "with the Syrens three," but the Sirens play no further part in the story. Comus possesses a new herb, haemony, more potent than moly (636), and with it and the wizard's wand, which has become part of the enchanter's equipment, he changes human beings into creatures with animal heads—a more convenient metamorphosis than a complete transformation, if the Masque is actually to be performed. Both the episode of Guyon in the *Faerie Queene* and the adventures of the Lady in the dark wood indicate that the myth of Circe has become a universally accepted, instantly comprehensible symbol of the conflict between reason and passion, virtue and vice, with the victory of reason and virtue to be anticipated as the outcome. And just as Spenser develops the manifold implications of temperance, particularly in its Aristotelian identification with the Mean, so Milton enshrines in *Comus* a Platonic virtue called "saintly chastity" (452) and "spare temperance" (766), which is obviously derived from sophrosyne.

In the Renaissance, as in antiquity, artistic exploitation of the figure of Odysseus kept pace with the literary and resulted in such complicated programs as that followed by Annibale Carracci in painting the ceiling of the Camerino Farnese in the Palazzo Farnese in Rome. The theme is virtue, and the central episode is the Choice of Hercules, but the lunettes at either end of the room show Odysseus with Circe and the Sirens, while in the corners of the vault are the cardinal virtues. Justice and Temperance frame the story of Circe, Fortitude and Prudence that of the Sirens. Above the Circe lunette is a personified Chastity, identified by her turtledove.[141]

The Elder Scipio

Scipio the Elder, to whose place of retirement at Liternum the triumphal procession of Chastity (with which we began) made its way, affords an example of a historical figure about whom legends clustered in his own lifetime, so that he quickly crossed

---

[141]The program was furnished by Fulvio Orsini; see John Rupert Martin, *The Farnese Gallery* (Princeton, 1965) 39. Figs. 17 and 18 show the scenes from the *Odyssey*.

the boundary that separates fact from myth.[142] He was celebrated in antiquity and thereafter for several Roman virtues, two of them facets of sophrosyne: *continentia* and *moderatio*. The first he displayed in his honorable treatment of the beautiful captive at New Carthage, whom he returned to her fiancé, the Celtiberian leader Allucius, along with the ransom offered by her relatives. He thereby won the young man's allegiance to Rome and—according to Polybius—the approval of his own troops for his *enkrateia* and *metriotês*.[143] Livy's account of this episode and the one immediately preceding it, when Scipio, yielding to the request of the wife of Mandonius, orders that the daughters of King Indibilis be treated with as much *verecundia* and *moderatio* as if they were the wives of Rome's allies, shows clearly that the historian has interpreted the virtuous conduct of the Roman general in the light of its effect on Rome's subject peoples. He in fact ascribes to Scipio complete awareness of the consequences of his moderate behavior, just as Cicero in the *Verrines* makes the younger Scipio point out to the people of Segesta the political implications of his own policy of *mansuetudo*, in contrast to the *crudelitas* of Phalaris.[144]

Scipio's treatment of the Spanish captive will remind any reader of the *Lives* of Alexander the Great of that conqueror's scrupulous behavior toward the female relatives of the defeated Darius.[145] One reader who was so reminded was Aulus Gellius. After recording that Alexander was said to have refused even to look at the wife of Darius, Gellius suggests as the topic for a little declamation (*declamatiuncula*) the question which was *continentior*, Alexander in that episode, or Scipio in the story of the Celtiberian captive. He then proceeds to quote some verses of Naevius about the scandalous youth of a great general and maintains that Valerius Antias had referred them to Scipio and had for that reason rejected the account of Scipio's *continentia* accepted by all other

---

[142]Consult R. H. Haywood, *Studies on Scipio Africanus* (Baltimore, 1933) 9–29, for the sources of various legends about Scipio. See also H. H. Scullard, *Scipio Africanus: Soldier and Politician* (London, 1970), especially Chapter XII.

[143]Polybius 10. 19. 7. Cf. Livy 26. 50; Valerius Maximus 4. 3. 1; Florus 1. 22. 40.

[144]*Verr.* 2. 4. 33. For Cicero's views on the political value of moderation, see *De Imp. Cn. Pomp.* 14. 41.

[145]For example, Plutarch, *De Alex. Fort.* 2. 6 and the *Life* 21. 11 and 30. 10. Cf. also the story of the captive Panthea in Xenophon, *Cyropaedia* 6. 1. 47.

historians. Antias held rather that the girl had been *in deliciis amoribusque usurpata* by Scipio (7. 8)—a conclusion which, a recent biographer of Scipio observes, reflects on the morals of Antias rather than on those of Scipio.[146]

The political consequences of ostentatious morality are prominent in Livy's account of the famous rebuke delivered by Scipio to Masinissa for marrying Sophoniba, the daughter of Hasdrubal and former wife of the defeated Scyphax. Here, too, Livy emphasizes the *temperantia* of Scipio, recalling his self-restraint when he was a *iuvenis* in Spain and putting into his hero's mouth a diatribe on the danger of yielding to pleasure and the supreme value of *temperantia*, which Scipio says he prizes more highly than his military virtues. *Qui eas [voluptates] temperantia sua frenavit ac domuit multo maius decus maioremque victoriam sibi peperit quam nos Syphace victo habemus.* ("He who by his temperance has bridled and mastered these pleasures has won for himself a much greater glory and a greater victory than we have as a result of Scyphax's defeat" [30.14].)

These three stories are chiefly responsible for Scipio's persistent fame as an *exemplum temperantiae*, and they inspired many works of art. Florentine cassoni, which often portray exemplars of chastity because they are intended as hope chests or wedding presents, provide numerous illustrations of the *continentia* of Scipio, usually the story of the Spanish captive, but sometimes the episode of Masinissa and Sophoniba.[147]

Scipio's fame as an exemplar of *moderatio* is based on his refusal to accept the excessive honors offered him by the Senate after his victory over Hannibal (Livy 38. 56. 10–13, Valerius Maximus 4. 1. 6). His retirement to Liternum, while explained by Livy as the result of his prosecution by the Petilii (38. 52), which he did not deign to answer, also came to symbolize restraint of ambition.

[146]Scullard, *op. cit.*, 292, note 182. Polybius, whose version of the story is like Livy's, nevertheless remarks that Scipio was known to his friends as *philogynês*, a lover of women (10. 19. 3).

[147]See Schubring for many examples. Nos. 141, 142, 302, 486, 541, 612 depict the Spanish captive; 485 portrays Sophoniba. Alexander and the wives of Darius figure in No. 544. The most popular subject is Lucretia, but other exemplars of chastity are Tuccia, Hippo, Verginia, Penelope, Claudia Quinta, Susanna, Judith, and Daphne, most of them assembled in the Triumph of Chastity.

(Milton cites it as such in his *Second Defence*, when he attempts to establish a parallel between Scipio and Sir Thomas Fairfax, who had withdrawn from the Puritan army because of his revulsion from Cromwell's policies.)[148] Seneca did much to popularize this point of view through an *Epistle to Lucilius* (86) written while he was actually staying *in ipsa Scipionis Africani villa*. He comments on the statesman's *egregia moderatio pietasque* and his decision to withdraw from public life rather than endanger the *libertas* of Rome by impairing her laws. Because of Scipio's moderation and piety, rather than his generalship, Seneca is convinced that *animum . . . eius in caelum, ex quo erat, redisse* ("his soul has returned to heaven, whence it came").

This letter was known to Petrarch, who, after the death of Laura, copied in the margin of his text of Virgil the phrase *animam . . . eius . . . in celum*.[149] Another letter of Seneca may have been in his mind when he described Pudicizia in the *Triumph* as coming ashore at Baiae, after the voyage from Cyprus, and then proceeding *dritto a Literno*. In *Epistle* 51, Seneca discusses places proverbial for immorality or morality, mentioning Baiae among those that promote *luxuria* and Liternum as an honorable contrast. In the exuberant expansion of the theme of the Triumph, artists sometimes portrayed Scipio as a prominent member of the procession, riding horseback beside the unicorn chariot of Chastity.

The *temperantia* both practiced and counseled by Scipio, according to these traditions, was highly valued by Cicero, who shared Isocrates' belief that the ethos of a whole society reflects that of its leaders and who regarded *temperantia* as a key virtue in the statesman or general, indispensable for conciliating allies and subject peoples (*Ep. ad Q.F.* 1. 1. 22). He ascribes this *temperantia* to the Younger Scipio in several notable passages in the *Verrines*, but the Elder Scipio also figures as an exemplar, and his most interesting appearance is in the *Somnium Scipionis*, which had enormous influence in the Middle Ages. In this treatise the Elder Scipio

---

[148]*Complete Prose Works* (New Haven and London, 1966) IV, 669.

[149]Cf. the Budé edition, *Lettres à Lucilius* (Paris, 1965) vol. 3, page 138, note 1. I owe this reference to Seneca, *Ep.* 86, to an anonymous referee for the Cornell University Press.

expounds to the Younger the Platonic doctrine that by keeping the soul free from contamination with bodily pleasures the statesman who has cared for the *salus patriae*—the welfare of his country—will more quickly fly *in hanc sedem et domum suam* (9. 21)—precisely the same notion of the flight to the fatherland as Plotinus links with the Voyage of Odysseus.[150] The vast prestige of the *Somnium* and the popularity of Macrobius' *Commentary* help explain the profound reverence with which the Elder Africanus was regarded in the Middle Ages and early Renaissance. Petrarch's epic poem *Africa,* with Scipio as hero, was the occasion of his coronation on the Capitoline in 1341.[151]

Another source of Scipio's popularity in the Renaissance was the *Punica* of Silius Italicus, the manuscript of which was found by Poggio ca. 1417. Book XV relates the story of the Spanish captive and compares Scipio favorably with Agamemnon, Achilles, and indeed all the Greeks at Troy, whose tents were full of captive women (15. 274–282). At the beginning of this book, Silius describes the dream of Scipio, not the Ciceronian dream, but one in which Scipio is visited by two women, Virtus and Voluptas, who invite him to choose between the ways of life they represent. The Choice of Hercules is reenacted in Roman terms, with emphasis on glory and victory as the rewards of virtue. Not only does Virtus have much to say about chastity as characteristic of the life to which she summons the hero (101), but she herself resembles the popular concept of a personified Sophrosyne or Temperantia. She has a simple coiffure, a modest expression, a manlike gait and countenance, and a pure white garment.[152] The most famous reflection of this scene in art is Raphael's little painting, now in the National Gallery in London, long known as the Dream of a Young Man, which Panofsky identified as the Dream of Scipio.[153]

[150]Plotinus, *On the Beautiful* 1. 6. 8. Cf. Cicero, *Hortensius* 2. 24: *facillimum ascensum et reditum in caelum* and the comment of Seneca about Scipio's return *in caelum.*

[151]Scullard, *op. cit.,* 242, comments on the interest in Scipio's life evoked in the early Renaissance, including its significance for Dante and Petrarch. See also Aldo Bernardo, *Petrarch, Scipio, and the "Africa": The Birth of Humanism's Dream* (Baltimore, 1962).

[152]15. 28 ff. Cf. the description of Sophrosyne in Gregory of Nazianzus, *Carmen* 45. 229 ff. (*P.G.* 37) and see below, Chapter 4, note 21.

[153]Panofsky. *Hercules am Scheidewege* (above, note 74) 76–81. See also Wind, 81–82, for the suggestion that the source is Macrobius' Commentary on the *Som-*

Plate III. Fortitude and Temperance with representative heroes (Samson and Scipio
ricanus?), detail of *The Seven Virtues* by Francesco Pesellino (ca. 1460). Samuel H.
ess Collection, Birmingham Museum of Art, Birmingham, Alabama.

Scipio's reputation for *temperantia* and its component virtues was so persistent that in the art of the Renaissance he is more likely than any other pagan hero to appear as her historical representative. In Perugino's painting of the Cardinal Virtues on the wall of the Cambio in Perugia (the source of Raphael's inspiration, according to John Pope-Hennessy),[154] Scipio is accompanied by two other typical figures, Pericles and Cincinnatus, but in some other instances he is the sole exemplar. A notable example is a cassone from the Spiridon Collection in Paris, which shows the cardinal and theological virtues personified as enthroned women with their human representatives seated at their feet. A helmeted figure, identified by an inscription as Scipione Africano, sits at the feet of Temperantia.[155] The same iconographic scheme appears on another cassone, by Francesco Pesellino (1422–1457), now in Birmingham, Alabama, where, however, there is no identifying inscription, and the figure at the feet of Temperantia, holding a book, looks more like a philosopher than a soldier (Plate III).[156]

It is appropriate that the chief historical exemplar of sophrosyne in the Renaissance tradition should be a statesman, because its origins as a cardinal virtue are inextricably linked with the fifth-century *polis* and the ideal constitutions of Plato. Chapter 2 will explore some aspects of the career of sophrosyne as an *aretê politikê* in the Greek world.

---

nium Scipionis. In Cicero, however, it is the Younger Scipio who dreams; hence derivation from the *Punica* is preferable, since there the dreamer is the Elder Scipio and some details correspond to Raphael's painting. On the fusion of Scipio with Hercules in the *Punica,* see Edward L. Bassett, "Hercules and the Hero of the *Punica,*" in *The Classical Tradition: Literary and Historical Studies in Honor of Harry Caplan,* ed. Luitpold Wallach (Ithaca, N.Y., 1966) 258–273.

[154]*Raphael* (London, 1970) 130.

[155]Van Marle, II, Fig. 47, and Schubring, No. 340.

[156]Schubring, No. 275, formerly in the Wittgenstein Collection, Vienna, now Samuel H. Kress Collection 541. A similar figure (Solon?) sits at the feet of Prudentia. For a useful collection of ancient, mediaeval, and Renaissance references to Scipio Africanus as a model of several virtues, including *temperantia* and *moderatio,* and photographs of important works of art portraying the principal episodes in his career as a moral *exemplum,* see Mab Van Lohuizen-Mulder, *Raphael's Images of Justice, Humanity and Friendship: A Mirror of Princes for Scipione Borghese* (Wassenaar, 1977). The appearance of historical exemplars of sophrosyne/*temperantia* in art is discussed in Chapter 4, below.

2

Politics and Education

Εὐνομία τε σαόφρων
ἁ θαλίας τε λέλογχεν
ἄστεά τ' εὐσεβέων
ἀνδρῶν ἐν εἰρήνᾳ φυλάσσει

(Good Order, sound of mind,
who possesses feasts
And guards in peace
The cities of pious men)
—Bacchylides, 13. 186–189 Snell

Protagoras the Sophist, in the speech at the house of Callias ascribed to him in Plato's dialogue, begins, as we did in Chapter 1, with myth. "Once upon a time," he says, the gods existed, but not yet mortal creatures. He tells how all other living things were created and endowed with the various means of life and survival, and then how Prometheus gave to mankind fire and technical competence (*entechnos sophia*), which he stole from Hephaestus and Athena. Nevertheless, human beings were still in danger of extinction, because they lacked *sophia politikê* (political competence), which dwells with Zeus. Hence they could not live in cities without wronging one another. Zeus therefore sent Hermes to give man a sense of mutual respect (*aidôs*) and fairness (*dikê*), so that these qualities might be "orderers of cities and bonds of friendship, drawing men together" (*πόλεων κόσμοι τε καὶ δεσμοὶ φιλίας συναγωγοί*). He specifically instructed Hermes that these gifts should be distributed to all men, for otherwise cities could not exist. And that is why, Protagoras explains, when men confer about *politikê aretê*, which requires *dikaiosynê* and sophrosyne, they do not consult just a few experts (as they would about building or some other craft), but everyone, on the assumption that all men must share this *aretê*, else there would be no cities (323A).

The use of a myth to introduce or conclude a discussion of political and ethical doctrine is characteristic of the Sophists, as well as of Plato, and whether the content of this myth actually goes back to Protagoras or is entirely Platonic, it illustrates what the previous chapter called philosophical myth, the kind that builds on familiar elements—in this case the myth of Prometheus the culture hero—in order to create a new entity that will in some way reinforce the doctrine to be presented. What is significant in this myth and its explication is the belief that an *aretê politikê* is essential to the very existence of the city, that its function is to promote order and friendship within the community, that it must belong to all the citizens, and that one of its two primary forms is sophrosyne, here identified as the successor to the archaic *aidôs* (as *dikaiosynê* succeeds *dikê*).

It is also significant that Plato attributes this insight to a member of the first generation of Sophists, thereby fixing in the period just before the outbreak of the Peloponnesian War a recognition of the political implications of sophrosyne. That he is not guilty of anachronism in this respect is clear from a tendency noticeable in the thirties and twenties of the fifth century to relate this virtue to social and political issues, as they are reflected in comedy and tragedy as well as in historical writing.[1]

In 432 B.C., the dramatic date of the *Protagoras*, and again when Plato actually wrote the dialogue (perhaps 390 or thereabouts), sophrosyne was perceived as an excellence profoundly affecting the conduct of the individual in his relation to his fellow citizens and therefore setting a certain stamp on the community as a whole. But the precise nature of this *aretê politikê* would have been perceived differently at these two dates, less than half a century

---

[1]For some pertinent passages, see North, 72–73 (Euripides) and 85–120 (the Sophists, Aristophanes, Thucydides). Some of the material considered in the first part of this chapter has already been discussed in *Sophrosyne*, where, however, it is scattered through nine chapters. I hope that it will prove useful to bring together in more compact form what I still regard as the most important evidence for sophrosyne as an *aretê politikê*, before proceeding to subjects not previously considered.

apart. The years between had spanned the Peloponnesian War, the Revolutions of the Four Hundred and the Thirty Tyrants in Athens, the heyday of the Sophists, the burgeoning of Attic oratory, and the career of Socrates. They were years of extraordinarily rapid change and growth in Greek political thought, and sophrosyne was but one of a cluster of related ethical concepts that were analyzed, debated, defined, and redefined. Under the pressure of historical events and theoretical speculation alike, sophrosyne was, by the early years of the fourth century, understood by politicians, Sophists, historians, philosophers, and ordinary citizens in ways significantly different from those familiar two generations earlier. It is the purpose of this chapter to review the career of sophrosyne as an *aretê politikê* in the Greek world and then to consider two special topics closely related to this subject, the concept of the *sôphronistês,* the prudent counselor, in Greek political thought, and the attempts made by various Greek cities, especially Athens, to instill virtue in their citizens through legal enactments.

SOPHROSYNE AS AN *ARETÊ POLITIKÊ*

A recurring phenomenon in every society is the acquisition of political significance by concepts that originally had none. Because of specific historical events or more nebulous historical forces, an idea hitherto neutral will become, for a time at least, so profoundly political as to operate almost as a shibboleth and even arouse passions that would have been incomprehensible a short time before. Such has been the fate of "law and order" in American political life since the mid-sixties, and such was the fate of sophrosyne, a somewhat analogous concept, beginning in the middle of the sixth century B.C. In its first, Homeric appearances the word had no political implications whatsoever, but it became a form of political excellence in the archaic and classical periods, at first in the conservative, oligarchical, Dorian politics reflected in the poetry of Theognis and to some extent Bacchylides and Pindar, and later in democratic Athens.

The basic, etymological meaning of sophrosyne is "soundness (or health) of mind"—or rather of the *phrenes,* an organ of uncertain location. It makes no difference, for our present purposes, whether the *phrenes* were originally the lungs or the midriff.[2] What matters is that healthy *phrenes*, which make their owner "sound-minded" or "safe-minded," thereby protect him against various conditions that Homeric society regarded as unhealthy or dangerous. One such condition is *hybris*, which may occur, as we learn from the *Iliad*, when Zeus sends Atê (Infatuation) to such heroes as Agamemnon (9. 18) or Achilles (19. 270). Their *phrenes* become maddened (24. 114), their *thymos* (passion) is aroused (19. 271–272), and they commit acts that offend the gods and their fellowmen. Since self-restraint on such occasions may enable one to avoid *hybris, saophrosynê,* probably by a gradual process over a long period of time, took on this meaning, without, of course, losing its original connotations of good sense, soundness of mind. Self-restraint manifested itself in a reluctance to overstep boundaries, whether set by the gods or by society. It is in the *polis* civilization of the seventh and sixth centuries that this kind of inhibition seems first to acquire political significance, as a means of restraining the aggressiveness of the citizens, who without such restraint would make life unlivable for one another. This is what Plato's Protagoras means when he says in his myth that the early specimens of mankind injured one another (ἠδίκουν ἀλλήλους). What enabled them to curb their destructive aggressions was the practice of self-restraint and justice, the acceptance of mutually protective inhibitions. This we learn, not only from the *Protagoras,* but even more specifically from the *Gorgias,* where Callicles, in his eloquent attack on conventional morality, reserves his contempt for precisely these two inhibiting virtues, while he values the other two members of the cardinal tetrad, courage and intelligence (*andreia* and *sophia*), because, in his view, they serve their possessor, rather than society, and enable him to achieve power and gratify his appetites.[3]

But in addition to self-restraint, leading to moderation, sophrosyne may also imply prudence or shrewdness, usually in one's own interest or to secure one's own safety or advantage. This kind of sophrosyne results in efficient administration of the household

[2]See R. B. Onions, *The Origins of European Thought* (Cambridge, Eng., 1954) 23–43.
[3]See especially 491B-C, 492A ff.

and the state and is linked with *aretê politikê,* certainly in the fourth century, perhaps as early as the latter part of the fifth.

The career of sophrosyne in Greek political thought falls into four divisions, roughly chronological, but with considerable overlapping:

1. The period in which it is identified with an aristocratic system of values and an oligarchic or at least conservative type of constitution (sixth and fifth centuries B.C.).

2. The fifth and fourth centuries, in which it is increasingly involved with the development of moderate democracy in Athens, particularly as reflected in the speeches of the Attic orators of the fourth century.

3. The time of philosophical speculation in the fourth century, when sophrosyne attains a greatly expanded significance in the ideal constitutions of Plato.

4. The Hellenistic and Graeco-Roman ages, during which it finds a special context in theories of kingship, in rhetorical applications of the *topos* of the cardinal virtues to the *basilikos logos* (the address to a ruler) and related types of epideictic oratory, and in the peculiar developments surrounding the virtues of the Roman emperor.

In all four categories sophrosyne as an *aretê politikê* is an exclusively masculine virtue, yet occasions arise when the conduct of women is seen to have important consequences for the state; hence the sophrosyne proper to them becomes a concern to lawmakers and political philosophers, although it remains a private, feminine *aretê.*

The earliest political (or semipolitical) allusions to sophrosyne exploit its fundamental meaning of soundness of mind. *Sôphrôn* in fact resembles our word "sound" in being for the most part neutral, but in a political context usually equivalent to "conservative." The *saophrones* in the elegies of Theognis, writing in Megara in the sixth century, are those who think sound thoughts about the state, that is, accept the traditional arrangements and are conservative in their orientation, as is Theognis himself.

This poet, in spite of his intensely reactionary politics, is a brilliant innovator where sophrosyne is concerned: the first to personify the virtue, the first to cite a mythical exemplar—

Rhadamanthys—and the first to treat sophrosyne as the antithesis to *hybris* in public life, an event of far-reaching importance in Greek political philosophy. Responding to the growing power of the poor and hitherto landless members of society, Theognis speaks for the conservative Dorian nobility and warns the young friend to whom he addresses his elegies that trouble is at hand: "Cyrnus, this city is in labor and I fear that it will bring forth a chastiser[4] of our wicked *hybris*. For the townspeople are sound [*saophrones*], but the leaders are inclined to fall into great wickedness [*kakotês*]" (39–42). We do not know who the leaders were or what particular situation inspired these verses, but for the first time the *saophrones* are placed in a political context and their condition is opposed to *hybris* and *kakotês*.[5] Elsewhere in Theognis the antithesis between sophrosyne and *hybris* need not be political, although it seems likely to be so in the famous reproach to Zeus: "How then, son of Cronus, can your mind bear to hold wicked men in the same category [*moira*] as the one who is just [*ton dikaion*], whether the mind of men be turned to sophrosyne or toward *hybris*, persuaded by unjust [*adikois*] deeds?" (377–380).

It is important also that in this passage sophrosyne is allied with justice. Since it had usually been *dikê* that earlier poets, especially Hesiod, opposed to *hybris* in the great structural pattern defining archaic morality, sophrosyne could only gain strength as a civic virtue from being associated with the just man and contrasted with unjust deeds. The joint opposition of the two forms of *aretê politikê* to *hybris* forecasts the great development of this theme in Aeschylean tragedy and still later in Plato.

Other political concepts that Theognis relates to sophrosyne

[4]εὐθυντῆρα. The word *sôphronistês*, which would be appropriate to the context, is not attested before Thucydides. An early date (in the 630s) is proposed for Theognis by M. L. West, *Studies in Greek Elegy and Iambus* (Berlin and New York, 1974) 65–71.

[5]An imitator responsible for vv. 1081–1084 later in the corpus attempts to bring the situation and the contrast into sharper focus and also introduces the concept of *stasis*, civil war, to specify the kind of *hybris* the poet had in mind: ὑβριστήν, χαλεπῆς ἡγεμόνα στάσιος ("a man of wanton violence, leader of harsh civil strife"). Plutarch, *Mor.* 295C, says that the Megarians ἐσωφρόνησαν κατὰ τὴν πολιτείαν ("became moderate in their constitution," or perhaps, "gained a sound government") after the expulsion of the tyrant Theagenes.

include Good Faith in abiding by oaths (Pistis), a matter of crucial importance in cities torn by factional strife, and Piety (Eusebeia), also a form of political excellence in the sixth century.[6] Eunomia (Good Order), which is central to Solon's political thought, is not mentioned by name in Theognis,[7] but this Hesiodic sister of Dikê and Eirênê (Peace) begins to draw close to sophrosyne in lyric poetry of the fifth century. Both Pindar and Bacchylides use the phrase *saophrôn eunomia*. Bacchylides personifies the concept (in the Hesiodic tradition) and says that she guards in peace the cities of pious men (13. 183–189 Snell), while Pindar concludes a paean with a prayer to Apollo to crown the children of Thebes with the blossoms of *saophrôn eunomia* (1. 10)—remarkable as the first recorded prayer to Apollo for sophrosyne. We note that Bacchylides is celebrating Aegina, a Dorian city, mythologically the sister of Dorian Thebes. If we add these facts to the Dorian background of Megara, we may conclude that in the late sixth century and early fifth, sophrosyne, in alliance with such qualities as *eunomia*, *dikê*, and *eusebeia*, was part of the Dorian political ethos. The earliest recorded allusion to the entire canon of cardinal virtues occurs in an ode of Pindar, the *Eighth Isthmian*, which celebrates the mythical heroes of Aegina, the Aeacids, as possessing the special forms of excellence that developed in the archaic and early classical period out of the needs of the city-state.[8]

The most Dorian of the Dorians, of course, were the Spartans, and it occasions no surprise that sophrosyne came to be considered as quintessentially Spartan a trait as courage or hardiness. The evidence connecting sophrosyne with Sparta in the fifth century and thereafter is much more abundant than that which links

[6]1135–1142. This is the passage in which the Hesiodic prediction of the departure of Aidôs and Nemesis at the close of the Iron Age is brought up to date, Sophrosyne replacing Aidôs, as in the *logos* that explicates the myth of the *Protagoras*. On the political significance of *eusebeia* consult Friedrich Solmsen, *Plato's Theology* (Ithaca, N.Y., 1942) 3–14.

[7]Unless we accept the emendation of Herwerden at v. 1142 (*eunomias*), where most editors retain the MS reading, *eusebias*.

[8]See North, *A.J.P.* 69 (1948) 304–308. Of the five virtues ascribed to the Aeacids, two (sophrosyne and *eusebeia*) are referred to by some form of the name that later became canonical, while the others (justice, courage, wisdom) are described in action or referred to by Homeric equivalents of their classical names.

the virtue with other Dorian cities in the archaic age. Thucydides, Critias, the tragic poets, and the orators provide ample evidence. But it was believed in antiquity that Spartan sophrosyne went back to a very early period indeed, being one of the products of the constitution of Lycurgus, who cannot be dated later than the early seventh century.[9] Plutarch, writing in the second century of our era, summed up the tradition when he said that Cleomenes III (the reforming Spartan king of the third century B.C.) sought to bring back the *sôphrôn* and Dorian way of life of Lycurgus.[10] In his *Life of Lycurgus*, Plutarch maintains that the great lawgiver who, significantly, obtained the sanction of Apollo at Delphi for his constitution, aimed to render the Spartans free (*eleutheroi*), self-sufficient (*autarkeis*), and self-restrained (*sôphronountes*) for as long a time as possible (31); here Plutarch betrays the almost universal admiration felt by the Greeks for the stability of the Spartan way of life, irrespective of its quality.

The element in the Lycurgan constitution later considered responsible for the sophrosyne of the whole state was the Gerousia, the Council of Elders, which supplied an obviously aristocratic factor in the mixed constitution ascribed to ancient Sparta from the fourth century B.C. on.[11] Of the Gerousia, Plato says in the *Laws* that the *sôphrôn* power inherent in old age was mingled with the bold strength of the monarchy, and he offers this Lycurgan device as an example of moderation (*to metrion*), observing that if *to metrion* is neglected, the result is injustice, child of *hybris* (691C-E).

Another institution, at once social and military, adapted by Lycurgus as an essential part of his system, was the common meal (*syssition*), which Plutarch calls a school of sophrosyne, because it was there that boys, who were allowed to be present, heard politi-

---

[9]Consult W. G. Forrest, *A History of Sparta 950–192 B.C.* (London, 1968) 60.

[10]*Cleomenes* 16. Polybius complains that while Lycurgus produced sophrosyne in the private life of the Spartans, he failed to endow them with a *sôphrôn* ethos in foreign affairs (6. 48. 8). Strabo says that the Spartans ἐσωφρόνουν, "used to behave with moderation," before Lycurgus, because they did not engage in wars abroad (8. 5. 5).

[11]For example, Aeschines 1. 180–181, Plutarch, *An Seni* 789E, Cicero, *De Sen.* 6. 20.

cal discourse.[12] We should mark this opinion well because of the contrary view expressed by Plato, when in the *Laws* he advocates official use of the symposium (drinking party), an Ionian institution, instead of the *syssition*, as a device for instilling sophrosyne in both young and old.[13]

The sophrosyne that Thucydides considers a dominant Spartan trait and that he contrasts throughout the *History* with typical Athenian qualities has two principal facets: in domestic affairs, rigid discipline and obedience, and in foreign affairs, a kind of conservatism, aloofness, reluctance to act, what the Spartan king at the outbreak of the war calls caution and the waiting game (τὸ βραδὺ καὶ μέλλον) and equates with prudent restraint (*sôphrosynê emphrôn*, 1. 84. 1). Closely akin are the two qualities that the fifth century knew as *apragmosynê* (well-bred aloofness) and *hêsychia* (tranquillity)—highly valued by admirers of conservative politics and aristocratic behavior, both of them antitheses to *polypragmosynê*, meddling, being a busybody.[14]

By contrast, Thucydides portrays the Athenians as restless, self-confident, aggressive, full of what he calls *to drastêrion* (the active principle) or even—just once—*polypragmosynê*, converting to a term of praise the word that is so invidious in most fifth-century sources (6. 87. 2).[15] One would hardly guess from Thucydides that sophrosyne had strong political ties with Athens as well as with Sparta. When he refers to Athenian moderation he

---

[12]*Lycurgus* 12.

[13]Plato considered that Spartan education not only failed to instill sophrosyne (in this context, temperance), but actually promoted drunkenness (*Laws* 637A-B). In this respect he disagreed with his kinsman Critias, the philolaconian oligarch, who in his poem on the Spartan constitution praised Spartan drinking habits as moderate and in tune with Sophrosyne, the neighbor of Piety (Frg. 6 D-K).

[14]On *apragmosynê* and *polypragmosynê* consult Victor Ehrenberg, *J.H.S.* 67 (1947) 46–67, and North, 102–103. For a more detailed analysis of Thucydides' use of sophrosyne and related words see Pierre Huart, *Le vocabulaire de l'analyse psychologique dans l'oeuvre de Thucydide* (Paris, 1968) 469–475.

[15]Necessity has compelled the Athenians to do many things—*polla prassein*—and this behavior on their part benefits most of the Greeks, because the fear of Athenian intervention compels the wrongdoer to control himself—*sôphronein*—even against his will. The Aeschylean undertones of this passage are full of irony, as is the conversion of *polypragmosynê* (6. 87. 3) into a source of sophrosyne for others.

always uses some variant of the words *metrios, metriotês* (literally, "being in the middle"), and in general acquiesces in the prevalent belief that sophrosyne is a Spartan slogan and a Spartan virtue. The supreme expression of Athenian *aretê* and *politeia* at the beginning of the war—Pericles' Funeral Oration—never mentions sophrosyne. Yet as early as the middle of the sixth century, Athenian sepulchral inscriptions begin to use a formula by which the dead man is praised as *agathos* and *sôphrôn* or is honored for his possession of *aretê* and sophrosyne. Since we do not have an equal number of contemporary inscriptions from any other one city to compare with the Athenian lot, it is hard to estimate the significance of this evidence, but Paul Friedländer's remark, "The combination of bravery and soundness of mind seems to be an Attic ideal,"[16] can hardly be contested, although it is impossible on the basis of the evidence to tell how widespread the ideal was.

The metrical inscriptions dating from the seventh century to the fifth collected by Gerhard Pfohl[17] number just under two hundred, of which one hundred are non-Attic, ninety-seven Attic. Of the total, only ten contain certain or conjectural references to sophrosyne or *sôphrôn;* of these ten, nine are Attic; of these nine, six are from the sixth century. The data are indeed scanty, and their interpretation is controversial,[18] but such as they are, they do suggest that sophrosyne was already, in the middle and late sixth century, a quality valued in Athens, and valued there more than elsewhere. Its appearance on epitaphs in conjunction

[16]Paul Friedländer, *Epigrammata: Greek Inscriptions in Verse from the Beginnings to the Persian Wars* (Berkeley and Los Angeles, 1948) p. 79 on IG I.² 986. See also p. 15 on IG I.² 988: "It will be no accident that it is an Attic inscription that thus takes a moral turn in place of the stricter epical norm of Doric countries."

[17]Gerhard Pfohl, *Greek Poems on Stones*, Vol. I: *Epitaphs from the Seventh to the Fifth Centuries B.C.* (Leiden, 1967).

[18]M. B. Wallace, *Phoenix* 24 (1970) 100, notes that three out of four *aretê kai sôphrosynê* epitaphs of the Peisistratid period were probably the work of one stonecutter, Aristion of Paros, and concludes that they do not entitle us to regard the union of the two virtues as anything but a vogue among the rich ("noble families on good terms with the tyrants," p. 101), who could afford monuments at the Dipylon made by Aristion. In fact, only one of the three inscriptions cited (Pfohl, 35) actually bears the name of Aristion; a second (Pfohl, 37) has the letters . . . *arios,* and the third (Pfohl, 63) only a sigma. In this inscription, *sôphrôn* is also restored. There are two other Dipylon inscriptions of the late sixth century (Pfohl,

with one other "value-term" denoting courage makes it seem likely that sophrosyne had already begun to designate a form of excellence essential in peacetime, corresponding to courage in time of war. The polarity of these two virtues and the importance of their being interwoven in the fabric of the state constitute a major theme in the political works of Plato, but their close association as an Athenian ideal begins in the latter half of the sixth century.

To call sophrosyne a political excellence at this early date goes beyond the available evidence, if by "political excellence" we mean what the term would imply to Plato or Aristotle, but if *aretê politikê* can be construed as meaning an excellence to which a given *polis*—or an influential group of its citizens—pays conspicuous tribute in a context that isolates and thereby celebrates a very small number of virtues, then it may be said that sophrosyne emerges as an *aretê politikê* on the strength of the Attic epitaphs, even before Aeschylus in the *Oresteia* establishes it together with *sebas* (reverence) as a source of happiness and prosperity for the Athenians (*Eumenides* 1000: *sôphronountes;* 1019, *sebontes;* the two participles occupy corresponding positions in the strophe and antistrophe).

Still earlier, at the beginning of the sixth century, Solon (archon in 594 B.C.) by his insistence on moderation in all his reforms had become the first champion of Attic sophrosyne, at least in the view of later interpreters, although the word itself does not appear in any extant fragment of his verse, which emphasizes instead *dikê, kosmos,* and *eunomia.* Subsequent writers, ancient and modern, take it for granted that Solon was himself an exemplar of sophrosyne and that he sought to impress this virtue on his fellow citizens. Just as Lycurgus had done, Solon went to Delphi and, according to Plutarch, received a significant oracle ("Sit in the

36, 48) which refer to sophrosyne (or *sôphrôn*) with *aretê;* for neither is any connection with Aristion alleged. The other Attic epitaph from this period referring to sophrosyne (Pfohl, 67) does not come from the Dipylon. The one relevant non-Attic epitaph (Pfohl, 156) is Argive, ca. 525–500. The dead man, called an *anêr agathos* in line 2, is commended in line 4 as *sôphrôn, aethlophoros* (prize-winning), *sophos.* The second adjective in this list would be surprising in Athens, but the technique of listing attributes is known in Attica too, ca. 500 B.C., cf. Pfohl, 67.

middle of the boat").[19] Aeschines credits him, as we shall see, with specific legal enactments intended to protect and foster soph-rosyne in its various aspects—moral purity in women and boys, orderly conduct, decent behavior in general. Solon shares with the rest of the Seven Wise Men (all ten or eleven of them) a reputation for sophrosyne,[20] derived from the fact that all support the Del-phic code and express its morality in their legislation.

It is important to remember how scanty our evidence is for the sixth century and how shaky are the proofs that one concept or another was definitely connected with Dorian, or Ionian, or Athenian ethics and politics. Solon's political vocabulary includes key words that we find also in Theognis a little later, not to men-tion Pindar and Bacchylides in the next century—words like *eunomia* and *hêsychia*—yet it gradually becomes evident (especially after the Persian Wars, when the Greeks grew more self-conscious about the contrast not only between Greeks and barbarians, but between Dorians and Ionians) that Athens was developing a brand of sophrosyne different from that of Sparta.

Several reasons for this development and this difference have been suggested; proof is in no case possible. The rise of the mer-cantile middle class, favored by the reforms of Solon, has been cited as a likely reason.[21] Hatred of tyranny, whose outstanding characteristics were perceived as being *pleonexia* (overreaching) and *hybris,* antithetical to sophrosyne, may have enhanced the value of this virtue in Athenian eyes, especially in the fifth cen-tury, when the stereotype of the hybristic tyrant was well estab-lished, as we learn from Aeschylus and Herodotus. After the Per-sian Wars, popular opinion tended to relate the victory of the Greeks to their sophrosyne, justice, and piety, as opposed to the

[19]*Solon,* 14. 6.

[20]*Anth. Pal.* 7. 81: πάντας ἀριζάλου σωφροσύνας φύλακας: "all guardians of admirable moderation." Pittacus of Mitylene was the only Wise Man who actually referred to sophrosyne in one of the sayings ascribed to him (10. 13 D-K). Myson was pronounced most *sôphrôn* by the Delphic oracle, according to Hipponax, 63 West.

[21]See, for example, George Thomson, *Aeschylus and Athens* (London, 1941) 283, 350; Gregory Vlastos, *C.P.* 41 (1946) 65–83, especially 81–82, on the needs of the trading class and the ways in which "the whole of Solon's polity, with its peculiar blend of radicalism and conservatism, answers admirably the needs of this 'middle class.'" For objections to this explanation, see Wallace, *art. cit.* (above, note 18).

hybris of the enemy,[22] a theme important to Aeschylus in the *Persians* in 472. Toward the middle of the fifth century, when he wrote the *Oresteia*, it was possible for him to represent sophrosyne as one of the cornerstones of Athenian democracy, the bulwark against both tyranny and anarchy.[23] As such, the word clearly denotes moderation: sophrosyne is the Mean between the two dangerous extremes that threatened the Athenian *polis*.

The other aspect of sophrosyne as an *aretê politikê*, its self-regarding, self-protective side, also made it attractive to Athens, a great mercantile city whose prosperity depended on skillful administration. *Euboulia* (good planning) is a quality in which the Sophists were keenly interested; it is one of the ways in which intelligence manipulates nature and overcomes fortune (a favorite theme of Thucydides). There are passages in Thucydides and Aristophanes in which *euboulia* and sophrosyne are treated as synonyms, or are closely related, and both terms imply intelligent management.[24] Moreover, sophrosyne can be explicated by some form of the word *dioikein* (to manage, administer). This development comes later than the political interpretation of sophrosyne as moderation; most instances belong to fourth-century authors, such as Plato and Xenophon.[25] But there is a curious forerunner in the late fifth century. Orestes in the *Electra* of Euripides (386–387) refers to good administration (*eu oikein*) of cities and households and cites as the virtue by which a man proves himself most excellent and capable of such administration the self-restraint of the Peasant who is married in name only to Electra. In this passage the words *euandria* (367), *agathos* (378), and *aristos* (382) are used to commend him for his restraint. Elsewhere in the play he and his conduct are described as *sôphrôn* (53, 261). A. W. H. Adkins, who comments on the novelty of the point of view ex-

---

[22]See the skolion cited by Werner Peek, *Hermes* 68 (1933) 118–221, and for the stereotype of the hybristic tyrant see Aeschylus, *Prometheus* 240–241, 939–941, 970.

[23]*Eumenides* 516–537, 681–706, 1000. Sophocles, Frg. 622 Nauck, links the safety of the *polis* with the practice of justice and sophrosyne.

[24]Thucydides 1. 78. 1–4 (*euboulia* vs. *tychê*) compared with 4. 18. 4 (sophrosyne vs. *tychê*). Aristophanes, *Birds* 1540, lists among the equipment of the oligarchs sophrosyne, *euboulia*, and *eunomia*.

[25]Plato, *Meno* 73A6 ff., Xenophon, *Oec.* 7–8.

pressed in these lines, observes that Euripides' tone suggests that he is advancing an unfamiliar thesis.[26]

A further step in the development of this line of thought may be seen in Isocrates' praise of Theseus in the *Helen* (ca. 370 B.C.) for being *sôphrôn*. His sophrosyne is not self-restraint or moderation, but wise administration (*dioikein*) of the *polis* (31). Plato, who connects sophrosyne with the intelligent regulation of cities and households in several dialogues, usually does so, as we shall see, in a context relating sophrosyne to some form of intellectual virtue, such as *epistêmê* or *phronêsis*, which makes its function in administration more comprehensible.

The fourth century is the age in which Athenian sophrosyne as a self-consciously democratic value reaches its peak, although if we were to believe the orators we would have to locate its heyday in the time of Solon or during the supremacy of the Areopagus, and in fact, the democratic sophrosyne celebrated by fourth-century authors is usually an *aretê politikê* compatible with a moderate, not a radical, democracy, hence a virtue that would probably have pleased Solon and the members of the Areopagus in their prime. What is most intriguing is the reason why, quite abruptly, after the turn of the century, the *aretê* that had generally been conceded to the Spartans and had been as a political term suggestive, not only of conservatism, but of aristocracy or oligarchy, began to be appropriated by the Athenians and even spoken of as if it were a hallmark of democracy.

Two reasons seem plausible. One is the conspicuous failure of the Athenian policy based on activism (*to drastêrion*) and driven to the extreme of *pleonexia* (overreaching) in the later years of the Peloponnesian War. It is not only Thucydides who blames the collapse of Athens on the excessive ambition and self-interest of her leaders after the death of Pericles (2. 65. 9, 3. 82. 8). Fourth-century writers, looking back at the fifth century, criticize the failings of the democracy and recommend heavy doses of sophrosyne to cure the ills brought on by *hybris* and *polypragmosynê*.[27] There is much evidence of disillusionment and disenchantment

---

[26]A. W. H. Adkins, *Merit and Responsibility* (Oxford, 1960) 176-177, 195 ff.

[27]Plato and Isocrates agree at least on this prescription. Cf. Isocrates, *On the Peace* 30, 58, 119, with Plato's defense of sophrosyne against the attack of Callicles in the *Gorgias*.

with the values of the generation just past, which had led to such disastrous results.

The other reason is connected with the disgrace which the oligarchs suffered after the Revolution of the Thirty Tyrants in 404 B.C., when their pretensions to sophrosyne and related aristocratic values were discredited. The phrase *sôphrôn aristokratia* referred to by Thucydides (3. 82. 8) as a slogan of the oligarchs ceased to have any meaning. Critias with his collaborators had proved the reverse of *sôphrôn*. The time came when the return of the democracy after the expulsion of the tyrants could be described, in distant retrospect, as the restoration of a *sôphrôn politeia*.[28] Henceforth sophrosyne could plausibly be claimed by the democrats, who had, after all, opposed the *hybris* and violence of the Thirty, and so in the fourth century it became a democratic *aretê politikê*. That as a private, individual virtue it had always been valued by both parties doubtless made the transfer easier.

In the transitional period, early in the fourth century, sophrosyne had a special link with the concept of concord or reconciliation (*homonoia*), the ideal of those who sought to bind up the wounds of civil war and restore harmony among different parties in the state. The two concepts are united in the speech of Andocides "On the Mysteries," delivered in 399 B.C., when reconciliation or amnesty would have been much to the speaker's advantage.[29] The *homonoia* phase is brief, however. Far more persistent is the tendency traceable in the speeches of Lysias and Isaeus that reveal, even more convincingly than do sophistic showpieces or model orations, precisely what Athenian juries well down into the fourth century were willing to believe about the *sôphrôn* citizen. There is a sharp distinction between the earliest of the Attic orators, Antiphon and Andocides, whose interpretation of sophrosyne is akin to that of Aristophanes, Thucydides, and Euripides, and the fourth-century orators, who reflect a stereotype of the *sôphrôn* citizen that could only have come into existence after the oligarchic revolution of the Thirty and the ruin of the high hopes that had foundered with the collapse of Periclean Athens.

The dominant characteristic of the *sôphrôn* citizen of the

---

[28]Aeschines 2. 176 (delivered in 343 B.C.): σωφρόνως πολιτευθέντες.

[29]For example, 109, 140. Cf. the fragment of Thrasymachus, *On the Constitution*, from a somewhat earlier date (ca. 411 B.C.), 1 D-K.

fourth-century orators is that he is a democrat through and through. Only democrats are loyal Athenians. Oligarchs are traitors, and the antithesis between the two provides a *topos* that recurs long after the political events that gave it birth had receded into the past. Both Demosthenes and Aeschines, as a matter of course, couple sophrosyne with democracy and *hybris* with oligarchy—and this in the middle of the fourth century or even later.[30]

The second notable trait of the *sôphrôn* citizen is that he is *chrêstos*, "useful" to the *polis* in various ways. *Chrêstos* and its frequent synonym *spoudaios*, "serious, responsible," had always been terms of praise in fifth-century Athens, often implying good birth and wealth, suggesting, at the very least, that this was a man you could count on, and it is likely that association with the condition of being *chrêstos* strengthened the position of sophrosyne as a political excellence in both fifth and fourth centuries.[31] The proof that one has been *chrêstos* increasingly often, in the fourth century, takes the form of listing the "liturgies" one has performed for the *polis*—financing the production of dramatic festivals, building warships, and the like. There is even a *topos* according to which the most laborious liturgy is to be a *sôphrôn* citizen. As we shall find in Chapter 3, this argument is considered efficacious for persuasion through ethos.[32]

Thirdly, the *sôphrôn* citizen is quiet, inoffensive, and minds his own business. He never initiates litigation, but is driven to the courtroom by his rapacious, violent, hybristic opponent. *Apragmosynê* and *hêsychia* are the closest synonyms here; they appear with sophrosyne in what Chapter 3 will identify as the *apragmosynê-topos,* a device regularly used in the proem of a speech to secure the sympathy of the judges. Isaeus in his first oration has his client maintain that he and his brothers were brought up in so

---

[30]For example, Demosthenes, *Against Timocrates* 75 (ca. 353 B.C.); Aeschines, *Against Ctesiphon* 168 (330 B.C.).

[31]On the implications of *chrêstos* in its moral, social, and civic connotations see W. Robert Connor, *The New Politicians of Fifth-Century Athens* (Princeton, 1971), especially 88, note 2. Plutarch links *chrêstos* with both *sôphrôn* and *epieikês* (reasonable) in *Mor.* 806F-807A.

[32]See below, Chapter 3, on the practice of Lysias and Isaeus.

respectable a fashion[33] that they never entered the lawcourt, even as listeners. Obviously, the inactive principle had for the time being at least come to dominate the ideal of the Athenian citizen.

Among the fourth-century orators Isocrates stands out, partly because of his determination to elevate sophrosyne to a position of real significance in foreign policy. His conception of it as a virtue of the individual is remarkable, not for any originality (it has much in common with the views ascribed to the Just Argument in Aristophanes' *Clouds*),[34] but for the consistency with which he expresses it throughout a tremendously long lifetime and the connection he sees between the old-fashioned virtues and his own type of *paideia*. He is also responsible, more than anyone else, for fostering the myth of the golden age of sophrosyne in domestic and foreign policy in the Athenian past, and he even cites as an exemplar one of the very statesmen whom Socrates in the *Gorgias* condemns for lack of sophrosyne and for leaving the Athenians worse than he found them—Pericles, in the *Antidosis* 111.

The political sophrosyne that Isocrates would exercise in foreign affairs, unlike the domestic brand, undergoes a sharp change in the course of his career. In the *Panegyricus* (380 B.C.) it is considerate treatment of the allies and is linked closely with concord (*homonoia*) on an international scale.[35] In the oration *On the Peace* (355 B.C.), composed after the collapse of the Second Athenian Maritime Confederacy, it means giving up any thought of having allies, abandoning the hope of preserving an empire. According to Isocrates in this address, recent, disastrous Athenian policy can be accounted for in the simplest of moral terms. He says, in so many words, "Wantonness [*akolasia*] and *hybris* have proved to be the cause of our woes, sophrosyne of our blessings" (119).[36] Here,

---

[33]1. 1 (σωφρόνως ἐπαιδευόμεθα). Cf. 4. 28–30, a contrast between the *kosmioi* and the *philopragmones* (meddlers). On the *topos* of the *sôphrôn (metrios, kosmios) bios* see North, 136–137.

[34]Cf. *Clouds* 962, 1067, with *Areopag.* 4, 13, 20, 37, 48.

[35]3, 104, 173. This is not the same as the domestic *homonoia* referred to by Andocides (see above, note 29).

[36]Cf. 30, 58. Isocrates' advice amounts to a recommendation that Athens content herself with the kind of foreign policy suitable for a second-class power, such as Thucydides had commended in the case of Chios (8. 24. 4–5).

too, as in the stereotype of the private citizen, the inactive principle had for the time being triumphed.

There is little to suggest that Isocrates' political advice had much influence in Athens. But, ironically, generations yet unborn were to be influenced by his invention of the *basilikos logos,* the address to the ruler, embodying both encomium and advice to princes. This was a pseudo-oration, a literary convention that proliferated from the early fourth century till the end of the Renaissance and profoundly affected both prose and verse in many vernaculars. Isocrates' *Evagoras* and to some extent also his *Nicocles,* honoring the rulers of Cypriote Salamis, served later ages as models for this type of address, in which the virtues of the ruler were systematically eulogized and illustrated by appropriate achievements.[37] On many occasions, what appeared on the surface as praise was in fact intended as advice or exhortation. Thus Isocrates himself, in the *Antidosis,* maintains that his purpose in writing the *Nicocles* was to give counsel to the king on how best to rule the citizens and to secure for Nicocles' subjects the mildest possible reign (67–70). The sophrosyne prominent among the kingly virtues is paradigmatic self-restraint or else something close to the later Roman concept of *clementia* as an imperial virtue. The sophrosyne supposedly instilled in the subjects of the ideal king is little more than obedience, or, at best, restraint and moderation of appetite and passion, in accordance with the supposed example of the ruler.

Some of the tendencies evident in Athenian interpretations of sophrosyne as a political excellence in the late fifth and early fourth centuries have their most important consequences in Plato's *Republic* and *Laws.* Both versions of the ideal state establish the virtue as a cornerstone of the constitution and both make serious efforts to coordinate it with the active principle, thus restoring the balance that had been lacking in Athenian political life during the war with Sparta and its aftermath. Even as early as the *Apology* Plato had been deeply aware of the political orientation of all the cardinal virtues. Erwin Wolff's Berlin monograph many years ago drew an analogy between Socrates and Amphiaraus and

[37]For the topic of the virtues in epideictic oratory, see Chapter 3.

showed how each of the virtues was ascribed to Socrates in the
Apology, as to the seer in the *Seven against Thebes,* and in each case
had a value for the state, unlike the same virtues in Xenophon's
Apology, where they are interpreted merely in the context of individual ethics.[38] Plato's suggestions for the role that sophrosyne
should play in the state are too complex for a brief summary. It
must suffice here to mark the principal stages in the progress of
this Platonic *aretê politikê* and to suggest some possible links with
what went before and what came after.

In his earliest, presumably most Socratic dialogues, Plato maintains the intellectual view of sophrosyne, as in the *Charmides,*
where it is equivalent to self-knowledge. Socrates says that the
state (like the household) ruled by the *sôphrôn* person would be
well administered (καλῶς οἰκεῖσθαι), because he would know
what he could and could not do (171D–172A). The advantageous
situation in which every person does what he is best qualified to
do is, of course, identified with *dikaiosynê* in the *Republic,* but in
the *Charmides,* where the notion first appears, this benefit is conferred by sophrosyne. The link between *oikonomia* and sophrosyne (alluded to in passing by Isocrates in the *Helen* 31), is
made to seem more natural when Plato defines sophrosyne as a
form of knowledge, *epistêmê* or *phronêsis,* as he does here in the
Charmides and again in the *Symposium* (209A 6–8). There Diotima
holds that the greatest and finest kind of *phronêsis* is that concerned with the *diakosmêsis* (regulation) of cities and households,
to which is given the name of sophrosyne and *dikaiosynê.*

In both the *Gorgias* and the *Republic,* sophrosyne is viewed as
order, harmony, *symphônia,* a bold extension into the political
sphere of the popular definition of the virtue as control of pleasure and the appetites (for example, *Gorgias* 491D). The equation
of sophrosyne in the *Gorgias* with order and *kosmos* (and its identification with the principle of order that holds together heaven
and earth, gods and men) is the most important of Plato's innovations and the most influential for later political theory, since it
prepares the way for the microcosm-macrocosm theory adopted
by Plato himself in the *Timaeus* and elaborated by the Stoics, and it

[38]Erwin Wolff, *Platos Apologie* (Berlin, 1929), 75 ff.

transforms sophrosyne and justice from ordinary civic virtues into organizing principles akin to the principle of order in the universe. One consequence of this approach is the function assigned to sophrosyne in the *Republic:* it is a harmony sounding the same note in perfect unison throughout the whole, a *symphônia* of the naturally inferior and the naturally superior on the question which should rule (432A). On it ultimately depends the unity of the state.

It is important to observe that in the *Republic,* sophrosyne is an excellence required of all three classes in the state and all three faculties in the soul. It is not the virtue simply of the third class (the craftsmen) and the third part of the soul (the appetitive faculty), but in post-Platonic political theory, even when the tripartite soul is maintained, and with it the three classes in society, philosophers often restrict sophrosyne to the third and lowest element in each category.[39] As an *aretê politikê* it is then construed as obedience, orderly conduct, much as in the Dorian vocabulary of the sixth and fifth centuries B.C. This change does not result from any radical rethinking of Plato's political theories. It simply reflects actual political conditions in the Graeco-Roman world and, moreover, accepts as the essential sophrosyne what Plato regarded as the lowest rung on the ladder of perfection. Very early in his consideration of *aretê* in the state and in the soul he had begun to distinguish levels of each virtue, according to the motives for its practice. Inferior motives for self-restraint (such as love of money or ambition) produce only an inferior virtue, in contrast to that achieved by the person who renounces appetite and passion because of his love of wisdom (*Phaedo* 82C). It is actually possible, Plato observes, to be *sôphrôn* by reason of a kind of wantonness (*Phaedo* 68C-E), and this *sôphrosynê dia akolasian,* which Plato terms "demotic"—bourgeois—*aretê,* has only the name in common with the perfected, philosophical *aretê* of the rulers in the *Republic* or the members of the Nocturnal Council in the *Laws.* The difference between Plato and his successors in this regard is that they usually accept the "demotic" virtue as the only attainable, or even desirable, *sôphrosynê politikê,* while Plato sets at

[39]For some instances, see North, 225, 234, note 105.

the top of the ladder of virtue a philosophical *aretê*, in which sophrosyne, wisdom, justice, and courage are all encompassed by the Idea of the Good.

Amid the prodigal abundance of the *Republic*, one concern stands out, in Books 2 and 3, as especially characteristic of Plato's approach to civic virtue—his recognition of the need to blend the two antithetical temperaments, the gentle (*praos, sôphrôn*) and the spirited (*megalothymos*) in the souls of the citizens and thus in the state as a whole. When these traits have been harmonized by the proper education in music and gymnastic (this is the primary subject of Books 2 and 3), the soul and the state become *sôphrôn* and brave. The description of the corrupt constitutions in Book 8, which must have drawn upon the history of the civil wars in the preceding generation for many of its vivid details, shows that when the harmony of the political organism—its sophrosyne— disappears, the opposite process is set in motion: the cycle of decay begins, the first stage of which sees the triumph of the spirited element over the *sôphrôn* and of passion over reason (547E).

In the *Statesman*, Plato again selects for special attention this very problem, the opposing temperaments and the urgent need to harmonize them in the state. He even makes the radical suggestion that the opposition between the two is based on a fundamental hostility between the very Forms of sophrosyne and *andreia* (307C). His description of the consequences for the state when either of the two dispositions dominates the other—an unwarlike attitude resulting ultimately in slavery, when the state suffers from a surplus of the *sôphrôn* temperament, excessive militarism leading to constant warfare and also resulting in slavery, when the aggressive trait is dominant (307E-308A)—reads like a commentary on certain passages in Thucydides, in which the equally dangerous political extremes represented by Nicias and Alcibiades are exposed.[40]

The *Laws*, too, recognizes the need to harmonize the moderate

[40]See North, 109-110. J. B. Skemp, *Plato's Statesman* (London, 1952) 66, note 5, suggests that Plato has in mind the political situation in Athens during the last years of the Theban supremacy and is inspired by the equally dangerous policies of the moderate Eubulus and his opponents.

and the spirited principles in the soul and the state, focusing attention in this case on the antithetical types of music and dance, which the legislator must employ in order to blend the two traits of temperament (802D-E, 815D). Sophrosyne and *andreia* are earlier identified as the characteristic virtues of peace and war, hence the qualities aimed at, respectively, by the newly founded Cretan city and the traditional Spartan system. The most original sections of the first two books of the *Laws* are those that deal with ways of testing natural sophrosyne in the young and developing it in conformity with the laws of the new state into civic sophrosyne. It is here that Plato advises the legislators to employ carefully regulated drinking parties as an instrument for training in virtue. Here, too, he makes a detailed comparison with the Spartan system of common meals (*syssitia*), which, by prohibiting wine, not only fails to promote sophrosyne but actually leads to the opposite extreme of drunkenness (637A-B). Throughout the *Laws* Plato reveals a heightened concern for sophrosyne as a quality of the ideal state, a consequence, it seems, of the increased interest of his later dialogues in movement and change, hence in the passions and appetites that represent movement in the soul. It is for this reason that sophrosyne tends to replace justice as the focus of his attention, but it is either "natural" or "demotic" virtue that Plato usually discusses, rather than the philosophical *aretê* that is one with *phronêsis* and the rest of the tetrad.

Nevertheless, this supreme and unified *aretê* remains, in the *Laws,* as it was in the *Republic,* the object of contemplation by the heads of state, here the members of the Nocturnal Council,[41] who are charged with the safety of the constitution (963A-966B). One of their functions is to visit the prisoners in the *Sôphronistêrion,* the House of Correction, to which are condemned criminals guilty of impiety by reason of folly, not wickedness of character (908E). The name of this institution, one of Plato's most original conceptions,[42] and the responsibility of the Nocturnal Council to "soph-

---

[41]For the philosophic virtue, still recognized as supreme, see *Laws* 710A5 ff., 964A4 ff.

[42]Consult Glenn Morrow, *Plato's Cretan City* (Princeton, 1960) 491, on Plato's originality in proposing a prison for corrective purposes. Already in the *Protagoras* 324A-C the deterrent function of punishment had been noted (itself a highly original idea), but the word used is *kolazein,* not *sôphronizein.*

ronize" its inmates by persuasive discourse, contribute to the impression conveyed by many passages in the *Laws* that Plato now sees sophrosyne as the greatest source of safety and stability for the state. It can scarcely be an accident that the Athenian statesman Lycurgus, whom tradition represents as a pupil of Plato, seems to have considered it his function to "sophronize" the demoralized state of which he was the chief financial officer and effective leader for twelve years (338–326). One of the ways he sought to achieve his purpose was through the institution of the officers known as *Sôphronistai*, if indeed they were his creation (they do not appear in inscriptions before 334/333 B.C.). Their function was to supervise the morals of the ephebes during their period of training.[43] In Platonic terms, the young men would be learning to convert a natural tendency toward sophrosyne into the civic virtue which it was the purpose of the *Laws* to instill.[44] A like result is ascribed by Xenophon to the ten-year ephebate served by the young Persians whose education he portrays in the *Cyropaedia;* they spend their time on guard duty to protect the city and to achieve sophrosyne (1. 2. 9).

Civic or bourgeois sophrosyne is the kind of political excellence that Aristotle also aims to encourage in the state. Although his political and ethical theories are dominated by the concept of moderation, he never applies the vocabulary of sophrosyne to this concept as it affects the state, any more than Solon had, but always speaks of *mesotês*, the *mesos bios*, the *mesoi*, or the *mesê politeia*, which he considers the best (*Pol.* 1295a25 ff.). Clearly, Aristotle regards sophrosyne as a virtue of the individual, difficult to relate to the *polis*, even though like most Greeks he tends to identify political and personal morality and says, for example, that the state needs the same virtues as the individual—courage and hardiness in times of activity, love of wisdom in times of leisure, sophrosyne and justice in both seasons, but especially in times of peace and leisure, because they who enjoy prosperity have need

[43]See below, on the reforms of Lycurgus.

[44]In view of Plato's decisive influence on the development of sophrosyne it is fitting that this should be the first word in the first epitaph for him quoted by Diogenes Laertius, 3. 43.

Σωφροσύνῃ προφέρων θνητῶν ἤθει τε δικαίῳ
ἐνθάδε κεῖται ἀνὴρ θεῖος Ἀριστοκλέης . . .

of great sophrosyne and justice (1334a22-34). In this commonplace, which goes back in sentiment if not in specific phraseology at least to Hesiod (*Erga* 214 ff.), Aristotle recalls the old-fashioned concept of sophrosyne, familiar especially in tragedy, as the antithesis to *hybris* (the child of *koros*—abundance—according to Solon 6. 3 West). But generally he gives the word a more limited function in the *Politics* (as indeed he does also in the *Ethics*): restraint of appetite (essential for slaves if they are to do their work properly, 1260a36), not being talkative (essential for women, 1277b17 ff.), self-restraint where women are concerned (noble—*kalon*—for citizens, when the woman belongs to someone else, 1263b9-11).

At the close of Book 1 of the *Politics,* Aristotle comes to grips with the question whether those who are ruled possess the same kind of sophrosyne (and other moral virtues) as does the ruler—a problem destined to arise again and again in the coming centuries of absolute rule by Hellenistic monarchs and Roman emperors. He concludes that the ruler must have moral virtue in its entirety, whereas slaves, women, and children need have only what is appropriate to their respective conditions. Sophrosyne is not identical for the two groups. For the ruler it is (like *andreia*) conducive to command (ἀρχική), for the subject it is conducive to subservience (ὑπηρετική, 1260a20-24). Since submission to authority had been regarded as a virtue proper to women (and young people of both sexes) from early times and was often equated with sophrosyne (for example, Euripides, *Troad.* 654-656, Xenophon, *Cyrop.* 1. 2. 8), Aristotle here, as often, identifies himself with traditional and popular views. It would be immensely interesting if he had included at this point or elsewhere in the *Politics* some discussion of the sophrosyne of the ruler—in what way precisely it is "conducive to command"—but for this we look in vain. Instead Aristotle develops the subject of distinction in virtue based on distinction in sex, associating himself with Gorgias rather than Socrates (as both are portrayed in Plato's *Meno* 74B ff.) and endorsing the "enumeration" of the virtues in preference to the doctrine of their unity. In support of the Gorgianic view, Aristotle quotes the comment of Sophocles' Ajax: γυναιξὶ κόσμον ἡ σιγὴ φέρει ("On women silence confers adornment," *Ajax* 293), implying that the most obvious sign of feminine sophrosyne is the absence of talkativeness.[45]

The same assumption comes to the surface in a later discussion of the *aretê* of the ruler and the subject in Book 3, which, moreover, shows that Aristotle finds it natural to think of sophrosyne as a feminine virtue. He maintains once more that sophrosyne and justice differ in ruler and subject and adds that sophrosyne and courage are different in men and women, "for a man would seem cowardly if he were only as brave as a brave woman, and a woman would seem talkative [*lalos*] if she were only as discreet [*kosmia*] as a good man" (1277b17-24).[46]

Among the later philosophical schools only the Stoa maintained the Platonic doctrine that virtue is one and the same wherever it is found, whether in gods or mortals, men or women. The Stoics therefore held that the virtue of the ruler did not differ in kind from that of the subject. Actually, the old Stoa did not believe it to be a function of the state to instill virtue in its citizens. There is considerable evidence that the early Stoics, like the Cynics, considered organized society a positive hindrance to the achievement of virtue.[47] Some members of the school, however, took a strong interest in politics. Zeno, the founder, wrote a *Politeia,* and at least three of his pupils, Persaeus, Cleanthes, and Sphaerus, are reported to have written treatises on kingship. None is extant, but from other writings of the Old Stoa it is inferred that they upheld the doctrine of the identity of virtue wherever found. That is, all men who are wise share in the divine reason immanent in the *kosmos.* If kings are not wise, they must be taught by wise coun-

[45]Cf. Sophocles, Frg. 61 Nauck. For some consequences in iconography, see below, Chapter 4, notes 90, 101.

[46]There is a wealth of precedent for the assumption that sophrosyne is peculiarly feminine; we need look no farther than Plato's identification of a certain kind of music as both feminine and *sôphrôn* (*Laws* 802E). Sophrosyne as the *virtus feminarum* is discussed in greater detail in my article "The Mare, the Vixen, and the Bee: *Sophrosyne* as the Virtue of Women in Antiquity," *Illinois Classical Studies* 2 (1977) 35-48.

[47]Consult Margaret Reesor, *The Political Theory of the Old and Middle Stoa* (New York, 1951) 11, note 5.

selors, just as ordinary men must be (a doctrine that lent support
to the conception of the *sôphronistês* as a commonplace of
Graeco-Roman political thought).

The Neopythagoreans, on the other hand, advanced the theory
that the king was "animate law" (*nomos empsychos*) and directly
imitated divine virtue, while his subjects could only imitate him.[48]
This doctrine, too, might have consequences in political life, providing a philosophical basis for the flattery of the ruler expressed
in so many encomia and treatises on kingship. It is already implicit, although in an entirely nonmystical fashion, in Isocrates'
expectation that the *aretê* of Evagoras or Nicocles will serve as an
incentive to the practice of virtue by their impressionable subjects.

The final and most prolonged period in the political career of
sophrosyne coincides with the Roman imperial age, when the continued influence of the fourth-century Greek encomium, the
vigorous tradition of the native Roman *laudatio funebris,* the interest of several philosophical schools in the relation between ethics
and political action, and the practical requirements of Roman
politics converged on the topic of the virtues of the emperor. In
this context the Platonic canon suffered drastic changes, one of
which may be seen in the makeup of the quartet of virtues ascribed to Augustus when the Senate in 27 B.C. dedicated the
clupeus aureus in the Basilica Julia in honor of his *virtus, clementia,
iustitia,* and *pietas.* If *clementia* here takes the place of sophrosyne
(for which *temperantia* would be the normal Latin translation), the
ethical tradition of the Stoa makes the change an easy one, for
clementia is one of the virtues subordinate to *temperantia* both in
the writings of the Middle Stoa and in the doctrine of its Roman
imitators.[49] But it is political necessity that really dictates the
change—the necessity of fostering the reputation of the absolute
ruler for mildness and compassion and of utilizing every
device—from the coinage to the *basilikos logos*—to spread the notion abroad. Hence, although *temperantia* is entirely absent from

[48]See North, 235-236 and note 110. Ps.-Ecphantus is the writer who is most
explicit about the difference between the virtue of the king and of his subjects. See
Plutarch, *Numa* 20. 8, on the subjects who voluntarily practice sophrosyne
(ἑκουσίως σωφρονοῦσι) when they behold the ruler's example.

[49]See North, 271, 301.

imperial coins, *clementia* often appears, beginning with Tiberius, and in literary sources goes back even before the Principate, to Cicero's eulogy of the *clementia Caesaris* in his speeches of the year 46 B.C. Two years later the Senate authorized a temple to the *Clementia Caesaris*. The abuse of the word in connection with Julius Caesar may account for the tendency of some Augustan authors—Virgil and Propertius among them—to avoid it and use *pietas* in its stead,[50] but its eclipse was temporary, and *clementia* remains the most prominent political aspect of sophrosyne in the imperial age. It is closely followed by *moderatio*, which also finds mention on a coin of Tiberius and which dominates the *Panegyric of Trajan* by the Younger Pliny.[51]

Pliny's *Panegyric*, which is to later Roman panegyric what the *Evagoras* of Isocrates had been to the Greek *basilikos logos*, preserves the pattern of the school encomium, but adds a great many more virtues to the Platonic canon, although this canon is clearly basic.[52] More interesting than the speech itself is what Pliny says about it in a letter to Vibius Severus (3. 18. 1-2), which describes his motives for embellishing and publishing the original, much shorter speech of thanks addressed to the emperor when Pliny assumed the consulship. He says that he believed it most suitable for a *bonus civis* to strengthen the emperor's virtues by honest words of praise and to use his example for the instruction of future emperors. To teach what a prince ought to be is indeed *pulchrum*, he adds, but also *onerosum ac prope superbum;* to praise an excellent prince and thus show his successors a guiding light is just as useful and much less arrogant (3-4). Pliny thus takes upon himself the traditional role of the wise counselor—the

---

[50]The relation of *pietas* to *clementia* is discussed by Inez Scott Ryberg, in *The Classical Tradition: Literary and Historical Studies in Honor of Harry Caplan*, ed. Luitpold Wallach (Ithaca, N.Y., 1966) 235-236.

[51]For example, 3. 2, 9.1, 16. 1-3, 17. 4, 54. 5, 55. 5. *Modestia* is also prominent (3. 2, 21. 1, 47. 6, 58. 2). The third facet of sophrosyne that serves the purposes of imperial propaganda on coins and in eulogies is *pudicitia*. On the political exploitation of all these virtues, see North, 300-311.

[52]Verbal echoes of the *Panegyric*, especially the first half, in the Latin Panegyrists of the fourth century are traced by Josef Mesk, *W.S.* 34 (1912) 246-252. For Pliny's use of traditional topics of encomium see Mesk, *W.S.* 33 (1911) 71-100, and Marcel Durry, *Pline le Jeune, Panégyrique de Trajan* (Paris, 1938), passim.

sôphronistês—but cloaks his advice in flattery, much as Isocrates had done in the *Nicocles*.[53]

SÔPHRONISTÊS

Graeco-Roman treatises on kingship, such as the first four addresses of Dio Chrysostom (all intended, it seems, for Trajan), reveal another facet of the politically oriented literature of the Empire. They are usually based on Platonic and Cynic-Stoic commonplaces regarding the ruler and his relation to his people and to the gods, and, like the outright encomia, normally recognize the cardinal virtues as the basic *virtutes principum*. Sophrosyne tends to describe the ruler's control of appetite and passion, a personal characteristic that becomes significant politically when it enables the king to serve as an example to his people in restraining wantonness (*akolasia*, for example, Dio, 3. 67, 10), but it is also responsible, in some cases, for the ruler's obedience to the gods (for example, Dio 2. 70–71), and often it has a strong flavor of the Cynic *autarkeia* (independence) and *philanthrôpia* (roughly equivalent to the Latin *clementia* and prominent among the virtues of the ruler from the time of Isocrates' *Evagoras*). Dio is one of those who use the word *sôphronistês* to designate the adviser to a king. He applies the term to Homer, who is praised in the second discourse *On Kingship* as the most competent *sôphronistês*, because one who heeds him will become a most excellent and fortunate king (2. 54).[54]

Dio does not venture to call himself a *sôphronistês*, but his four orations *On Kingship* fall into the category of the *speculum principis* (to use a Latin term)—the Mirror of the Prince, which might almost as well be classified as a *sôphronizôn logos* (a speech designed

---

[53]See *Antidosis* 67–70. Cf. Erasmus' explanation of his panegyric of Philip of Burgundy (to present in the guise of flattery the pattern of a good prince), cited by Lester K. Born, *A.J.P.* 55 (1934) 35.

[54]The *sôphronistês* need not instill sophrosyne alone; Dio says that Homer teaches that the most kingly forms of excellence are *andreia* and *dikaiosynê*. We note, however, that the passages immediately preceding and following the praise of Homer deal exclusively with Homeric examples of discipline and self-restraint in the army (53) and with the king's responsibility for banishing from his soul and his realm everything wanton and indecent in music, literature, and the dance (55–56)—functions, not of *andreia* or *dikaiosynê*, but of sophrosyne.

to correct—*sôphronizein*—or to instill virtue). This phrase properly describes the Cynic diatribe of the third century B.C. and is appropriate to the *speculum principis* because so many of these addresses show the influence of Cynic political doctrine and employ anecdotes (like that of Diogenes and Alexander), mythical paradigms (Heracles, Odysseus), and interpretations of Homer developed and popularized by the Cynics.[55] In a fragment of Lycophron's *Menedemus* the diatribe is actually termed a *sôphronistês logos*,[56] and it would not be inappropriate to call the adviser to the prince a *sôphronistês*, although the word appears only sporadically in this connection and (it should be emphasized) never becomes even a semitechnical term in ancient political philosophy. Nevertheless, it provides a convenient designation for a minor, yet persistent, theme in writings about the state in the time after Plato, and it calls attention to the relation between this theme, that of the prudent counselor to the young ruler, and Plato's emphasis on sophrosyne in the *Laws*.

The noun *sôphronistês* first occurs in a political context in Thucydides, where it has no fixed connection with any faction or class, but is used collectively of the oligarchs (as correctors of the democrats in Plataea) and of the democrats (as correctors of the oligarchs), while the Sicilians at Camerina are warned in 415/414 that it is too late for them to try to act as *sôphronistai* for the Athenians.[57] The emphasis on civic sophrosyne which we have already noted in Plato's late dialogues and his theory of remedial punishment are both reflected verbally in his coinage of the name *Sôphronistêrion* for the House of Correction in the *Laws*. To the extent that the members of the Nocturnal Council are charged with converting the prisoners they are *sôphronistai*, in a literal

---

[55]For example, Dio, *Or.* 4. 14, on Diogenes' advice to Alexander, which Dio develops into a sermon on the nature of kingship, emphasizing the need for Alexander to be *sôphrôn* (21); *Or.* 2. 54, on Homer, and *Or.* 1, on Heracles as the model ruler. Dio does not confine his function as *sôphronistês* to discourses addressed to rulers. He describes as a *sôphronizôn logos Or.* 32, to the Alexandrians on their disorderly behavior in the theater and the stadium, which repeatedly refers to his wish to "sophronize" them (30, 32–33, 37, 73, 80, 95). Cf. Julian's *Misopogon*, addressed to the people of Antioch, especially 342D–343C, 345B, 354B, 364D.

[56]Frg. 3 Nauck.

[57]See 3. 65. 3; 6. 87. 3; 8. 48. 6–7.

sense. But they are also *sôphronistai* in a broader sense, if, as Glenn
Morrow suggests, they do for the ideal Cretan city what Plato
wished the Academy to do for Athens, namely, "to apply philosophy to the saving of the city-state."⁵⁸ Only later does the word
sôphronistês imply this kind of activity, rather than the strictly
etymological "correct," "instill discipline in," for which the common synonym in Attic oratory is *kolazein*,⁵⁹ but the germ of the
later development is to be found in Plato.

One passage in the *Laws* became a kind of *locus classicus* for the
description of the wise counselor. It is that in which the Athenian
Stranger, discussing the young tyrant who could most easily effect
a change in government in the direction of either *aretê* or *kakia*,
says that the tyrant would be lucky if he lived at the same time as a
great lawgiver, and shortly afterward remarks that Nestor excelled all other men in eloquence and sophrosyne. If such a man
should come again, blessed would be those who heard the words
from his prudent lips (ἐκ τοῦ σωφρονοῦντος στόματος, 711E).
Plato does not call either Nestor or the great lawgiver a *sôphronistês*
(in the context of the *Laws*, *nomothetês* is the natural choice,
710A-711E), but it would be easy for his readers to draw the
conclusion that the wise counselor ideally associated with the
young tyrant should be like Nestor, eloquent and *sôphrôn*, and such
a lawgiver would easily be considered a *sôphronistês*. Familiarity
with the word itself must have been enhanced, at least in Athens,
after the institution of the office of *sôphronistês* (sometime before
334/333 B.C.), especially since many ephebic inscriptions mentioned it in a prominent position.⁶⁰

Aristotle, in a fragment thought to derive from his lost treatise

---

⁵⁸*Op. cit.*, 509-511.
⁵⁹See, for example, Lysias 22. 20, 27. 5. Plato uses *sôphronistês* in the narrow
sense in *Rep.* 471A, and *sôphronizein* (to punish, correct, bring to one's senses), in
Gorg. 478D, *Rep.* 471A, *Phaed.* 69A, *Laws* 854D, and *Critias* 121C. In *Rep.* 471A,
which contrasts the attitude of Greeks at war with other Greeks to that of Greeks
fighting against non-Greeks, *sôphronizein* is distinguished from *kolazein* and
sôphronistês from *polemios*: εὐμενῶς δὴ σωφρονιοῦσιν, οὐκ ἐπὶ δουλείᾳ κολάζοντες
οὐδ' ἐπ' ὀλέθρῳ, σωφρονισταὶ ὄντες, οὐ πολέμιοι ("they will correct, in a spirit of
benevolence, not punishing with a view to enslavement or destruction, being cas-
tigators, not enemies"). For the rare Dorian word *sôphronistys* (castigation), see
Laws 934A1.
⁶⁰For the ephebic *sôphronistai*, see below, pp. 124-125.

On Kingship, says that to be a philosopher is a handicap to a ruler, but the ruler should listen to philosophic counselors (Frg. 647R³). His own relation to Alexander caused him to figure in many later works on kingship, such as Dio's second oration, which closes with a speech by Philip in which he praises Aristotle for teaching Alexander about rule and kingship, whether by interpreting Homer or in any other fashion (79). Several members of the early Stoa also "conversed" with kings (Zeno with Antigonus Gonatas) or interested themselves in the topic of the ruler.[61] Chrysippus taught that the wise man should take part in politics either by ruling a kingdom himself or by assisting the ruler (*SVF* 3. 693; cf. 691, 692). Sphaerus influenced Cleomenes III, the reforming king of Sparta in the third century B.C., whom Plutarch praised for his sophrosyne (*Cleomenes* 13). According to Plutarch, Sphaerus visited Sparta, concerned himself with the young men and ephebes, and became the adviser of Cleomenes. He helped the king reform the *paideia* and *agôgê* and restore the orderliness of the *syssitia* (11), which Plutarch elsewhere calls a school of sophrosyne. In the *Life of Lycurgus,* Plutarch mentions the great demand for Spartan commanders in other cities, and these he calls not only "harmosts"—the technical term—but *sôphronistai* (30), possibly because of his persistent tendency to ascribe sophrosyne to Lycurgan Sparta.

The Academy itself supplied political advisers to a number of cities that sought constitutions or counsel. The Platonic *Sixth Epistle* mentions the two, Erastus and Coriscus, who went to advise Hermeias of Assos, and Plutarch tells of others.[62] In his little essay, "That a Philosopher Ought to Converse Especially with Men in Power," he makes a Platonic comparison of the philosopher to a physician. Just as the physician will be particularly eager to cure the eye which "sees for many and watches over many," so the philosopher will be particularly eager to attend to the soul of the ruler, who must be wise and self-restrained and just (*phronein kai sôphronein kai dikaiopragein*) in behalf of many (776D). Anaxagoras and Pericles, Plato and Dion, Pythagoras and

[61]Consult Reesor, *op. cit.* 14 ff.
[62]*Adv. Colotem* 1126C–D; consult Glenn Morrow, *Studies in the Platonic Epistles* (Urbana, 1935) 134.

the Greek leaders in South Italy, Athenodorus and Cato, Panaetius and Scipio are the pairs listed here. Polybius left his own account of his relation to the young Scipio Aemilianus, who specifically asked the Greek historian to help him to speak and act in a way worthy of his ancestors—that is, to gain a reputation for sophrosyne, *kalokagathia*, and *andreia* (31. 24–30).

Such a responsibility might readily be assumed by a Stoic. It is more surprising to find an Epicurean interested in these matters, but the fragments recovered from the library of Piso at Herculaneum include parts of a treatise by the Epicurean Philodemus, "On the Good King according to Homer," which offers standard advice on how to apply the cardinal virtues to the task of ruling, advice colored by the conditions of the Roman world. A traditional element is the appearance of Nestor as a mediator of opposing factions.[63]

The concept of the wise adviser or warner goes back to Homer (Polydamas warning Hector) and is important in tragedy (Amphiaraus, Teiresias) and in Herodotus, where the pattern requires that a seer or wise man, such as Solon, warn a tyrant who is on the verge of committing *hybris*. Wolff has pointed out that Aeschylus develops the Homeric warner in the direction of civic virtue by having Amphiaraus in the *Seven against Thebes* issue warnings on the subject of *dikê*.[64] But it would be even more accurate to identify him as a *sôphronistês*, since the contrast between Amphiaraus and the six hybristic, boastful attackers of Thebes is based primarily on his sophrosyne. This, too, is a civic virtue in Aeschylus' interpretation of the myth.

If we were to extend the concept of the *sôphronistês* to poets who seek to instill virtues allied with sophrosyne in the rulers to whom they address their verse, we might begin with Pindar, whose odes to Hieron of Syracuse contain, as one commentator has put it, "a note of exhortation, as if the poet were striving to improve the moral tone of the tyranny."[65] All these poems, but especially the

[63]Oswyn Murray, *J.R.S.* 55 (1965) 178, suggests that the work was written to celebrate Piso's election to the consulship in 58 B.C.

[64]*Op. cit.,* 78–83. See also Richmond Lattimore, *C.P.* 34 (1939) 24–35, and Charles Segal, *W.S.* 84 (1971) 39–51.

[65]R. W. B. Burton, *Pindar's Pythian Odes: Essays in Interpretation* (Oxford, 1962) 125–126. See also David C. Young, *Pindar Isthmian 7, Myth and Exempla* (Leiden, 1971) 37–38. on the device of the negative paradigm.

second *Pythian*, convey with every device available to the victory ode the need for the ruler to cultivate modesty—awareness of the transience of mortal achievement and respect for the power of the gods. The mythical *exempla* mentioned in Chapter 1—the "negative paradigms" of hybristic heroes—function as *sôphronistai:* Ixion on his "winged wheel" (*Pyth.* 2. 22), Tantalus, who could not endure his great prosperity (*Ol.* 1. 56). The myths themselves, the gnomic phrases that accompany them, and the ethical terminology, studded with words like *olbos, koros, hybris,* and *atê,* are appropriate to the kind of poetry and the kind of political situation that Pindar knew, and his salutary advice reflects the kind of sophrosyne familiar in late archaic and early classical Greece, a moral virtue that becomes in some sense political when the person addressed is a tyrant.

A very different nuance of sophrosyne, appropriate to a very different political orientation, finds expression in some of the most splendid poetry of the Augustan age. Horace and Virgil in particular are widely believed to have exerted a moderating influence on the emperor, Horace, for example, seeking to instill *clementia* (a virtue closely allied with *temperantia* in Stoic doctrine) through his great Pindaric ode, *Descende caelo* (3. 4), where, as noted in Chapter 1, he employs the myth of the Gigantomachy in his plea for mercy for the defeated Antonians after Actium.[66] As advisers to Augustus, Horace and Virgil must be recognized as the most tactful *sôphronistai* on record, models for later poets at other courts, from antiquity to the Renaissance, whose verse was increasingly cross-fertilized by the topics and motives of panegyric oratory, philosophy, and Christianity.

An unusually explicit instance from the fifteenth century in Spain is that of Juan di Mena, whose poem *El Laberinto de Fortuna,* dedicated to King Juan II of Castile, has been interpreted as an effort to change the character of the king through an elaborate allegory associating the cardinal virtues with the planetary spheres, which are filled with exemplary figures, good and bad. The relative weight assigned to the various virtues is surprising.

[66]On the relation of *clementia* to sophrosyne or *temperantia,* consult North, 300–301. For a discussion of the political influence of Horace and Virgil and an extensive bibliography on the subject, see Kenneth J. Reckford, *Horace* (New York, 1969), especially pages 77–84 and note 1, page 157.

The first three circles (those of the Moon, Mercury, and Venus) all have to do with aspects of sophrosyne/*temperantia:* the other three cardinal virtues have one circle each. The sphere of Saturn, which Dante assigns to the ascetics (*Paradiso* 21), is here reserved for the man who possesses all four cardinal virtues; this model statesman is described as "riding Fortune's horse . . . with a tight rein," that is, like the charioteer in Plato's *Phaedrus,* exercising sophrosyne.[67]

Allied with the Greek philosophical tradition of the *sôphronistês* is the biblical tradition of the prophet who fearlessly denounces an erring king. St. Ambrose in his rebuke to Theodosius I for the massacre in Thessalonica presents the most celebrated example of a Christian bishop functioning as *sôphronistês* to a ruler. In *Epistle* 51 he bids the emperor repent, citing examples of royal sinners who confessed their sins (David, Job), and he threatens to bar the emperor from Holy Communion unless he does penance. It is evident that Ambrose is very conscious of his likeness to the Hebrew prophets (rather than the Greek philosophers), for when he says, in the *Peroratio,* that God wishes to correct (*castigare*) his servants, not destroy them, he compares himself to the prophets, the emperor to repentant sinners who are saved: *Istud mihi commune est cum prophetis, et tibi erit commune cum sanctis.*[68] The funeral oration delivered by St. Ambrose over Theodosius in 395 refers to the emperor's willingness to heed Ambrose *magis arguentem quam adulantem* (rebuking, rather than flattering him, 34). One of the most significant passages in this influential address is the digression on the finding of the True Cross by St. Helen (40–51). From two of the nails she caused to be made a diadem (symbolizing faith) and reins (suggesting *iusta moderatio*). So important was this element in the tradition that the heroic statue of St. Helen in St. Peter's Basilica shows her holding the nails in one hand, while with the other she supports the cross. St. Ambrose interprets the

[67]See Luis Beltrán, *Speculum* 46 (1971) 318–332. The Moon represents chastity (defined as *temperantia* is defined in Cicero, *De Inv.* 2. 54. 164), Mercury avarice, and Venus virtuous love.

[68]Consult Franĭšek Dvornik, *Early Christian and Byzantine Political Philosophy* (Washington, 1966) 784, on Ambrose; on St. John Chrysostom rebuking the Empress Eudoxia, see pages 698–699.

holy relic *super fraenum* as an injunction to the emperors to curb their *insolentia*, check their *licentia*, and follow the example of Constantine, rather than of the Neros and Caligulas. It is tempting to suppose that this vivid digression fostered the wide use of the bridle as an attribute of *temperantia* in mediaeval and Renaissance art (we shall see some examples in Chapter 4), but the frequency with which *temperantia* is explicated by words related to *frenare* (to bridle, rein in) forbids us to assume that there was any one predominant source of the imagery.

A contemporary of St. Ambrose, the Neoplatonist Bishop of Ptolemais in Cyrene, Synesius, harks back more consciously to the Greek tradition. In the Proem of his address to Arcadius, *On Kingship*, in 399, he describes his own words as being, not flatterers, but teachers and *sôphronistai*, and he reminds the emperor of his need for good advice. In a passage full of Platonic reminiscences he compares flattering words to unhealthful food, his own counsel to medicine or gymnastic.[69] In 399, to be sure, Synesius had not yet become bishop, but the courage with which he criticized conditions at court and even the conduct of the emperor himself ("You live the life of a sea anemone"—βίον... θαλαττίου πνεύμονος), not to mention the feeblemindedness of his favorites ("counterfeits of humanity, pin-headed and dim-witted"—μικροκεφάλους τε καὶ ὀλιγογνώμονας) suggests that the people of Ptolemais knew what they were doing when they called him to be their bishop, much against his will, in 410.[70] As bishop he found it necessary to excommunicate Andronicus of Berenice, Praeses of Libya Superior, who used torture to extort money from the provincials,[71] and in the brief period of his episcopacy (he died in 413), he was obliged, like the Platonic philosopher-king, to sacrifice his treasured *bios theoretikos* and plunge completely into the *bios praktikos* to meet the needs of his people. To an extraordinary

[69]*Peri Basileias*, ch. II, p. 7 Terzaghi.

[70]For his scruples about becoming bishop when he could not fully accept all the popular beliefs of his people, see the famous Letter 105.

[71]Letter 58; see also Letters 72 and 90. For Synesius as defender of his people against the state, consult Kenneth Setton, *Christian Attitude towards the Emperors in the Fourth Century* (New York, 1941) 152-162, and for his courage in demanding reforms, some of which were granted, see Charles H. Coster, *Late Roman Studies* (Cambridge, Mass., 1968) 145-182.

degree he exemplified, in his self-proclaimed role of *sôphronistês*, both the original meaning of the word (castigator) and its developed significance (teacher of salutary lessons).

LEGAL ENACTMENTS DESIGNED TO INSTILL SOPHROSYNE

Aristotle in the *Nicomachean Ethics* says flatly, "Lawgivers make the citizens good by training them; to do this is the wish of every lawgiver; those who do not do it well are in error. Herein differs a good constitution from a bad one" (1103b 3–6). And later, "Since living with sophrosyne and hardiness is not pleasant to the many, particularly the young, upbringing and education should be laid down by the laws, which will not be painful when they have become habitual. . . . Since they ought to practice these habits when grown up too, we should need laws for these matters also, and indeed for the whole of life generally" (1179b 33 ff). A translator of the *Politics,* setting this down as Aristotle's main political principle, denounces it unequivocally as bad.[72] Bad or good, it is a principle to which most Greeks (except, as noted above, some Cynics and Stoics) subscribed, and it is, above all, the principle that supported the whole tremendous structure of Plato's *Laws.* Because Plato prefaces his legislation with persuasive and explanatory proems, there is no doubt about the intent behind it—to instill the civic virtues. Actual laws in Greek history are rarely so explicit, yet it is possible to cite several specific laws or types of law that were thought to instill sophrosyne, or to aim at this result.

Formal schooling was, of course, the responsibility of the parents, rather than the *polis,* in most states for which we have any evidence in the classical period, but from the earliest expression of Greek thought on the subject it was nevertheless assumed that each state must and will somehow stamp its values on the young and thus form their character. *Polis andra didaskei* (The city is man's teacher) was a gnomic saying with which few Greeks disagreed. The first legal enactment that might qualify as a *nomos peri sôphrosynês,* a law concerned with sophrosyne (to use an expression current in the fourth century), is the famous law of Pittacus, ty-

[72]Richard Robinson, *Aristotle's Politics, Books III and IV* (Oxford, 1962) xxv.

rant of Mitylene in the early sixth century B.C., which doubled the penalty for any offense committed in a state of intoxication.[73] Whether drunkenness was more of a problem on Lesbos than elsewhere, it is impossible to say. Violence growing out of drinking parties is certainly known elsewhere in the archaic age, and not just in the myth of the Lapiths and the Centaurs. But Pittacus was famous for his interest in sophrosyne, and this regulation may be one outcome.[74]

The legislation of other archaic lawmakers aims at comparable goals, if we consider, not just sobriety, but orderly behavior, absence of extravagance, and protection of women and boys from sexual abuse as objects of *sôphrôn* legislation. We have already noted that the constitution of Lycurgus in Sparta was thought to instill sophrosyne (in the sense of discipline and endurance), especially through the institution of the common mess. Solon, the architect of Athenian sophrosyne, was thought to have promoted the virtue in a greater variety of ways. Our most fertile source is Aeschines, in the *Oration against Timarchus,* whose subject (prosecution on a charge of male prostitution) makes it inevitable that we should hear a good deal about laws meant to protect virtue and morality. Aeschines develops at prodigious length the topic of the *exemplum,* seeking to show the value placed on chastity by the great Athenians of old, and he asks the clerk to read aloud certain laws that illustrate Solon's concern for sophrosyne *peri paidôn* (in the case of boys) and that show the function of the laws to be that of instilling discipline (*sôphronizein,* 7, 20, 139).

The laws regulating the conduct of schoolmasters and requiring that a *chorêgus* (director of a chorus) be over forty ("the most *sôphrôn* time of life") are interpreted as showing the foresight concerning sophrosyne exhibited by Solon, Dracon, and other early legislators (7–12). Laws requiring the prosecution of panders, laws relieving boys of the obligation to support parents who had hired them out as prostitutes, laws against wanton violence (*hybris*), laws forbidding free persons who have become prostitutes to serve as archons, heralds, or ambassadors, or to address

---

[73]Aristotle, *Pol.* 1274b 18 ff.
[74]See above, note 20.

the Council or the Assembly (21)—all these are termed by Aeschines *nomoi peri sôphrosynês*, laws concerned with chastity or decency.

Aeschines' concept of a golden age of Athenian morality echoes that of Isocrates, who more tirelessly than any other fourth-century writer embellished this myth and advocated a return to the standards of the past, when the Areopagus supervised the sophrosyne and *eukosmia* of the young.[75] Soon after the disaster of Chaeronea, during the dominance of Lycurgus (338–326 B.C.), an attempt was actually made to revive these standards through a reform of the *ephebia*, the system of military training that in some form or other had long been provided for male Athenians when they reached the age of eighteen. The Areopagus was in charge of this program, but more directly involved were the officials known as *sôphronistai*, who were elected, one from each tribe, to supervise the moral and civic training that was now added to the traditional instruction in hoplite drill and the use of weapons. The *Constitution of the Athenians*, in the first literary allusion to the *sôphronistai*, mentions the requirement that they be over forty (like the *chorêgus* in the laws of Solon) and be regarded by the fathers of the ephebes as "best and most suitable to oversee [*epimelesthai*]" the young men. Their first act was to take their charges on a circuit of the temples, after which garrison duty began. The only other specific responsibility listed by Aristotle for the *sôphronistês* was to buy provisions for all the ephebes of his tribe out of the money (four obols a day) allotted to each one by the state, "since they mess together [*syssitousi*] by tribes." It seems as though an effort was being made to secure for the young Athenians some of the advantages supposedly conferred on their Spartan counterparts by the *syssition*, the common mess. Aristotle concludes by saying that the *sôphronistês* "looks after everything else" (42. 3). Some light is cast on what this statement means by the series of tribal inscriptions, beginning in 334/333 and continuing until 303/302, which honor the ephebes and their officers, often recording the award of a golden crown of specified value to the *sôphronistês* and

[75]*Areopagitica* 37, 46, and passim.

praising him for instilling in his charges such virtues as sophrosyne, *eukosmia,* and the like.[76]

Only in Athens is the term *sôphronistês* used for such officers, and there is no reason to suppose that any comparable institution existed elsewhere, although an inscription from Tenos describes a gymnasiarch as a guardian of good discipline (*medeôn sôphrosynês*).[77] In the light of other evidence suggesting the austerity of Lycurgan Athens,[78] it seems likely that a conscious effort was made to restore something resembling the *archaia paideia,* which, as all readers of the *Clouds* will recall, was supposed to be redolent of sophrosyne.[79] That Lycurgus is represented by tradition as a pupil of both Isocrates and Plato helps explain his concern for the civic virtues and perhaps accounts for the prominence of sophrosyne, evinced by the very name *sôphronistês,* as well as by the stock phrases employed in the honorary inscriptions. It is not without interest, in this connection, that the shrine of Amphiaraus at Oropus became during this period a center of ephebic activity,

[76]The Pseudo-Platonic *Axiochus* 367A names the Areopagus and the *sôphronistai* as jointly responsible for supervising the ephebes. See J. Oehler, PW, *s.v. Sôphronistês* for literary and epigraphic evidence. On the development and organization of the *ephebia* consult O. W. Reinmuth. *The Ephebic Inscriptions of the Fourth Century B.C.* (Leiden, 1971), and Fordyce Mitchel, *T.A.P.A.* 92 (1961) 347-357, and *Hesperia* 33 (1964) 349-351. Reinmuth conjectures that organized military training for the young men of Athens began soon after the Persian Wars, when the Areopagus was powerful (p. 137), but on the basis of an inscription of 361/360 assigns the *ephebia* as a formal institution to the first quarter of the fourth century (p. 124). He emphasizes that the *sôphronistai* appear only in 334/333 and disappear after 303/302, being created in order to instill the civic virtues and then dropped because "this invasion of the parental domain seems to have evoked a negative reaction" (p. 135). The *sôphronistai* were revived under Hadrian and are mentioned on inscriptions down to A.D. 263, but their organization and function are obscure. The *sôphronistai* referred to on an inscription of 325/324 B.C. from Axione (*IG* II[2] 1199) are not ephebic.

[77]Kaibel, 948.

[78]The austerity of Lycurgan Athens and the interest in sophrosyne and allied virtues evinced by Lycurgus himself are discussed by V. Tandoi, *Studi Italiani di Filologia Classica* 42 (1970) 154-178. See also Fordyce Mitchel, *Lycourgan Athens: 338-322* (Cincinnati, 1970), and Robert F. Renehan, *G.R.B.S.* 11 (1970) 219-231 (citing passages in the *Oration against Leocrates* that seem to reflect the *Laws* of Plato).

[79]*Clouds* 962, 1024-1027.

the find spot of several inscriptions and the site of festivals celebrated with particular magnificence. It has even been suggested
that the stimulus for the reform and extension of the *ephebia*
under Lycurgus was not dismay over the defeat at Chaeronea, but
a new spirit of national exuberance caused by the recovery in
338/337 of Oropus, a frontier town symbolizing Athenian
hegemony in Greece.[80]

Further references to laws about *eukosmia*, in Aeschines' Timarchus oration, have to do, not with the moral training of the young,
but with orderly conduct in the assemblies. They include the pro-
vision that older men have priority in speaking. In this connection
Aeschines recalls the *sophrosyne* of the old-fashioned
statesmen—Pericles, Themistocles, Aristides—who were such
models of decorum that they were never seen to speak with an
arm outside their cloak. The statue of Solon in the agora at
Salamis, Aeschines tells us, shows him in this decorous attitude
(25).[81]

Another and very much more important category of *nomoi peri
sôphrosynês* would include Athenian laws providing for the
punishment of adulterers, who in the fifth century B.C. could be
put to death by the citizen responsible for the woman concerned
(her *kyrios*, lord) if they were caught in the act, or subjected to
various kinds of humiliating punishment, referred to with relish
by the comic poets.[82] Aristotle says in the *Ethics* that the law prescribes certain conduct: that of the brave man (not to leave the
line of battle), that of the *sôphrôn* (not to commit adultery or
violent assault, 1129b 19 ff.). As often, he chooses for his examples what must seem to him and his Athenian readers the most
important and obvious civic virtues that the laws can instill.

And what of the women, not just those taken in adultery, but

---

[80]The suggestion is made by Reinmuth, *op. cit.*, 70–71.

[81]See Plutarch, *Nicias* 8. 6, for Cleon as the first orator to slap his thigh and
stride up and down while addressing the people. Thus he stripped *kosmos* from the
speaker's platform. Another kind of regulation that in the past secured sophrosyne on the part of speakers before the Areopagus was the prohibition against
speaking *exo tou pragmatos* (off the subject)—a measure designed to prevent emotional appeals. Cf. Aristotle, *Rhet.* 1. 1. 5 (1354a21–25); and see Lycurgus, *Vs.
Leocratem* 11.

[82]Consult K. J. Dover, *Aristophanes, Clouds* (Oxford, 1968) on 1027, 1083.

that whole half of the human race in the Greek world whose fundamental virtue was assumed to be sophrosyne? Were legal enactments of any consequence where they were concerned? Could the proverb have been changed to read, *Polis gynaika didaskei* ("The city is woman's teacher")?

There certainly were laws in Athens designed specifically with women in mind. Solon's sumptuary legislation was aimed at regulating their dress and behavior on public occasions, especially funerals and festivals (almost the only occasions when they could be much in evidence). According to Plutarch, Solon forbade them to go out on these occasions wearing more than three himations (the normal outer garment) or carrying more than one obol's worth of food or drink. They could not, at funerals, lacerate their flesh or use set lamentations, sacrifice an ox at a grave, or visit tombs of any but their own kin, save at the time of burial (21). Not chastity, obviously, but decorum is the aim of such laws, which Plutarch calls legislation to prevent disorderly and wanton behavior (*to atakton kai akolaston*). Solon's real purpose was evidently to curb the ostentation and check the expenditure of the rich, aristocratic families, which would be manifested especially at funerals.[83]

Aeschines, still in the inexhaustible *Oration against Timarchus*, gives us a glimpse of laws protecting feminine chastity. The most mysterious is the "Law of the Ancestors" that allowed a father whose daughter had been seduced to wall her up in an empty house with a horse, which was expected to kill her (182). The law was no longer in effect in the fourth century, for Aeschines merely says that the foundations of the house still stand and the place is named for the Horse and the Girl.[84] From Plutarch's statement that a virgin could not be sold into slavery it has been inferred that according to the laws of Solon an unmarried girl who had been seduced could be sold.[85] As for married women, Aeschines reports still another law of Solon (on the *eukosmia* of women) that forbids adulteresses to adorn themselves or attend

[83]W. K. Lacey, *The Family in Classical Greece* (Ithaca, N.Y., 1968) 87.

[84]The tradition goes back to Hippomenes, who punished his unchaste daughter Leimone in this fashion. Marcel Détienne, *History of Religions* 11 (1971) 170, suggests that the horse symbolizes both the seducer and the infernal powers.

[85]Lacey, *op. cit.*, 289, note 102 (on Plutarch, *Solon* 23. 2).

public sacrifices. If such a woman appears on such an occasion, any man who wishes may tear off her jewels and clothes and beat her, but not to death (184). This law, like many cited by Aeschines, has for its purpose what the orators call, in one of their favorite topics of the epilogue, *sôphronizein tas allas*, to set an example for the other women, enforcing a legal or social standard in such a way as to lead those who observe it to abide by the rules themselves. It shows, as W. K. Lacey notes,[86] a good deal of psychological insight, since getting dressed up and going out must have constituted one of the greatest pleasures available to housebound Athenian women. In fact, the ways in which the expression "to go out" (*exienai*) is used in poetry and legal prose contribute something to our appreciation of the restrictions placed on Athenian women.[87]

In contrast to the severe punishment that could be inflicted on a man taken in adultery (with a free woman in the legal control of a citizen),[88] the woman herself—apart from the prohibition on appearing at sacrifices—was merely supposed to be divorced, and she could take her dowry back when she left her husband's house.[89] The comparative mildness of her punishment is surprising because of the grave consequences of her behavior: the wife's adultery cast doubt on the legitimacy of any children she might have and thus imperiled their rights of citizenship, of inheritance, and of sharing in the cult of their kinship group. As Lacey points out, it was the overwhelming importance of being able to prove legitimacy for reasons connected with civic rights and inheritance of property that made the Athenians (in his view) "excessively preoccupied with the chastity of their womenfolk."[90] But the same considerations account for the treatment of the guilty wife. She

---

[86]*Op. cit.*, 309.

[87]See, for example, Kenneth Reckford, *T.A.P.A.* 99 (1968) 329–359, on the implications of ἐξῆλθον δόμων (*Medea* 214); Aristotle, *Pol.* 1300a 4–8, on the ἐξιέναι of poor women, and Plutarch, *Solon* 21. 5 on the laws about ταῖς ἐξόδοις τῶν γυναικῶν (the goings out of women).

[88]Demosthenes 47. 53–56; Aristotle, *Ath. Pol.* 57. 3; Lacey, *op. cit.*, 113 ff.

[89]Demosthenes 59. 64–71. See A. R. W. Harrison, *The Law of Athens: The Family and Property* (Oxford, 1968) 55–56.

[90]*Op. cit.*, 113. He also makes the odd suggestion (page 288, note 97) that the ease with which women in heroic times (Penelope excepted) seem to have been seduced may have made the Greeks of classical times suspicious.

was allowed to retain her dowry because of the primary importance of protecting the *oikos*, thus keeping the wife's property under the control of her family, to which it belonged. This concern took precedence over any other motive, including the punitive.

Aristotle in the *Politics* refers to the existence of *gynaikonomoi* (superintendents of women) in some cities, but comments that they can exist only in aristocratic societies. It is impossible in a democracy to keep the women of the poor from "going out"— *exienai*—while in an oligarchy the women are too spoiled to put up with the institution (1300a 4–8). He is highly critical of the failure of the Spartans to control their women properly and even ascribes to this failure the decline of the Spartan system in the fourth century.[91] That Spartan women were deficient in chastity had been an Athenian commonplace in the fifth century; now Aristotle charges them with lack of discipline and excessive concern for riches, absence of sophrosyne in a broader sense and one that is intimately connected with the corruption of the *polis*.

At some time after Aristotle had commented on the existence of *gynaikonomoi* elsewhere, such officers began to operate in Athens, too, instituted perhaps by Demetrius of Phalerum under the influence of Aristotle himself.[92] The activity for which they are best known, thanks to allusions by the comic poets, had nothing to do with the supervision of feminine conduct, but rather with the limitation of expenditure at feasts. According to Athenaeus, they allowed no more than thirty guests, while according to the historian Philochorus, they shared with the Areopagus the responsibility for curbing luxury.[93] Elsewhere in the Hellenistic world, boards of *gynaikonomoi* seem to have performed the same function in supervising girls as did the *paidonomoi* in the case of boys,[94] but there is no reason to suppose that they were anywhere comparable to the Athenian *sôphronistai*.

[91]*Pol.* 1269b 13 ff.; cf. *Rhet.* 1. 5. 6 (1361a 9–11) and see Plato, *Laws* 806C.

[92]For this suggestion see Georg Busolt and Heinrich Swoboda, *Griechische Staatskunde* (Munich, 1920–1926) I. 493–494.

[93]Consult Athenaeus 6. 245. See also PW, *s.v. Gynaikonomoi* (Boerner).

[94]For example, at Magnesia on the Maeander; see Wilhelm Dittenberger, *Sylloge Inscriptionum Graecarum* (Leipzig, 1915–1924) II, 589, and cf. Menander Rhetor, 3. 363 Spengel.

Dionysius of Halicarnassus, in his description of early Rome, discusses efforts made by various states to ensure sophrosyne and *eukosmia* on the part of women. Some states, he maintains, have established many laws to serve as *sôphronistai* for women and have even appointed a magistrate to supervise their conduct. He pronounces this device ineffective and prefers the law of Romulus that prescribed an especially holy and indissoluble form of matrimony (*confarreatio*), by virtue of which a woman became a partner in her husband's property and shared his religious rites. When he died, his wife, provided that she had been *sôphrôn* and obedient to her husband, inherited his property. Dionysius attributes to this law of Romulus Rome's alleged freedom from divorce for 520 years[95]—a wildly unhistorical claim, since as early as 451 B.C. the Twelve Tables had included some reference to the legal formula with which a husband could dismiss a wife (Cicero, *Philipp.* 2. 28, 69).

Cicero prefers a different Roman solution to the problem of guaranteeing good conduct on the part of women. In *De Republica* he rejects the Greek institution of the *praefectus* (*gynaikonomos*) appointed to oversee women and recommends instead a censor, who would teach men how to control (*moderari*) their wives (4. 6. 6). Evidently he found it repugnant that a Roman husband should assign to a magistrate the right to supervise his wife's conduct, and as far as his preference for the censor is concerned, he always tends in *De Republica* to exalt traditional Roman institutions, even while giving them nontraditional functions.[96]

To carry much further into the Roman world our study of measures designed by the state to instill sophrosyne in women would unduly prolong this chapter, but two additional topics warrant at least brief mention because of the light they shed on characteristically Roman approaches to the problem. Rome from the beginning preferred to leave to the *paterfamilias*, sometimes

---

[95]*Ant. Rom.* 2. 25. According to Dionysius, Romulus permitted the Romans to punish with death adultery and wine drinking, in the belief that *methê* (drunkenness) is the cause of adultery. See 2. 26–27 for laws devised by Romulus to instill sophrosyne in young persons, especially males.

[96]Cicero's description of the duties of the censors in *De Legg.* 3. 3. 7 does not include the supervision of feminine conduct.

advised by the family council, the responsibility for punishing immorality on the part of wives and daughters, and thus in effect "sophronizing" other women in the family, yet in the course of time legal institutions were thought necessary to reinforce the waning authority of the *pater*. Some of these laws belonged to a category described by Greek observers as laws concerning sophrosyne. Religion, too, had a powerful influence in directing attention to desirable norms of conduct, and beginning in the late fourth century B.C., Rome had a cult of Pudicitia with shrines, images, and heroines intended to impress on women the advisability of practicing this virtue.

Greek historians of Roman institutions generally apply the term *nomoi peri sôphrosynês* to laws concerned with marriage and adultery (called by the Romans themselves *leges de pudicitia* and *de adulteriis*) and sumptuary laws (*leges sumptuariae*). Plutarch, who cites Sallust as his authority, says that the dictator Sulla imposed on the Romans laws about marriage and sophrosyne. He does not describe these *leges Corneliae,* but to judge by the context in which he refers to them, they were sumptuary as well as *leges de pudicitia.* He comments, that is, on the paradox by which Sulla, although wanton and extravagant himself, instilled discipline in the citizens (ἐσωφρόνιζε τοὺς πολίτας), whereas Lysander, with whom Sulla is compared, became general when Sparta was at the very peak of her *eunomia* and sophrosyne and was himself indifferent to wealth, but corrupted his country by sending home for public use the riches and spoils that he had acquired. Thus by his lack of avarice he injured Sparta more than Sulla by his greed injured Rome.[97]

Sumptuary laws in Rome go back at least to 215 B.C., when the Lex Oppia *de Luxu Feminarum* forbade women to possess more than one-half ounce of gold, wear multicolored dresses, or ride in two-horse vehicles within the city (Livy 34. 1–8).[98] Augustus in-

---

[97]*Comparison of Lysander and Sulla,* 3. 2–5.

[98]The Lex Oppia was repealed in 195 B.C., over the vigorous opposition of Cato the Censor, who described the agitation of Roman women in favor of repeal as *consternatio muliebris* (female madness), likened it to the secession of the *plebs* in 494 B.C., and warned Roman men that if they yielded to the demands of the *matronae* they would never again be able to control feminine *licentia* and *luxuria* (Livy 34. 1–4).

cluded both sumptuary laws and *leges de adulteriis* and *de pudicitia* in the legislation with which he sought to enforce his moral reform (Suetonius, *Aug.* 34. 1),[99] and it has been suggested that he also revived the ancient cult of Pudicitia, which, although in origin a private rather than a public cult, had important consequences for the whole state and moreover represents a peculiarly Roman effort to instill in ladies of the patrician and plebeian castes the kind of sophrosyne required of women.[100]

The honors paid to Pudicitia have been traced back to the mysterious affair of 331 B.C., described by Livy (8. 18), when the licentiousness of a group of patrician women was held to be a threat to the safety of the state (as well as to their husbands, some twenty of whom died of poison administered by their wives). Not only was a Roman court established for the first time to hear accusations of poisoning (170 women were convicted), but efforts were made to encourage regard for chastity through the foundation of a cult of Pudicitia Patricia, a private cult open only to patrician women married once to patrician men. It was matched, some thirty-five years later, by a cult of Pudicitia Plebeia, set up in 296 B.C., and open to similarly monogamous plebeian women (Livy 10. 23. 1–10). Still later, in 215 B.C. (the year of the Lex Oppia), a contest was held to select the *pudicissima* woman in Rome, a competition open to both castes and won by Sulpicia, daughter of a patrician, but wife of a plebeian. Sulpicia dedicated a statue to Venus Verticordia (Turner-of-hearts-to-chastity), a ceremony that has been viewed by R. E. A. Palmer as an affirmation of unity among the women of both castes "at the lowest point in Roman morale during the Hannibalic war."[101] Venus Verticordia did not receive a temple until 114 B.C., when one was erected to atone for the crime of three Vestals, convicted of breaking their vows of chastity.[102]

---

[99]On the provisions of legislation *de pudicitia,* consult PW, *s.v. Stuprum* (Pfaff).

[100]See the article by Robert E. A. Palmer, cited in Chapter 1, note 63, which brings together the information about the cults of Pudicitia and offers conjectures about their foundation, restoration, and survival in various guises until the papacy of Innocent I.

[101]Ibid., 136.

[102]The feast day of Venus Verticordia was April 1, when Joannes Lydus, *De Mensibus* 4. 65, p. 119 Wuensch, records the rites performed by women for the

Whether or not the cult of Pudicitia was in fact restored by Augustus during his consulship in 28 B.C. (when he held censorial powers), it attracted enough notice in the early Empire to inspire satirical comments in the poetry of Propertius and Juvenal.[103] What is more, the memory of the shrines, images, and heroines of Pudicitia survived the centuries, thanks to such writers as Livy and Valerius Maximus, to achieve a different kind of celebrity in the *Triumphs* of Petrarch. As we saw in Chapter 1, the *Triumph of Chastity*, composed about 1344, takes the personified Pudicizia and her attendants to Scipio's Liternum and then to Rome, where they first visit the temple of Venus Verticordia, *che dedicò Sulpizia* (Petrarch conflates the dedication of the statue in 215 B.C. with the foundation of the temple in 114 B.C.) and then reach their destination at the shrine of Pudicitia Patricia (*non di gente plebeia, ma di patrizia*).[104] By this time, the authentic ancient observance, whatever it may have been, had long since been forgotten, and the participants had been augmented by mythical and historical figures derived from many sources—including even Dante's Piccarda Donati, the Florentine nun ravished from her convent[105]—but the kernel of Petrarch's narrative is embedded in the events of 331 B.C. in Rome. This accumulation of typical figures and exemplary anecdotes and their unpredictable recombination in Petrarch's verse[106] constitute but one of many instances in which traditions related to sophrosyne persist, however changed, and contribute to the representation in literature and art of moral values that have meaning for a society centuries removed from that which gave birth to Sophrosyne herself and her Roman siblings. This survival, with the changes that made it possible, is probably the most interesting, as it is certainly the most enduring, of the consequences of the long career of sophrosyne. Yet before we examine in greater detail the iconography that

---

sake of concord and chastity (περὶ ὁμονοίας καὶ βίου σώφρονος). See also Sir James Frazer on Ovid, *Fasti* 4. 157.

[103]Propertius 2. 6 and 7; Juvenal 6. 306-313, cited by Palmer, 137-138, 143-144.
[104]183.
[105]*Paradiso* 3. 34 ff.
[106]For the iconography of the Triumph of Chastity see below, Chapter 4, and Plates I, X, and XI.

enables us to trace the ebb and flow of interest in this virtue, which persisted in some form until the emblem books of the baroque period, another topic invites attention, because it demonstrates the ways in which an ethical concept, growing and changing in sensitive response to the growth and change of the Greek *polis*, affected one of the most essential institutions of that *polis*, its oratory.

3

Eloquence

τρόπος ἔσθ' ὁ πείθων τοῦ λέγοντος
οὐ λόγος

(It is the character of the speaker that persuades,
not his speech.)

—Menander, Frg. 407, 7 Koerte

The day-to-day operation of the dominant institutions of fifth-century Athens—the courts, the Assembly, the Council—and of their counterparts in other democratic cities endowed the art of persuasion with steadily increasing influence. If sophrosyne in one of its most prominent aspects is an *aretê politikê*, a product of the *polis*, as Chapter 2 suggests, we should expect to find it reflected in the oratory of the period, which is necessarily shaped, in its moral dimension, by the ethics both of the orators themselves and of their audiences. In fact, the speeches of the fifth century, together with the speeches and rhetorical handbooks of the fourth, enable us to see with unusual clarity and detail how a great many ethical concepts were expressed in language calculated to appeal to popular audiences and how they were in various ways manipulated for the sake of persuasion. Among them sophrosyne plays a notable role, corresponding to its central position in the stereotype of the *chrêstos politês*, the useful citizen, whose virtues, in addition to being eulogized in judicial and epideictic oratory, often provided the model after which the orator himself molded his public persona. Changes in the interpretation of sophrosyne, especially fluctuations of meaning in response to social and political developments, quickly become apparent in oratory, which also

affords some evidence of the impact that certain mythical exemplars discussed in Chapter 1 had on audiences of the classical
period.

Among such exemplars, Nestor is conspicuous for his combination of sophrosyne and eloquence.[1] Although never described as
sôphrôn in the Homeric poems, which know only a limited range of
meanings for this word, he is later considered not only *sôphrôn*
but, as we saw in Chapter 2, a *sôphronistês,* one who imparts
moderation or virtue in general. The source of his later reputation for sophrosyne is the prudent counsel that he offers to
younger, usually more impassioned, men. Hence Plato, after recommending that a young tyrant, himself endowed with kingly
qualities, find a wise lawgiver to advise him (*Laws* 710C-D),
shortly afterward cites Nestor as an example of eloquence and
sophrosyne combined and describes as blessed (*makarioi*) those
who heed his counsel (711E). Nestor's "most excellent advice"
(*aristê . . . boulê, Il.* 9. 94) is the fruit of vast experience, stretching
over three generations, and there is a close correlation between
his extreme longevity and his powers of persuasion. His speeches
are full of references both to his venerable age and to the de-
ference paid to him by heroes of the past. Thus he offers the first
recorded example of an orator's reliance on what the Greeks of
later times were to call *axiôma* and the Romans *auctoritas,* terms
describing the personal repute and moral weight that lend persuasive power to a speaker by making him, in Aristotle's word,
axiopistos, worthy of being believed.

Nestor's eloquence is in fact distinguished by an early form of
what rhetoricians later termed ethos, the systematic exploitation
of the speaker's character as an aid to persuasion. This technique
goes through three distinct stages of development: the prerhetor-
ical, when orators like Nestor in the *Iliad* or the infant Hermes in

---

[1]For Nestor's eloquence, see *Iliad* 1. 248-249, for his advisory speeches, 2.
434-440, 4. 310-316, 9. 79, 179; for his wise counsel, 9. 94. The reliance of
Homeric orators on personal authority is discussed by Kennedy, I, 37; see also 90-
92 on persuasion through ethos. The standard work on this subject is Wilhelm
Süss, *Ethos: Studien zur alteren griechischen Rhetorik* (Leipzig, 1910). See also E. M.
Cope, *An Introduction to Aristotle's Rhetoric with Analysis, Notes, and Appendices* (Lon-
don, 1867) 108-113, 245-246, and *Commentary* (revised by J. E. Sandys), vol. II
(Cambridge, Eng. 1877) 5-6.

the *Homeric Hymn* (4. 368–386) refer with apparent artlessness to some aspect of their past life in order to win the hearer's confidence; the sophistic, when the persuasive value of the orator's reputation is manipulated, not perhaps more consciously than before, but in accordance with recognized topics that are now part of a systematic pattern; and the Aristotelian, which requires ethos to be evinced by the speech itself and furthermore elevates this mode of persuasion to a parity with logical argument and emotional appeal.

Another early development in Greek oratory was the praise of heroes according to canons of excellence reflecting the values of their society, values that changed as society changed, but continued to be designated by the word *aretê*. A reversal of the canon automatically provided a framework for invective. Praise (*epainos*) and blame (*psogos*) formed the basis of honor and dishonor in Homeric society; the *klea andrôn* (glories of men) celebrated by Achilles in *Iliad* 9 undoubtedly rested on the concept of *aretê* which the hero himself had learned from his elders. What that concept was we are soon told by Phoenix, who reminds Achilles of its twofold content: to be a speaker of words and a doer of deeds (*Il.* 9. 443). This, the earliest formulation of a concept of excellence including eloquence[2] as well as prowess in battle, was the first of many lists or canons of *aretai* that were to provide guidance for eulogy or invective, first in poetry, then in the prose of the fifth century, when sophistic rhetors converted the topic of *aretê* into an oratorical commonplace. Finally, in the fourth century, Aristotle designated *aretê* and *kakia* as the basic material of epideictic oratory, and this principle was thereafter enshrined in treatises and handbooks to the end of antiquity.

The topic of *aretê* and the use of ethos as a mode of persuasion deserve recognition as the two principal debts that ancient rhetoric owes to ethics. Aristotle, who classed rhetoric as an offshoot of ethics as well as of dialectic,[3] called attention not only

---

[2]Eloquence is included in canons of excellence in the fifth and fourth centuries under the influence of sophistic rhetoric and Attic oratory; see, for example, Euripides, *Autolycus*, Frg. 282. 23-28 Nauck, Anon. Iamb., D-K 89, p. 400; Aeschines, 3. 168.

[3]*Rhet.* 1. 2. 7 (1356a 25-33).

to the importance of epideictic oratory and ethical persuasion, but also to their common dependence on a knowledge of *aretê* and *kakia*. He was the first to insist that the character of the speaker constitutes a mode of persuasion on a par with the logical and emotional methods, and he was also the first to divide oratory into what came to be called the *tria genera causarum,* deliberative, judicial, and epideictic, the third of which has for its subject praise and blame and therefore requires a knowledge of virtue and vice.[4] On two occasions in the *Rhetoric* he links by cross-reference his discussions of ethos and epideictic, pointing out that their material is the same. It is the chief purpose of this chapter to study the development of the theory of persuasion through ethos, but the topic of *aretê* will also be considered, especially as it becomes a recognized resource of orators engaged in ethical persuasion. For both subjects—ethos and the *topos* of *aretê*—sophrosyne and closely related virtues will furnish much of the evidence.

Because the establishment of the three modes of persuasion is fundamental to the structure of Books 1 and 2 of the *Rhetoric,* Aristotle defines them promptly in chapter 2 of Book 1 (his real beginning), saying that of the proofs furnished by the speech itself (the *entechnoi,* artistic, proofs), the first depends on the *êthos tou legontos,* the character of the speaker. Persuasion is effected through ethos whenever the speech is delivered in such a way as to make the speaker seem worthy of trust (*axiopistos,* a term that is immediately glossed by the word *epieikês,* reasonable, equitable). Such persuasion must be achieved through the speech, he insists, not through any preconceived opinion of the speaker's character. Those writers of handbooks who hold that the speaker's *epieikeia* contributes nothing to his persuasiveness are wrong. Ethos actually has the most sovereign power to persuade; to achieve it, one must understand characters (*êthê*) and virtues (*aretai*).[5]

Although we have no clue to the identity of those writers of handbooks who denied any oratorical value whatsoever to ethos or *epieikeia,* we do know that Gorgias, Isocrates, and the author of the anonymous *Rhetorica ad Alexandrum* endorsed the view that

[4]For Aristotle's originality in these respects, consult Friedrich Solmsen, *A.J.P.* 62 (1941) 35–50, 169–190.

[5]1. 2. 4, 7 (1356a 1–27).

the past life of the speaker was the key to persuasive ethos, and this theory may accordingly be recognized as sophistic.

For Aristotle in the *Rhetoric* it was almost equally urgent to classify the three types of oratory, and this is what he does in the next chapter (1. 3), dividing the entire field into the *tria genera causarum*, distinguished according to the three kinds of audience: the spectators (of epideictic) and the judges—of what is past (judicial) and what is yet to come (deliberative). The epideictic kind is duly considered in chapter 9, where Aristotle observes at the outset that virtue and vice, the noble and the disgraceful, are the aim of those who assign praise and blame and that discussion of this subject will also cast light on ethical persuasion, since by the same methods we will be able to make ourselves and someone else seem worthy of credence where virtue is concerned (*axiopistos pros aretên*). Since Aristotle is here embarking on an analysis of *aretê* for the benefit of the epideictic orator, it is most probable that by "someone else" he means the subject of an encomium, rather than a client for whom a speech is to be composed by a professional logographer. He is not, that is, talking either about *êthopoiia* (portrayal of character) in a speech written for a client to deliver himself, which must therefore be composed in something like that person's own style of speaking, or about a situation in which it is necessary to distinguish between the ethos of an advocate and that of the litigant for whom he speaks. The *Rhetoric*, as is well known, virtually ignores the latter situation, which, though common in Rome, occurred but rarely in Athens.[6]

A more detailed but still very brief discussion of ethos occurs at the beginning of Book 2, where Aristotle makes a transition from the principles of logical persuasion (the final topic dealt with in Book 1) to those concerned with ethical and emotional persuasion. In Book 1 he has explained how to make the speech itself *apodeiktikos* (demonstrative) and *pistos* (convincing); he now points out that it is also necessary for the speaker both to show himself to be of a certain character and to get the hearer into a certain frame

---

[6]See Elaine Fantham, *Phoenix* 27 (1973) 262–275, and Kennedy, II, 139, and *A.J.P.* 89 (1968) 428–436. The *Rhetorica ad Alexandrum*, however, appears to contemplate a situation in which a speech is to be delivered by an advocate for a client (1442a 7 ff.).

of mind. It makes a great difference with regard to credibility (*pistis*), Aristotle observes, especially in deliberative, but also in judicial, speeches, that the speaker appear to be a certain kind of person and that the hearers consider him to have a certain attitude toward them. It is important, furthermore, that the hearers have a certain attitude toward the speaker. The apparent character of the speaker is of greater value in deliberative oratory, the disposition of the hearers in judicial.[7]

Turning first to ethos, Aristotle says that speakers appear credible for three reasons, apart from their use of demonstrative argument: because of intelligence (*phronêsis*), moral virtue (*aretê*), and good will (*eunoia*). For the first two, *phronêsis* and *aretê*, he refers to his discussion of the *aretai* in Book 1, under epideictic, observing again that by the same means one will make himself or someone else seem intelligent (*phronimos*) and virtuous (*spoudaios*). For good will (now designated as *eunoia* and *philia*) he refers to his forthcoming discussion of the emotions.[8] *Philia* is indeed discussed in 2. 4 (1380b 35 ff.), among the *pathê*, but nothing more is said about its relation to ethos, an indication of the ambiguity of the whole concept of *eunoia* and the difficulty of separating the projection of *eunoia* by the speaker from the desired consequence, a corresponding *eunoia* (or *philia*) on the part of the audience.

That *philia* and *eunoia* are virtually interchangeable is evident from the passage in the *Politics* (5. 7. 14 [1309a 33–39]) in which Aristotle lists the three qualities essential for a holder of high office: *philia* toward the established constitution, *dynamis* (capacity) with respect to the tasks involved in leadership, and *aretê* and *dikaiosynê*, considered as one virtue. Here we see almost the same set of *aretai* as in *Rhetoric* 2. 1. 5, but from a slightly different point of view (politics rather than persuasion).

The choice of just these qualities (*phronêsis, aretê,* and *eunoia*) as productive of credibility gives us a glimpse of the foundations on

[7] 2. 1. 2–4 (1377b 23–33).

[8] 2. 1. 5 (1378a 7)–7 (1378a 19). Aristotle's vocabulary in these chapters constitutes a guide to the terminology of ethical persuasion in fourth-century oratory. *Epieikês* is the favorite term for the person regarded as *axiopistos;* common synonyms are *spoudaios* and *chrêstos.* For the meaning of these and related terms in Aristotle consult Gerald Else, *Aristotle's Poetics: The Argument* (Cambridge, Mass., 1967) 73–78, 457.

which Aristotle was building. They recall, as has often been observed, the attributes on which Pericles bases his claim to *pistis* in Thucydides 2. 60. 5–6: γνῶναί τε τὰ δέοντα καὶ ἑρμηνεῦσαι ταῦτα, φιλόπολίς τε καὶ χρημάτων κρείσσων ("to know what is needed and communicate it, and to be patriotic and immune to the corruptions of wealth").[9] They also echo the requirements laid down by Socrates in the *Gorgias* (487A-B) when he tells Callicles, in effect, that he finds trustworthy only the speaker who is equipped with *epistêmê* (knowledge), *eunoia,* and *parrhêsia* (outspokenness, which in this instance implies the absence of any impediment to telling the truth and is therefore equivalent to the *aretê* and *dikaiosynê* of the *Rhetoric* and the *Politics*).[10]

Obviously, Aristotle was not the first to take thought about *axiopistia,* although he may have been the first to use the word in a technical sense. His originality consists in his analysis of the relation of this to other aims of the orator and his definition of the *êthos tou legontos* as the way to achieve it. The extent to which he depends, for his actual doctrine of ethos, on cross-references to his treatment of epideictic in Book 1 and emotional persuasion in Book 2 (as well as the brevity of his remarks) suggests that—from a purely chronological standpoint—ethos was one of the last subjects to be worked out, or that—from a methodological point of view—he was able to explicate the subject in this context in terms of other subjects he had already discussed. When he came to consider its ramifications, he had merely to refer to material already organized under other, more traditional headings. As is well known, attempts to influence the emotions of the hearers, especially through appeals to anger and compassion in the epilogue of a speech, had been reduced to formulae by earlier rhetoricians, among whom the name of Thrasymachus is the best known, and there must have been considerable doctrine on which to draw. Epideictic, too, although first elevated to a high level of theoretical importance by Aristotle, was far from being his own

[9]See Cope, *op. cit.,* 246, note 1, and Cope and Sandys, *Commentary* on *Rhet.* 2. 1. 5, for the parallels in the *Politics* and Thucydides.

[10]Consult Antje Hellwig, *Untersuchungen zur Theorie des Rhetorik bei Platon und Aristoteles, Hypomnemata* 38 (Göttingen, 1973), 280 ff., for the parallel in the *Gorgias* and for analogous passages in other works of the fourth century.

invention, and, as I have suggested, the topic of *aretê* had already undergone a long period of growth and change. A brief account of the principal stages of this development may help us to appraise Aristotle's originality in this area also and to determine at what point the topic of *aretê* (particularly the cardinal virtues) became part of the arsenal of the rhetoricians.

THE *TOPOS* OF *ARETÊ* BEFORE ARISTOTLE

Even in the Homeric poems it is easy to perceive a broadening in the scope of the concept of *aretê* beyond the physical prowess that guarantees success in battle (the principal early meaning of the word), and the advances made by the *Odyssey* over the *Iliad* in this respect are too well known to require demonstration. But a much more complex development occurred in choral lyric, the most important forerunner of the later prose encomium. Simonides is reputed to have been the first to write poetic encomia of actual persons (rather than of gods and mythical heroes), but Pindar in his victory odes offers the closest extant parallel to the epideictic oratory of Isocrates, who boasts that he is the first to celebrate the *aretê* of a man in prose (*Evagoras* 8).

In Pindar's *epinikia* both the concept of *aretê* and the word itself are prominent, and the word now conveys a wide range of implications. Pindaric eulogy honors both physical and mental qualities in the athletic victor, and, what is more, celebrates, in addition to the virtues of the individual, what might be called civic virtues, or, better, desirable conditions of civic life, such as the Hesiodic trinity of *eunomia, dikê,* and *eirênê* (*Ol.* 13. 6–7). Many different groupings of *aretai* are employed, suited to the particular hero, and in one case Pindar even alludes to the virtues that were later to be canonized as cardinal, ascribing them to the Aeacids, in the *Eighth Isthmian* (24–29).[11]

Tragedy also has much use for groups or canons of virtue, both to describe individual heroes like Amphiaraus in the *Seven against Thebes* (610) and to eulogize cities, particularly Athens, whose praise constitutes a favorite theme for choral odes. Euripides in particular is wont to cast into poetic form topics already well estab-

---

[11]See North, *A.J.P.* 69 (1948) 304–308.

lished in the official funeral oration of the Athenian *polis*, the *epitaphios logos*.[12] This, the earliest surviving type of prose encomium, goes back at least to the first half of the fifth century[13] and, if we may judge by the six examples still extant, developed a rigidly conventional form. Of the three typical sections (*epainos*, praise, *thrênos*, lament, *paramythia*, exhortation), the first always consists of panegyric of the ancestors and of the dead men themselves. The essential topics are their courage and their benefactions to Athens (sometimes also to the rest of Greece)—a theme summed up in the word *euergesia*. It is here that a *topos* concerning *aretê* first becomes a formal requirement in a recognized type of oration. No fifth-century *epitaphios logos* includes the canon of cardinal virtues, but in the fourth century the tetrad is borrowed from other types of prose encomium and at last finds its way into the *epitaphios* as well.[14]

Who it was who first employed the cardinal virtues in epideictic oratory is impossible to establish, but it would be hard to find a more attractive candidate for the role of *patêr tou logou* than Gorgias. Not only did he specialize in epideictic, including the festival oration and the eulogy of mythical figures, but his pupils and imitators give a prominent position to precisely these virtues in their *epainos*. Isocrates, in a very early courtroom speech, *De Bigis* (ca. 397 B.C.), praises Pericles for possessing three of the four cardinal virtues, sophrosyne, *dikaiosynê*, *sophia* (28), and in the Cyprian orations of his maturity (ca. 372–365) develops the *topos* of *aretê* around the entire group of four. The speech of Agathon in Plato's *Symposium*, which is extremely Gorgianic in style and parodies the Gorgianic perverseness in argumentation, eulogizes Eros as the possessor of all four cardinal virtues (196B–197A). Gorgias himself associated *aretê*, as a topic in mythical eulogy, with the praise of achievement, maintaining in the *Helen* (1) that virtue constitutes adornment (*kosmos*) for action (*pragma*). Although the

---

[12]See Burgess, 154, for many examples, and consult Gunther Zuntz, *The Political Plays of Euripides* (Manchester, 1955) 16–20.

[13]For various estimates of the date of the earliest *epitaphios logos* see Kennedy, I, 154 (475 B.C.) and Felix Jacoby, *J.H.S.* 64 (1944) 37–66 (464 B.C.).

[14]For example, Plato, *Menexenus* 246D–248A, Hypereides 6. 8 (sophrosyne and courage), Ps.-Demosthenes 60. 3, 6, 17.

praiseworthy things (*epaineta*) in Gorgianic eulogy are not, for the most part, moral virtues,[15] the bond between *aretê* and achievements (usually *praxeis* or *erga*), once established, became virtually indissoluble. Thus Isocrates, in his own oration on *Helen* (ca. 380 B.C.), eulogizes Theseus with respect to four virtues, three of the cardinal tetrad and piety (*eusebeia*), which here, as often, takes the place of *dikaiosynê* (31). The claim made for each of the virtues is supported by a recital of Theseus' achievements. A decade or so later, when Isocrates praises Evagoras and Nicocles of Cyprus, he links each virtue with the appropriate time of life and illustrates them all with the appropriate *praxeis*. By this time not only is the portrayal of *aretê* firmly established as the main purpose of epideictic,[16] but the nucleus of the topic consists of the cardinal virtues, with whatever additions or substitutions are appropriate to a given case.

Plato's contribution to the growth of the *topos* of *aretê* was influential out of all proportion to his presumed intent, for it was his authoritative definition of the tetrad of virtues in Book 4 of the *Republic*—for purposes unrelated to rhetoric—that determined which of the fluctuating group of *aretai* long cherished by the Athenian *polis* should be canonized in philosophy, handed on to the Stoics to become the nucleus of their ethical system, and finally transmitted to the Romans (as well as the Greeks of Hellenistic and imperial times) as the special group of virtues enshrined in epideictic oratory. Moreover, Plato was the first to insist that the *epaineta* must always be the "goods of the soul"—the virtues—not those of the body or of external fortune, which sophistic encomium admitted.[17] Plato's more rigorous concept of what is to be praised was maintained by Aristotle, who, however, did not limit to Plato's four the virtues that inspire *epainos*. In the *Rhetoric* he lists no fewer than nine,[18] and these are the virtues to which he refers the student of ethical persuasion, without specifying which, if any, are especially useful to this end (although he notes that the

[15]Consult Vinzenz Buchheit, *Untersuchungen zur Theorie des Genos Epideiktikon von Gorgias bis Aristoteles* (Munich, 1960) 173 ff. For the virtues in Gorgias' *Epitaphios*, see North, pages 93–95.

[16]Burgess, 126, note 4 (an analysis of the *topoi* used in the *Evagoras*).

[17]See Buchheit, *op. cit.*, 91–92, on the significance of *Theaet.* 173C ff.

[18]*Rhet.* 1. 9. 5–6 (1366b 1–3) and cf. *Eth. Nic.* 1. 12 (1101b 32).

virtues that confer the greatest benefits on society, and are therefore the most honorable, are courage, justice, and liberality).

Aristotle's most important contribution to the treatment of the
topos of *aretê* is not his definition of each virtue in the oratorical
context (useful though this is), but his integration of the *topos* into
a system which bestowed rhetorical effectiveness upon many
hitherto unrelated devices. His success in relating the parts to the
whole and proceeding from a knowledge of the nature of his
subject to a demonstration of its structure, powers, and functions
marks him as the embodiment of the philosophical rhetor described by Socrates in the *Phaedrus* (269E–270D).

In marked contrast to his treatment of moral virtue in the
Ethics, Aristotle's definition in *Rhetoric* 1. 9. 4 (1366a 36 ff.) is
precisely oriented toward the pragmatic aims of the orator. Now
aretê is a faculty of conferring benefits (*dynamis euergetikê*),[19] and
the definitions of the individual virtues tend to emphasize utility
in a political or social context. The recognition of *euergesia* as the
essence of virtue, for the purpose of persuasion, and the choice in
Rhet. 2. 1. 5 of *phronêsis*, *aretê*, and *eunoia* as the qualities that the
orator should attempt to "project" are largely responsible for the
air of pragmatism that distinguishes these sections of the treatise.
Here, the reader feels, we are in contact with the real world of
Attic oratory, and we wonder how much can still be resurrected of
the foundation on which Aristotle built. For ethical persuasion, as
for the topic of *aretê*, the foundation was laid by Homer.

ETHICAL PERSUASION BEFORE ARISTOTLE

Since many ancient commentators regarded Homer as the supreme teacher of rhetoric, it is natural to inquire whether the
extravagantly admired orators of the *Iliad* and the *Odyssey* employed ethical persuasion.[20] As I have indicated in connection

---

[19]Or a faculty providing and preserving good things (*dynamis poristikê agathôn kai phylaktikê*). Recent comments on the relation of the *Rhetoric* to the rest of Aristotle's work show a welcome tendency to recognize the serious philosophical purpose that shapes the *Rhetoric*. See especially William M. A. Grimaldi, S.J., *Studies in the Philosophy of Aristotle's Rhetoric* (Wiesbaden, 1972), and Eugene E. Ryan, "Aristotle's *Rhetoric* and *Ethics* and the Ethos of Society," *G.R.B.S.* 13 (1972) 291–311.

[20]Ancient critics show no interest in this aspect of Homer's eloquence, their chief concern being to identify the *tria genera dicendi* in the speeches of Odysseus, Nestor, and Menelaus. See George Kennedy, *A.J.P.* 78 (1957) 22–25.

with Nestor, a kind of ethos is visible, but it is closer to the type
that I have called sophistic than to the Aristotelian, since it consists
in the reminder of *res gestae,* the assertion of *auctoritas,* not in the
pure *êthos tou legontos,* evinced through the speech itself. An
example is Nestor's address to Patroclus in *Iliad* 11, which not
only alludes explicitly to the heroic values of which Phoenix and
Ajax have already reminded Achilles in the Embassy of Book 9,[21]
but embeds them in an account of the warlike exploits performed
by Nestor as a young man in Pylos. He stirs up Patroclus' thirst for
glory with a reminiscence of what Peleus said to Achilles when he
sent him off to war (to be always best in battle and preeminent
among all others, 11. 784) and intensifies the effect of the reminder by setting it in the perspective of the heroic generations that
have gone before. This is an entirely successful speech, Nestor's
finest, and it is crucial to the plot of the *Iliad,* whose final great
episode it initiates.

   Nestor employs the same technique in his speech to the in-
furiated chiefs, Achilles and Agamemnon, in Book 1, when he
prefaces his advice with a catalogue of the legendary fighters who
had respected his judgment: "And they listened to the counsels
that I gave and heeded my bidding" (1. 273). We note that the
verb *peithesthai* (to be persuaded, heed, obey) occurs three times in
one and one-half lines at the climax of Nestor's exhortation
(273-274). Here and elsewhere (as in his advice to Agamemnon in
Book 9), Nestor carefully establishes his credentials before proceeding to his specific counsel: "I shall speak as seems to me to be
best, for no one else will think a thought better than what I am
thinking" (9. 103-105)—a claim that seems designed to assure
the audience of his *phronêsis* and *eunoia.* His *aretê* is implicit in the
res gestae to which he alludes.

   Closer to what Aristotle had in mind in recommending persuasion through the speech itself, rather than the past life of the
speaker, is the kind of *pistis* achieved by Odysseus in his en-

----

[21]The appeal to accepted ethical or moral values is an important element in
Homeric eloquence, but it belongs in most instances to the realm of emotional, not
ethical, persuasion. Thus Phoenix and Ajax emphasize *aidôs* (the sense of decency
or obligation) in *Il.* 9. 506-509, 640, as does Priam in his appeal to Achilles in *Il.*
24. 503-504.

counter with Nausicaa. Just as Nestor, with three generations of *res gestae* to call upon, is a textbook example of sophistic ethos, Odysseus—unknown, nameless, naked, bereft of the least trace of *auctoritas*, hence obliged to convey an impression of *axiopistia* solely through his speech—is close to the Aristotelian ideal. In thirty-six lines, the terrifying, salt-encrusted creature from the sea establishes his *eunoia*, conveys an impression of *aretê*, especially piety and reverence, and manages to suggest a past in which he was a man of substance, although now in urgent need of pity and assistance (*Od.* 6. 149–185).[22]

Still richer and more highly developed is the *êthos tou legontos* encountered in Attic tragedy. This is only to be expected. Even though plot is the soul of tragedy, as Aristotle says in the *Poetics* (1450 a 38), *deuteron de ta êthê* ("character comes next"). It is the task of the dramatic poet to project a convincing character through words, and there is no reason why orators could not have profited from studying the techniques employed with such sovereign effectiveness in the theater of Dionysus.[23] Not only is *êthopoiia* essential for the craft of the dramatist, but there are many passages in extant tragedy in which a character conveys through his speech alone what Aristotle calls *axiopistia*, or at least impresses the audience with his *auctoritas*. Several Aeschylean speeches rich in such ethos could be cited: Prometheus' descriptions of his beneficence (*euergesia*) toward both Zeus and mankind (*P.B.* 216 ff., 442 ff.), a *topos* indispensable in courtroom oratory; Darius' advice to the Persian Elders and the Queen (*Pers.* 680–842), freighted with insight from beyond the grave and laden with gnomic observations about the destiny of mankind—their effectiveness enhanced by the Chorus' praise of the old king's *phila . . . êthê* (kindly disposition) even before his ghost appears (648); Apollo's reminder, at the beginning of his speech in de-

[22]Aristotle found in the Phaeacian episode an illustration of ethical and emotional persuasion suitable to the proem of a speech; see *Rhet.* 3. 14. 11 (1415b 25–28). For an instance of ethical persuasion in behalf of someone other than the speaker himself, see *Od.* 2. 230, 234, where Mentor tries to persuade the Ithacans to protect the interests of Odysseus against the suitors by portraying him as a kind, gentle, fatherly ruler.

[23]Aristotle in the *Rhet.* often cites examples from tragedy; see 3. 16. 8 ff. (1417a 16 ff.) on ethos in the *Diêgêsis* (Statement of the facts).

fense of Orestes before the Areopagus, that he will speak justly
because, being a seer, he cannot lie and has never, in all his oracu-
lar utterances, said anything except what Zeus himself com-
manded (*Eumen.* 614–618)—a transparent bid to establish both
phronêsis and *aretê*. The advice of Danaus to his daughters about
how to address the Argives so as to win their protection (*Supp.*
197–203) constitutes a veritable set of instructions on persuasive
ethos, such as would not be out of place in a rhetorical handbook
of much later date. Danaus reminds the girls that modesty becomes the suppliant and bold talk is offensive; he even warns
them to be neither too fast nor too slow in their speech, since the
Argives are quick to take offense.[24]

In the time of Sophocles and Euripides audiences at the tragic
contests could hear many superbly effective speeches, constructed
according to the principles then being used in the lawcourts and
doubtless being taught by some rhetors.[25] Attempted persuasion
through ethos now becomes very common indeed, always mingled with emotional persuasion. Since this is a subject familiar to
all who read Greek tragedy, I shall mention only three examples,
all from the period between 431 and 428 (just before the first visit
of Gorgias to Athens) and all dependent, as it happens, on appeals
to the concept of sophrosyne, each time in a different aspect.

In Euripides' *Medea,* Jason's speech of self-justification attempts to establish for the speaker an ethos that is prudent (both
sôphron and *sophon*) and well-disposed to Medea and their children (545 ff.). It also makes the notorious claim to beneficence
(*euergesia*) in his having brought Medea to Hellas, where she has
enjoyed the advantages of civilization. In the *Hippolytus* by the
same poet, the hero's speech of self-defense before Theseus emphasizes his sophrosyne (here, "chastity") and opens with one of

---

[24]On modesty (*sôphronein*) as proper to strangers see Menander, *Monostichae*
545.

[25]The historians also offer many examples of effective use of ethical persuasion
in speeches. See, for one example, the speech of Artabanus in Herodotus, 7. 10, in
which, after establishing his *eunoia* and *phronêsis* by reminding Xerxes of his prudent advice to Darius in the past, he warns the young king against attacking
Greece and supports his advice with gnomic observations about divine jealousy.
Thucydides' mastery of ethos in such speeches as those ascribed to Archidamus (1.
80–86) and Pericles (2. 60–64) needs no demonstration.

the most familiar of all topics of the proem: "Unaccustomed as I am to public speaking . . ." (considered below as part of the *topos* of *apragmosynê* or *apeiria*, "inexperience").[26] When Creon in Sophocles' *Oedipus Tyrannus* refutes the charge that he sought to overthrow the king, he does so by claiming for himself certain moral virtues, one of which is sophrosyne (here, "modesty, lack of ambition," 584 ff.). That in each of these cases the speech fails to persuade the person to whom it is addressed (Medea, Theseus, Oedipus) and at the same time has the dramatic effect of under- lining the less attractive aspects of the speaker's ethos gives us some insight into the ironic possibilities of these *topoi* and shows, as well, the relatively early date at which they could be exploited in the theater.

Quite a different situation obtains in a play by Euripides from which we have substantial fragments, the *Hypsipyle,* produced around 410 B.C., probably in a trilogy with the lost *Antiope* and the extant *Phoenician Women.*[27] Twenty years or so after the *Medea* and *Hippolytus,* with their devastating attacks on heroes who claim to possess sophrosyne but prove to have only a partial or defective virtue, Euripides presents a character almost unparalleled among his masculine figures, a hero who announces that he is *sôphrôn,* persuades his listeners that this is indeed the case and wins an argument on the strength of his ethos.

The speaker is none other than Amphiaraus. On the way to attack Thebes with the rest of the Seven, he becomes involved at Nemea in the desperate plight of Hypsipyle, who has carelessly allowed her infant charge Opheltes, child of King Lycurgus and Queen Eurydice, to be killed by a snake while she is guiding Amphiaraus at his request to a spring in the meadow. He now pleads for her life before the baby's mother. First, he establishes his moral credentials: piety (*to eusebes*) and a sense of obligation for the service Hypsipyle has rendered him (for not to show gratitude would be *aischron,* disgraceful). He then bids for Eurydice's confidence by assuring her of his sophrosyne, which is (he says) much talked of by the Greeks (σῶφρον γὰρ ὄμμα τοὐμὸν

[26]Barrett (above, Chapter 1, note 24), cites Lysias 12. 3, 19. 2, Isaeus 8. 5, 10. 1, and Demosthenes 27. 2, 55. 7.
[27]See T. B. L. Webster, *The Tragedies of Euripides* (London, 1967) 163.

Ἑλλήνων λόγος πολὺς διήκει, Frg. 60. 44–45 Bond). He defines this *aretê* with two glosses: *kosmein emauton* (ordering, controlling myself) and *ta diapheronta horan* (seeing the essential things, what matters, 46). The first phrase defines sophrosyne in the sense that had become popular in the late fifth century. The second recalls the distinction between being and seeming that Aeschylus had ascribed to Amphiaraus in the *Seven against Thebes* (592). Eurydice's readiness to be persuaded is, as T. B. L. Webster observes,[28] remarkable. Clearly she is overwhelmed by Amphiaraus' *axiopistia*. She actually says, "You are not unworthy, *anaxios*" (Frg. 60, 54 Bond), as she bids him speak. Her only express reason is that since he lives near Argos she has heard from everyone that he is *sôphrôn*. Hence she even consents to unveil herself in his presence. When he has finished speaking, she explains what to look for in orators: men's nature and deeds and the behavior of the wicked and the good. She concludes by saying that it is right to have confidence in the *sôphrones*, but to have nothing to do with the unjust (115–117).[29]

If the final play of this trilogy was indeed the *Phoenician Women*, it helps to explain the extraordinary emphasis on sophrosyne throughout this scene. In the *Phoenician Women*, Euripides explicates the unblazoned shield of Amphiaraus as a symbol of his sophrosyne (1111–1112), picking out one of the four virtues assigned him in Aeschylus' *Septem* and equating with sophrosyne the preference for reality over appearance that was thereafter linked with this hero in the memory of Greece and Rome. Already in the second play of Euripides' trilogy, it seems, the poet calls attention to this virtue in the seer and makes it the basis of his powers of persuasion. Significant from a rhetorical point of view is the way the speaker reminds the hearer of his established reputation and then, by elements within his speech, confirms her preconceived notion.[30] He starts out, that is, with the Isocratean kind

---

[28]Ibid., 214.

[29]Even before the arrival of Amphiaraus, the Chorus links persuasion with sophrosyne, in this instance good judgment on the part of the listener. They assure Eurydice in the fourth episode that her noble words are persuasive to those who have good sense, ἐν σώφροσιν (Frg. 22, 9–10 Bond).

[30]For example, by the assurance that he would not tell a lie, because to do so would be to shame Apollo, the source of his prophetic power, and by the long

of ethos and finishes with the Aristotelian. Even more interesting is the difference between the impression made by Amphiaraus and that made by Hippolytus, although each states baldly that he is renowned for sophrosyne. Amphiaraus is like Theseus in Euripides' *Suppliants,* a hero whose sophrosyne is one of the unalterable data of the myth, not to be attacked even by such an iconoclast as Euripides.[31] The entire episode affords a glimpse of the courtroom technique available in 410 or thereabouts, in which ethos could be the dominant mode of persuasion.

Such familiar devices inevitably found reflections in Old Comedy. The classic study of rhetoric in Aristophanes,[32] which offers a detailed analysis of the defense of Dicaeopolis in the *Acharnians,* calls attention to the attempt in the Proem to remove prejudice (*diabolê*). This is a favorite topic of ethical persuasion in Attic oratory, usually combined with the assertion of some positive virtue.[33] It is prominent in the defense of the dog Labes in the mock trial of the *Wasps.* His advocate, Bdelycleon, begins by saying that it is hard to speak in defense of a dog that has been slandered, then proceeds boldly to the topic of *euergesia,* maintaining that Labes is *agathos* because he chases wolves away and *aristos* among all dogs now in existence by reason of his proficiency at herding sheep, and that he guards the door and is excellent in all other respects as well (950–958). The abundant use of rhetorical devices in Old Comedy proves, if proof were needed, that Athenian audiences were sufficiently familiar with such techniques to recognize them instantly and find amusement in their

---

consolatio on the death of the baby, which is based on the commonplace of sophrosyne according to which suffering is the lot of mankind.

[31]Eteocles, on the other hand, is endowed by Euripides with an ethos entirely different from that of the Aeschylean character in the *Septem;* in the *Phoenissae* he is greedy for power (*philotimos*) and willing to commit injustice in order to achieve it (523–525, 532, 554).

[32]Charles T. Murphy, *H.S.C.P.* 49 (1938) 69–113.

[33]The *Rhetorica ad Alexandrum,* which knows nothing of ethos as a separate mode of persuasion, yet insists repeatedly on the need to remove prejudice (*diabolê*). See especially chs. 29 (demegoric oratory) and 36 (dicanic). In both types of address the removal of prejudice is a function of the proem. Aristotle, *Rhet.* 1. 1. 3–4 (1354a 11–18) complains that earlier handbooks deal with matters outside the issue, such as *diabolê.*

parody. Again we get a date in the mid-twenties for the parody of
ethical persuasion because the *Acharnians* was produced in 425
B.C., the *Wasps* in 422.

AXIÔMA

During the same period, concern began to be expressed about
the persuasiveness attached to what was called *axiôma* (high repute). Thucydides, in his famous assessment of the reasons for
Pericles' influence in Athens, says that he owed it to his *axiôma*
and *gnômê*, as well as to his incorruptibility (2. 65. 8).[34] He did not
say anything just to please the Athenians, but was able to oppose
them even to the point of enraging them because of his high
repute (*axiôsis*, 2. 65. 9). For Thucydides the words *axiôma* and
axiôsis seem to have no derogatory connotations, but Euripides, in
the *Hecuba* and the *Suppliants,* reflects contemporary fears that
the *axiôma* of a speaker might overwhelm the audience's good
judgment, even though the speaker's advice is bad. Hecuba says to
Odysseus, "Your *axiôma,* even if you speak badly, will carry conviction, for advice [*logos*] from those in ill-repute and from those
in good repute does not have the same effect" (293–295). The
Herald in the *Suppliants* conceives of a situation even more
dangerous, one in which a wicked man actually achieves *axiôma* by
wooing the *dêmos* with his tongue (423–425).[35] Both the *Hecuba*
and the *Suppliants* may be dated between ca. 425 and 420.

Clearly, then, *axiôma* and its synonyms in the last quarter of the
fifth century implied the possession of the kind of popular esteem
that would normally enhance the powers of persuasion. *Axiôma* is
thus close to the Roman concept of *auctoritas,* and indeed the
word chosen to translate *auctoritas* in the Greek version of the *Res
Gestae* of Augustus (34. 3) is *axiôma*. If this is not precisely the
Aristotelian *êthos tou legontos,* it approximates the sophistic conception of the rhetorical effectiveness of the speaker's past life.
Since we know the names of sophistic rhetoricians who at this very

[34]Cf. Aristotle's three requirements for *axiopistia* (2. 1. 5 [1378a 6–8]) and consult Cope and Sandys (above, note 9).

[35]J. H. Finley, Jr., *H.S.C.P.* 49 (1938) 42–43. calls attention to the likeness
between Euripides and Thucydides in these passages and concludes that both
writers have lost faith in debate. Cf. Sophocles, Frg. 622 Nauck.

time were developing the arguments from probability, nature, and advantage, or the appeals to pity and other emotions, it is natural to ask whether there were no Sophists famed for exploiting the persuasive possibilities inherent in *axiôma*. The answer is that no name is identified with the early technical approach to ethos, and the reason is undoubtedly that this kind of persuasion had not yet been clearly distinguished from persuasion through emotional appeals. Yet in addition to Aristotle's emphatic rejection of an approach to ethos that is satisfied with a preconceived notion of the speaker's life (*Rhet.* 1. 2. 4), there is other evidence that the value of ethos (or *axiôma*) in a rhetorical context was appreciated and that some instruction was available on how to exploit it.

Since early rhetorical teaching made much use of model speeches, we may regard a passage in the *Defence of Palamedes* by Gorgias as a demonstration of how to derive persuasive effect from a good reputation.[36] Palamedes offers his past life (τὸν παροιχόμενον βίον) as witness to the truth of what he says (15) and maintains that to deserve trust (*pistis*) is what makes life worth living (21). Instruction in the form of handbooks comes later, and the *Rhetorica ad Alexandrum,* which (whatever its date) certainly reflects a tradition going back to the Sophists,[37] gives every evidence of sensitivity to the importance of *axiôma*. The previous life of the speaker (according to this handbook) contributes to persuasion (*to peithein*) and to the achievement of a reputation for being equitable (*doxa epieikês*). If ethos and actions are closely correlated, the chances of carrying conviction are good (ch. 38).

The most successful heir of Gorgias, Isocrates, refers to this subject in the *Antidosis* (ca. 354), using the same phrase (*doxa epieikês*) as the author of the *Rhetorica ad Alexandrum* and stating his own position in a way that highlights the originality of Aristotle. He explains that one who wishes to be persuasive will not neglect *aretê*, but will especially attend to it, so that he may achieve a reputation as equitable as possible among his fellow citizens, for

---

[36]The date is uncertain. Cf. James Coulter, *H.S.C.P.* 68 (1964) 300 (before 411) and Charles Segal, *H.S.C.P.* 66 (1962) 137 (later).

[37]On the probable date and sophistic antecedents of the *ad Alex.* see Kennedy, I, 114–122.

who does not know that speeches seem more true when spoken by those who are well thought of than when spoken by those in ill repute? The proofs afforded by one's life (*pisteis ek tou biou*) have greater force than those that come from the speech (*ek tou logou*, 278).

ARISTOTLE, *RHETORIC* 3

Aristotle, as we have seen, takes a position exactly opposite to that of Isocrates: the *êthos tou legontos* must be achieved through the speech itself, not through a preconceived notion of the speaker's character. His demand is a consequence of his basic distinction between *atechnoi pisteis*, inartistic or nontechnical proofs, lying outside the art of the speaker (such as witnesses, oaths, and the evidence of slaves under torture) and *entechnoi*, artistic proofs—those achieved through the art of rhetoric itself. According to this view, the former life and *doxa epieikês* of the speaker are as much outside the subject (*exo tou pragmatos*) as an affidavit or an oath. It would, of course, be a grave mistake to suppose that Aristotle expected the orator to renounce the exploitation of *axiôma;* part of the speaker's task would always be to remind the audience in any way he could of whatever reputation for *epieikeia* he might possess. Aristotle's concern is simply to establish what lies within and what without the competence of rhetoric as a *technê*.

In practice the difference between the sophistic and the Aristotelian types of ethical persuasion would seldom be clear-cut. Cicero subscribes to the Isocratean view, according to which favor is secured by *dignitas, res gestae,* and *existimatio vitae,* but he actually tells us much more specifically than Aristotle does what the speaker should do to enhance an already favorable impression. It seems to be principally a matter of delivery (one of the *officia oratoris* not developed in any detail until the time of Theophrastus). In *De Oratore*, Antonius explains that one should use a gentle voice, a modest expression, pleasant words, and an air of doing reluctantly and against one's will what one is actually eager to do (2. 182). He adds that the orator should show the marks of affability, liberality, mercy, piety, and a nature that is pleasing, not greedy or avaricious. The qualities of men who are upright and modest, not harsh, insistent, litigious, or bitter, win good will. (We note that only the ethos of the speaker himself can easily be conveyed in this way, not that of a client.) Cicero's advice recalls a passage in the *ad Alexandrum* in which the speaker using a type of oratory called "investigative" (*exetastikon*) is urged to employ an ethos that is not bitter (*pikron*), but gentle (*praon*); thus his speech will become more persuasive and arouse the least prejudice (ch. 37).

Such a comment in the one remaining complete sophistic handbook shows that rhetoricians were not unaware of the effect that ethos within the speech itself might have, even though they stopped short of the Aristotelian perception of ethos as a separate mode of persuasion, on a par with *logos* and *pathos*. The advice that they offered their pupils was, if we may judge by the *ad Alexandrum*, organized according to the various parts of the oration (*moria logou*), just as early rhetorical schemes for appealing to the emotions tended to locate such appeals in the proem and the epilogue. Valuable traces of pre-Aristotelian ethical persuasion are to be found in Book 3 of the *Rhetoric*, which incorporates in chapters 13-19 elements of a sophistic handbook linked with Isocrates' pupil Theodectes and organized according to the traditional *moria logou*.

Theodectes is elsewhere credited with defining the task of the orator in terms of four parts of the oration (the four usually referred to Isocrates in the later tradition). According to this scheme the proem aims at securing good will (*eunoia*), the narrative at plausibility (*pithanotês*), the proof at persuasiveness (*peithô*), and the epilogue at indignation (*orgê*) or compassion (*eleos*).[38] Aristotle maintains that only two parts are really essential (narrative and proof), but reproduces the rival scheme and in so doing includes advice about ethos which often parallels comments in the *Rhetorica ad Alexandrum*, organized throughout on the *moria logou* principle.

In discussing the proem, for example, Aristotle speaks of *eumatheia* (willingness to learn, *docilitas*) as desirable in the judges. It is necessary for the orator to appear *epieikês*, for the judges pay

[38]*Anon. Proleg.* 32, 216 Rabe.

more attention to such persons (3. 14. 7 [1415 a 38 ff.]).[39] In the narrative (*diêgêsis*), one should "slip in from the side" (*paradiêgeisthai*) whatever has a bearing on one's own *aretê* (16. 5 [1417a 3 ff.]). More precisely, narrative will be ethical if it reveals moral purpose (*proairesis*, 16. 8 [1417a 16-19]). The orator should try to give the impression that he speaks because of this and not from calculation (*apo dianoias*). Thus he will seem to pursue, not his own advantage, but what is noble (*kalon*, 16. 9 [1417 a 24 ff.]).[40] Here Aristotle provides sample phrases likely to secure the desired effect, pointing out that they imply prudence (*phronêsis*) and virtue (the *agathon*); the reader recalls that *phronêsis* and *aretê* are necessary to achieve *axiopistia* (2. 1. 5 [1378a 6-8]). Both narrative and proof should evince a moral character, for which maxims (*gnômai*) will be helpful, since they reveal ethos (3. 17. 9 [1418a 17-19]).[41] One should not introduce rhetorical syllogisms (enthymemes) into a speech that has an ethical cast, because demonstration (*apodeixis*) has no moral character and shows no moral choice (17. 8 [1418a 15-17]). In the proof, ethical persuasion may in some instances be of greater value than logical argument. If you have arguments, Aristotle says, you may speak ethically and demonstratively; if you do not have enthymemes, speak *êthikôs*. It is more suitable for a person who is *epieikês* to appear *chrêstos* (useful) than for the speech to be elaborately worked out (17. 12 [1418 a 38 ff.]). In the epilogue, one important aim is to show the speaker as *agathos* (and his opponent, naturally, as *kakos*, 19. 1 [1419b 16-17]).

What is striking in these "Theodectean" chapters—apart from their intensely pragmatic character—is the lack of any coherent

---

[39]The reference here is to forensic oratory; epideictic draws its proems from praise and blame (3. 14. 2 [1414b 30 ff]). *Rhet. ad Alex.* 29 deals with the function of the proem in a demegoric speech and the ways of maintaining or producing *eunoia* in the audience. Chapter 36 discusses the same challenge in forensic oratory.

[40]Cf. *Rhet.* 3. 2. 4 (1404b 18-21) on the need to conceal artifice (compared to mixing drinks). See Dionysius of Halicarnassus, *Lysias* 8, on the advantage of seeming not to calculate an effect.

[41]For the use of maxims see *ad Alex.* 11, 22, 32. Ethos is not mentioned, but in 22 maxims are recommended for all parts of the oration, so that the speech may be urbane (*asteios*). Urbanity, it is implied, constitutes a desirable form of ethos.

frame of reference that would permit the reader to relate the scattered admonitions to a single body of doctrine. The absence of a definition of ethos or a recognition that it constitutes an independent mode of persuasion means that the odd bits of traditional advice have no impact beyond the part of the address for which they are intended. No conception of how to project and sustain a convincing characterization emerges. Aristotle's own achievement becomes all the more impressive when we realize that, brief as his treatment of ethical persuasion actually is, he endowed its wraithlike form with a new and very substantial body of material simply by observing that this mode of persuasion has much in common with epideictic oratory, for which there was already a well-developed series of *topoi* dating at least from the time of the Sophists. And by directing his readers to that part of his discussion of epideictic which dealt with the virtues, Aristotle indicated the mother lode from which future prospectors could mine their most precious ore. This is precisely what Cicero did, centuries later, when he said in *De Oratore* (quoting the Academic philosopher Charmadas) that philosophy, not rhetoric, is the source from which the orator must learn to seem to his audience as he wishes to seem and to move them as he chooses. This knowledge, he says, lies *penitus in media philosophia retrusa atque abdita* ("hidden and stored away deep in the core of philosophy," 1. 87).[42]

In addition to linking ethos with the topic of *aretê,* and thereby providing it with additional substance, Aristotle advances the understanding of ethical persuasion in still another direction in *Rhetoric* 3 by his study of *lexis êthikê,* style that reveals (or expresses) character. Chapters 1 and 7, which relate *lexis* to each of the Aristotelian *pisteis,* are of far-reaching importance. Here, too, Aristotle builds upon a perception much earlier expressed by Plato, when in the *Laches* the title character admits that he is *philologos* (a lover of both speech and reason, since *logos* implies both), provided that the speaker and what he says are suitable to each other and in harmony (πρέποντα ἀλλήλοις καὶ ἁρμόττοντα,

---

[42]See also *Orator* 118 on the *philosophiae . . . locos,* including those *de virtutibus aut vitiis.*

188C–D).[43] The concept of the *prepon* (suitable, fitting) is central
to Aristotle's discussion of style in 3. 7 (1408a 10 ff.), where he
shows that the persuasiveness of all three *pisteis* depends on the
use of an appropriate style. In the case of ethos, he recommends
suiting the style to such categories as age, sex, nationality, and
moral dispositions; this discussion, which has much in common
both with *Rhetoric* 2. 12–17 (on the characteristics associated with
times of life and states of fortune) and *Poetics* 15 (on characterization in tragedy), has an obvious bearing on *êthopoiia* and is therefore helpful, not only for the *logographos* writing a speech to be
delivered by a client, but also for any writer concerned with the
portrayal of character in any genre. Nevertheless, Aristotle is
primarily interested in the ways in which style makes the *pisteis*
credible in oratory, and this chapter is particularly successful in
showing how the integration of all three types of proof may be
accomplished through an appropriate style.

ETHICAL *TOPOI*

The absence of any substantial remains of technical treatises
dealing with ethos before Aristotle's *Rhetoric* and the *Rhetorica ad
Alexandrum* lends special significance to the model speeches devised by the Sophists, whether for display or for instruction, and
we shall now turn to the *topoi* used in such orations. If the three
Tetralogies that have come down under the name of Antiphon
could be established as authentic and dated around 440 or soon
thereafter, we could be certain that, in this relatively early stage of
rhetorical teaching, *topoi* designed to demonstrate a certain kind
of ethos were already located in the parts of the oration where
they later became fixed and where they were calculated to evoke
standard reactions connected with familiar ethical values. Since,
however, the date and authorship of the *Tetralogies* are alike disputed,[44] with estimates of their composition ranging from 440 to
around 400, it is rash to assume that they reflect an extremely
early state of instruction, although it is probable that they precede

---

[43]The relation of ethos and *lexis* in *Rhetoric* 3 is discussed by Father Grimaldi, *op.
cit.*, 50–51, and Hellwig, *op. cit.*, 267 ff.

[44]For the wide variation in suggested dates and the arguments on each side
consult K. J. Dover, *C.Q.* 44 (1950) 56–59.

most of the model speeches ascribed to Gorgias, Antisthenes, and Alcidamas.[45] Under the circumstances, in citing elements conducive to ethos in the *Tetralogies* or other model speeches, we can make only the modest suggestion that they demonstrate the kind of instruction available in the last third of the fifth century. After a brief survey of these elements, I shall summarize the categories of ethical *topoi* actually used by the Attic orators and relate them, as far as possible, to the parts of the oration in which they regularly occur.

The *Tetralogies*, three sets of four speeches each, two for the defense, two for the prosecution, deal with cases of homicide and exemplify different ways of arguing from the same premises. Their approach to ethos may be summarized as follows:

1. All three *Tetralogies* make a conscious effort to establish a persuasive ethos, usually in the Proem, always early in the speech, and they do so in one of two ways: the speaker represents himself as inoffensive and nonlitigious, or else he cites the usefulness of himself and his family to Athens. The first method exemplifies what we may call the *apragmosynê-topos*,[46] the second the *euergesia-topos*.[47] Since it is the defendant who is most in need of establishing an ethos that will conciliate the judges, we find these *topoi* in the second speech of each *Tetralogy* (1. 2. 12; 2. 2. 1, 10; 3. 2. 1). The relation to *eunoia* is obvious.

2. In a reversal of the topic of *aretê*, they accuse the opponent of wickedness, most often audacity (*tolmê, anaideia*) and wanton insolence (*hybris, akolasia*). This *topos* usually occurs in the body of the speech, but may open the second speech for the prosecution,[48] as a counter to the ethical persuasion used in the first speech for the defense. Since the material for such attacks on the character of the opponent comes from the sphere of epideictic

[45]See the works cited in notes 36 above and 53 below for the range of dates suggested for these model speeches.

[46]For example, 1. 2. 12 (*apragmosynê*, avoidance of meddling, is implicit in the claim that wealth comes not from litigation [*polypragmosynê*, meddling], but from hard work). *Apragmosynê* is highly regarded in a society that counts *polypragmosynê* a fault. On the history of both concepts see Victor Ehrenberg, *J.H.S.* 67 (1947) 46–67.

[47]For example, 1. 2. 12; 2. 2. 3.

[48]For example, 2. 3. 1, 2, 5, 6; 3. 3. 1.

oratory, with its concern for virtue and vice, we are reminded of how natural such borrowings were, long before Aristotle prescribed them in the *Rhetoric*.

3. The *Tetralogies* locate in the epilogue claims that the speakers were defenders of justice and piety, and they appeal to these virtues in the judges.[49] This combination of ethical and emotional appeals proves to be one of the most enduring techniques in Attic oratory. It occurs in all three *Tetralogies*, and in the second it figures in three of the four speeches.

4. The third *Tetralogy* demonstrates how to apply the argument from probability to a situation revolving around the presence or absence of sophrosyne. The issue is whether the young defendant or the elderly victim is more likely to have caused the fatal altercation, and the decision depends on which is more likely to possess self-restraint, the young or the old (3. 3. 2; 3. 4. 2). The argument is of interest for two reasons. First, it illustrates the combination of *eikos* (probability) and ethos that is the principal mode of defense in certain types of courtroom oratory (such as Gorgias' *Defence of Palamedes* and Plato's *Apology of Socrates*), wherein the accused seeks to establish a specific ethos and relate to it the probabilities in a given case. Secondly, it justifies Aristotle's inclusion in *Rhetoric* 2 of his celebrated sketch of the characteristics of the young, the elderly, and the middle-aged (chs. 12–14). Not only is it important for the orator to know how to appeal to the interests and emotions typical of different age groups, but it may also be essential to paint a convincing picture of the ethos of a client or an opponent, and the age group to which he belongs may be the determining factor. The *êthopoiïa* in which Lysias excelled sometimes exploited precisely this technique.[50]

Although justice, piety, and sophrosyne all figure separately in the *Tetralogies*, they are not organized in anything like a canon, and there is no indication that the author is familiar with such a grouping. The same is true of the model speeches that have come down under the names of Gorgias, Antisthenes, and Alcidamas. All, however, pay attention to certain individual forms of *aretê*, and some show what appears to be a strong interest in *êthopoiïa*.

---

[49] 1. 1. 9–10; 2. 13; 2. 2. 12; 3. 11; 4. 10; 3. 2. 9; 4. 1. The usual phrase is *dikaiôs kai hosiôs*.

[50] For example, *Or.* 24. 15 (an old man), 16. 11 and 18. 20 (young men).

The *Palamedes* of Gorgias, the most valuable of the model speeches from this point of view, has the accused man himself set forth his virtues in a section toward the close of the oration, rather than in the Proem, the usual locale. Yet the Proem does present him as a man who fears dishonor more than death; it introduces the issue of justice, and it suggests that the accuser, Odysseus, is *kakistos,* an utter villain (1-3). In the address to the judges that follows the Refutation, Palamedes maintains that his life has been blameless, that he has been a great benefactor of the Greeks and indeed of all mankind, that he has preferred *aretê* to wealth, and that he has not been useless in deliberation or idle in war (29-32).

Here we recognize two of the most important commonplaces employed in ethical persuasion by fourth-century orators (already observed in the *Tetralogies*): the *apragmosynê-topos* and the *topos* of *euergesia* (or *opheleia,* helpfulness). Moreover, as we have noted, Palamedes offers his past life as a witness to the truth of what he has been saying (15) and, like Socrates in the *Apology,* combines the argument from probability with the portrayal of ethos, for his defense consists essentially of the effort to convince the judges that it is not likely (*eikos*) that a man of such character as he claims for himself would have committed the crime of which he is accused. He even calls the recital of his virtuous life a *sêmeion,* in technical terms a "sign" that he cannot be guilty of disgraceful and evil deeds (31).[51]

The two model speeches attributed to Antisthenes, the *Ajax* and the *Odysseus,* are even more exclusively concerned with the topic of virtue, being (as George Kennedy points out)[52] studies in *êthopoiia.* In each case the ethos portrayed consists of a particular form of *aretê: andreia,* the excellence of Ajax, and *sophia,* Odysseus' special quality. Each oration contains a series of amplifications of the topic of virtue; what is most significant is their focus on the contrast of values, as seen through the lens of mythology. Another reflection of this concern, probably a little later in the fourth century, is Plato's *Gorgias,* where, however, the values are embodied in near-contemporary figures.

Still another model speech dominated by concepts of *kakia* and

---

[51]For the relation of the *Palamedes* to Plato's *Apology* see Coulter, *art. cit.,* (above, note 36).
[52]I, 172.

aretê is the *Odysseus* ascribed to the Sophist Alcidamas.[53] The Proem employs the *opheleia-topos* and defines the *agathos kai dikaios anêr* (the man who is noble and righteous). These two subjects constitute the entire appeal for *eunoia*. The *eugeneia-topos* is used in reverse in an attack on the character of Palamedes' father (13–21).[54] The Epilogue contains a warning that acquittal will encourage others to do wrong (a version of the *sôphronizein tous allous topos*).[55] The last two *topoi* are more characteristic of the fourth century than of the fifth.

When we turn from model speeches to those apparently intended for actual delivery, we find the same *topoi* enlisted in the service of ethical persuasion, now clothed in more realistic detail, but in general located in the same parts of the oration and seeking to arouse the same responses in the jury. The ethical topics are dominated by the concept of *euergesia*. In full accord with Aristotle's conception of how *aretê* should be interpreted in oratory, virtue is regularly portrayed by the Attic orators as a faculty of conferring benefits, and the greatest virtues are those most useful to others. In one respect, however, they do not agree completely with Aristotle.

In his view, justice, courage, and liberality are the most honorable forms of *aretê*, being most useful to others.[56] Sophrosyne, defined in the *Rhetoric* as the virtue that disposes men in regard to the pleasures of the body as the law commands, is less obviously useful to others, and Aristotle tends to treat it as a quality of the individual, difficult to relate to the *polis*.[57] Yet certain facets of sophrosyne are in fact indispensable to fourth-century oratory, which frequently employs it (or one of its siblings, *epieikeia, metriotês, kosmiotês, apragmosynê*) as a term of praise and even more frequently ascribes one of its antitheses (often *akolasia* or *hybris*) to the opponent. Plato in the *Laws* pronounces both sophrosyne and

---

[53]For a suggestion that this speech be attributed to some pupil of Gorgias, see Kennedy, I, 173.

[54]Cf. the attack on the elder Alcibiades in Lysias, *Or.* 14. 30–40.

[55]See below, on topics of the epilogue.

[56]*Rhet.* 1. 9. 6 (1366b 5 ff.).

[57]Probably for the same reason, *temperantia*, the usual Latin translation of sophrosyne, is absent from the Roman imperial coinage, which celebrates other aspects, especially *clementia*, that have a more obvious relation to public life.

phronêsis to be goods which the possessor can share with others and which are therefore deserving of *epainos* (730E), and Isocrates in the *Nicocles* describes justice and sophrosyne as the most valuable virtues because of the benefit they bestow on mankind (29-30). The benefits emphasized by the orators include being nonlitigious (hence minding one's own business), behaving with scrupulous respect for the highest standards of sexual morality, and instilling in others such virtues as orderliness, respect for the laws, and good behavior in general. The last of these functions gives rise to one of the favorite topics of the epilogue, that which includes some variant of the expression *sôphronizein tous allous*— "teach the rest a lesson." Like the *topos* of *euergesia* or *opheleia,* which dominates the proem of many speeches, this clearly owes its existence, or at least its remarkable prominence, to the orator's need to emphasize service to the *polis* or to the common interest (*koinon*), and it brings sophrosyne well within the boundaries of Aristotle's definition of *aretê* as a faculty of conferring benefits.

For the sake of brevity, I shall now present in summary form the types of argument related to ethical persuasion in Attic oratory of the fifth and fourth centuries, noting the moral values appealed to and indicating the part of the oration considered appropriate for each *topos.*

Proem

In the proem, the overwhelming favorite is the "Unaccustomed as I am" (*apragmosynê*- or *apeiria*)-*topos,* in which the speaker pleads inexperience in speaking, thus appealing for sympathy and attempting to disabuse the judges of the notion that he is a practiced orator, one who is *deinos legein.* Antiphon employs this device in two of his three genuine orations and in the second of these amplifies it at great length (*Herodes* 1-5).[58] In fourth-century oratory it often involves a claim to sophrosyne, *hêsychia* (quietness), or *kosmiotês* (orderliness), all implying the well-bred aloofness and absence of *polypragmosynê* (meddling) that survived as a desideratum even in democratic Athens. What began as a simple disavowal of skill or oratorical experience turned into a

---

[58]An extremely adroit variation on this *topos* opens Plato's *Apology.*

claim to possess certain forms of *aretê* traditionally valued by Athenian juries.

Also in the proem belongs the boast about benefactions performed for the *polis,* the *euergesia-topos.* The words *chrêstos* (useful) and *opheleia* (helpfulness) often occur in this connection. We have already noted that the first *Tetralogy* supplies an example, when the defendant offers a list of "liturgies" as proof of his beneficial ethos (1. 2. 12). Very soon this topic expands to include the ancestors. Andocides, in *On His Return,* describes the services to Athens performed by his forefather Leogoras (26) and in *On the Mysteries* lists the *agatha* of his *progonoi* (ancestors) in general (141). The topic of *opheleia* has as a prominent subdivision the rehearsal of particular liturgies—paying for the performance of a tragic or dithyrambic chorus, building a warship, putting on a torchlight procession, and the like. Some of the orators use a special variant, according to which the most laborious liturgy is living a *sôphrôn* life (Lysias 21. 19; Isaeus, Frg. 30, Demosthenes 38. 26).

Narrative

It will be recalled that Aristotle in *Rhetoric* 3. 16. 8 (1417a 16 ff.) recommends several ways of rendering the *diêgêsis* ethical and indeed gives the impression that this is the really critical part of the oration for persuasive ethos. Such is obviously the case in encomiastic oratory, which would usually include in the *Narratio* references to *aretê* and proofs of moral choice, but the other *genera causarum* often exploit the same technique, especially when they adopt elements of encomium or invective. Thus Lysias in his prosecution of Eratosthenes not only describes the conduct of the members of the Thirty in vivid detail, but points out that their behavior constituted a revelation of their character (*tropos*); in the next breath he reminds the jury of the admirable behavior of his murdered brother and himself: performing liturgies, conducting themselves with *kosmiotês,* and ransoming Athenians from the enemy—the standard proofs of *euergesia* (21).[59]

With the elaboration of various forms of epideictic oratory in

---

[59]For the doctrine of the *Narratio* based on persons, as worked out in Hellenistic rhetoric, see the *Rhetorica ad Herennium* 1. 8. 13.

the Graeco-Roman period the *topos* of *aretê* occupied ever more space in the *Narratio*. An encomium would praise the parents of the subject and his education (*paideia, trophê*), as well as his *praxeis* in maturity, which demonstrated his possession of the virtues. These *topoi* are clearly defined already in the *Evagoras* of Isocrates, which describes the *trophê* of the king (marked by the physical advantages of beauty and strength and the moral virtue of sophrosyne, 22). That the correlation of *trophê* and sophrosyne was common practice seems evident from the *ad Alexandrum*, where we read, however, that the orator should say little about the early stages of a person's life, since people think that for children to be *kosmioi* and *sôphrones* is a credit to those who brought them up, rather than to themselves (35).

Still another technique conducive to ethical persuasion that was often employed as part of the *Narratio*, although it could be introduced elsewhere, was the use of historical or mythical exemplars of virtue or vice. These served particularly to magnify the glorious *aretê* of Athens in the Golden Age and to point up the contrast with the degenerate present. A notable instance, chosen from the interplay between Demosthenes and Aeschines, is the response of Demosthenes to his rival's remarks about Solon as a model of decorum. In contrast to the immodest Timarchus, who had recently thrown off his cloak and allegedly addressed the Assembly half naked, Solon (like Pericles, Themistocles, and Aristides) had been so modest (*sôphrôn*) that he would not deliver an oration while holding even one arm outside his garments. In such a pose of the utmost decorum he was portrayed by a statue in the marketplace of Salamis (1. 25–26). Demosthenes, in *On the False Embassy*, responds sharply that it would be better for the Athenians if Aeschines imitated the spirit (*psychê*) and intellect (*dianoia*) of Solon instead of the attitude of his statue; he then describes the moral qualities of Solon as a statesman, which Aeschines has utterly failed to reproduce (251 ff.). This counterattack suggests how the *dokein-einai* (appearance-reality) antithesis, which Aeschylean tragedy had symbolized in the shield of Amphiaraus and which had long since become a commonplace in philosophy, could filter down to the particular, often trivial terms of the courtroom.

Both Aeschines and Demosthenes in these corresponding passages use one of the fundamental techniques of epideictic, *syn-krisis* (comparison), mentioned by Aristotle as a means of securing amplification (*auxêsis*), the commonplace most appropriate to epideictic (*Rhet.* 1. 9. 38–39 [1368a 10 ff.]; cf. *ad. Alex.* 3). *Synkrisis* (already a convention in Pindar's victory odes) was indispensable in any kind of oration that included elements of encomium or invective and ultimately became one of the standard *progymnas-mata* (preliminary exercises) in the rhetorical schools of the Empire. Wherever it appeared, it was inseparable from the topic of *aretê*.

Proof

A *topos* favored in the proof or refutation in forensic oratory is the assertion that the virtue of one's previous life provides a reason for acquittal. This, the sophistic version of ethical persuasion (relying on a preconceived notion of the speaker's *epieikeia* to secure the judges' favor), is very common indeed. Aeschines remarks complacently in *On the Embassy* that because of his *sôphrôn* life the Athenians refused to believe Demosthenes' accusation that he had abused the Olynthian captive woman at the court of Philip. He commends the present jury for putting more faith in the past life of those on trial than in the charges of their enemies (4–5). More common even than this *topos* in Attic oratory is its reversal by prosecutors. Licentiousness, insolence, immoral conduct of various kinds are produced as reasons for conviction, and this type of personal attack becomes much more frequent as the fourth century wears on.[60] The integration of the *topos* of virtue and vice with attempts at persuasion through ethos is evidently complete by the time of Aeschines.

Epilogue

The favorite ethical *topos* in the epilogue is the reminder of the justice and piety of the speaker and the appeal to these qualities in the judges. No one cliché is more ubiquitous than the phrase *dikaiôs kai hosiôs* (in accord with justice and piety) in this part of the

[60]For example, Andocides, *On the Mysteries* 124–131; Ps.-Andocides, *Against Alcibiades* 13–33; Lysias 14. 25–29; Aeschines, *Against Timarchus,* passim; and Demosthenes, *Against Meidias,* passim.

oration. But another favorite device, whose terminology changes before our eyes in the transition from "Antiphon" to the later orators, is the one that we have called *sôphronizein tous allous* (teach the others a lesson), naturally a topic of the prosecution. Already in the first of the *Tetralogies* we are told (in the Epilogue of the second speech for the prosecution) that conviction will reduce the number of plotters, increase those who practice piety, and rid the community of pollution (1. 3. 11). This topic develops into the plea, used freely by Lysias, Ps.-Andocides, Demosthenes, and Aeschines, that the jury convict the accused, so as to deter other wrongdoers and instill in them sophrosyne. The wide use of the verb *sôphronizein* to express this idea may be another sign of the special value attached to sophrosyne in fourth-century Athens.[61]

The interplay between Aeschines and Demosthenes over this *topos* shows both how an orator could exploit it and how his opponent could counter it. Aeschines in the *Oration against Timarchus* spends the entire Epilogue exhorting the jury to condemn the accused in order to prevent others like him from flourishing and to instill virtue in the young—young citizens only, by the way. Aeschines specifically invites Timarchus and his kind to turn their attention to seducing foreigners and resident aliens and leave Athenians alone (195). Later, in the *Oration on the Embassy,* he introduces, as part of his record of *euergesia* toward the *polis,* the boast that his prosecution of Timarchus had served as a summons to purity (*paraklêsis tês sophrosynês*), for which all who had sons or young brothers should be grateful (180–181). Demosthenes' response in his speech *On the False Embassy* doubtless expresses the impatience with which the Athenian audience suffered this boast. Aeschines did not prosecute and ruin Timarchus in order to make our children *sôphrones,* Demosthenes protests. They are *sôphrones* already, and God forbid that Athens should come to such a pass that the young should need Aeschines as *sôphronistês* (285–286).

[61]"Antiphon" suggests that risk and disgrace suffice to curb (*sôphronisai*) someone in the grip of passion (*Tetr.* 1. 3. 3), but *sôphronizein* in this semitechnical sense tends to occur mainly in Demosthenes and Aeschines. Earlier orators use various forms of the adjective *sôphrôn* (in such phrases as *poiein sôphronesterous,* to make better-behaved); see Lysias 14. 12 (not, however, in the Epilogue) and Ps.-Andocides, 4. 40.

Allied with this *topos* in the epilogue is that of *sôtêria*, safety resulting from the practice of sophrosyne. This is not the same as *euergesia* or *opheleia*. Whereas that topic usually occurs early in the speech, as a device to secure good will, or in the proof, as an argument for acquittal, this topic belongs to the closing argument and is partly ethical, partly emotional. "If you fail to convict Meidias," says Demosthenes, in his prosecution of the man who had attacked him while clad in his choregic robes, "each member of the jury may expect to be assaulted with impunity by his personal enemies. Only by punishing him can you walk home from this courtroom without glancing anxiously behind you" (219–222). The next to the last sentence of the speech urges the jury to cast one vote that will simultaneously assist Demosthenes, gratify the people, *tous allous sôphronisai* (teach the others a lesson), and guarantee for themselves a life of perfect safety thereafter.[62] The very last sentence of all invokes piety and justice in the jury's deliberations (227).

ETHOS AFTER ARISTOTLE

Hellenistic rhetoric evidently ignored Aristotle's doctrine of ethos and *pathos* as distinct modes of persuasion. The rejection of *pathos* we can understand because the Stoics were on principle hostile to it, and some influential rhetors of the Hellenistic age—Hermagoras especially—were sympathetic to Stoicism. But it might seem that ethos should flourish in Stoic rhetoric, if anywhere. Was it not on ethos that the defense of Rutilius Rufus, the Roman Socrates, depended? Yet to judge by what we can learn of his trial, Rutilius not only refused to exploit emotional appeals (*nemo ingemuit*, Cicero observes disapprovingly), but also made little attempt to persuade through ethos, except that implicit in his former life;[63] he used, that is, the sophistic *axiôma*, not the Aristotelian *êthos tou legontos*. Actually, the disappearance of ethical

[62]This *topos* can equally well be applied to the safety of the whole state or indeed of all the Greeks. See Lycurgus, *Against Leocrates* 146–150; the last word in the speech is *sôtêrias* (safety). This *topos* is not exclusively forensic, but when employed in other *genera causarum* it is not limited to the epilogue. It is common in the praise of Athens in the *epitaphios logos* and allied panegyrics. See Isocrates, *Panegyr.* 80–82; Hypereides, *Epitaph.* 4.

[63]Cicero, *De Or.* 1. 229–230; cf. *Brutus* 114–115.

persuasion probably resulted from the simple fact that in spite of Aristotle's efforts it had not been completely disentangled from *pathos.* When *pathos* went out of style (in theory, that is—it can never have disappeared from actual oratory), so did ethos. When *pathos* returned, so again did ethos, but not the Aristotelian ethos. It was a milder form of *pathos,* the *leniores affectus,* that Cicero established as one of the three modes of persuasion, and this only in his mature rhetorical works.

Neither Cicero in *De Inventione* nor the *Auctor ad Herennium* (each reproducing Hellenistic rhetorical doctrine with some traces of a Stoic bias) considers ethos a separate mode of persuasion. But after he has rediscovered Aristotle, Cicero reintroduces the Aristotelian *pisteis,* assigning to each *pistis* responsibility for one of the three functions of the orator that he now distinguishes: to prove (*probare*), to please (*conciliare, delectare*), and to move (*permovere*). According to this doctrine, which appears in *De Oratore* (55 B.C.) and the *Brutus* and *Orator* (both 46 B.C.), it is the task of ethos to win over the hearers. *Conciliare* is the term preferred in *De Oratore, delectare* in the *Brutus* and *Orator.*[64] But this is essentially the function of the proem in the old, sophistic doctrine of the parts of the oration, as prescribed, for example, by Theodectes (προοιμιάσασθαι πρὸς εὔνοιαν), acknowledged by Aristotle (*Rhet.* 3. 14. 7 [1415a 34–36]), and preserved unchanged throughout the history of Greek and Roman rhetoric.[65] To secure the *eunoia* of the audience through a variety of methods, including presentation of the ethos of the speaker and his opponent, is necessary in the proem, Aristotle reluctantly concedes, because of the deficiencies of the hearers, who cannot concentrate simply on the logical content of the speech (3. 14. 8 [1415b 4–6]); the devices of the proem may be prolonged throughout the entire address and used wherever they are needed, especially those intended to secure attention (3. 14. 9 [1415b 9 ff.]). Cicero amplifies the importance of one function—securing *eunoia, benevolentia*—and expands it so that it dominates the whole speech. Even so, he maintains

---

[64]*De Or.* 2. 115, 121, 128; *Brutus* 185, 187–188, 197, 276; *Or.* 69. See Fantham, *art. cit.* (above, note 6) 273–275, for possible reasons why Cicero substituted *delectare* for *conciliare* in the later treatises.

[65]Consult Cope and Sandys, *Introduction.* 331 ff., for many references.

the view that the proem is the best place to evince an ethical quality, observing in *De Oratore* 2. 317 that here one should not require vigor (*vis*) so much as charm (*delectatio*).[66]

The quality especially calculated to achieve *delectatio* is *lenitas*, gentleness, Cicero's favorite translation of *epieikeia*.[67] Ethos itself is now interpreted as appealing to the *leniores affectus*, the milder emotions. In contrast to the emotional style, which is *intenta ac vehemens*, the ethical style is described as *placida, summissa, lenis*,[68] but it is nonetheless an appeal to the emotions, not, as in Aristotle, an independent mode of proof. Cicero's most original contribution to the doctrine of the three *pisteis* comes in the *Orator*, where he equates the three traditional styles (the plain, the middle, and the grand) with the three functions of the orator and thus with the three kinds of proof.[69] According to this new scheme, the middle style is the one proper to ethical persuasion, with its aim of winning favor. Describing what the Greeks call *êthikon*, Cicero says that it is *come, iucundum, ad benevolentiam conciliandam paratum* ("easy, pleasant, well suited to winning approval," *Or.* 128). His own oration on the Manilian Law provides him with an example of the middle style. This speech is in form deliberative, but in content epideictic (*fuit ornandus . . . Pompeius*, Cicero explains, *Or.* 102), and it relies heavily on the techniques of ethical persuasion, including a long section devoted to the *topos* of *aretê* (10. 27–16. 48). Not only is *temperantia* prominent among the virtues ascribed to Pompey, but Cicero in retrospect describes the style of the address as *temperata*.[70]

---

[66]In *De Or.* 2. 184, Antonius says that *exprimere mores* has such effect in *prooemium, narratio*, and *peroratio* that it often is more effective than the *causa* itself. *Exprimere mores* designates the descriptive function of ethical persuasion (see Fantham, *art. cit.*, 272–273), but Latin rhetoric never found a universally satisfactory translation for the other implications of ethos.

[67]*De Or.* 2. 182–184; cf. Quintilian 6. 2. 8–10. For a discussion of the nuances of *lenitas* and the extent to which they differ from those of *epieikeia*, see Fantham, *art. cit.*, 262–263.

[68]*De Or.* 2. 183; cf. 211.

[69]On his originality here consult A. E. Douglas, *Eranos* 55 (1957) 18–26.

[70]*Or.* 102. Another masterpiece of the *genus medium* is the *Pro Caelio*, which is also heavily dependent on the *topoi* of virtue and vice. See R. G. M. Nisbet in *Cicero*, ed. T. A. Dorey (London, 1964) 69, on the stylistic character of this speech.

The conception of the middle style as a mixture of the qualities identified with the two extremes, the *grande* and the *tenue,* is naturally expressed in such terms as *mixtum, medium, temperatum,* and the like. Thus in *Orator* 20–22 Cicero first describes the grand and the plain styles, then pronounces the third to be *interiectus inter hos medius et quasi temperatus* ("located between them in the Mean, like a mixture"). This style, he says, flows in one tenor, bringing nothing except ease and smoothness (*facultas, aequalitas*) or else it adds certain nosegays, as in a garland, and marks the whole speech with modest (*modicis*) ornaments of thought and diction. (In the vocabulary used to characterize the middle style, ethical and technical nuances are interwoven more closely than is the case with the other two. Partly for this reason, perhaps, Nestor, the model of sophrosyne/*temperantia* in the moral sphere, is a favorite exemplar of the middle style.[71]) Cicero's formulation became proverbial: there are as many characters of style as there are functions of the orator: the plain style for proof, the middle style for winning favor, the grand style for swaying the emotions. The man who commands all three is called *moderator ille et quasi temperator* ("one who controls and blends, as it were") (*Or.* 69–70).[72]

Such a formulation is very different from Aristotle's, even though the revival of the three Aristotelian *pisteis* lies behind Cicero's innovation. Once the ethical mode has been virtually limited to winning favor, it becomes far more a matter of style and delivery than of ethical doctrine, and it is significant that in Cicero's rhetorical works the close connection that Aristotle had established between ethos and epideictic oratory (because both are based on a theoretical grasp of the virtues and vices) disappears from view. A second major difference between Cicero and Aristotle is that the appeal to ethos now includes the speaker's *auctoritas* as well as the ethos inherent in the speech itself, a reversion to the

[71]See Aulus Gellius 6. 14. 7 for Nestor and the *mixtum moderatumque genus.*

[72]*Temperator* (a Ciceronian coinage) recalls the radical meaning of *temperare* (to mix, mingle), but by this time *temperare* and *sôphronizein* had been linked in rhetorical and philosophical terminology long enough for *temperator* to have some flavor of *sôphronistês,* especially when coupled with such a word as *moderator.* On the interaction of ethical and technical connotations in this complex of terms see North, *C.P.* 43 (1948) 11–12.

sophistic practice. This change was inevitable, given not only Cicero's affinity for Isocrates, but the overwhelming importance for the Romans of *auctoritas, dignitas, res gestae,* and the like.[73]

Cicero actually owes more to the vigorous tradition of Roman oratory than to any Greek precedent, for the Romans had always employed ethos more freely than the Greeks and had combined it with *pathos* in such a way that the two were more than usually indistinguishable.[74] And it should be remembered that, just as Cicero's practice regularly goes beyond the rhetorical precepts he received from the Greeks, so, too, he goes beyond his own rhetorical precepts, even those set forth in *De Oratore.* He manipulates the topics of ethical persuasion with the utmost skill, by no means confining them to the proem, whether he is portraying the virtues of a client or impressing the jury with his own admirable qualities. The importance of the role of the advocate in the Roman legal system lends to the problem of persuasion through ethos a complexity for the most part lacking in the Athenian courts. Nowhere is Cicero more effective than when, as in the *Pro Caelio,* he employs ethos in such a way as to establish one type of characterization for himself, the advocate, and a totally different one for his client, both of them magnificently suited to the demands of all four elements in the forensic situation—the client, the opponent, the charge, and the jury, as he defines them in his discussion of the full-scale, formal proem in *De Oratore* (2. 321).[75]

Quintilian restores some of the territory that Cicero in theory had removed from the province of ethos, although he, too, considers it to be essentially a milder form of *pathos.* His major account of ethos comes in Book 6, whose subject is the *Peroratio,* where *pathos* had always been supreme, and it is for this reason

[73]Consult Richard Heinze, *Vom Geist des Römertums,* 3d ed. (Stuttgart, 1960) 43–58, on the history of *auctoritas.*

[74]For examples of Cicero's skillful use of ethos and the superiority of his practice to his theory, see George Kennedy, *A.J.P.* 89 (1968) 429–435.

[75]Cicero's reference to the client (*reus*) shows the influence of the typical situation in the Roman courts, whereas what he says in *De Inv.* 1. 22 (where ethical *topoi* are to be drawn from the orator's own person, the judges, the adversary, and the case) restates the advice of Aristotle, *Rhet.* 3. 14. 7 (1415a 26–28). Quintilian 4. 1. 6–12 recognizes the role of the *actor causae,* the advocate, in securing *benevolentia,* while in 13 he discusses the *litigator,* the client. See note 6 above for *ad Alex.* ch. 36 (on how to secure good will, *eumeneia,* for a client in forensic cases).

that he devotes such careful attention to distinguishing between the functions proper to the two types of *affectus*. The uncertainty that rhetoricians continued to feel about the nature of ethical persuasion is evident in his remark that the meaning is not sufficiently clear from the term ethos itself (6. 2. 13). His analysis takes into account all possible connotations, including even the exercises in *êthopoiïa* current in the schools, which he had already discussed in Book 1 (9. 3). Quintilian's consideration of ethos is the most thoughtful and in general the most helpful available in Roman rhetoric. His critical survey of the views of earlier technical writers and his concern for defining the relation of ethos to *pathos* enable him to make several illuminating observations in Book 6, in addition to his earlier discussion in Book 4 of the place of ethos in the *Exordium* and the *Narratio*, the parts of the oration for which ethical persuasion had traditionally been most important.

Rejecting the notion that the ethical quality is merely *mite ac placidum,* mild and peaceful, Quintilian looks for something more positive, which he describes as *humanum, amabile, iucundum* (6. 2. 13). He assigns to the ethical mode responsibility for irony (15) and for at least one of the usual functions of *pathos* in the *Peroratio,* arousing *odium*—in this instance, through indirect and devious means rather than the more straightforward approach available to *pathos*. *Odium* may be aroused against the opponent through ethos by seeming to bow to his violence and thus revealing it more effectively than if one had denounced him openly (16). Quintilian insists that the orator must evince the same virtues he praises in his client (18); by his own *bonitas* he will secure *fides* for the case.[76] Like Antonius in *De Oratore,* he emphasizes the need to avoid any appearance of arrogance: *nihil superbum, nihil elatum saltem ac sublime* ("nothing haughty, nothing, to say the

---

[76]Cf. 4. 1. 6 ff (see note 75, above). Of Quintilian's further remarks on ethos, one of the most interesting, for its stylistic implications, is his comparison of ethos to comedy, *pathos* to tragedy (6. 2. 20). G. M. A. Grube, *The Greek and Roman Critics* (London, 1965) 86, note 1, points out that *êthikos,* as opposed to *pathetikos,* "came to refer to a lower emotional level as well as writing in character." Aulus Gellius (6. 14. 6-7) quotes Varro as identifying the comic poet Terence with the middle style (*mediocritas*), while the tragic poet Pacuvius exemplifies the grand (*ubertas*) and the satirist Lucilius the plain (*gracilitas*).

least, uplifted and proud"), and, like Cicero in the *Orator*, he recommends the *medius modus* as the style suitable for ethos (19).[77]

Thus the Roman understanding of persuasion through ethos moves away from the Aristotelian perception that ethos and epideictic have much in common because both are based on knowledge of *aretê*. When some stoicizing rhetor of the Hellenistic period transferred the discussion of the virtues from the neighborhood of epideictic to that of deliberative oratory (as in *De Inventione* and the *ad Herennium*),[78] there was no corresponding movement of doctrine on ethos over to the side of deliberative, although this could have occurred without offending the shade of Aristotle, who had all along recognized that ethos was especially effective in deliberative oratory. Ethos was temporarily overlooked. What did emerge in Roman rhetoric, partly as a consequence of the link established between ethos and the doctrine of the proem (as designed to produce *eunoia*), partly as a result of Cicero's identification of ethos, *conciliare,* and the middle style, was a new emphasis on one particular virtue, *modestia, moderatio,* sophrosyne in its Latin dress, still regarded as the antithesis to *hybris, superbia.*[79]

Martianus Capella, whose rhetorical doctrine includes a detailed and schematic presentation of the doctrine of ethos as *conciliatio* of the audience by means of *dignitas* arising from the hearer, the client, the orator, or the opponent, says that such *conciliatio* is achieved through the orator when he speaks of himself *non superbe, sed moderate* (5. 502–503). This complex of ideas was, as suggested above, reinforced by Cicero's recommendation

[77]Hermogenes, the most influential rhetorician of the Second Sophistic, regards ethos as one of the Ideas or Forms of Style; he includes *epieikeia* as the means by which the speaker may ingratiate himself with his audience. See Annabel M. Patterson, *Hermogenes and the Renaissance: Seven Ideas of Style* (Princeton, 1970) 118, for some consequences in Renaissance satire.

[78]The discussion of the *genus demonstrativum* still contains a treatment of the virtues, however; see *De Inv.* 2. 59. 177 and *ad Her.* 3. 6. 10. In *De Or.* Cicero adopts the Aristotelian system and considers the topic of the virtues in relation to epideictic (2. 343 ff); so also *Part. Or.* 74 ff.

[79]This virtue, more than any other, is deemed proper for the proem, according to sources ranging from fifth-century Athens to mediaeval Europe. On the "modesty-*topos*" see Ernst Robert Curtius, *European Literature and the Latin Middle Ages,* trans. W. R. Trask (London, 1953) 83–85.

of the middle style in connection with ethos, since the vocabulary applied to this style (*medius, temperatus*) was a constant reminder of the virtue of moderation and temperance. Yet the link between this virtue and this mode of persuasion goes much farther back than Cicero; we have only to remember that extraordinary scene from Euripides' *Hypsipyle* in which Amphiaraus wins over Eurydice through ethical persuasion based on sophrosyne alone.[80]

And so we return one last time to the paradigmatic figure who haunts these pages. Commended by Eteocles in Aeschylus' *Seven against Thebes* with one of the earliest recorded references to the canon of cardinal virtues (610) and described by the Scout as an *anêr sôphronestatos*, a man of the utmost sophrosyne (568), Amphiaraus exemplifies this quality in a sense especially appropriate to the dramatic situation. He behaves with the modesty and self-knowledge that proceed from unflinching insight into reality, in pointed contrast to the hybristic, self-deluding boastfulness of the other attackers. Furthermore, his rebuke to Tydeus and Poly-neices for their wicked violence (571–586) establishes him as a classical type of the warner, a precursor of what would later be called a *sôphronistês*.

Some sixty years later, in two plays full of fascinating variations on Aeschylus, Euripides not only reinforces the Aeschylean characterization, but develops it in a direction dictated by contemporary interest in the relation between character and oratorical effectiveness. In the *Phoenissae*, Amphiaraus continues to be described in terms that emphasize his notable restraint, as Antigone marvels at the calm and steady (*sôphrona*) goads with which he drives his chariot horses (177–178), while in the *Hypsipyle* (perhaps from the same trilogy) he performs his miracle of persuasive oratory on the strength of his reputation for sophrosyne.

But the most influential Euripidean gloss on Aeschylus is the explication of the unblazoned shield as itself a sign of sophrosyne. Aeschylus had already implied as much when the Scout explained the shield in terms of its bearer's wish to be, not just to seem, *aristos* (σῆμα δ' οὐκ ἐπῆν κύκλῳ / οὐ γὰρ δοκεῖν ἄριστος, ἀλλ᾽ εἶναι θέλει, *Sept.* 591–592), one of the most frequently quoted passages

---

[80]See above, pp. 149–151.

in all Aeschylean tragedy.[81] Now Euripides spells out what Aeschylus had merely implied: "The seer Amphiaraus [approached] with no hybristic devices, but weapons modestly [σωφρόνως] unblazoned" (1111–1112). Thus the shield becomes a symbol of the virtue, and so it remains, even when, in some later versions of the story, it perversely acquires a blazon. In the *Thebais* of Statius, for example, the seer is said to "flash forth the conquered Python on his shield" (*clypeo victum Pythona coruscat*, 4. 222). This device still proclaims Amphiaraus a servant of Apollo and alludes significantly to the defeat of a monster notoriously symbolic of disorder and chaos.[82]

In the great central scene of the *Seven*, with its description of the Argive attackers and their shields, Aeschylus adapts a technique long since perfected by Homer in *Iliad* 18, where the scenes and persons supposedly depicted on the Shield of Achilles are brought before the reader's inward eye. Imitations of the Homeric shield—by Hesiod, by Virgil, by innumerable lesser poets—serve infinitely varied purposes, but nowhere is the device employed in a more concentrated and telling fashion than in the *Seven*, where, moreover, the actual blazons of archaic shields are vividly recalled.[83]

In Chapter 4 we shall find that shields, disks, and other circular objects remain favorite locations for symbolic representations of the virtues and vices in painting and sculpture, as well as in literature. But the shield symbol is only one of a tremendous variety of ways invented in late antiquity and thereafter to suggest the nature, the effects, and the shifting relationships of Temperantia, Pudicitia, Clementia, Moderatio, and the other Latinized sisters of Sophrosyne.

[81]See, for example, Plato, *Rep.* 361B, 362A, *Apol.* 36D, Plutarch, *Aristides* 3. 5, Sallust, *Cat.* 54.

[82]See above, Chapter 1, note 4.

[83]The best discussion of the scene in the *Seven* remains that by Helen Bacon referred to in Chapter 1, note 35.

4

The Iconography
of Sophrosyne

Hanc prope temperiem praebens Moderatio stabat
Fortia frena vehens sive flagella manu,
Quis pigros stimulet, veloces temperet...

(Near her, proffering temperance, was standing Moderation,
Holding in her hand strong reins or scourges,
With which to prick the indolent, control the headstrong...)
—Theodulf of Orleans

"Lady Sophrosyne, daughter of great-souled Aidôs," begins the
epitaph of Cleidemus from the Dipylon in Athens, in the fourth
century B.C., and "Hail, divine Euteleia, child of glorious Sophrosyne," writes Crates the Cynic a century later.[1] Starting with
Theognis in the archaic age, Greeks of every period personified
Sophrosyne and linked her in various ways with a wide range of
other abstractions: not only Aidôs (Restraint) and Euteleia (Frugality), but Pistis (Good Faith), the Charites (Graces), Eusebeia (Piety), Hasychia (Quietness), Aretê (Courage), Hagneia (Purity), and
Hygieia (Health).[2] Yet there is no extant representation of her

[1]The notes to this chapter are disproportionately voluminous, compared with
those to the other three chapters, because here I hope to provide as much detailed
information as possible for the benefit of nonspecialists, while realizing that at
every point art historians will be able to correct and amplify my findings and, I
hope, explain some of the puzzles (such as the origin of the "Rouen iconography")
that have so far defied solution.

[2]For the references to the stele of Cleidemus, Crates, and Theognis and for the
association of Sophrosyne with Eusebeia, Hasychia, Aretê, and Hygieia consult

in ancient art, nor does any literary allusion dating from the classical period suggest that there was a recognized type of Sophrosyne, as there was, for example, of Eirênê (Peace), Hygieia, or Nemesis.[3]

In later antiquity, however, as the personification of ethical abstractions became increasingly popular in both literature and art, we find here and there a clue to the way in which Sophrosyne was visualized. Thus the *Pinax* of Cebes (dating probably from the first century after Christ and purporting to describe an allegorical

---

PW., *sv. Sophrosyne* (Türk). For Hagneia see Gregory of Nazianzus, *P.G.* 37, *Carm.* 45, vv. 229 ff. As late as the closing decades of the fourth century after Christ, an elegiac couplet on a floor mosaic of the Baths of Curium, Cyprus (where another mosaic perhaps bears witness to the Christianity of the builder), refers to Aidôs, Sophrosyne, and a third virtue whose name is lost (Eunomia? Eusebeia?) as sisters who preside over the exedra. See T. B. Mitford, *The Inscriptions of Kourion* (Philadelphia, 1971) No. 203. Many literary and epigraphic references to the personified Sophrosyne are listed in W. H. Roscher, *Ausführliches Lexikon der griechischen und römischen Mythologie* (Leipzig, 1884–1937), *s.v.* Sophrosyne. F. W. Hamdorf, *Griechische Kultpersonifikationen der vorhellenistischen Zeit* (Mainz, 1964), cites evidence for the representation of such groups as Themis, Dikê, Aidôs, and their kin, but none for Sophrosyne, who in fact received cult worship only in the imperial age and then only in a few places in Asia Minor and Syria (see North, 254–255). Consult W. K. C. Guthrie, *Orpheus and Greek Religion* (New York, 1966) 260 and Plate 14, for the altars to Aretê and Sophrosyne in the precinct of Demeter at Pergamum.

[3]Eirênê: cf. Pausanias 1. 8. 2 and see PW., *s.v. Eirene* (Waser). Hygieia: many cult statues survive, chiefly from shrines of Asclepius. Cf. PW., *s.v. Hygieia* (Tamborino). Nemesis: Pausanias 1. 33. 3 ff.; cf. PW. *s.v. Nemesis* (Herter) and *Bulletin de correspondance hellénique* 88 (1964) 496–506. Personified abstractions appeared in Greek art as early as the seventh century B.C., for example, on the Chest of Cypselus, where Dikê (Justice) was represented as dragging, throttling, and beating Adikia (Injustice) (Pausanias 5. 18. 2). A red-figured vase, now in the Kunsthistorisches Museum in Vienna, shows Dikê striking Adikia with an ax: see *History of the Hellenic World: The Archaic Period* (Athens and London, 1975) 183. Among the Platonic virtues, only Dikaiosynê had anything like a recognized "type" in ancient art. Aulus Gellius 14. 4 records the description of Justice by Chrysippus as she was portrayed *a pictoribus rhetoribusque antiquioribus:* he emphasizes her stern appearance and keen gaze, rather than any specific attributes. For the type representing Dikaiosynê on Greek coins of the Roman imperial age (with scales, scepter, or cornucopia) consult PW., *s.v. Dikaiosyne* (Waser). An early example of the monumental representation of a group of four related virtues is the set of statues adorning the Library of Celsus in Ephesus, the originals of which may go back to A.D. 117–125. They portray Aretê, Sophia, Epistêmê, and Ennoia (Insight). See *Forschungen in Ephesus*, Vol. V. Part I, *Die Bibliothek,* 47 ff. I am grateful to George M. A. Hanfmann for calling my attention to these personifications.

painting deposited as a votive-offering in a temple of Cronus) refers to Sophrosyne as one of the eight sisters of Epistêmê (Wisdom)[4] and says that they were all good to look upon, well-behaved, dressed in modest and simple garments, unaffected and not heavily made up, as were certain women depicted elsewhere in the painting who represent the vices (20. 203). Gregory of Nazianzus in the fourth century gives a more specific account of Sophrosyne's appearance in his poem *De Seipso,* concerning a dream in which he saw her together with Hagneia. Both were beautiful women, clothed in white garments and veils and characterized by that *akosmia* (lack of adornment) which is equivalent to *kosmos*—a condition approved by the Fathers and their forerunners of the Cynic-Stoic school. They had no golden ornaments, no jewels, no silken clothing or soft linen, no golden curls tumbling over their shoulders for the winds to play with. Their eyes were fixed on the ground, the blush of modesty (*aidôs*) could be glimpsed through their veils, and they were silent, their lips closed like rosebuds.[5] The description in some respects anticipates the

[4]The others are Andreia, Dikaiosynê, Kalokagathia, Eutaxia, Eleutheria, Enkrateia, and Praotês. E. H. Gombrich, *J.W.C.I.* 15 (1952) 254–256, suggests that the dialogue may have described a real painting and postulates an ancient tradition of ethical allegory in art, such as might lie behind the Lydian tombstone of the first century after Christ which shows Asôtia (Profligacy) and Aretê on either side of the Pythagorean Y, a visual reminder of Prodicus' Apologue. (See Panofsky, *Tomb Sculpture,* 33 and Fig. 23.) The Pythagorean, Cynic-Stoic, and other elements in the *Pinax* are discussed by Robert Joly, *Le Tableau de Cébès et la philosophie religieuse* (Brussels, 1963); for its place in the tradition of the emblem book see Reinhart Schleier, *Tabula Cebetis, oder "Spiegel des menschlichen Lebens darin Tugent und Untugent abgemalet ist"* (Berlin, 1973). Lucian in the second century after Christ puts Sophrosyne with Aretê, Dikaiosynê, Alêtheia (Truth), and other related qualities in the train of Philosophia (*Piscator* 16). Byzantine examples include Eustathius Makrembolites, *Hysminê and Hysminias* (twelfth century), where four allegorical figures painted on a wall—Phronêsis, Ischys (Strength), Sophrosyne, and Themis—are described in detail (*Erotici Scriptores Graeci,* Hercher, 2. 2–6) and the elaborate account of the personified virtue in the early fourteenth-century poem of Meliteniotes, *To Sophrosyne,* ed. M. Miller, *Notices et extraits des manuscrits de la Bibliothèque impériale et autres bibliothèques* 19 (1858) II, 1–138, where Sophrosyne herself, her garden, castle, and a host of mythical and historical representatives receive allegorical interpretation.

[5]*P.G.* 37. *Carmen* 45, vv. 229 ff. The derivation of this poem from Prodicus' Apologue is discussed by M. C. Waites, *H.S.C.P.* 23 (1912) 1–46. The paradoxical phrase *kosmos akosmos* or some variant goes back to Sophocles (Frg. 762 Nauck) and has different implications according to its context. An epigram ascribed to Greg-

formulae for depicting Pudicizia and Castità prescribed in the
Iconologia of Cesare Ripa[6] over a thousand years later, and it is
doubtless an accurate reflection of the way in which Sophrosyne
would have been portrayed at almost any period. It is especially
consistent with the popular interpretation of the virtue in the
Hellenistic and Graeco-Roman ages, when the word sophrosyne
normally implied self-control or chastity, rather than moderation,
soundness of mind, self-knowledge, or any of the wider range of
meanings more common in the classical era.

The imagery employed by ancient authors in connection with
sophrosyne[7] and the animals thought to possess the virtue in some
of its many aspects forecast the mediaeval and Renaissance
iconography of the concept (or its principal Latin equivalents,
temperantia, pudicitia, moderatio). A persistent image likens sophrosyne to the control of a wild or unruly beast, to be mastered by
a bit, bridle, or yoke. Plato makes frequent use of the image of the
beast in order to represent the passionate and appetitive elements
in the soul. The most influential example is the myth of the
Charioteer with his two horses in the *Phaedrus*, often imitated by
Patristic writers. Another commonplace in ancient literature is the
comparison of passion (especially sexual passion) to a raging fire,
which it is the function of sophrosyne to extinguish. The flame
alone figures in most love poetry from Sappho onward, where the
passion of love is represented as being triumphant, but sometimes
Sophrosyne (in Latin Temperantia, Pudicitia, Castitas, or even
Sobrietas) is personified as the foe of Eros (Amor) and Aphrodite
(Venus),[8] and occasionally the act of extinguishing a flame is described. Such a symbolic deed is implied by Apuleius in the story
of Cupid and Psyche, when Venus appeals to her worst enemy,
Sobrietas, to deprive Cupid of his weapons and quench the flame

---

ory of Nazianzus refers to a statue in the church of St. Basil in Caesarea, depicting
the tetrad of life-giving virtues (ζωογόνων ἀρετῶν τετραχτύος, *Anth. Pal.* 1. 93).
There is no indication of how they were portrayed.

[6]See below, pp. 250–260.

[7]For categories of imagery used in Greek and Latin literature to suggest
sophrosyne or *temperantia*, consult North, 380–386.

[8]For this theme in the Greek Anthology see, for example, *Anth. Pal.* 9. 132. For
Sobrietas as the enemy of Venus, see Apuleius, *Metam.* 5. 30.

of his torch (*taedam deflammet*). The Byzantine prose romance by Eustathius, *Hysminê and Hysminias,* depicts the warfare between Eros and Sophrosyne in similar terms: Eros kindles the fires of passion, but Sophrosyne sprinkles dew from heaven and puts out the flame (4. 23). Another favorite device in ancient discussions of the virtues employs various types of imagery derived from military equipment.[9] The sword represents aggression or severity; hence a sheathed sword symbolizes moderation or clemency, as in Seneca's eulogy of Nero. All three images—the bridle, the extinction of a flame, and the sheathing of a sword—were destined to take artistic shape in the Middle Ages and to become familiar as symbols of sophrosyne/*temperantia.*

Ancient literature is prone to associate various animals, birds, and even fishes with moral qualities, either on the theory that a given animal may possess *aretê* of a physical type (as the Neoplatonists taught that cattle possess sophrosyne, lions courage, storks justice, and cranes wisdom)[10] or merely as symbols of the virtues and vices. In the Middle Ages and the Renaissance a very long list of animals came to represent various facets of sophrosyne/*temperantia* and the opposing vices. Some had already

[9]The most famous of all such metaphors is that of St. Paul, *Eph.* 6. 13 ff., which found imitators in literature and art throughout the Middle Ages. See, for example, Alain de Lille, *Anticlaudianus* 8. 324–333, where the virtues supply armor and weapons to the perfect man, Prudence giving him a helmet, Reason a sword, Peace a set of greaves, etc. For the sheathed sword, see Seneca, *De Clem.* 1. 1. 3. Virtue herself is already a soldier in Seneca, *De Beata Vita* 15. 5. Using still another kind of military symbolism, Poseidonius compared the *sôphrôn* Q. Fabius Maximus to a shield, the bold (*andrikos*) Marcellus to a sword (Plutarch, *Marcellus* 9. 6–7 and *Fabius* 19. 4). As early as the *Seven against Thebes,* 375 ff., the warrior's shield afforded an opportunity for the literary depiction of symbols of virtue and vice, sophrosyne and *hybris;* see above, pp. 175–176. Cf. the shield of Turnus, *Aeneid* 7. 789 ff. For the shield blazons in archaic vase painting, consult G. H. Chase, *H.S.C.P.* 13 (1902) 61–127. On the use of shields or disks to display emblems of the virtues in Gothic art, see below, p. 196. Rubens' painting *The Majority of Louis XIII,* in the Medici Gallery of the Louvre, depicts the Queen handing over the tiller to her son, in a boat rowed by four personified virtues, Strength, Faith, Justice, and Prudence, identified through the attributes depicted on shields that are fixed, Viking fashion, on the side of the boat. I owe this reference to the Presidential Address of Harry Levy, at the annual meeting of the American Philological Association, 1974.

[10]See, for example, Olympiodorus, *In Phaed.* 45 Norvin.

been mentioned in this context in antiquity. Thus the turtledove is
a symbol of marital chastity because it purportedly takes but one
mate. The salamander indicates resistance to passion because it
can live unharmed amid flame. The elephant is renowned for
modesty because he begets young only in secret, so that offspring
may not fail, and then only after his mate has presented him with
a mandrake root. Even certain species of fish won praise for sophrosyne because of their supposedly monogamous habits.[11] The
tortoise represents feminine sophrosyne because, by carrying its
house wherever it goes, it teaches that a *sôphrôn* woman stays at
home in seclusion. A characteristic transformation from pagan to
late baroque iconography occurs when the Elean Aphrodite of
Phidias, portrayed with one foot resting on a tortoise, reappears

[11]Some ancient references to these animals and their sophrosyne include: the
turtledove: Aelian. *De Nat. Anim.* 10. 33 (σώφρων ἐστὶν ἡ τρυγών), cf. 3. 5 on the
pigeon and 3. 44 on the ringdove (for which see also Porphyry, *De Abstin.* 3. 11);
Pliny the Elder, *H.N.* 10. 52. 104 (*columba ... plurima pudicitia*); Gregory of
Nazianzus, *Car. Mor.*, *P.G.* 37, 620, vv. 536-539. The salamander: Aelian 2. 31;
Pliny 10. 86. 188; Gregory, *op. cit.*, 624, vv. 580-582, and *Oratio funebris in laudem
Basilii Magni*, *P.G.* 36, 524; see Kurt Weitzmann, *Greek Mythology in Byzantine Art*
(Princeton, 1951) 27, for references to the salamander and Fig. 28 (from Morgan
Library Codex 652, Fol. 381ʳ) for a picture of a salamander in the flames. The
elephant: Aelian 8. 17; Pliny 8. 5. 13. Neither refers to the mandrake, however.
This detail occurs in the *Physiologus;* see W. S. Heckscher, *Art Bulletin* 29 (1947)
173, note 93, for references, including Honorius Augustodunensis, *P.L.* 172, 443.
See also Hugh of St. Victor, *De Bestiis*, *P.L.* 177. 72-73, 25, 26. The fish: Aelian 1.
13 (on the sophrosyne of the "Etna-Fish"—αἰτναῖος—which consists in
monogamy); cf. Gregory of Nazianzus, *Car. Mor.*, *P.G.* 37, 621, vv. 543-545. As an
allusion to fasting the fish appears in a German tapestry of the fifteenth century
now in Ratisbonne (Tervarent). See also the engraving by Aldegrever (Bartsch).
The fish persists into modern times as a type of sophrosyne, but of *sobrietas*, rather
than *pudicitia* (yet consider the implications of the phrase "cold fish"). The Temperance Monument in Washington, D.C. (Pennsylvania Avenue and 7th Street),
has two entwined dolphins with an ibis and papyrus on top of the monument. The
colloquial expression "drinks like a fish" would seem to deny the fish its status as a
symbol of sobriety, but it probably alludes to habitat and implies that because the
fish is immersed in water it drinks constantly—the nature of the drink being
irrelevant to the meaning of the expression. The *Physiologus*, which originated in
Alexandria in the second century after Christ, and the *Hieroglyphics* of Horapollo
(perhaps the fourth century) relate certain animals to sophrosyne, but in very
different ways. The *Physiologus* considers animals to possess the virtues in some
fashion, but Horapollo merely uses them as symbols. The influence of the
Physiologus was felt throughout the Middle Ages, while the *Hieroglyphics* was not
known in the West until the sixteenth century.

as the Pudicitia of Ripa, a veiled nun, who also rests one foot on a tortoise.[12]

Latin literature carries on and extends the Greek habit of personifying ethical abstractions. No precise and universally adequate Latin equivalent for sophrosyne existed (even as Greek could find no wholly satisfactory translation for *clementia* or *frugalitas*), but by the time of Cicero a wide variety of well-established Latin abstract nouns could render the different nuances of sophrosyne. Among them were *temperantia, moderatio, modestia, pudicitia, sobrietas, clementia,* and *frugalitas,* of which only *pudicitia* and *clementia* have any importance for iconography in the ancient period. *Temperantia,* which Cicero established as the usual equivalent of sophrosyne in philosophical contexts, never appears on Roman coins or in any other form of imperial propaganda, probably because it was considered too personal and individual a virtue to be useful for this purpose. St. Augustine observes in the *City of God* that the Romans never deified *temperantia,* even though some Romans practiced the virtue (4. 20). They did deify Pudicitia, however, and we hear of the shrines in her honor, one patrician, the other plebeian. If they held statues of the goddess, she was probably represented as in the portrait bust found in the excavations under St. Peter's Basilica and the statue discovered in Ostia.[13]

Both as a masculine virtue (from the time of Hadrian) and as the principal excellence ascribed to empresses, Pudicitia is frequently referred to on coins. Those of Plotina, wife of Trajan, show an altar, designated as that of Pudicitia; those of Hadrian's wife Sabina show the personified virtue holding before her face

[12]This transformation and the stages by which it was achieved are discussed by W. S. Heckscher, *Phoenix* 7 (1953) 105–117. See Plutarch, *Coniug. Praec.* 142D; cf. *Mor.* 381E.

[13]The shrines: Livy 10. 23. 3–10, Festus 242, 236, 237, Juvenal 6. 308. The article by R. E. A. Palmer cited in Chapter 1, note 63, discusses the evidence for the shrines and for the continuity of the tradition connecting Pudicitia with the area of the *Vicus Longus.* The bust: consult Jocelyn Toynbee and John Ward Perkins, *The Shrine of St. Peter and the Vatican Excavations* (London, 1956) 95 and Plate 30. The statue: see Raissa Calza, *Bolletino d'Arte* 35 (1950) 201–207 and Figs. 1–4; here it is suggested that the statue represents Fausta, the wife of Constantine, in the guise of Pudicitia.

the veil that has always been the chief attribute of modesty and allied virtues.[14] Clementia, which was named, with Virtus, Iustitia, and Pietas, on the *Clupeus Aureus* presented to Octavian in 27 B.C., is also represented on coins as a personified figure and is further suggested by scenes on reliefs, including those of the so-called Marriage Sarcophagi, which portray four virtues, not the Platonic tetrad, but a distinctively Roman quartet very close to that of the *Clupeus Aureus:* Clementia, Virtus, Pietas, and Concordia. A supplication in which a conquered barbarian is spared by a victorious Roman general indicates Clementia.[15] On coins the

[14]See Harold Mattingly, *Coins of the Roman Empire in the British Museum,* Vol. III (London, 1936) 291, Nos. 405–414 and Plate 54. 10 and 11. Such coins inspired Ripa's conception of Pudicizia; he mentions those of Sabina and Otacilia Severa in connection with the veil which he prescribes for pictures of this virtue. The gesture of holding up the veil or drawing it away from the face in the presence of the bridegroom is at least as old as archaic representations of the marriage of Hera and Zeus, as seen on the metope from Temple E at Selinus, now in Palermo. Consult M. E. Mayo, "The Gesture of Anakalypsis" (abstract), *A.J.A.* 77 (1973) 220. Penelope's gesture of holding her veil before her face in the presence of the suitors (*Od.* 1. 334) is cited by Julian, *Or.* 3. 127D as an indication of her sophrosyne. For the representation of Pudicitia on coins consult PW., *s.v. Pudicitia* (Radke). For Pudicitia on imperial medallions honoring empresses of the third century, see Jocelyn M. C. Toynbee, *Roman Medallions* (New York, 1944) 164. The *pudicitia* type was employed in antiquity and thereafter in a variety of ways, as, for example, on the Antioch mosaic of Hippolytus and Phaedra, in which Phaedra's effort to overcome her passion is suggested by her use of the *pudicitia* gesture of holding up her veil. Panofsky, *Titian,* 145, calls attention to a mediaeval Danae modeled on Pudicitia and to Jan Gossart's development of this type for his Danae, but in both cases it is the tower, not the veil, that identifies Danae/Pudicitia. The tower also serves as a popular emblem of chastity (see Appendix), and Danae even acquires the unicorn chariot of Pudicitia in the *Hypnerotomachia Poliphili* illustrations at the end of the fifteenth century; see Madlyn Millner Kahr, *Art Bulletin* 60 (1978) 43–55. Wolfgang Stechow, *Rubens and the Classical Tradition* (Cambridge, Mass., 1968) Figs. 46 and 48, identifies as Pudicitia Mary Magdalene in Rubens' painting of the Holy Women at the Sepulchre. Harold L. Axtell, *The Deification of Abstract Ideas in Roman Literature and Inscriptions* (Chicago, 1907) briefly discusses Pudicitia (39) as well as Clementia (32, 35) and Mens Bona (24, 77). Although Mens Bona is not normally a Roman equivalent to sophrosyne (Plutarch, *de fort. Rom.* 5 translates by *Gnômê*), in at least two passages in Roman poetry the concept seems to be assimilated to Sophrosyne: Ovid, *Amores* 1. 2. 31–32 (the inspiration of Petrarch's *Triumphs*) and Propertius 3. 24. 19.

[15]The personified virtue does not herself appear in these scenes. For a bibliography of works on the Marriage Sarcophagi see Elaine Loeffler, *Art Bulletin* 37 (1957) 195–208. For photographs of sarcophagi belonging to this type in Mantua, Florence, and Los Angeles, consult Inez Scott Ryberg, *Rites of the State Religion in*

most common type shows the personified Clementia seated, holding a scepter or a *patera.*[16]

The partial identification of Clementia with Sophrosyne rests
mainly on the evidence that in Roman Stoicism this virtue was
considered a subdivision of *temperantia.*[17] It is true that Greek
writers who sought to translate the Latin word *clementia* more
often rendered it as *philanthrôpia* or *epieikeia* than as sophrosyne,[18]
but the Emperor Julian praises the sophrosyne of Constantius in
situations where *clementia* would be the appropriate Latin term,
and Claudian assigns to the personified Clementia the cosmic
function—bringing order out of chaos—which is part of the
Greek concept of sophrosyne.[19] Julian also compares the Empress
Eusebeia to a statue of Sophrosyne.[20] Although he gives no hint of
the form or attributes that would distinguish such a statue, it is
clear that he can readily conceive of its existence, and we cannot
rule out the possibility that he had himself seen an image of Sophrosyne, comparable, perhaps, to the statue of Annia Regilla, wife
of Herodes Atticus, which once stood near the fountain of Pirene
in Corinth and was described in a dedicatory inscription as an

---

Roman Art (Rome, 1955) Plate LVIII. Further information about the Roman virtues on sarcophagi is supplied by Anne Ruggles Bromberg, "Concordia: Studies in
Roman Marriage under the Empire" (Ph.D. dissertation, Harvard University; for
abstract see H.S.C.P. 66 [1962] 249–252). The Clementia panel of Marcus Aurelius in the Conservatori Museum, Rome, is discussed by Ryberg, *Panel Reliefs of
Marcus Aurelius* (New York, 1967) 9–15, see Plates II, III. Similar scenes on the
columns of Trajan and M. Aurelius are discussed by Richard Brilliant, *The Arch of
Septimius Severus in the Roman Forum* (Rome, 1967) 238.

[16]Mattingly, *op. cit.* I, 384, No. 78 (Vitellius); IV, 101, No. 702, and Plate 15. 1
(Antoninus Pius). Consult PW., *s.v. Clementia* (Aust). The word *Moderationi(s)* ap-
pears on coins of Tiberius, but without a representation of the personified virtue.
See Mattingly, I, 132, No. 90, and Plate 24.5.

[17]Cicero, *De Inv.* 2. 164. Seneca, *De Clem.* 1. 11. 2.

[18]For example, the Greek translation of the word *clementia* on the *Clupeus Aureus*
in the *Res Gestae.* Jürgen Kabirsch, *Untersuchungen zum Begriff der Philanthropia bei
dem Kaiser Julian* (Wiesbaden, 1960) 15–25, discusses the efforts of Greek writers to
render the Latin *clementia.*

[19]Julian, *Or.* 1. 17A, 41C-D, 2. 95A, 100C. Claudian, *De Con. Stil.* 2. 22. 6.
Claudian has the makings of a *psychomachia* in his list of Stilicho's virtues (Iustitia,
Patientia, Temperies, Prudentia, and Constantia) and of the vices which he avoids
(Avaritia, Ambitio, Luxuries, and Superbia) 2. 22. 100–122. The degree of per-
sonification varies, Luxuries being more completely visualized than the others.

[20]*Or.* 3. 123A (ὥσπερ ἐν ἱερῷ καθιδρυμένον ἄγαλμα σωφροσύνης).

εἰκὼν σωφροσύνης (*IG* IV. 1599). It is more likely, however, that Julian had in mind a statue of Pudicitia, whose natural Greek rendering would be Sophrosyne.

Late antiquity, as is well known, indulged lavishly that taste for the personification of ethical and religious qualities which the Romans of the classical period had always enjoyed, even more than had the Greeks. In pagan Latin literature of the imperial age, an important example (in addition to the works of Claudian) is the fifth-century *Marriage of Mercury and Philology* by Martianus Capella, in which the cardinal virtues are introduced into the chamber of the bride. They are described collectively as worthy *matronae* of sober mien, unadorned with makeup, but glowing with a kind of simple charm (the *kosmos akosmos* again, Latinized as *sobrio decore*, 2. 127–130). Although the function of each virtue is explained, no separate attributes are listed. An influential Greek Christian work of the second century is the *Shepherd of Hermas*, which records a vision of seven women, all of them personified virtues, who support the tower of the church (*Vis.* 3. 8. 1–7). The virtue most closely akin to Sophrosyne is the second of these, Enkrateia (Self-Control), who is said to be well-girded (περιεζωσμένη) and dressed like a man (ἀνδριζομένη).[21] Tertullian's *De Spectaculis,* in a passage pregnant with significance for the future, pits four personified virtues against the corresponding vices. They are Castitas, fighting against Impudicitia, Fides against Perfidia, Misericordia against Saevitia, and Modestia against Petulantia (29. 5). In Tertullian's diatribe against the circus and the amphitheater, the struggle between the virtues and the vices is conceived as an athletic or gladiatorial one, but their contest plainly forecasts the military combat soon to be described by Prudentius.[22]

[21]The other virtues are Pistis, Haplotês (Simplicity), Epistêmê, Akakia, Semnotês, and Agapê. Elsewhere Hermas beholds twelve beautiful maidens building the Tower, contrasted with twelve women clothed in black. Again Enkrateia is the second of the maidens; opposed to her is Akrasia (*Sim.* 9. 15. 1–3). The notion that Virtue must somehow resemble a man appears also in Silius Italicus' version of the Choice of Heracles, his Dream of Scipio (*Punica* 15. 18 ff.). Here *Virtus* is said to be *et ore incessuque viro propior,* 29–30; compare ἀνδριζομένη in the *Shepherd of Hermas.*

[22]See Aimé Puech, *Prudence: Etude sur la poésie latine chrétienne au IV͏ᵉ siècle* (Paris, 1888) 245–246, for Tertullian as the inspiration for Prudentius, and pages 241 ff.

In art, both pagan and Christian, the same taste for allegory and symbolism reveals itself. The mosaics that survive from ancient sites do not, as it happens, include any representation of Sophrosyne, but this circumstance may be no more than accidental, since comparable personifications occur, notably that of Megalopsychia (Greatness of Soul). Moreover, scenes of chariot races and of the hunt, popular in mosaics and on sarcophagi, have been interpreted as graphic demonstrations of such virtues as *andreia* (courage) and *megalopsychia,* even in the absence of personified abstractions. Hippolytus, the *sôphrôn* huntsman, is a favorite type whose appearance may symbolize victory over passion or some other form of the irrational.[23] A few paintings from late antiquity also preserve traces of personified virtues. Those of the Coptic necropolis at El Baḳawāt in the Oasis of Khargeh (late fourth or early fifth century) include figures labeled Eirênê (Peace), Dikaiosynê (Justice), and Euchê (Prayer).[24] Still later, manuscript illuminations employ these subjects, the best-known

---

on Latin allegory in the fourth century, especially that of Claudian. Athletic imagery depicting the struggle between virtue and vice is discussed by Colin Eisler, "The Athlete of Virtue," in Meiss, I, 82–97.

[23]Consult Doro Levi, *Antioch Mosaic Pavements* (Princeton, 1947) I. 339–345, Glanville Downey, *T.A.P.A.* 76 (1945) 279–286, and Ernst Kitzinger, *Dumbarton Oaks Papers* 6 (Cambridge, Mass., 1951) 117–118. For sarcophagi decorated with scenes suggesting self-restraint or control of the passions, see Panofsky, *Tomb Sculpture,* 30 (an Etruscan urn with the Actaeon motif), and 34 (garland sarcophagi whereon winged cupids bridle goats, lions, bulls, and boars. Saxl, I, 179, interprets in the same way the emblematic bull tamed by a putto, ubiquitous on Borgia monuments). Panofsky. *Tomb Sculpture,* 31, describes a Roman sepulchral altar bearing attributes of Diana (see Fig. 94), which he regards as a tribute to the virtue of the deceased woman. Consult Carl Robert, *Die antiken Sarkophag-Reliefs,* III. 2 (Berlin, 1904) 169–219, for scenes alluding to the myths of Actaeon, Bellerophon, Hippolytus, Icarus, and Alcestis, all of which may imply sophrosyne. For Hippolytus and Bellerophon, see Chapter 1 above.

[24]C. K. Wilkinson, *Bulletin of the Metropolitan Museum of Art* 23 (1928) sec. 2, pp. 29–36. See also Künstle, 37 ff.; cf. Van Marle, II, 18 ff., and Katzenellenbogen, 28, and consult Glanville Downey, *T.A.P.A.* 69 (1938) 355, note 13, on the Khargeh paintings and those at Bawit (Faith, Hope, Charity, Patience) and Saqqara (these four, plus Prudence, Fortitude, and others unidentified). Jacques Schwartz, "Nouvelles études sur des Fresques d'el-Bagawat," *Cahiers archéologiques* 13 (1963) 1–11, suggests that the figures of Euchê, Dikaiosynê, and Eirênê which are associated with a picture of Daniel in the Lions' Den actually apply to three separate episodes in the life of Daniel, among which the story of Susanna and the Elders is linked with Justice. (I am indebted to George M. A. Hanfmann for calling my

examples being the Vienna Dioscorides (ca. 512), on the title page of which Megalopsychia and Phronêsis (Prudence) flank the Empress Anicia Juliana, and the manuscripts of the *Scala Paradisi* by John Climacus, which show a great number of personified virtues assisting the soul to climb the ladder to Heaven. Sophrosyne and Apatheia (the Stoic condition of being dispassionate) help it up the fourteenth and fifteenth rungs of the ladder.[25] Western art in the Middle Ages was to employ all three of these methods of depicting the virtues (personified figures, genre scenes, and mythical exemplars).

The precise extent to which Greek or Byzantine influences may have affected the portrayal of the personified virtues in the Latin West is still uncertain, but after the time of Prudentius there is no need to look further for the inspiration that populated Carolingian, Romanesque, and even Gothic art with virtues and vices, shown at first in combat, later with the virtues triumphant. While pictures of the battle scenes described in the *Psychomachia* (ca. 410) owe much to illustrations of the last six books of the *Aeneid*, the depiction of the virtues themselves with their attributes (especially in the earlier manuscripts) is remarkably faithful to the literary source.[26]

THE *PSYCHOMACHIA*

Among the seven major virtues[27] taking part in the *Psychomachia*, two represent important facets of the Greek sophrosyne

---

attention to this article.) For the association of Susanna with *castitas* in later biblical exegesis, see North, 365–366.

[25]The treatise itself dates from the seventh century. Illustrated MSS survive from the eleventh. See J. J. Tikkanen, *Ein illustrierte Klimaxhandschrift der Vatikanischen Bibliothek* (Helsinki, 1890), and John Rupert Martin, *The Illustration of the Heavenly Ladder of John Climacus* (Princeton, 1954) Figs. 45, 107, and consult Katzenellenbogen, 22–24.

[26]On the illustrated Prudentius MSS and their antecedents in Roman art consult Katzenellenbogen, 1–13. For reproductions of scenes in which the Pudicitia-Libido and Sobrietas-Luxuria contests occur, see Richard Stettiner, *Die illustrierten Prudentius-Handschriften* (Berlin, 1905), and Helen Woodruff, *The Illustrated Manuscripts of Prudentius* (Cambridge, Mass., 1930).

[27]The pairs of adversaries are Fides-Veterum Cultus Deorum, Pudicitia-Libido, Patientia-Ira, Mens Humilis-Superbia, Sobrietas-Luxuria, Operatio-Avaritia, and Concordia-Discordia. They are based on no systematic theological or moral program, and the list is therefore readily expanded, contracted, or otherwise altered,

and are in fact among its common Latin representatives in the classical period: *pudicitia* (chastity) and *sobrietas* (temperance in eating and drinking). Pudicitia and Libido (Lust or Lechery) are the second pair of combatants to take the field. Chastity is a warrior-maiden, dressed in armor, with shining weapons; she is attacked by Lust, girt with torches, who hurls flaming and smoking firebrands at the face and eyes of her adversary. Pudicitia strikes the hand and the fiery weapons of Libido with a stone and pierces her throat with a sword (40–52), which she then washes in the Jordan and lays on an altar (98–108). The description of the combat echoes *Eph.* 6. 16—Prudentius even borrows the words *tela . . . ignea,* fiery darts, from the Vulgate—but it also exploits the imagery traditional in poetic allusions to sexual passion, being a literal interpretation of the metaphor that equates lust with a raging fire. The victory speech delivered by the triumphant virtue explicates the meaning of the battle, as Pudicitia recalls the defeat of Holophernes by Judith (a symbol of the triumph of sophrosyne over lust in Patristic exegesis)[28] and crowns her own victory with allusions to the Virgin Birth (58–69, 76–88).

Sobrietas and Luxuria (whom later authors more often designate as Temperantia and Gula)[29] constitute the fifth pair of com-

---

according to the needs of the artist or the medium. For a suggestion relating Prudentius' list of virtues and vices to Cyprian, *De zelo et livore,* 16, consult Ralph Hanna, III, *C.P.* 72 (1977) 108–115.

[28]See especially Ambrose, *De Hel.* 9. 29 and *De Vid.* 7. 40. According to Frances Godwin, *Speculum* 26 (1951) 609–614, Judith is first portrayed in art as a representative of *temperantia* in the Belleville Breviary (first half of the fourteenth century), yet the picture of Judith in the Romanesque mosaic pavement of Sta. Maria Maggiore at Vercelli may, Porter suggests (I, 383), represent the struggle of *temperantia* against *intemperantia. Somme le roi* MSS show Judith decapitating Holophernes as an illustration of Chastity triumphant over Lust. Consult Réau, II, 331–335, for a catalogue of scenes portraying Judith (not always as a representative of *temperantia*).

[29]Gula (or *ventris ingluvies,* as Gregory, *Moralia in Job,* 31. 45, *P.L.* 76, 620–622, and his imitators also call it) is distinguished from Luxuria by Ps.-Hugh of St. Victor (*De Fructibus Carnis et Spiritus* 9–10), who equates Luxuria with what Prudentius calls Libido. At Laon the *psychomachia* sculpture (1190–1200) includes Sobrietas versus Hebetatio, as well as Castitas versus Luxuria (Künstle, 159). Hebetatio (dullness) is an unusual opponent for Sobrietas, but the explanation may lie in passages like Claudian, *De Con. Stil.* 2. 22. 132–133: *luxuries . . . hebetat . . . sensus.* For the origin of the Laon group of virtues in the series known as the "Gift-virtues" (deriving from the Gifts of the Holy Spirit, Isaiah 11) consult Tuve, "Virtues," II, 64.

batants. Luxuria has come to the field of battle directly from an
all-night banquet (depicted in lively fashion by many of the manuscript illustrators), and throughout this episode the pleasures of
taste are paramount. When Luxuria has been defeated and is
forced to chew on the bloody pulp of her own tongue (smashed by
a rock which Sobrietas has hurled at her mouth), caustic remarks
are made about the contrast between this mouthful and what she
has lately been swallowing (427–431). She arrives on the scene in a
chariot, throwing violets and roses[30] at her adversaries, who are
on the verge of surrender when Sobrietas rallies them with an
exhortation recalling episodes from the Old Testament concerned with abstinence and repentance for gluttony (371–406).
Having no weapon of war, Sobrietas holds the standard of the
Cross in front of the chariot horses. They promptly bolt, throw
Luxuria from the car, and crush her beneath the wheels. The
personality and attributes of Luxuria are amplified by the description of her attendants—Iocus, Petulantia, Amor, Pompa,
Venustas, Discordia, and Voluptas—all of whom flee after her
defeat, scattering their possessions as they go (433–446).[31]

[30]Contrary to convention, the flowers associated with Luxuria include lilies as
well as roses (354–355). Literature and art perennially oppose the "lilies and lan-
guors of virtue" (to quote Swinburne, "Dolores") and the "roses and raptures of
vice." (Note Chesterton's response: "And if you think virtue is languor just try it
and see.") The lily symbolizes virginity in Patristic writing (for example, Jerome,
adv. Jovin. 1. 285, a passage alluded to by Ripa in describing Pudicizia) and is
therefore ubiquitous in pictures of the Annunciation. For the association of roses
with luxury or voluptuousness, see Horace, *Odes* 1. 38. 3–4 with many other
allusions almost as memorable (1. 5. 1, 1. 36. 15, 2. 3. 14, 2. 11. 14, 3. 19. 22, 3. 29.
3). The personified Sophrosyne of Eustathius (note 4, above) omits roses from her
garland because "there is nothing common to sophrosyne and the rose," 2. 6. Yet
roses may symbolize Christ and the Blessed Virgin (Réau, I, 133), and white roses
are emblems of purity. In the *Psychomachia* itself, the scepter of Sapientia sprouts
both roses (symbolic of martyrdom) and the lilies of *pudicitia* (881–883). The
fifteenth-century spiritual encyclopedia described by Saxl, *J.W.C.I.* 5 (1942) 82–
142, includes a *psychomachia* scene in which seven vices attack a castle defended by
seven virtues, who are armed with roses and even fire roses from a cannon (p. 104,
Plate 25a). The contrasting symbolism of the red rose and the white is exploited
equally by Baciccio in the Temperantia painting in Sta. Agnese in the Piazza
Navona and the nineteenth-century romantic poet, John Boyle O'Reilly, in "A
White Rose."

[31]The attributes of this group are cymbals, the bow, arrows, and quiver of
Amor, garlands, and jewels. Breaking or otherwise damaging the bow of Cupid is

The illustrated manuscripts of the *Psychomachia*, ranging in time from the ninth century to the twelfth (but going back, it has been suggested, to an archetype of the fifth),[32] depict these combats with great fidelity and maintain many of the literary attributes of the virtues and vices. Pudicitia and Sobrietas are shown as warrior-maids, the first with a sword and a stone, the second with a cross and a rock. Libido is armed with torches (as many as three in some illustrations), and Luxuria is a voluptuous figure, first at the banquet table,[33] later in the chariot. Few works of literature in

---

a symbol of the triumph of Chastity which goes back to the Greek Anthology; see, for example, *Anth. Pal.* 5. 179, a threat to throw the bow and arrows of Eros into the fire. Cf. Ovid, *Remedia Amoris* 139: *Otia si tollas periere Cupidinis arcus* (the motto used by Mantegna in his Triumph of Wisdom over Vice) and Apuleius, *Metam.* 5. 30: *Sobrietas . . . arcum enodet.* Petrarch revives it in the *Triumph of Chastity,* and thereafter it appears often in paintings related to this theme (for example, the *Triumph of Chastity* by Lorenzo Lotto in the Palazzo Pallavicini in Rome and that by Signorelli in the National Gallery in London). Pompê (Procession) is occasionally personified in Greek vase painting, where she conveys no more derogatory implications than does Eros, the prototype of Amore. A red-figured oinochoe of the late fifth century in the Metropolitan Museum in New York shows Pompê and Eros in company with Dionysus. See PW., *s.v.* Pompa (Boemer). Petulantia (Wantonness) is personified as the foe of Modestia in Tertullian's *De Spectaculis* 29. For Eros as the adversary of Sophrosyne in the Greek Anthology, see *Anth. Pal.* 9. 132; in Byzantine literature, Eustathius, *op. cit.*, 4. 23. Silius Italicus, in the *Dream of Scipio,* makes Ebrietas, Luxus, and Infamia the *comites* of Voluptas (*Punica,* 15. 96 ff.).

[32] Katzenellenbogen, 4.

[33] In mediaeval and Renaissance art the personification of gluttony (*gula, intemperantia, ventris ingluvies,* rather than *luxuria*) is often shown (apart from the context of the battle) seated at table, either gorging herself or repelling a beggar who hopes for a morsel from her intemperate feast. See Katzenellenbogen, 13, note 1, for an eleventh-century Paris MS (Bibl. nat. MS lat. 2077) which shows Gula thus gorging at table, while Luxuria is depicted loosening her girdle at the approach of her lover. Scenes of gluttony appear frequently in fourteenth-century moral treatises, such as the picture of Intemperance illustrating Ser Zucchero Bencivenni, *Lord's Prayer,* in Mario Salmi, *Italian Miniatures* (New York, 1954) Plate XVIa. Gula in the act of vomiting is also an iconographical type with a very long history, ranging from a boss on the south wall of Lincoln Cathedral, cited by E. W. Tristram, *English Wall Painting of the Fourteenth Century* (London, 1955) 96–97, to the emblem books. Spenser describes Gluttony thus in *F.Q.* 1. 4. 21 ("He spued up his gorge"). Temperantia, too, could be shown at table, presumably avoiding the gluttony suggested in the *Intemperantia* scenes. A MS of *Somme le roi* (1295) represents her thus; see below p. 216. In tapestries of the fifteenth century. Temperantia is glorified through scenes reprehending intemperance at meals. Van Marle, II, 102, lists tapestry cycles of this nature. See Joan Evans, *Monastic Iconog-*

all history can have had such direct and immediate influence on art as did the *Psychomachia,* which inspired the portrayal of virtues and vices (not always the same pairs as those of Prudentius) in mosaic pavements, on reliefs over church and cathedral portals, on baptismal fonts, column capitals, and stained glass windows, and on innumerable objects such as portable altars, ivory caskets, and tapestries. Since this subject has been extensively treated in the standard works on iconography, it will suffice here to record some of the more significant changes in the portrayal of Pudicitia, Sobrietas, and other virtues allied with sophrosyne, which appear in the context of the *Psychomachia* between the Carolingian period and the thirteenth century, when the popularity of the theme declines.

The earliest extant sources are the illustrated manuscripts, but in the Romanesque period mosaic pavements and reliefs, especially above church portals, often employ the motive of the *psychomachia,* as do various types of small objects. usually religious in nature. At first the influence of the poem was powerful enough to focus attention on the actual combat. The twelfth-century ivory cover of the Melisande psalter is a late example. Six scenes from the life of David (whose combat with Goliath was in itself a popular symbol of the *psychomachia*) are interspersed with scenes of warfare between pairs of virtues and vices, who include Pudicitia versus Libido and Sobrietas versus Luxuria, in each case faithful

---

raphy in France (Cambridge, Eng., 1970) Plate 30, for a sculptured allegory of Temperance from the refectory of the Benedictine Abbey of Saint-Bénigne, Dijon, and pages 14–15 for the iconography derived from New Testament repasts. When Luxuria is depicted on Romanesque capitals, she is portrayed in terms of lust, rather than gluttony, and is represented as a woman whose breasts are devoured by snakes (Mâle I, Figs. 264, 265; Van Marle, II, Figs. 86, 87; consult Réau, I, 168 ff.) or as one who rides a goat or a ram (see Richard Hamann, *Burlington Magazine* 60 [1932] 91 ff., for this motive at Auxerre, Freiburg, Arles, and elsewhere, and consult Folke Nördstrom, *Virtues and Vices on the Fourteenth-Century Corbels in the Choir of Uppsala Cathedral* [Stockholm, 1956] 94–103). In the Gothic age Luxuria is often suggested by a scene in which two lovers embrace (Chartres, Amiens) or a courtesan admires herself in a mirror (Notre Dame). A very early forerunner of the first of these scenes occurs on the Lydian tombstone cited in note 4, above, where it illustrates Asôtia (Profligacy).

to the text of Prudentius.[34] Many examples of this dynamic representation of the spiritual conflict exist, even well into the Renaissance,[35] but inevitably the moment of triumph came to seem more significant and interesting than the actual fighting, and already in the twelfth century the virtues were beginning to be shown in a static portrayal, triumphant over the vices (who are sometimes crouched at the feet of their adversaries or are being trampled by them). Among early examples of this type of iconography are the twelfth-century Norman fonts in two neighboring English churches, St. Leonard's in Stanton Fitzwarren (Wiltshire) and St. Peter's in Southrop (Gloucestershire). In Stanton Fitzwarren there are eight pairs of Virtues and Vices. Among them Temperantia (replacing Sobrietas in Prudentius' list) tramples on Luxuria, and Pudicitia on Libido, both virtues being depicted as warrior-maidens. Temperantia carries a lance and a banner; Pudicitia's weapons are missing. A third pair, belonging to the same sphere of morality, has been added: Modestia triumphing over Ebrietas. The crouching vices are identified by name, but are not characterized by attributes. The font at Southrop represents the same type of *psychomachia,* but with certain differences, the most notable being the smaller number of pairs and the portrayal

[34]See Van Marle, II, Fig. 4. David, the favorite Carolingian model of kingliness, is linked with the cardinal virtues by Ambrose, *De off. min.* See 1. 6. 21 and 2. 22. 115 for his *temperantia.*

[35]The theme of the *psychomachia* was revived in the fifteenth century, when it was combined with other, post-Romanesque ways of depicting the virtues and vices. A notable example from the sixteenth century is Mantegna's painting for Isabella d'Este, now in the Louvre, which shows Wisdom, Philosophy, and Chastity putting to flight the Vices, including Lust, Sloth, Avarice, and Gluttony, while three cardinal virtues, including Temperance with her two vessels, watch the conflict from a cloud in the sky. The relation of this device to a pageant performed at Ferrara in 1502 for the marriage of Lucrezia Borgia and Alfonso d'Este is explained by E. Tietze-Conrat, *Mantegna* (London, 1955) 29. Taddeo Zuccari's Psychomachia in the Vatican is more traditional than Mantegna's scene, in that it has seven pairs of combatants, although they are not distinguished by recognizable attributes. All the virtues are winged, armed, and helmeted; they impale on their lances vices in the form of devils, having animal heads and bat wings, tails, and even in some cases pitchforks. See Van Marle, II, Figs. 6 and 8. Other sixteenth-century paintings of the *Psychomachia* are Perugino's *Combat of Love and Chastity* and Baccio Bandinelli's *Combat of Ratio and Libido* (Seznec, 109–111, and Fig. 38).

of the Virtues as knights, rather than as warrior-maids. There are only five pairs of combatants here, still including Temperantia (with a banner) standing on the stomach of Luxuria, and Modestia with a sword, stabbing Ebrietas in the throat (Plate IV). A subtle touch is the spelling of the names of the vices backward, in letters that are themselves reversed.[36]

Romanesque church doorways, especially in France, very often employ the motive of the *psychomachia,* usually in the form of virtue triumphant over vice. The portal now becomes the conventional location for this part of the *speculum morale,* although column capitals within the church also employ the motive, as do frescoes of the same period.[37] In the thirteenth century the repre-

[36]For photographs of the two fonts see E. S. Prior and A. Gardner, *An Account of Medieval Figure Sculpture in England* (Cambridge, Eng., 1912) Figs. 31, 171. The eight pairs at Stanton-Fitzwarren are Largitas-Avaritia, Humilitas-Superbia, Pietas-Discordia, Misericordia-Invidia, Modestia-Ebrietas, Temperantia-Luxuria, Patientia-Ira, and Pudicitia-Libido. The five pairs at Southrop are Patientia-Ira, Largitas-Avaritia, Temperantia-Luxuria, Misericordia-Invidia, and Modestia-Ebrietas; here the cycle is augmented by a relief of Moses between Ecclesia and Synagogue. Elsewhere in England the *psychomachia* theme appears on reliefs at Salisbury, Exeter, and Malmesbury. The virtues and vices portrayed on the arch of the doorway of the Chapter-house at Salisbury Cathedral (1260–1270) are particularly lively and show many divergences from Prudentius. Consult Rosalie Green, *J.W.C.I.* 31 (1968) 148–158, for solutions to some iconographical puzzles and a suggestion that the north side of the arch represents the Seven Deadly Sins with their *remedia* and the south side the cardinal and theological virtues with their opposing vices, in a scheme like that of the North Porch at Chartres. At Claverly (Shropshire) a Romanesque fresco shows the Virtues as fifteen knights on horseback; consult Edgar Antony, *Romanesque Frescoes* (Princeton, 1951) 195 and Fig. 481. The *psychomachia* theme was the subject of several Gothic wall paintings in England, including those at Chalgrove (Shropshire) and in the painted Chamber at Westminster.

[37]Consult Réau I, 177–179, for a list of twelfth-century church portals that employ the *psychomachia* theme, and for a detailed study of one such portal, see E. L. Mendell, *Romanesque Sculpture in Saintonge* (New Haven, 1940). The favorite location is on an archivolt of the main portal, and the number of combatants is usually six pairs (ibid., 144). When the motive appears on column capitals, the number is reduced to four pairs, whose content varies. The virtues combined with the seasons on portals of Cluniac churches are discussed by Joan Evans, *Cluniac Art,* 114; see pages 80–81 for the virtues and vices as represented in churches of this order. At Saint Lazare in Autun some notable examples of personified virtues and vices are preserved; consult Denis Grivot and George Zarnecki, *Gislebertus Sculptor of Autun* (New York, 1961) Plates 19a-c (Avaritia-Largitas, Ira-Patientia) and K and Q (Luxuria, a woman bitten by snakes). For Romanesque frescoes

Plate IV. Modestia triumphant over Ebrietas, Church of St. Peter, Southrop, Gloucestershire (twelfth century). Photograph by the author.

sentation of the virtues in triumph goes a step further. They still
appear near church doorways, but the vices have been removed to
a separate scene, in which they are shown in action, rather than as
personified figures like the virtues. The scenes are now drawn,
not from the Bible or history, but from daily life, and Temperantia is omitted from the cycle, her place being taken by Chastity
(Pudicitia or Castitas). The earliest of these Gothic cathedral
groups is that on the west façade of Notre Dame in Paris (dating
from the early thirteenth century), where Chastity, framed in a
medallion and seated on a throne, holds a shield bearing a
much-disputed emblem, a bird surrounded by flames, which is
thought by some to be a mediaeval attempt to depict a salamander
and by others to be the legendary bird Charista, said by Solinus to
fly unharmed among flames.[38] Beneath the figure of Chastity was
a scene from daily life representing lechery, probably a courtesan
looking into a mirror (restored as a figure holding a pair of
scales). There are twelve Virtues in all, corresponding to no
known moral treatise. The number is doubtless dictated by the
fact that the virtues are placed under statues of the Apostles,
twelve in number.[39] Slightly later versions of the same scenes at
Amiens and Chartres correspond closely to the prototype at
Notre Dame, except that the scene portraying lust consists of a
young man caressing a courtesan.[40]

---

employing the *psychomachia* theme consult Réau, I, 177, and Antony (*op. cit.*,
above, note 36). Bronze doors of Romanesque churches sometimes used this
theme; one such is the door of St. Sophia, Novgorod (cast 1152–1154 in Mag-
deburg), where virtues clad in armor trample on vices. See Hans Weigirt,
Romanesque Sculpture (London, 1962) 100. For an example of a Romanesque altar
with personified virtues, including Modestia, but without vices, see the Lisbjerg
Altar, Copenhagen (ibid., 42–43). An exhaustive list and description of objects
(portable altars, shrines, reliquaries, fonts, crosses, book covers, chalices, and other
liturgical vessels) decorated with the cardinal virtues (usually in medallion frames)
may be found in Katzenellenbogen, 45–51.

[38]Mâle, II, 120, discusses the possibility that the creature is a phoenix or a turtledove, or that the artist gave the salamander the shape of a bird; cf. Réau, I, 180 f.
For the bird Charista, see Evans, *Mediaeval*, 97, Réau, I, 88, Katzenellenbogen,
75–81, and note 1, page 76.

[39]Mâle, II, 114, note 6 and Réau I, 181. See Tuve, "Virtues" I, 227 and note 25,
on the derivation of the group from subdivisions of the cardinal virtues, according
to the lists in Cicero and Macrobius, plus the seven "Gift-Virtues" and the theological virtues.

[40]All three cycles (at Notre Dame, Amiens, and Chartres) are discussed by Mâle,
II, 110–130. See also Réau, I, 190, on Gothic reliefs and stained glass employing

The cycle resembling that of Notre Dame appears on the south porch at Chartres. The north porch (also of the thirteenth century) has a different set of Virtues and Vices on the third archivolt of the left portal, eight in number, rather than twelve, consisting of the three theological virtues, the four cardinal virtues, and Humility. Here Temperantia (rather than Castitas or Pudicitia) appears, and instead of being a seated, veiled figure, enclosed in a medallion (like the Chastity of the south porch) she is a standing female figure, unarmed, holding a bird (perhaps a dove as in the *Somme le Roi* MS of 1295).[41] At her feet is a crouching figure of a woman tearing her garments, who, if we can judge by the corresponding pair of figures in Giotto's cycle in the Arena Chapel in Padua, must be Ira (Wrath).[42] The series represented on the north porch at Chartres reflects a systematic theological treatise which builds its program, not on a haphazard collection of virtues and vices (as in the *Psychomachia* of Prudentius and the cycles at Notre Dame and on the south porch at Chartres), but on the integration of the four pagan cardinal virtues (long since baptized by the Fathers) with the Pauline triad (a synthesis that was not achieved until close to the middle of the twelfth century) and the addition to these seven of humility, named by St. Augustine the root of the tree of virtue[43]—the *arbor bona,* which now begins to enjoy enormous popularity in moral treatises and in art.

---

the *psychomachia* motive, and consult Katzenellenbogen, 75–81, Künstle. 159–161, and Van Marle, II, 62–63, and Figs. 96–97, 100–101, 104.

[41] Henry Martin, *La miniature française du XIIIe au XVe siècle* (Paris and Brussels, 1923) Plate 2.

[42] R. Freyhan, *J.W.C.I.* 11 (1948) 79, suggests that the virtues and vices of the Arena Chapel are founded on the cycle of the north porch at Chartres. Giotto's Temperantia is unlike her Chartres counterpart in having two attributes, a bit in her mouth and a sheathed sword. Both can be traced to the imagery of sophrosyne/ *temperantia* in ancient literature, and both have great influence on the iconography of this virtue in Italy, especially the sheathed sword, which often appears in Florentine art of the Trecento. The seated figure identified as Temperance in a Giottesque panel of the Madonna and Child with Saints and Virtues, ca. 1330, "probably held two jugs" according to the Catalogue of the exhibition "The Italian Heritage" at the Wildenstein Gallery, May 17–August 29, 1967. No trace of any attribute is now visible.

[43] Consult William M. Green, *University of California Studies in Classical Philology* 13 (1949) 407–431. According to Katzenellenbogen, *Chartres,* 56–67, the iconography of the left portal of the north porch is indebted to a ninth-century letter of Pseudo-Jerome, which dealt with the Assumption of the Virgin and attributed to her all the virtues, and an eleventh-century sermon by Fulbert of Chartres on her

Before considering the ramifications of the *arbor bona* and some
other consequences of the treatises produced in the twelfth and
thirteenth centuries by such seminal writers as Peter Lombard,
Hugh of St. Victor, Herrad of Landsberg, Honorius Augustodunensis, and St. Thomas Aquinas, we must review the history
of the four cardinal virtues in Carolingian and Romanesque art,
since their career is separate from that of the virtues involved in
the *Psychomachia,* even though Temperantia (or one of her equivalents) belongs to both groups.

THE CARDINAL VIRTUES

The cardinal virtues appear as personifications in Carolingian
miniatures, without any opposing vices and without either the
accessory virtues of the *Psychomachia* or the three Pauline virtues.
They are often connected with rulers, either kings or high
ecclesiastical dignitaries, and in this way are true to their Greek
origin, for in the ancient world the cardinal virtues—wisdom,
justice, courage, and moderation—developed in the context of
the *polis* and achieved philosophical significance as the excellences
of the ruler, whether a Platonic philosopher-king or a leader of
the Roman *Optimates.*[44] They were known to the Carolingian Age
through a variety of sources, Cicero himself and such inter-
mediaries as Macrobius, Martianus Capella, Ambrose, Gregory,
and Isidore of Seville. In the ninth century the doctrine of the
four virtues was restated by Alcuin in several influential
treatises.[45] But for iconography the most important of the

Nativity, which specifically ascribed to her the four cardinal virtues, with faith,
charity, and humility. For the Temperantia-Ira pair, see Etienne Houvet, *Cathédrale
de Chartres, portail nord* (Chelles, Seine & Marne, 1919) I, 85.

[44]Plato, *Republic* 4, and Cicero, *De Officiis,* are the most important sources.
Alcuin's two influential treatises on the cardinal virtues are dedicated to rulers,
Charlemagne himself and Duke Wido of Brittany.

[45]Alcuin's sources (John Cassian, Isidore of Seville, Gregory the Great) are
discussed by Luitpold Wallach, *Alcuin and Charlemagne* (Ithaca, N.Y., 1968), chapter XII. Alcuin's treatise *De Virtutibus et Vitiis* (*P.L.* 101, 613 ff.) exemplifies the
way in which authors who knew both the *Psychomachia* tradition, with its flexible
list of opposing virtues and vices, and the classical tradition, with the four Platonic
virtues, might use both without an effective integration of the two systems. Alcuin
lists eight pairs of opposed vices and virtues, Prudentian in derivation, with
superbia-humilitas the fundamental pair, and keeps the notion of warfare alive by

Carolingian writers is Theodulf of Orleans, who in one of his poems describes a plaque (*discus*) in the palace of Aachen, depicting personifications of the liberal arts and the virtues. According to Theodulf, the picture showed a tree, rooted in a globe, supporting on its branches the figures of the arts and the virtues. The second group is listed as Prudentia, Vis, Iustitia, and Moderatio. Two of these terms—Vis instead of Fortitudo, Moderatio for Temperantia—are unusual, but not unprecedented. Martianus Capella refers to Vis in his description of the personified virtues, while giving sophrosyne the normal Ciceronian name, Temperantia (2. 128–129). Cicero himself in *De Officiis* translates sophrosyne by the two words *moderatio modestiaque* (1. 159), and Macrobius lists *moderatio* under *temperantia*.[46]

More important than the names given to the virtues by Theodulf are the attributes assigned to them. Prudentia holds a book, Vis is identified by her arms and armor (a dagger, a shield, and a helmet), Iustitia has a sword, a branch of palm, a set of balances, and a crown, and Moderatio *frena* and *flagella,* bridle and scourge, symbols of the twofold function of this virtue, which restrains what is excessive and stimulates what is deficient. The symbolism is explained as follows:

> Hanc prope temperiem praebens Moderatio stabat
> Fortia frena vehens sive flagella manu,
> Quis pigros stimulet, veloces temperet, et quis
> Aequus ut aequatis cursibus ordo meet.[47]

---

the use of such terms as *bellatores* and *duces.* He adds that among these leaders of the Christian religion, four most glorious commanders stand out: *prudentia, iustitia, fortitudo, temperantia*—an obvious attempt to unite the two sets of virtues. In *De Animae Ratione* Alcuin lists seven vices, omitting *ira* (*P.L.* 101, 640D). He derives them from the corruption of the three Platonic divisions of the soul, which, properly governed, produce the cardinal virtues.

[46]*In Somnium Scipionis* 1. 8; *moderatio* is one of the nine subdivisions of *temperantia*. The sixth-century *Formula Vitae Honestae* of Martin of Bracara, derived from Seneca's lost *De Officiis*, emphasizes the need for moderation in the practice of all four cardinal virtues and even includes a chapter on due measure (*mediocritas*) in the practice of each one (6–9, ed. Barlow), but the Latin rendering of sophrosyne here is *continentia*.

[47]*De Septem Liberalibus Artibus in Quadam Pictura Depictis (M.G.H., P.L.A.C.,* ed. Dümmler, vol. I, XLVI. 57). The bridle recalls the imagery of curbing or restrain-

Near her was standing Moderation, offering temperance,
Holding in her hand strong bridles or scourges
With which to prick the indolent, control the headstrong, and with which
To maintain an even tenor, as if with balanced course.

As both the word Moderatio and its explication disclose,
Theodulf is closer to the ancient conception of sophrosyne than
are most of the writers in the tradition of Prudentius, who make
the control of appetite and passion the essence of the virtue and
restrict its scope to *sobrietas* and *pudicitia*. In this respect Theodulf
resembles Alcuin, who also knew that Temperantia enshrines the
principle of the Mean and repeatedly links the virtue with the
Terentian proverb, *Ne quid nimis*, the Latin form of the Apolline
Mêden agan.[48] When, much later (in the fifteenth and sixteenth
centuries), the bridle becomes a widely used symbol of Temperantia, it is rarely accompanied by *flagella* or any equivalent, except
possibly the spurs on the heels of Temperantia in the Rouen
iconography, which, however, more likely symbolize the young
knight's maturity, in the chivalric tradition.

The chief Carolingian and Ottonian representations of the cardinal virtues include some of the most sumptuous manuscripts of
the middle or late ninth century: the Bible of Count Vivian or
first Bible of Charles the Bald (843–851), with its portrait of David
accompanied by figures of soldiers, musicians, and cardinal virtues; the Bible of San Callisto (876–888), written by Ingobert for
Charles the Bald, on the dedicatory page of which a portrait of

---

ing a headstrong animal so often related to sophrosyne in ancient literature. An
early symbolic use occurs in the myth of Bellerophon to whom Athena Chalinitis
gave the bridle with which he mastered Pegasus (cf. Pindar, *Ol.* 13 and see Chapter 1). Ambrose in his Funeral Oration for Theodosius introduces the discussion
of the ruler's *temperantia* with a digression on the finding of the True Cross, one of
the nails from which was worked into a bridle for Constantine's horse (41–51).
Many definitions of *temperantia* involved such words as *frenum* or *frenare;* for
example, Isidore of Seville says it is the virtue by which *libido concupiscentiaque
rerum frenatur* (*Etymologiae* 2. 24. 6). Cf. also Martin of Bracara, *Formula* 4: *Impone
concupiscentiae frenum*. Latin elegy refers disapprovingly to the *frena pudoris* (Propertius 3. 19. 3)

[48]For citations see Wallach, *op. cit.*, 69–70. On the relation of the Mean to
Christian ideas of *temperantia* consult Viola B. Hulbert, *Studies in Philology* 28
(1931) 184–210.

the king shows him with personifications of the four virtues in the niches of his throne; the Cambrai Gospels (second half of the ninth century), with a portrait of an unidentified king, again accompanied by the cardinal virtues; and the Marmoutier (or Autun) Sacramentary (ca. 850), which shows Abbot Raganaldus, in a large central medallion, blessing the people, while smaller medallions in the corners of the page contain personified virtues, each with its identifying attributes. The same general pattern of iconography is maintained well into the twelfth century by such manuscripts as the Book of Pericopes of Henry II (1012), the Missal of St. Denis (mid-eleventh century), and the Rhenish Lectionary (ca. 1130),[49] but the attributes of Temperantia exhibit considerable variety from one miniature to another. Clearly, in the case of this virtue, no single type had yet been established, and indeed it is sometimes only by the labeling of the personifications that one virtue is distinguished from the others. In the Vivian Bible all four virtues hold palm branches; in the Bible of San Callisto Temperantia has outstretched hands; in the Cambrai Gospels and the Marmoutier Sacramentary she holds a torch and a jug, while in the Rhenish Lectionary her attributes are two vessels, whose function is explained by the inscription, *Fervorem vite* [=*vitae*] *discretio temperet in te:* Let discretion temper the ardor of life in you.[50]

It is the last two of these devices that hold the greatest promise for the future. The torch and jug derive from some such description as that by Julius Pomerius of a principal activity of *temperantia*, extinguishing the flames of passion.[51] The two vessels imply

---

[49]The Carolingian, Ottonian, and later miniatures are described and some of them reproduced by Katzenellenbogen, 30–36 and Figs. 32–38, and Van Marle, II, Fig. 13. See also, for the Vivian Bible, Wilhelm Köhler, *Die Karolingischen Miniaturen* (Berlin, 1930–1960), I, Plate 72, and Réau, II, 20; the San Callisto Bible, *Art Bulletin* 55 (1973) Plate 58; the Marmoutier Sacramentary, John Beckwith, *Early Mediaeval Art* (New York, 1964) Fig. 51, Köhler, Plate 68b; the Missal of St. Denis, Beckwith, Plate 171. Consult North, "Temperance," 371 and see Fig. 1 (the Marmoutier Sacramentary).

[50]*Discretio* is the *genetrix, custos,* and *moderatrix* of all the virtues in the influential *Conlationes* of John Cassian (2. 1–4).

[51]*Vita Contemplativa* 3. 19 (*P.L.* 59, 502). See Katzenellenbogen, 55. On the popularity of this late fifth-century work, consult M. L. W. Laistner, *The Intellectual Heritage of the Early Middle Ages* (Ithaca, N.Y., 1957) 40–56. The significant phrase

the mingling of water and wine and thus allude to the root meaning of the verb *temperare* (to mix or mingle). This symbol is by all
odds the most popular in the mediaeval and Renaissance iconography of the virtue, being the simplest and easiest to understand
on the basis of etymology. No other cardinal virtue was capable of
being represented in such radical terms. The quenching of the
flame is also a recurrent theme, but a minor one compared with
the two vessels and (especially in the Renaissance) the bridle. It is
surprising that Carolingian miniatures neglect the imagery of the
bridle, to which Theodulf's poem must have given wide currency.

CORRESPONDING GROUPS OF FOUR

The iconography of *temperantia* and the other cardinal virtues
was inevitably affected by the theory of the macrocosm and the
microcosm, popular in the early Middle Ages, which found correspondences and parallels among many significant groups of four,
one of the best examples of this type of correlation being Radulphus Glaber's *Historia Sui Temporis* (1057). This treatise begins
with a discussion of the "divine quaternity" and proceeds to
equate a number of tetrads: the Evangelists, the cardinal virtues,
the elements, four of the senses, the Rivers of Paradise, and the
ages of human history.[52] According to Radulphus' ingenious interpretation, the Gospel according to Mark has a special link with
temperantia because it contains an account of the baptism of John.
The related physical element is naturally water, the corresponding sense that of taste, the River is the Gehon, and the age that of
the Patriarchs (both of the last two correlations go back to Ambrose, *De Paradiso*, probably by way of Walafrid Strabo).[53] Radul-

---

for *temperantia* is *Ignem libidinosae voluptatis extinguit* ("She quenches the blaze of
lecherous pleasure"). Sometimes Temperantia holds a spray of flowers along with
a vessel; see Katzenellenbogen, 33, note 2, and 34, note 3. Tervarent (*Supplement,
s.v. Mors*, p. 437) reports the appearance of the bridle in twelfth-century miniatures, but the attribute does not become common until popularized by Raphael.

[52]*P.L.* 142, 613–615. The mystical significance of the number four in late an-
tiquity and the Middle Ages and its influence on iconography are discussed by
George M. A. Hanfmann, *The Season Sarcophagus in Dumbarton Oaks* (Cambridge,
Mass., 1951) I, 198 ff. See Réau, I, 67–69 and 75, for a bibliography on the subject.

[53]On the sources used by Radulphus consult Evans, *Cluniac Art,* 112. The cardinal virtues and the elements are related intermittently and variously in Western
thought. For Robert of Grosseteste's comparison of moderation to coldness, hence

phus explains that as water is to the physical world, so is *temperantia* to the intellectual. It is the nurse of good things, bearing an abundance of virtues and preserving faith through a yearning for divine love.

As Joan Evans has demonstrated, this treatise and its quaternities influenced the iconography of Cluniac churches in the Romanesque period.[54] The identification of the Rivers of Paradise with the cardinal virtues is the most enduring of the correlations listed above; it originates with Philo Judaeus and is carried on by the Latin Fathers, although the correspondence between individual Rivers and cardinal virtues is not the same in Philo as in Ambrose and Augustine.[55] In art the two quaternities are often related or identified. The choir mosaics of 1107 in the church of San Savino in Piacenza depict both tetrads, the cardinal virtues being suggested by genre scenes (less common for virtues than for vices).[56] In the scene at the lower left of the mosaic a man stands unsteadily, holding in his left hand a staff, in his right an overflowing goblet. A second figure stands upright beside him,

---

to water, consult Siegfried Wenzel, *Speculum* 43 (1968) 10. See Frances A. Yates *J.W.C.I.* 17 (1954) 115–173 and 23 (1960) 1–44, on the relation of Ramon Lull's theory of the elements to his system of virtues.

[54]Evans, *Cluniac Art*, 110 ff. Of special interest for *temperantia* is the mosaic of ca. 1151 in the oratory of San Martino in the Cluniac church of San Benedetto Polirone, near Mantua, which portrays the four personified virtues as women standing in niches, crowned and bearing palm branches, and identified by inscriptions. To the left, a youth enclosed in a medallion transfixes a monster in a second medallion, while to the right are two additional medallions, one of which (next to the figure of Temperantia) contains a unicorn. Consult Porter, III, 361, on this mosaic and I, 335, on other instances of the unicorn in Lombard art. If the unicorn of San Benedetto is intended to enhance the representation of *temperantia*, it is one of the earliest datable examples of what later becomes a commonplace. An earlier instance of the unicorn with a lady, in the crypt mosaic in San Savino, Piacenza (dated in the late eleventh or early twelfth century by Porter, III, 274; see Plate 186.8) need not be connected with *castitas* or *temperantia*. Katzenellenbogen, *Chartres*, 130, note 55, cites relief sculpture at Laon (ca. 1190), where the unicorn and the lady symbolize the virginity of the Blessed Mother. On the subject in general, consult Odell Shepard, *The Lore of the Unicorn* (London, 1930). See Tuve, "Virtues," II, 62–63, for the unicorn as a symbol of pride.

[55]Philo, *Legg. All.* 1. 14. 43 identified the Tigris with sophrosyne, Ambrose, *De Par.* 3., *P.L.* 14, 296 ff., the Gehon. Augustine, *De Gen. contr. Man.* 2. 10. 13–14 follows Ambrose.

[56]Yet see the west portal at Reims (Réau, I, 182) and the miniatures discussed below, in connection with *Somme le Roi*.

while a third sprawls drunkenly on the ground. It has been conjectured that the upright figure represents *temperantia*, while the other two demonstrate the results of intemperance,[57] much as in later minatures and tapestries *temperantia* is glorified by scenes showing the consequences of gluttony and insobriety at table. Frescoes at Civate represent the Rivers flowing from the feet of Christ, and several other quaternities—Evangelists, virtues, archangels—are also present.[58] On the Romanesque capitals at Vézelay and Cluny the cardinal virtues are associated, not with the Rivers, but with another familiar tetrad, the four seasons.[59]

The thirteenth-century baptismal font at Hildesheim offers one of the most elaborate examples of the combination of the Rivers and the virtues, together with the prophets and the symbols of the Evangelists. Temperantia is depicted mingling water with wine, and she alone has an inscription drawn, not from the Bible, but from a pagan text: *Omne tulit punctum, qui miscuit utile dulci* ("He has won every vote who has mingled the useful with the delightful," Horace, *Ep.* 2. 3. 343). Another inscription clarifies the relation of the Rivers to the virtues, employing in the case of Temperantia the etymological explanation proposed by Ambrose: *Temperiem Geon terrae designat hiatus* (Temperance is represented by Gehon, which means "hole in the ground"). Ambrose had observed that just as a hole absorbs offscourings and filth, so *castitas* is wont to destroy all bodily passions. In the vocabulary of Ambrose *castitas* and *temperantia* are both used to translate the Greek sophrosyne.[60]

The fusion of the theme of the *Psychomachia* with the group of virtues comprising the Platonic tetrad, the Pauline triad, and humility represents one of the most important stages in the iconography of *temperantia*. As we have seen, it is an accomplished fact on the north porch of Chartres in the thirteenth century (where, Adolf Katzenellenbogen maintains, the association of these specific virtues with the Blessed Virgin is inspired by a ser-

[57]Porter, III, 275; see Plate 183. For a different interpretation, see William L. Tronzo, *Gesta* 16 (1977) 15–26.

[58]Porter, I, 371.

[59]See Evans, *Cluniac Art*, 113–115.

[60]See *De Virginitate* 1. 17–18, ed. Cazzaniga. For the Hildesheim font consult Erwin Panofsky, *Die deutsche Plastik* (Munich, 1924) Plate 47, and pages 110 ff.

mon of Fulbert of Chartres, who died in 1028), and it is found in such twelfth-century documents as the *Hortus Deliciarum* by Herrad of Landsberg. This popular encyclopedia, written between 1159 and 1175, was designed to provide an allegorical interpretation of history from the Creation. The famous illustrated manuscript destroyed by fire at Strasbourg in 1870 contained a miniature which portrayed eight virtues and eight vices according to the convention of the *Psychomachia* as warrior-maidens. Superbia, the captain of the vices, on horseback, led seven figures clad in chain mail against a procession of armor-clad figures designated as Humilitas, Fides, Spes, Caritas, and the four cardinal virtues. Temperancia brought up the rear, carrying a vessel which she emptied into a bowl. Her sword, like that of Justicia, remained in its scabbard.[61] Such miniatures account for the continuing popularity of the *psychomachia* in the twelfth century, when it still appears with great frequency, both in church decoration and in illustrated moral treatises.

Alcuin, as we have seen (above, note 45), had already in the ninth century listed eight virtues and eight vices, of which humility and pride, respectively, were the source, but his other seven virtues were not the cardinal and theological groups. Rather, they were a set obviously derived from the *Psychomachia* and merely substituting for the Prudentian nomenclature equivalents popular in the ninth century, such as *gula* and *abstinentia* in place of *luxuria* and *sobrietas*, or *fornicatio* and *castitas* in place of Prudentius' *libido* and *pudicitia*. The grouping employed by the Abbess Herrad, while it does not entirely replace the flexible Prudentian list, nevertheless gains steadily in favor from the thirteenth century onward and ultimately sweeps the field.

Its source is the highly influential twelfth-century treatise *De*

[61]See Herrad of Landsberg, *Hortus Deliciarum (Garden of Delights)*, Commentary and Notes by A. Straub and G. Keller, ed. and trans. Aristide D. Caratzas (New Rochelle, N.Y., 1977) Plates XLIII and XLIV. Note also Plate XLVII (Luxuria driving a jeweled chariot in which ride fifteen armored and mail-clad warriors identified by the names of sister vices, including the *comites Luxuriae* of Prudentius), XLIX (Temperancia defeating Luxuria and putting her *comites* to flight), XLV (Sobrietas piercing the stomach of Gluttony). The *Hortus Deliciarum* popularized still other ways of portraying the virtues, including the ladder of virtue (Plate LVI) and the seated, enthroned virtue holding disks or medallions inscribed with the names of related qualities (Plate LII).

Fructibus Carnis et Spiritus by Pseudo-Hugh of St. Victor. Here are described the two trees, the *arbor bona* and the *arbor mala,* the one rooted in humility and the other in pride. From the *arbor bona* spring the three theological and the four cardinal virtues and from the *arbor mala* the capital sins. One of the most arresting features of Ps.-Hugh's treatment is his list of the *comites* of each virtue and vice, a literary commonplace going back to antiquity but now, in the age of monasticism, producing new associations. The *comites* of Temperantia (who includes within her sphere both Sobrietas and Pudicitia) are *discretio, morigeratio* (obedience), *taciturnitas, jejunium, sobrietas, afflictio carnis,* and *contemptus saeculi.* Those of Luxuria are *voluptas, lascivia, ignavia, petulantia, titubatio* (staggering), *blanditiae,* and *deliciae,* a group corresponding in part to the companions of Luxuria in the *Psychomachia,* but introducing some novelties as well. Ps.-Hugh's definition of *temperantia* relates it firmly to the Pauline triad, which it is the function of this virtue to guide and moderate (*ne excurrent in nimia et ne incompetenter intra suos terminos coarctentur . . . temperantia moderatur et discernit*).[62] We note here the same awareness of the relation between the fourth cardinal virtue and the principle of moderation or due measure as led Theodulf of Orleans to equip Moderatio with the twin attributes of *frenum* and *flagellum* and inspired an eleventh-century illustrator of the Codex Aureus in the Escorial to conceive of Temperantia as being *inter agnum et leonem media,* midway between lamb and lion.[63]

THE *ARBOR BONA*

The conception of the virtues and vices as growing in the form of a tree, basic to Ps.-Hugh of St. Victor's discussion in *De Fructibus,* now began to enjoy a vigorous life in both literature and art. It takes two principal forms. In one, all seven virtues are thought

[62]"So that they will not run to excess nor be improperly confined within their own boundaries, *temperantia* guides and directs them" (*P.L.* 176, 997–1006). For an illustration of the *arbor bona* in a MS of Ps.-Hugh's treatise, dating from the second quarter of the twelfth century, see Katzenellenbogen, Fig. 67. *Temperantia* is again interpreted in the context of monasticism in Hugh's treatise *De Claustro Animae* (*P.L.* 176, 1052–1053), where he advises tempering the harshness of monastic life for those who need such concessions.

[63]Katzenellenbogen, 32, note 1.

to grow on a single tree, whose root is humility. In the other, each virtue is portrayed as a separate tree growing in the Paradise of the soul. The notion of identifying virtues with trees or plants of some kind is ancient. In classical Greek literature, the luxuriance and exorbitant growth of the vices inspired the use of this metaphor in connection with *hybris* and *atê* (as in Aeschylus, *Septem* 601, *Suppliants* 106, and Sophocles, Frg. 718 Nauck), but occasionally the same idea is applied to one of the virtues, as when Democritus speaks of sophrosyne as the flower (*anthos*) of age (Frg. 294 D-K). Philo Judaeus developed in great detail the allegory of the trees of virtue, inspired by the account in Genesis of the Tree of Life and the Tree of the Knowledge of Good and Evil. The four cardinal virtues are for him four trees in the Garden of Eden. St. Paul contributed to the spread of the metaphor with *Gal.* 5. 22 on the fruits of the Holy Spirit. Methodius in the *Symposium* (8. 3. 83) conflated Philo's Tree of Sophrosyne in Paradise with the myth of the charioteer of the soul from Plato's *Phaedrus*. Augustine often refers to the *arbor bona*, rooted in *humilitas*, and the *arbor mala*, rooted in *superbia*;[64] his influence, above all, is

[64]For example, *P.L.* 44, 370, 461, 667, 668, 672, 754, and *P.L.* 45, 1454-1458. For Philo see *Legg. All.* 1. 14. 43-45, 1. 17. 56-58. On the popularity of the concept of trees of virtue and vice in the twelfth century, see Saxl, *art. cit.*, 107-115, and on its origins, development, and influence, consult E. S. Greenhill, *Traditio* 10 (1954) 323-371. The metaphor is developed at length by Lambertus in the *Liber Floridus*, an illustrated MS of which in Ghent (ca. 1120) portrays the virtues as fruits of the *arbor bona*, whose root, in this instance, is not *humilitas* but *caritas*. Various plants and shrubs spring from the virtue medallions: from *continentia* sprouts a rose, from *castitas* the olive, from *sobrietas* the fir, from *modestia* the balsam (see Katzenellenbogen, Fig. 64, and consult pages 63-68 for evidence concerning the contrasted trees in the twelfth century). Mâle, II, 108, discusses the elaboration of this theme in *Somme le Roi* (1279): seven trees (the virtues), seven springs (the gifts of the Holy Spirit), seven maidens (the petitions of the Lord's Prayer). See also Tuve, *Allegorical Imagery*, 79-118, and "Virtues," II, note 93. Molsdorf, No. 1054 (p. 211) cites a comparison between virtues and plants on a reliquary of the thirteenth century, now in the museum of Darmstadt (inspired by *Ecclesiasticus* 24. 17-23); Temperantia is equated with the vine and is accompanied by the explanatory sentence, *Ego quasi vitis fructicavi suavitatis odorem* ("I, like the vine, have brought forth an odor of sweetness," *Ecclus.* 24. 23). See Katzenellenbogen, 68, note 2. A late and very elaborate version of the virtue-tree motive is described by Saxl (*art. cit.*, p. 109): in the Casanatensis MS of the fifteenth century, which has over twenty allegorical trees, the cardinal virtues are four columns supporting the Tower of Wisdom (see above, on the imagery used in the *Shepherd of Hermas*).

responsible for the popularity of the motive. From the wealth of examples, I shall select two dating from the twelfth century or the early years of the thirteenth: an illustrated manuscript of the *Speculum Virginum* and the relief sculpture on the Baptistery at Parma, both of which conflate the iconography of the *arbor bona* with still other methods of representing the virtues known to the twelfth century.

The *Speculum Virginum,* attributed to Conrad of Hirzau (1070–ca. 1150), exists in a number of manuscripts, one of which, MS 72 of the Walters Art Gallery, dating from the first half of the thirteenth century, combines in its illustrations many elements of the allegorical universe of the Middle Ages.[65] Relevant to our study is the page (fol. 12^r) that shows Paradise under a mystical form (Plate V). The Rivers of Paradise appear as male, horned figures, each one touching two medallions in which are pictured a Doctor of the Church and the symbol of an Evangelist. From the center of the picture rise four trees, at the summit of each a cardinal virtue, depicted as a young woman. Temperantia (between Jerome and the ox which symbolizes Luke) empties water from a vase into a bowl of wine. Eight virgins, two standing at the foot of each tree, represent the eight Beatitudes according to Matthew, which, with the four cardinal virtues, constitute the *ratio spiritualis disciplinae.* Other illustrations in the same manuscript show the Tree of Vice, bearing seven groups of sins, rooted in *superbia* and identified as *fructus carnis* (fol. 25^v), and the Tree of Virtue, also with seven major groups of offspring, rooted in *humilitas* and labeled *fructus spiritus* (fol. 26^r). Missing from the Walters MS, but present in Arundel 44 of the British Library, is an illustration of the Tree of Jesse, which is used as a means of depicting and relating all the essential elements in the treatise. The quaternities of Radulphus Glaber have now been replaced by septenaries. At the top of the Tree seven reeds (rising from the head of Christ) lead to seven heart-shaped leaves containing the names of the Seven Gifts of

---

[65]For a study of the iconography of this MS consult Arthur Watson, *Journal of the Walters Art Gallery* 10 (1947) 61–74. The Arundel MS 44 of the same treatise in the British Library is discussed by Watson in *Speculum* 3 (1928) 445–469. See also M. Bernards, *Speculum Virginum* (Cologne, 1955), and Greenhill, *art. cit.* (above, note 64).

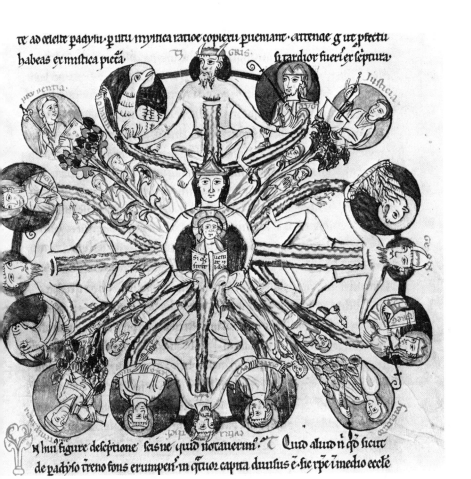

Plate V. Paradise under a mystical form, illustration from *Speculum Virginum* by Conrad ...irzau (first half of thirteenth century). Walters Art Gallery, Baltimore, MS 72, fol. 12ʳ.

the Holy Spirit and adjectives describing qualities related to each. Above these leaves and touching them are seven others, which contain greatly abbreviated references to seven of the eight Beatitudes according to Matthew, seven petitions of the Lord's Prayer, seven *Voces Domini* (Ps. 28), seven Triumphal crowns from Apoc. 2 and 3, seven articles of the Creed, seven sources of divine guidance, and seven virtues, the cardinal and theological. (Humility, the root of the *arbor bona* in the illustration of that metaphor, has to be omitted here—like the eighth Beatitude—because of the septenary scheme.)

The sixth pair of leaves contains the texts and allusions related to *temperantia*. The lower leaf refers to the *Spiritus Pietatis* and describes it as *Suavis* and *Benignus*. The upper leaf refers, in the first column, to *Et ne nos inducas* from the Lord's Prayer, then has the words *Beati mites* ("Blessed are the meek," Matt. 5:5), *Vox domini in magnificentia* (Ps. 28:4), and *Qui vicerit dabo ei sedere mecum in throno* ("To him that shall overcome, I will give to sit with me on my throne," Apoc. 3:21). In the second column are the words *Ascensio, Prophecie, Temperancia.* It would be futile to seek cogent reasons for each of these correlations. Given the desire to put together Beatitudes, Petitions, Gifts, and other septenaries, the author and illustrator were bound to execute the concept as best they could and with varying degrees of appropriateness. The Beatitude "Blessed are the meek" is not the one most often identified with sophrosyne/*temperantia,* but the correlation had been made long since by Gregory of Nyssa and is not intrinsically improbable.[66]

[66]Gregory of Nyssa, *De Beat., P.G.* 44, 1213 ff. "Blessed are the poor" and "Blessed are the poor in spirit" are related to *temperantia* by Ambrose, *Ex. in Luc.* 5. 64; "Blessed are the clean of heart" is linked with sophrosyne by John Chrysostom (*Hom. XV in Matt.*); "Blessed are they that hunger and thirst after justice" by Gregory of Nyssa, *De Beat., P.G.* 44, 1241. The mosaics of the cupola of the Ascension in St. Mark's, Venice (ca. 1200) portray a cycle of sixteen virtues, Pauline, cardinal, and Humility, plus Benignitas, Compunctio, Abstinentia, Misericordia, Patientia, Castitas, Modestia, and Constantia, many of them holding cartels that refer to the Beatitudes. Modestia carries a scroll that reads *Beati eritis vos cum oderint homines,* Castitas one with the legend *Beati mundo corde quoniam ipsi Dominum videbunt.* Temperantia has no legend, but is identified by her action of pouring from one vessel into another. The same cycle, with one additional figure (modeled after the Parma virtues, see below) is repeated on the archivolt of the second arch of the main portal (ca. 1230). Consult Otto Demus, *The Church of San Marco in Venice* (Washington, D.C., 1960) 157-161.

The Parma reliefs by Benedetto Antelami and his school (ca. 1196–1216) are four in number, two flanking the north portal of the Baptistery and two the west. Each shows a personified virtue, represented as a seated woman wearing a crown, who holds in either hand a flower from which grows a bust representing a related virtue. The four primary virtues are the Pauline triad, Spes, Fides, and Caritas, plus Castitas. Spes gives rise to Prudentia and Modestia, Fides to Justitia and Pax, Caritas to Pietas and Liberalitas, while from Castitas grow the daughter virtues of Patientia and Humilitas.[67] Only the motive of the growth of one virtue from another, like a plant of some kind, recalls the Pseudo-Hugonian system. The number of virtues (twelve) differs from his eight; the Parma group omits two of the cardinal virtues (*temperantia* and *fortitudo*) and substitutes for *temperantia castitas*,[68] which it puts on a par with the theological virtues, but the most striking disparity between Antelami's system and Ps.-Hugh's is the position of humility. Instead of being the root of all virtue, as in *De Fructibus*, it is now an offshoot of *castitas*. On the tabernacle of Or San Michele in Florence (1359) humility is subordinated to *temperantia*, but in that case the program is derived from St. Thomas Aquinas.

Iconographically, the Parma reliefs, as has been demonstrated by Geza de Francovich, belong to a type widespread in the eleventh and twelfth centuries, surviving both in manuscript illustrations

[67] Inscriptions identify the virtues concerned. For Castitas and her blossoms we read, *Ponitu[r in] medio virtus que casta [tuet]u', Cuius ad ornatū residet pacientia dextra Et facies humilē cognoscitur altera leva* (Porter, III, 146): "Placed in the middle is the virtue that guards chastity, for whose adornment patience sits on the right hand, and a humble aspect is recognized on the other, the left." See also Katzenellenbogen, 64, note 3. On the work of Antelami, consult Geza de Francovich, *Benedetto Antelami* (Florence, 1952).

[68] The appearance of *castitas* instead of *temperantia*, in a group of twelve virtues placed near the entrance to a church or baptistery, is, of course, reminiscent of the thirteenth-century reliefs on the portals of Notre Dame, Amiens, and Chartres. The Parma virtues are so similar to the twelve of the French cathedrals that Francovich (225) has suggested a common source, stemming from the Ile de France. There are, however, notable differences in iconography. The French virtues, for instance, hold disks, whose devices identify them, and there is no attempt to indicate the derivation of any of the virtues from any of the others. The French groups consist of the three theological virtues, chastity, and eight others; they include fortitude and omit justice, while the Parma group includes justice but omits fortitude. The Parma group, moreover, has no cycle of opposing vices.

and in a series of bronze liturgical basins found chiefly in northern and eastern Europe.[69] In this type a seated personification of a virtue or other abstraction (such as Philosophy or the Church) holds in each hand a disk or medallion, which contains either the name or the picture of a related entity. Antelami changes the disk to a flower, thus grafting this iconography onto the *arbor* motive of Ps.-Hugh and his imitators. The Walters manuscript of the *Speculum Virginum* employs both motives in its portrayal of the Rivers and Trees of Paradise, without, however, assimilating one to the other. Still a third mode of combining the two, yet without the evolution of disks into flowers, may be seen on the twelfth-century façade of the Romanesque church of San Pietro in Toscania (near Viterbo). Here two symmetrical vines arise on the left side (above a supporting figure of Etruscan origin); they entwine a series of medallions enclosing busts of the virtues, four in number, and two angels. The Mystic Lamb is placed among the leaves at the top. On the right is a corresponding pair of vines rooted in a three-headed Satan and containing symbols of the vices.[70]

GERMANIC ICONOGRAPHY

During the eleventh and twelfth centuries, when the attributes of the other three cardinal virtues were firmly established, those of *temperantia* continued to fluctuate, doubtless because the scope of this virtue was more difficult to define.[71] Temperantia is sometimes shown with a spray of flowers or a branch of palm, attrib-

---

[69]De Francovich, 225, cites as particularly close to the Parma type a Vienna miniature (Cod. vindob. 1367, fol. 921) of the mid-twelfth century, which shows a seated Caritas holding two medallions with busts of Fides and Spes. He also cites (471, note 23) the Arundel MS of the *Speculum Virginum* and (225, cf. p. 151, Fig. xxxvi) a miniature in the Reims Bible of St. Thierry (Philosophia and the liberal arts). Consult also M. Th. D'Alverny, *Mélanges dédiés à la mémoire de Félix Grat* (Paris, 1946) I, 264–265, table II. For the bronze basins see G. Swarzenski, *Bulletin of the Museum of Fine Arts* (Boston) 47 (1949) 74–76. Other attempts to account for the Parma iconography (as being inspired by Ps.-Hugh of St. Victor, or as reflecting the influence of the *Hortus Deliciarum*) are rejected by de Francovich, 224.

[70]See Hans Decker, *Romanesque Art in Italy*, trans. James Cleugh (New York, 1959) Plate 103, and consult page 59.

[71]See Katzenellenbogen, 55–56 and Figs. 33, 34, 37, 39. Even greater diversity existed in succeeding centuries. For some highly unusual attributes, see Appendix.

utes that could as well belong to any of the other members of the tetrad. The mixing of water with wine becomes a common clue to her identity; the bridle is extremely rare, and the hourglass has yet to make its debut. In the thirteenth century, as we have noted, the motive of the enthroned, crowned virtues, triumphant over the vices, prevails in French cathedral decoration, especially around the portals. Relatively few examples of this mode of representing the virtues occur in Germany or Italy, although there are some notable Italian cycles of the virtues, such as those on the Campanile at Florence, which, while lacking the scenes of vice in action, nevertheless owe something to the example of the French cathedral portals. In Germanic lands two developments occurred from the tenth century to the thirteenth that are rare in other countries: the association of certain virtues belonging to the sphere of *temperantia* with the Blessed Virgin and the portrayal of the cardinal virtues holding the instruments of the Passion of Christ.

The first of these types of iconography may be seen as early as the *Golden Book* of the Gospels of Echternach (983–991), in which the virtues of the Blessed Virgin are Virginitas, Sobrietas, Continentia, and Castitas. Each personification holds an identifying scroll; they have no distinctive attributes. Early in the eleventh century the Bible of Uta von Regensburg, Abbess of Niedermunster, shows the Blessed Virgin surrounded by eight women representing her virtues.[72] A series of eight personifications also surrounds the Virgin in a painting (ca. 1260) on the east wall of the Nuns' Choir at Gurk (Carinthia): Mary, enthroned as the *Sedes Sapientiae*, is flanked by Caritas and Castitas, and ranged with them are Solitudo, Verecundia, Prudentia, Virginitas, Humilitas, and Oboedientia, equipped with cartels giving the name of each virtue.[73] It is clear from other occurrences of this iconographical pattern that the virtues are linked with phrases from the story of the Annunciation in Luke. The same group in the cycle of the Liebfraukirche at Nuremberg carry scrolls identifying the allusions: thus Verecundia or Pudicitia refers to Luke 1:29 (*Turbata*

[72]See Hans Jantzen, *Ottonische Kunst* (Munich, 1947) Plate 94, p. 90.
[73]See Otto Demus, *Romanesque Mural Painting* (London, 1970) Plate 298, p. 39.

est in sermone eius) and Virginitas to Luke 1:34 (*Virum non cognosco*).[74]

In the Cathedral at Trier a ceiling painting shows figures representing the virtues holding the instruments of the Passion. Temperantia has the sponge and the spear, in an obvious allusion to the thirst of our Lord. The conception of the virtues of Christ, which He demonstrated through His passion and death, as being responsible in some sense for that death, develops from a sermon by St. Bernard in which he cites the charity, obedience, patience, and humility of the Crucified. A thirteenth-century German manuscript of the sermon shows these virtues personified and effecting the crucifixion.[75] Other virtues were added in later representations of the scene, and it was inevitable that the cardinal virtues should be given a share, although it was noted by at least one commentator that justice had no place on Calvary.[76]

THE VIRTUES IN FOURTEENTH-CENTURY FRANCE AND ITALY

In the fourteenth century the full effect of the thirteenth-century moral treatises makes itself felt in the iconography of the virtues. The combination of the cardinal and theological virtues into a set of seven, or, with the addition of humility, into eight, now becomes conventional. Doctrinally, the scheme of seven virtues received strong support from Vincent of Beauvais and St.

[74]See Künstle, 165–166, and Schiller, I, Figs. 47, 48. The Cistercian cloister of Bebenhausen, near Tübingen, used the same motive in a painting of 1334. The Virgin is enthroned, and below her throne is that of Solomon. Beside her are Misericordia and Veritas, and in niches stand the same six personifications as at Gurk, again identified by scrolls (Künstle, Fig. 44). On the middle portal of the west façade of the Cathedral of Strasbourg the same six virtues are again associated with the throne of Solomon. In an entirely different tradition we find seven virtues (cardinal and theological) linked with the Blessed Virgin in the City Hall of San Miniato al Tedesco (Tuscany); here the implications are political (Van Marle, II, 24).

[75]See Katzenellenbogen, 38–39, with Fig. 40, and Schiller, II, 137–140, on the literary sources of this iconography and its popularity in German convents in the thirteenth and fourteenth centuries, and for its development consult Saxl, *art. cit.* (above, note 64), 105. The fifteenth-century Casanatensis MS which he describes includes a picture of seven virtues crucifying Christ: St. Bernard's four, plus Faith, Hope, and Misericordia.

[76]Saxl, ibid., 106.

Thomas Aquinas, in the *Speculum Morale* and the *Summa* (*Secunda Secundae*), respectively, as well as from the Pseudo-Hugonian *De Fructibus* mentioned above. For iconography several works proved influential: two moral treatises, *Somme le Roi* (written in 1279 for Philip the Bold by his confessor, the Dominican Frère Laurent) and its direct descendant, *Le miruour du monde*, which appeared a century later, and two breviaries, the famous Belleville Breviary and the Breviary of Charles V,[77] both of the fourteenth century.

Illustrated versions of *Somme le Roi* depict Castitas and Luxuria side by side, and on another page, in a different context, Temperantia. Castitas is personified as a woman wearing a crown, holding a dove, and standing on a pig,[78] Luxuria as a woman holding a chain and a mysterious *chemise blanche*.[79] Underneath are two dramatic scenes (as on the cathedral portals), taken now, however, from the Old Testament rather than from daily life. The episode illustrating the effects of Chastity is the decapitation of Holophernes by Judith, whose literary association with the virtues of *pudicitia, sobrietas,* and *temperantia* goes back, as we have noted, to Ambrose,[80] and who now embarks on a long artistic career as the representative of these virtues.[81] Beside this scene

[77]On the sources of *Somme le Roi* (including the *Summa de vitiis et virtutibus* by Peraldus, a work of the second quarter of the thirteenth century), the reasons for its enormous popularity and translation into the vernaculars, and the representation of the virtues and vices in this and related books, see Tuve, *Allegorical Imagery*, 57–143. The relation between *Somme le Roi* and the *Miruour du Monde* and the influence of their iconographical tradition on the Belleville Breviary are discussed by Frances Godwin, *Speculum* 26 (1951) 609–614. For the Breviary of Charles V, see Mâle, III, 309.

[78]Martin, *op. cit.* (note 41 above) Plate 2 (opposite page 20).

[79]On Luxuria and her atrributes, see Tuve, "Virtues," II, 38. For the identification of the chemise as the "soul coat" or white garment of Scripture, see Ellen Kosmer, *Art Bulletin* 57 (1975) 1–8.

[80]See, for example, *De Hel.* 9. 29: *servavit pudicitiam, victoriam reciperavit.* Cf. *De Vid.* 7. 40, where Judith represents what are for Ambrose the two primary facets of *temperantia—sobrietas* and *castitas*.

[81]An earlier example of the use of Judith to suggest *temperantia* may be that in a Romanesque mosaic at Vercelli; see note 28 above. Although Philo and the Patristic writers find many examples of sophrosyne/*temperantia* in the Old Testament, iconography tends to confine itself to a few extremely familiar and easily interpreted groups: Judith slaying Holophernes (consult Réau, II, 1, 329–335), Susanna and the Elders (Réau, II, 1, 393–398), and Joseph and Potiphar's wife (Réau, II, 1, 163–165). An exception is the story of Tobit and Anna in the Vienna tapestry by

(underneath Luxuria) is a picture of Joseph and Potiphar's wife. Temperantia is grouped with the three other cardinal virtues on a single page—entirely separate from the portrayal of Castitas— and is shown as a woman seated with another woman at a table, beneath which kneels a beggar. The *Miruour du monde* of 1373 (Paris, Bib. nat. franç. 14939) offers advice to the illustrator on the best way to portray the virtues and for Atrempance (Temperantia) describes this very scene.

In the Breviary of Belleville (Paris, Bib. nat. ms. lat. 10483-4), dating from the first half of the fourteenth century, the two scenes (Judith and Holophernes, illustrating *luxuria* conquered by *castitas,* and the two women at table, demonstrating *temperantia* in action) are combined in a novel way. The Breviary contains marginal scenes illustrating the Psalter, composed in each case of a central picture representing one of the Sacraments, at the right a personified virtue, at the left a picture of the consequences of the opposed vice.[82] Since there are seven Sacraments, there are also seven virtues and seven vices. Temperantia is linked with the sacrament of marriage, which is represented by a picture of a couple standing before a church door; a monk leans down from the roof and points to a dove hovering between them. The bridegroom holds a scroll with the words *In timore Domini esto tota die.* At the right two women, one with crown and halo, sit at table. The one with the crown, obviously Temperantia herself, says to the other, *Estote sobrii et vigilate* (Peter 5:8).[83] At the left is the scene in which Judith prepares to decapitate Holophernes, lying in drunken slumber in his tent. The page is notable for two reasons: first, the artist has selected iconographical details known for at least a century in manuscripts of *Somme le Roi* and recombined

---

Bernard van Orley (Réau, II, 1, 322-323), but this is one part of an entire cycle devoted to the story of Tobit and Tobias. The episode of the blind Tobit and his wife Anna with the goat (*Tob.* 2. 11-14) is linked in the tapestry with *temperantia.* Katzenellenbogen, 57, describes two Ratisbon miniatures of 1165 which contrast virtues and vices, each personification accompanied by a representative scene from the Old Testament: Sobrietas, shown with the ascent of Elijah, is contrasted to Voluptas, shown with the death of Ahab and of Jezebel (Figs. 54, 55).

[82]See Godwin, *art. cit.* (above, note 28), Plate opposite page 609.

[83]This verse had been applied to Judith by Rabanus Maurus in the ninth century (*P.L.* 109, 539-559); see Godwin, *art. cit.,* 611.

them in such a way that the Judith scene is now connected with *temperantia,* rather than *castitas,* and the identification of the two virtues is thereby established; secondly, this is a very early example of the association of the seven virtues with the seven Sacraments, according to the system devised by St. Thomas in *De Sacramentis.* The famous correlation of the virtues and the Sacraments on the Campanile in Florence belongs to a slightly later date (1330–1340).[84]

The French virtue cycles of the thirteenth century are often reflected in Italian art of the fourteenth, which employs either the system of seven (or eight) virtues to which St. Thomas and Vincent of Beauvais had lent their authority or the fourfold system of antiquity, rarely the looser and more flexible *Psychomachia* group. After the Romanesque period, the most influential complete Italian cycle of the virtues is Giotto's series in the Arena Chapel in Padua (1306), which corresponds to the abbreviated version of the French cathedrals, as found on the north porch at Chartres. Among his eight virtues and eight vices Giotto portrays Temperantia with a bridle in her mouth and a sword sheathed in its scabbard—symbols of restraint whose meaning is amplified by the choice of an opposing vice—not Luxuria (as in the *Psychomachia* tradition) but Ira (Wrath), shown, as at Chartres, rending her garments in impotent fury. The opposition between *temperantia* and *ira* (or *furor*) in literature reaches far back into antiquity,[85] and, as we have seen, the bridle is a symbol of this virtue in art as early as the Carolingian period, if Theodulf's poem describes an actual picture, while the sheathed sword appears in a picture of Temperantia in a manuscript of the *Hortus Deliciarum* dating from the twelfth century. Giotto is the first to

[84]Godwin, *art. cit.,* 612. The absolute priority of the Belleville Breviary is disputed by Tuve, "Virtues," pointing to Simon Hinton's manual *Ad instructionem iuniorum* (ca. 1250), which correlates many groups of "Sevens" including the virtues and the sacraments.

[85]See, for example, *Aen.* 1. 57 (Aeolus *temperat iras*) and note 96 below. Sophrosyne opposes *orgê* (or *thymos*) in Greek literature; see North, 61, 64, 114. Furor tears open her coat of mail in the *Psychomachia* illustrations of the *Hortus Deliciarum,* Plate LI (above, note 61). For the symbolism of the sword, cf. Seneca, *De Clementia* 1. 1. 3; *conditum, immo constrictum, apud me ferrum est.* Spenser gives Mercilla a rusty sword (*F.Q.* 5. 9. 30) as an emblem of clemency.

combine the two attributes, of which the second, the sheathed sword, became a particular favorite in Florentine iconography in the fourteenth and early fifteenth centuries. Andrea Pisano's bronze door for the Baptistery provides the most conspicuous example (Plate VI).[86]

Giotto and his school are also influential in quite a different sector of the iconography of *temperantia*, that which includes the representation of *castitas*. From the beginning of the Christian era this facet of sophrosyne had been disproportionately exalted, and its presence among the three monastic vows (poverty, chastity, and obedience) gave it additional prestige. These vows became a popular theme in art with the spread of Franciscan spirituality and the illustration of the *Fioretti* of St. Francis. Probably the most famous portrayal of the personified Castitas is the allegory on the ceiling of the Lower Church in Assisi, by followers of Giotto (1320–1325), which shows Chastity in her tower, being presented with a crown and a branch of palm by angels, while the demonic Amor is driven away. Munditia (Purity) and Fortitudo are associated with Castitas by having their names inscribed beneath the window at which she sits. The other allegories on the ceiling represent Poverty and Obedience, both of whom also appear with Chastity in Sassetta's painting (ca. 1440–1444) of the Mystical Marriage of St. Francis and its companion piece, St. Francis in Ecstasy, which shows the saint triumphing over personified vices (Luxuria, Avaritia, Superbia), each accompanied by a symbolic animal. In the second of these paintings, Castitas, above the head of the saint, holds a spray of lilies; beneath his feet Luxuria admires herself in a mirror while reclining on a pig (see Plate II).[87]

[86]Andrea da Firenze's painting in the Chapel of the Spaniards, Sta. Maria Novella, and the Pazzi monument on the north porch of Sta. Croce also equip Temperantia with a sheathed sword.

[87]Both paintings were commissioned by the Church of San Francesco, Borgo San Sepolcro. For the *Mystical Marriage*, now in the Musée Condé, Chantilly, see Bernhard Berenson, *A Sienese Painter of the Franciscan Legend* (London, 1910) Frontispiece, and John Pope-Hennessy, *Sassetta* (London, 1939) Plate XXI. The triumph of St. Francis over the vices opposed to the Franciscan virtues constitutes a minor, but significant, theme in the history of sophrosyne and its Latin counterparts. Taddeo di Bartolo's altarpiece (1403) in the Umbrian Gallery at Perugia shows the saint trampling on figures representing Superbia, Luxuria, and Avaritia. Millard Meiss, *Painting in Florence after the Black Death* (Princeton, 1951) 51,

Plate VI. Temperance with sheathed sword by Andrea Pisano, detail of bronze south r of Florentine Baptistery (1333). Alinari/Editorial Photocolor Archives.

Even before the opening of the fourteenth century, Italian sculptors, notably the Pisani and their assistants, had begun to popularize cycles of the virtues, using diverse and original attributes and attitudes. In 1259–1260 Nicola Pisano adorned the hexagonal pulpit in the Baptistery at Pisa with six figures usually considered virtues, but variously identified because the iconography is so unconventional. Thus Temperance has sometimes been recognized in a hooded, barefoot figure (also identified as Humility), while Chastity has been seen in the guise of John the Baptist. It has lately been suggested that the figures are not virtues at all, but prototypes from the Old Testament and the New.[88] More securely identified are the eight personifications carved by the same sculptor on the octagonal pulpit in the Duomo in Siena (1268), since they have stronger affinities to well-established virtue types. Five show the influence of the French Gothic virtues, in being seated figures. The other three (including the Temperantia) stand, most of them holding scrolls; the attribute of Temperantia is far from usual, if it is properly identified as an incense boat.[89] But Giovanni Pisano's pulpit in the Duomo in Pisa (1310), which includes the four cardinal virtues, as well as the three theological, represents the most astounding break with the

note 154, suggests that Giovanni del Biondo's panel of St. John the Evangelist in the Uffizi may be the source of this iconography. Here the Evangelist (seated) has at his feet Superbia, an armed and helmeted soldier, Avaritia, a woman clutching a full moneybag, and Luxuria, a woman with an elaborate headdress, who reclines and looks into a mirror, in the immemorial attitude of Romanesque and Gothic figures of Luxuria (see Meiss, Figs. 69, 71). The same iconography appears in Sassetta's panel *St. Francis in Ecstasy*, now in I Tatti. Luxuria, again a young wanton, reclines on a pig. Superbia, portrayed as Alexander the Great in golden armor, is associated with a lion, and Avaritia, an old woman dressed as in Biondo's picture, but with an elaborate press in which she clamps shut the mouth of the moneybag, sits next to a wolf. The virtues, above the head of St. Francis, are (in addition to Chastity) Obedience with a yoke on her shoulders and her hands crossed on her breast, and Poverty, whose garment is patched. They recall the two virtues, Humilitas and Caritas, who hold back the drapery behind St. Zenobius, at whose feet are Superbia and Crudelitas, in still another work of Giovanni del Biondo in the Duomo of Florence (Meiss, Fig. 70).

[88]See Eloise M. Angiola, *Art Bulletin* 59 (1977) 1–27. For earlier views, identifying the figures with various virtues, see Pope-Hennessy, I, 176, and G. H. and E. R. Crichton, *Nicola Pisano and the Revival of Sculpture in Italy* (Cambridge, Eng., 1938) 60–61.

[89]See Enzo Carli, *Il Pulpito di Siena* (Bergamo, 1943) Plate 14, and pp. 22–23.

mediaeval iconography of Temperance. She now takes the form of a nude Venus Pudica, like the Medici Venus in the Uffizi, but gazing up toward Heaven (a change of attitude that effectively transforms the impression she makes on the viewer); she is the forerunner of a type that was much later to produce such graceful and seminude Temperantiae as those of the Chiaves tomb in the Lateran and the Sigismondo chapel in the Malatesta temple in Rimini, both in the middle of the fifteenth century.[90]

[90]For the Temperantia of the Pisa Duomo (without the veiling modestly imposed upon her in many pictures, such as Van Marle, II, Frontispiece, where the statue is misnamed Prudentia) see Adolfo Venturi, *Giovanni Pisano: La vita e l'opera* (Bologna, 1928) Plates 101–102. Pope-Hennessy, I, Plate 19, also identifies this statue as Prudentia, but cf. his text, page 12, and see Panofsky, *Studies*, 156–157 and note 97, and Kenneth Clark, *The Nude* (London, 1956) 89, who terms this statue "one of the most surprising false alarms in art-history . . . a complete anachronism." Giovanni Pisano's holy-water font in S. Giovanni Fuorcivitas, Pistoia, is so designed that the three Pauline virtues form a column supporting the basin, around which are arranged busts of the cardinal virtues, looking like figureheads on a ship: Temperantia holds a vessel; see Venturi, *op. cit.*, Plates 9–12. Still another iconographic type is represented by the Temperantia from the tomb of Margaret of Luxembourg, formerly in Genoa, only fragments of which now exist. This Temperantia (whose head is in a Swiss private collection) laid a finger to her lips. Consult Michael Ayrton, *Giovanni Pisano Sculptor* (London, 1969) 191, for the derivation of this gesture from the Epistle of St. James, ch. 3, where it refers to *mansuetudo,* a virtue subsumed under temperance by St. Thomas, and see Plate 189 for the head. On the significance of the gesture with the finger to the lips, in antiquity and thereafter, see note 101, below.

The Venus Pudica type is one of two modes of representing Venus that proved useful to iconographers of *temperantia* in the Renaissance. The other is the "Venus overthrown" type, employed in the *Triumph of Chastity,* in the Petrarchan series. She sometimes lies in the path of the triumphal chariot of Pudicitia (see Van Marle, II, Fig. 146, from a sixteenth-century tapestry). Comparable is the use of Eros (Cupid, Amor) in an attitude of defeat (fettered, or with broken bow), as in the *Trionfi* series or the paintings by Lorenzo Lotto and Luca Signorelli referred to in note 31 above. More limited in its usefulness is the Phidian type of Aphrodite with a tortoise, converted into an emblem of chastity. See note 12 above. In Greek antiquity the divine beings closely linked with sophrosyne in its various aspects were Apollo, Artemis, and Athena (see Chapter 1). In Rome, Apollo and Diana still represent more or less what they had in Greece, but Minerva is no longer so closely linked with sophrosyne/*temperantia*. Vesta, however, now becomes important. She herself does not symbolize purity (although her Greek counterpart, Hestia, is named in the *Homeric Hymn to Aphrodite* as one of the three goddesses impervious to love), but her priestesses, the Vestal Virgins, especially Tuccia, become types of *pudicitia*. In mediaeval and Renaissance iconography Apollo is of no special significance for *temperantia* or any of its aspects (except insofar as he is

Florence in the Trecento abounds in cycles of virtues, seldom accompanied by vices, but correlated, in at least some instances, with an intricate system of septenaries (replacing the quaternities of the Romanesque age). The amplest of these cycles is that on the Campanile, where the seven Sacraments, seven virtues, seven planets, seven liberal arts, and seven mechanical arts are portrayed in a great *summa* of human life. The Florentine attributes of Temperantia at this period show a refreshing variety. In addition to the sheathed sword already cited, there is the rare attribute of a compass in the hands of Temperantia on Orcagna's tabernacle in Or San Michele (1359), where, in conformity with the system of St. Thomas, she is shown with two accessory virtues, Humilitas and Virginitas. The compass is more often seen in the hands of Prudentia, among the cardinal virtues, or—in a different tradition—God the Father, but it begins to be associated with Temperantia when, in the late thirteenth century, *misura* (measure) once more becomes—as it was in antiquity—an important facet of temperance. Around this time the *Tesoretto* of the Florentine Brunetto Latini testifies that the people (*la gente*) are sometimes wont to call *Temperanza* by the name *misura*, and this tendency doubtless accounts for Orcagna's choice of attribute.[91] Although the compass never achieved great popularity as an attri-

---

the source of all four cardinal virtues, as of the liberal arts; cf. Seznec, 142–145), but Diana, Vesta, and Minerva often symbolize chastity or modesty. Chastity may be indicated by a classical Artemis/Diana, identified by her bow and arrows and short hunting dress, as well as by the new moon on her head. She often appears thus in the *Triumpn of Chastity,* as does Vesta or one of her priestesses, particularly Tuccia, identified by her sieve. See Chapter 1. Consult W. R. Valentiner, *Art Quarterly* 21 (1958) 137 and Fig. 15, for the Temperantia, perhaps inspired by a classical Diana, on the tomb of Cardinal Astorgio Agnense (ca. 1455), in the cloister of Sta. Maria sopra Minerva, Rome. For Minerva in the Triumph scene at Ferrara (Palazzo Schifanoia, 1467–1470) see note 141, below. The importance of Minerva/Pallas Athena in emblems having to do with chastity and the parallels between Britomart and Pallas in the *Faerie Queene* 5 are discussed by Jane Apteker, *Icons of Justice: Iconography and Thematic Imagery in Book V of the Faerie Queene* (New York and London, 1969) 102–103, 188–191. Various transformations of Minerva in Renaissance art are traced by Rudolf Wittkower, *J.W.C.I.* 2 (1939) 194–205. They include a Minerva Pudica which reconciles Castitas and Voluptas (pages 199–201) and another type combining Minerva with Venus (pages 202–203). For a different interpretation of some of Wittkower's examples, see Wind, 91, note 32.

[91] For the popular identification of *misura* with temperance and the consequent attribution to Temperantia of emblems of measurement, whether of space or time, and for the reference in the *Tesoretto,* see Lynn White, Jr., "The Iconography

bute of Temperance, it reappears, along with the by then conventional bridle, in a sixteenth-century Florentine statue by Giovanni Caccini, now in the Metropolitan Museum (Plate VII). Caccini's Temperantia was modeled on a bronze statue of the virtue by his teacher, Giovanni da Bologna, who in turn may have been influenced by his own teacher, Jacques Dubroeucq, sculptor of a Temperantia in the church of Ste. Waudru (Mons). Dubroeucq's Temperantia, however, has only the bridle; the compass appears to belong to a persistent Florentine tradition.

Another unusual Florentine attribute is the sickle in the hands of Temperantia in the fresco by Taddeo Gaddi on the ceiling of the Baroncelli chapel in Santa Croce (ca. 1335).[92] The more commonplace vessels for the mingling of water and wine identify Temperantia on both the Campanile (after 1336) and the Loggia dei Lanzi (1383–1391).

The cycle of virtues on the Loggia illustrates a tendency notable in the fourteenth century, especially in Italy, to display the cardinal virtues in places of civic and secular importance, as well as in a purely religious context. The political significance of the tetrad in antiquity was never entirely forgotten in later times, however radically the frame of reference might change. The Fathers had been keenly aware of the importance of the cardinal virtues for the emperor, in his official position, and in Carolingian times Alcuin directed to Charlemagne the first of many *specula principum* in which the *via regia* was paved with these virtues.[93] But it was in the

---

of *Temperantia* and the Virtuousness of Technology," in *Action and Conviction in Early Modern Europe*, ed. Theodore K. Rabb and Jerrold E. Seigel (Princeton, 1969) 204–208. For Orcagna's choice of virtues subsidiary to Temperantia from among those listed by St. Thomas in the *Summa*, 2. 2. 161, 152, 3 *ad* 2, consult A. de Surigny, *Annales archéologiques* 26 (1869) 162–165. On Caccini's Temperantia and its probable antecedents (see Plate VII), consult Olga Raggio, *Art News* 67 (1968) 45–49. The compass is included among the symbols of *Temperantia* by Barbier de Montault, *Traité d'iconographie chrétienne* (Paris, 1890) I, 215 ff., but it remains rare in this connection, except on printers' marks; consult Tervarent, *s.v. Compas.*

[92]The sickle may refer to pruning as a function of Temperance. Chew, 126–127, cites Phineas Fletcher, *The Purple Island* (ca. 1633), cantos ix–x, a *psychomachia* involving twenty-five virtues, each with a shield bearing her device, in which Temperance is symbolized by a hand from heaven pruning branches.

[93]See, for example, the funeral orations delivered by Ambrose for the Emperors Theodosius and Valentinian. In the first he emphasizes moderation in the administration of justice as the principal facet of *temperantia* (13, 14, 25, *CSEL* 73. 377

Plate VII. Temperance with bridle and compass by Giovanni Caccini (1583–1584). The Metropolitan Museum of Art, 67.208, Harris Brisbane Dick Fund, 1967.

fourteenth and fifteenth centuries that conditions in the Italian cities were ripe for the revival of the virtues as *aretai politikai,* and we find, especially in Florence, the most Athenian of the communes, many examples of their prominence in public places. Florentine instances included (in addition to the Campanile and the Loggia dei Lanzi, both of which add the theological to the cardinal virtues) Giotto's personified Commune accompanied by cardinal virtues, painted for the Great Hall of the Podestà, and the panels of the seven virtues by the Pollaiuoli and Botticelli, intended for the Mercanzia and now in the Uffizi (1469). At San Miniato al Tedesco the City Hall had a painting of the Blessed Virgin surrounded by the seven virtues (1393). In Venice the theological and cardinal virtues adorned the capitals of the columns of the Doges Palace, while the entrance through the Porta della Carta was guarded by statues of four virtues (a mixture of the two groups), by Bartolommeo Buon and Andrea Bregna, dating from the fifteenth century. Padua had the cycle designed by Miretto for the Sala Ragione (also in the fifteenth century), and in Rome the political posters of Cola di Rienzo exploited the cardinal virtues. In Perugia the late fifteenth-century paintings by Perugino in the Collegio del Cambio and the wood-carvings above the pulpit in the Collegio della Mercanzia set the cardinal virtues in a wholly secular environment. In Siena the reliefs by Jacopo della Quercia on the Fonte Gaia (1414–1419) include these virtues, which also appear on one of the benches in the Loggia della Mercanzia and in several paintings in the Palazzo Pubblico.[94] Of

---

ff.), while in the second he praises the emperor's sobriety and chastity (9, 10, 15-17, *CSEL* 73. 334-339). For the cardinal virtues in Alcuin's addresses and essays directed to rulers, consult Wallach, *op. cit.,* 230.

[94]Consult Anne Coffin Hanson, *Jacopo della Quercia's Fonte Gaia* (Oxford, 1965). Three theological virtues, four cardinal virtues, and Sapientia appeared on the original fountain (page 27). See Plate 48 for Temperantia (without attributes). In the Loggia della Mercanzia two benches, one with reliefs of the four cardinal virtues by Urbano da Cortona (1462), the other with five Roman heroes by Antonio Federighi (1464), suggest a close relation between the virtues and the state. Consult Hanson, 30. The frescoes by Taddeo di Bartolo in the antechapel of the Palazzo Pubblico (1406-1407) include representations of four virtues (Fortitudo, Prudentia, Iustitia, Magnanimitas) and a group of Roman heroes. Consult Nicolai Rubinstein, *J.W.C.I.* 21 (1958) 179-207, and Sibilla Symeonides, *Taddeo di Bartolo* (Siena, 1965) 138-153. The heroes of Magnanimitas are those often linked with

these the Frescoes of Good and Bad Government by Ambrogio
Lorenzetti constitute the most complex and original of the political cycles of virtues.

The great fresco in the Sala della Pace (1338–1339) has been
called a mediaeval *summa* in paint, a *summa* of government, which
represents the relations existing within the commune, the sources
of its authority, and the means of its operation.[95] The commune is
here personified as a male figure with the theological virtues
above his head; seated on either side of him are the four cardinal
virtues, with two additional personifications. Pax, Fortitudo, and
Prudentia are on his right, Magnitudo Animi, Temperantia, and
Iustitia on his left. In her right hand Temperantia holds an
hourglass, at which she points with her left. This is the earliest
surviving example of the emblem of time used to identify temperance, and it may, as Lynn White, Jr., points out, be a product of
the repainting of the fresco done in the later 1350s rather than
the original work two decades earlier. The opposing vices in the
corresponding Fresco of Bad Government elucidate the political
significance of the virtues. They are remote from the traditional

---

Temperantia (the two Scipios and Camillus). See Van Marle, II, 23–27, for the
civic context given to the virtues in some of the instances mentioned in our text.
Related to them are the cycles of the virtues in the great Renaissance palaces: the
inlaid wooden doorways at Urbino, the frescoes of the Colleone Palace in Bergamo, the cycle of the months in the Palazzo Schifanoia in Ferrara, the Raphael
virtues in the Stanza della Segnatura in the Vatican. Well-heads in private palaces,
like those in public piazzas, provided a favorite location for reliefs of the virtues (a
distant echo of the iconographic tradition of the Rivers of Paradise on baptismal
fonts?); for example, the well-head in the cortile of the Ca d'Oro in Venice (three
cardinal virtues, lacking Temperantia) and that in the Palazzo Morosini (Temperantia with two vessels). The Venetian tradition has continued into the present
century; the World War I memorial fountain in the Piazza Margherita is adorned
with cardinal virtues. A famous example from north of the Alps is the Renaissance
fountain of the cardinal virtues in the marketplace in Trier, by H. R. Hoffmann
(1595). Temperance by herself is a natural choice for a fountain figure; see, for
example, the Heiliggeist Brunnen in the Saalgasse, Frankfurt am Main (I am
indebted to Hilde D. Cohn for information about this fountain).

[95]George Rowley, *Ambrogio Lorenzetti* (Princeton, 1958) 99. On the significance
of the iconographical details, including the arrangement of the personifications
around the central figure, consult Rowley, 99–107 and see Plates 211 (Temperantia) and 175 (Furor). See also Rubinstein, *art. cit.* (above, note 94); consult White,
art. cit. (above, note 91), 208, on the probable date of the hourglass held by
Temperance.

vices of the Romanesque churches and the Gothic cathedrals, with their religious or personal implications. Instead they are so chosen as to emphasize the communal and civic aspects of vice: they are Guerra, Proditio, Divisio, Crudelitas, Furor, and Fraus, opposed, respectively, to Pax, Fortitudo, Providentia, Magnitudo Animi, Temperantia, and Iustitia. The choice of Furor as the antithesis to Temperantia recalls the Ira of Giotto's Arena Chapel, but Furor here is a vice of the mob, Virgil's *ignobile vulgus* (*Aen.* 1. 149), rather than of an individual. Indeed, the opposition of Furor to Temperantia is thoroughly Virgilian; we remember *impius Furor*, enchained within the temple of Janus, in *Aeneid* 1, a deliberate contrast to the three *exempla temperantiae* in nature and civil life, Aeolus, Neptune, and the Roman statesman.[96] Lorenzetti portrays Furor as a composite beast, not unlike a Centaur (a classical type of passion), but having the head of a wild boar, the torso and arms of a man, the forelegs of a horse, and the hind legs and tail of a dog. Again we are reminded of classical precedents, especially Plato's habit of likening the passions and appetites in man to unruly and sometimes hybrid beasts.[97]

TOMB SCULPTURE

A combination of the secular and the religious may also be seen in the vogue for cardinal virtues on sepulchral monuments, at first only those of churchmen, but later those of laymen as well. This development is one of the most characteristically Italian in the history of the cardinal virtues, although in fact the earliest

[96] *Aeneid* 1. 57 (Aeolus *temperat iras*) 146 (Neptune *temperat aequor*) 153 (the statesman *regit dictis animos*). *Furor arma ministrat* (150) and *fremet horridus ore cruento* (296). We note that the hybrid beast representing Furor in the Fresco of Bad Government carries a stone in one hand (cf. *Aen.* 1. 150: *faces et saxa volant*) and a knife in the other.

[97] For example, *Rep.* 588B ff., *Tim.* 70E ff., *Phaedrus* 230A. Rowley, *op. cit.*, 53, discusses the Madonna and Child in the loggia fresco of the Palazzo Pubblico, which included the cardinal virtues. See page 82 for a study of the Franciscan Martyrdom in the church of S. Francesco, Siena. The statuettes of women standing on pillars are interpreted by Rowley as personified virtues (Temperantia with two jugs, Plate 119, Castitas, a classical Diana with bow and arrow, Plate 120), but as vices by Maurice Shapiro, *Art Bulletin* 46 (1964) 367-371, who explains these two figures as Gluttony (with empty flagons and a bear at her feet) and Sloth (a Venus of the type described by Ovid, *Rem. Am.* 135-150).

recorded appearances of these virtues on tombs are not Italian at all. After the Roman sarcophagi, which employed complex and often esoteric symbolism to record the virtues of the dead, the motive of the virtues disappears from sepulchral art until the late Middle Ages. Then France in the twelfth century produced two similar tombs, that of St. Giles in St.-Gilles (Gard), destroyed in the French Revolution, and that of St. Junianus in St.-Junien (Haut Vienne). The tomb of St. Junianus (1160–1170) shows on the east end (ranged on either side of the *Maiestas Domini*) two sets of medallions containing busts of seven women; although they are without names or significant attributes, the number seven makes it tempting to identify them with the cardinal and theological virtues. These tombs were isolated examples and mark the founding of no school. Three-quarters of a century later the tomb of Pope Clement II in Bamberg (1237) was adorned with reliefs of the four cardinal virtues and showed Temperantia in the favored Carolingian attitude, pouring water into a vessel of wine.[98] Again the example is isolated and inspired no imitators. The great vogue for cardinal virtues in sepulchral sculpture blossoms in the fourteenth century, and Italy is its home. The earliest Italian example is actually from the thirteenth century, the arca of St. Dominic in Bologna (1267), made by the workshop of Nicola Pisano. It originally had the virtues as caryatids supporting the sarcophagus, an attitude comparatively rare in the north of Italy, but more common in Neapolitan tombs of the fourteenth and fifteenth centuries, where it was popularized by Tino di Camaino, the pupil of Giovanni Pisano. Presumably it was related to the virtue caryatids on such monuments by Giovanni as the font in Pistoia and the pulpit in the Duomo at Pisa.[99] When the virtues are used as caryatids on royal tombs, one is reminded of the statement by Rabanus Maurus that the virtues are columns upholding the *decus* and *honos* of the king.[100]

---

[98]See Van Marle, II, Fig. 16. Panofsky, *Tomb Sculpture*, 63, note 1, suggests that the reliefs reflect a prototype that may have been a memorial tablet similar to two twelfth-century miniatures described on page 60; see Fig. 240.

[99]Panofsky, *Tomb Sculpture*, 74. Consult Pope-Hennessy, I, 16–23, and II, 42, on Tino di Camaino and his work in Naples, and see s'Jacob, 209–211, on possible forerunners of the figures of virtues supporting monuments.

[100]*Tractatus de anima*, ch. 10 (*P.L.* 110, 1118).

The tomb of St. Peter Martyr in the church of S. Eustorgio in Milan, the work of Giovanni Balduccio (1339), also employs virtues (the usual seven, plus Obedience) as caryatids. Temperantia, crowned with ivy, performs the conventional act of mingling water with wine. More unusual are the two sphinxes on which she stands, symbols of that restraint of speech which is one of the primary aspects of *temperantia*.[101] Symbolic animals in association with personified virtues are less common in sculpture than in manuscript illuminations (where they more often symbolize the conquered vice than the victorious virtue), and they do not achieve much popularity until the time of the emblem books of the sixteenth and seventeenth centuries. The arca of St. Augustine in San Pietro nel Ciel d'Oro in Pavia, also by Balduccio or his school (1362), portrays the virtues, not as caryatids, but as statues in high relief around the sarcophagus. They include the conventional group of seven cardinal and theological virtues, augmented by Mansuetudo, Paupertas, Castitas, and Oboedientia. Again Temperantia holds the two vessels, an attribute that constitutes the almost invariable clue to her identity in Italian sepulchral sculpture of the Trecento.[102]

An exception is the Temperantia among the caryatids on the tomb of Queen Mary of Hungary, mother of Robert the Wise, by Tino di Camaino, in the church of Sta. Maria Donna Regina in

[101]Elsewhere restraint of speech may be symbolized by a bridle, especially if the bit is actually worn in the mouth. In antiquity the gesture of laying a finger to the lips might symbolize silence, or more generally restraint (consult J. M. C. Toynbee, *Essays in Roman Coinage Presented to Harold Mattingly* [Oxford, 1956] 215–216). Giovanni Pisano used this gesture to characterize Temperantia on the tomb of Margaret of Luxembourg; see note 90 above. It belongs to Patientia among the virtues of the Baptistery in Bergamo (1340), probably by Giovanni da Campione (Pietro Toesca, *Il Trecento* [Turin, 1951] Fig. 345). Beneath the virtue is a tiny figure representing the opposed vice, which resembles the Ira of Giotto in Padua (there considered the antithesis to Temperantia).

[102]In addition to those mentioned in the text, the most notable such tomb is that of Cansignorio Scaliger in Verona by Bonino da Campione (1374). See Fernanda de Maffei, *Le Arche Scaligere di Verona* (Verona, 1955) Plate 55. For photographs of the tombs of St. Peter Martyr and St. Augustine see Pope-Hennessy, I, Plate 57, Fig. 4, and Plate 58, Fig. 5. Plate 60, Fig. 77, shows the Scaliger monument. The two vessels identify Temperantia, as we have noted, in nonsepulchral sculpture of the fourteenth century also: the Florentine campanile and the Loggia dei Lanzi, the Baptistery in Bergamo, and many other monuments.

Naples (1326).[103] She holds in her left hand what has been interpreted as a struggling bird, a symbol of resistance to temptation.[104] The same attribute distinguishes Temperantia on the
tomb of Duke Charles of Calabria (son of Robert the Wise) in Sta.
Chiara in Naples, also the work of Tino (1333). Here the virtues,
not true caryatids, lean against the supporting pillars, the theological virtues crowned, the cardinal uncrowned, all of them
winged.[105]

The Neapolitan tombs are notable, as Panofsky observes,[106] for
ascribing the virtues to laymen and women, as well as to saints and
ecclesiastics. This innovation becomes a commonplace in the fifteenth century, as the Gothic gives way to the early Renaissance
style, and monuments of both religious and secular significance
employ the symbolism of the cardinal virtues, either alone or in
company with the Pauline triad, or less frequently with the liberal
arts.[107] In France the virtues are rarely associated with sepulchral
ornament in the fourteenth and fifteenth centuries, but very early
in the sixteenth are introduced by Italian artists, who brought

[103]W. R. Valentiner, *Tino di Camaino* (Paris, 1935) 104; see Plate 49c for Temperantia. A Florentine exception is the Pazzi monument by Alberto di Arnoldo on
the north porch of Santa Croce, which has the cardinal virtues as caryatids, among
which Temperantia is identified by the Giottesque sheathed sword. See Valentiner, Fig. 16.

[104]Ibid., 104.

[105]See Valentiner, Plates 60–61 and pages 125–126. For the influence that the
tomb of Charles of Calabria may have had on a mediaeval illustration of Hector's
Tomb, consult Hugo Buchthal, Meiss, 34–36.

[106]*Tomb Sculpture*, 74.

[107]Some fifteenth-century tombs that employ the cardinal virtues alone: the
ceiling of the chapel of the Cardinal of Portugal in San Miniato, Florence
(enameled terra cotta by Luca della Robbia, ca. 1466); the Chiaves monument in
St. John Lateran, Rome, by Isaia da Pisa (after 1447); the monument to Pope
Innocent VIII (died in 1492) by Pollaiuolo in St. Peter's, Rome; the tomb of Doge
Niccolò Marcello by Pietro Lombardo, Santi Giovanni e Paolo, Venice (1485–
1490); the tomb of Bishop Baglione (died 1451) by Urbano da Cortona in the
duomo, Perugia. Tombs having cardinal virtues augmented by two or three
theological virtues include the Foscari monument by Antonio Bregno in the Frari,
Venice (after 1457), the Tron monument by Antonio Rizzo in the Frari (1476–
1479); the Vendramin monument in SS. Giovanni e Paolo, Venice, by Tullio
Lombardo (1493). The cardinal virtues with the liberal arts: the tomb of King
Robert of Anjou, Sta. Chiara, Naples (1343–1345), and that of Pope Sixtus IV
(died 1484) by the Pollaiuoli, now in the Vatican Grottoes.

with them the attributes conventional in Italy, not without some initial compromise. Thus the earliest such tomb, that of Charles VIII (who died in 1498) at St.-Denis, had cardinal virtues of the Italian type, including a Temperantia with the two vessels of water and wine, but these were set among a total of twelve virtues, half-figures in circular reliefs, recalling the virtues of Notre Dame and Chartres.[108] The sculptor was Guido Mazzoni of Modena, who had worked in Naples before Charles VIII brought him to France in 1495.

Suddenly in the early sixteenth century an independent and highly original method of portraying the personified virtues appears on tombs designed by Michel Colombe and his followers. The most famous are those of Francis II of Brittany in the Cathedral of Nantes, begun in 1499, erected in 1507 (Van Marle II, Fig. 57), and the Cardinals d'Amboise in the Cathedral of Rouen by Rouland le Roux, begun in 1515 (Mâle, III, Fig. 175). In both instances Temperantia holds a clock in one hand, a bridle in the other.

The source of this iconography has generally been thought to be, in the phrase of Emil Mâle (III, 316) "quelque bel esprit de Rouen," who owed nothing to theological tradition, but was responsible for the illustrations of two fifteenth-century manuscripts, one a translation of Aristotle's *Ethics* by Nicole Oresme (1454) in the Rouen Library (Bibl. Munic. 927), the other Jehan de Courtecuisse's translation of Ps.-Seneca, *Formula Vitae Honestae,* made for the Duc de Nemours, Jacques d'Armagnac (Paris, Bib. nat. franc. 9186), and dated around 1470. In each manuscript the personified virtues are depicted, Temperantia wearing a clock on her head and holding in her mouth a bit to which are attached reins which she grasps with her left hand, while holding a pair of spectacles in her right. She wears spurs on her feet, which rest on a windmill.[109] The meaning of the attributes is

[108]Mâle, III, 323, note 1. See also Panofsky, *Tomb Sculpture,* 75 and Fig. 325, and Anthony Blunt, *Art and Architecture in France, 1500 to 1700* (London, 1953) 14.

[109]See Mâle, III, Fig. 168, for the Temperantia in the MS of the Duc de Nemours. The attributes of the other virtues include such objects as a coffin, a sieve, a mirror, and a moneybag (Prudentia), a press, an anvil, and a tower from which protrudes a dragon's head (Fortitudo). Justitia has the familiar sword and balance. Mâle, III, 313, note 2, cites explanatory verses.

explained by verses which accompany the pictures in the Paris manuscript:

> Qui a l'orloge soy regarde
> En tous ses faicts heure et temps garde,
> Qui porte le frein en sa bouche
> Chose ne dict qui a mal touche.
> Qui lunettes met a ses yeux
> Près lui regarde sen voit mieux.
> Esperons montrent que cremeur
> Font estre le josne homme meur.
> Au moulin qui le corps soutient
> Nul excès faire n'appartient.

> Who has regard for the clock
> In all his acts preserves the proper season.
> Who wears the bridle in his mouth
> Says nothing which pertains to evil.
> Who puts spectacles to his eyes
> Improves his vision of nearby things.
> Spurs show that fear
> Makes the young man mature.
> To the windmill which supports the body
> Belongs the rule of No Excess.

Recently a study of the two manuscripts cited by Mâle, in comparison with others containing moral treatises based on John of Wales's *Breviloquium de virtutibus* in different French translations, all illustrated by the "new iconography"—the Rouen iconography—and of manuscripts of Christine de Pisan's *Epître d'Othée* (written ca. 1400), which contain pictures of Temperantia adjusting a clock and attended by handmaidens representing facets of temperance (Frontispiece), led Rosemond Tuve to conclude that the new iconography originated earlier than Mâle supposed (before 1410) and not in Rouen, but more likely in the circle of the Dukes of Burgundy.[110]

---

[110]"Virtues," I, 264–289. This valuable article includes photographs of all the important miniatures showing the new iconography. For Temperantia regulating a clock in MSS of the *Epître d' Othée* see Plates 34b and c; consult page 282, note 36, for other *Othée* MSS, where the clock rests on the head of Temperantia and she is also equipped with a coffer and a pitcher, or where the Italian attribute of the two vessels prevails.

The motive of the clock as an attribute of Temperance first appears in the *Horologium Sapientiae* by the Dominican mystic, Heinrich Suso (ca. 1334), who introduces a personified Temperance equipped with a clock symbolizing order and regularity in life. To the obvious implications of the hourglass as an attribute of temperance (embodying a visual pun on the presence of *tempus* in *temperantia*), the mechanical clock, developed in the second quarter of the fourteenth century, added still more complex connotations, suggesting especially the harmony achieved when many moving parts work smoothly together. Nicole Oresme, whose translation of the *Ethics* of Aristotle for Charles V in 1370 is illustrated by the new iconography in the deluxe Rouen MS of 1454, was the first to use the metaphor according to which the universe is a vast clock created and set running by God. Christine de Pisan, whose father was physician and astrologer to Charles V, could have had the opportunity to become acquainted with the work of Oresme. It was certainly she who popularized the clock as an emblem of temperance; it appears frequently in illustrations of her *Epître d'Othée* (as it does in fifteenth-century manuscripts of Suso's *Horologium*). Christine identifies the goddess Othée as the wisdom of woman and says that Temperance should also be regarded as a goddess. "And because," she adds, "our human body is made up of many parts and should be regulated by reason, it may be represented as a clock in which there are several wheels and measures. And just as the clock is worth nothing unless it is regulated, so our human body does not work unless Temperance orders it."[111]

But there is no evidence that Christine was responsible for the other novelties in the new iconography, which, as a whole, had become available to illustrators by the middle of the fifteenth century. Lynn White, Jr., in his study of the relation between the iconography of temperance and the moral approval conferred on technology in the fourteenth and fifteenth centuries, finds it implausible that the "fantastic symbolism" of the new iconography could go back to Christine's time. The actual inventor still eludes identification. But White makes the important point that in con-

[111]See Tuve, *ibid.*, 289, and White, *art. cit.* (above, note 91), 209.

trast to the attributes of the other virtues, which are all objects familiar in antiquity, those of Temperantia (save for the bit) are recent inventions: the roweled spurs and the spectacles belong to the late thirteenth century, while the mechanical clock and the tower-mill are inventions of the fourteenth. Thus Temperantia alone is linked with progress in technology, and her status is correspondingly exalted. Through a complicated series of developments, which include the identification of temperance with measure (the supreme value of secular aristocracy in the thirteenth century), the revival of Aristotelian ethics, which identified virtue with the Mean, and the tendency to equate Temperantia with Sapientia (hence with Christ Himself) in explications of Proverbs 8:12-16, this virtue ceases to be (in White's phrase) "a wallflower at the scholastic ball" and becomes the most dynamic of all the virtues at a time when Western society was ready to acclaim the supreme importance of technological progress. Her enhanced value is revealed by the central position assigned to her amid cardinal and theological virtues in the illustration of Oresme's translation of the *Ethics* in the Rouen manuscript.[112]

The new iconography enjoyed a tremendous vogue, especially in France and the Netherlands, persisting for centuries in sepulchral sculpture, as on the sixteenth-century tomb of François de Lannoy in Folleville (Somme) (Plate VIII), but the complexity of the attributes was gradually modified by cross-fertilization with the Italian types. Thus the tomb of Francis II at Nantes, already referred to, mingles the two streams, having a Temperantia of the French type, with bridle and clock, a Fortitudo mainly French, with dragon protruding from tower, a Prudentia in the Italian style, and a Justitia which could be either, since here alone do the attributes coincide. In Spain, on the tomb of John II and Isabel of Portugal at Miraflores near Burgos (1489-1493), Temperantia herself mingles the two traditions, having a sundial on her head and a bridle around her face, but a bowl in one hand (the other hand is missing). In the first quarter of the sixteenth century the French influence is stronger; thereafter the Italian tends to pre-

[112]See White, ibid., Fig. 13, and consult especially pages 215-219 for the stages by which Temperantia over a period of two centuries becomes associated with the new technology of the later Middle Ages.

Plate VIII. Temperance with clock and bridle, detail of tomb of François de Lannoy, Folleville (Somme) (mid-sixteenth century). Photograph by the author.

dominate, as on the tomb of Louis XII at St.-Denis, designed by the Florentine Giusti brothers in 1531, where only Temperantia with a clock in her hand derives from the Rouen type. On Germain Pilon's tomb for Henri II at St.-Denis thirty years later, all four virtues are Italian. Temperantia by the position of her hands is judged to have held the two familiar vessels, but these are now lost.[113]

Of the attributes popularized by the new iconography, only the bridle and the clock retain any degree of vitality in sculpture. In painting and manuscript illumination, and even stained glass, it was easier to cope with the spectacles and the windmill, and these appear, for example, on the window of St. Romanus in the cathedral at Rouen. Bruegel's Temperance (1560) in his series of Virtues (cardinal and theological) is portrayed according to the new iconography, with clock on head, bit in mouth, reins in one hand, spectacles in the other, spur-clad foot resting on the fan of a windmill. She also wears a girdle of serpents and is surrounded by seven groups of people engaged in activities connected with the liberal arts, all of them portrayed as Children of Mercury in the astrological tradition.[114]

Both the bridle and the hourglass appear in Italian sepulchral ornament in the sixteenth century. Andrea Sansovino's Temperantia for the monument of Cardinal Girolamo Basso della Rovere in Sta. Maria del Popolo in Rome (ca. 1507) holds an hourglass, and Baldassarre Peruzzi's monument for Pope Adrian

[113]See Mâle, III, 324-325, for the tomb of Francis II and other tombs by Colombe and his school, and page 327 for the tomb of Henri II. Consult also Jean Babelon, *Germain Pilon* (Paris, 1927) Plate 14. For the Burgos tomb, see Harold E. Wethey, *Gil de Siloe and His School* (Cambridge, Mass., 1936) 34-38 and Plate 15a. The tomb of Louis XII is discussed by Panofsky, *Tomb Sculpture*, 75; see Fig. 324. Panofsky, *Titian*, 88-89, interprets the clock in the portrait of Eleonora Gonzaga in the Uffizi as a tribute to her temperance. White, *art. cit.*, 217, note 86, observes that in Holbein's portrait of the family of St. Thomas More, "a clock is placed almost directly over Sir Thomas's head, as though Temperantia were wearing her horological hat."

[114]See Ludwig Münz, *Bruegel: The Drawings, Complete Edition* (London, 1961) Plate 145, and H. Arthur Klein, *Graphic Worlds of Peter Bruegel the Elder* (New York, 1963) Plate 54; for the interpretation, consult Karl Tolnai, *Die Zeichnungen Pieter Bruegels* (Munich, 1925) 63. According to the *Dionysiaca* of Nonnus (14. 363, 15. 80, 33. 368, etc.), the Bacchae wear snakes around their waists, to protect them, even when asleep, from the lusts of men.

VI in Sta. Maria dell' Anima (ca. 1530) includes a Temperantia
with a bridle.[115] The same range of attributes occurs, of course, in
nonsepulchral statuary, reliefs, and paintings. The Temperantia
by Agostino di Duccio in the Sigismondo chapel of the Malatesta
Temple in Rimini holds two vessels, from one of which she pours
water into the other (Pope-Hennessy II, Fig. 106), while her counterpart by the same sculptor on the façade of S. Bernardino in
Perugia carries a bridle.[116] The hourglass remains the least com-

[115]For the della Rovere monument, see Pope-Hennessy, III, Fig. 58 and Plate
44. Pope-Hennessy compares this Temperantia with that of Isaia da Pisa on the
Chiaves monument in the Lateran (II, Fig. 108), suggesting that they may go back
to the same classical source (III, 55). For the tomb of Pope Adrian, see ibid. III,
Fig. 61. The virtues are rare in English sculpture. One notable example from the
early seventeenth century (1612) is the tomb of the first Earl of Salisbury in
Bishop's Hatfield, Hertfordshire, which has four kneeling virtues serving as
caryatids (Fortitude, Temperance, Truth, and Justice). Temperance pours from
one urn to another. See K. A. Esdaile, *English Monumental Sculpture since the Renaissance* (London, 1927) Plate VII, and Margaret Whinney, *Sculpture in Britain:
1530–1830* (London, 1964) Plate 13. The cardinal virtues also appear on two
English tombs by Nicholas Stone (1586–1647), pupil and son-in-law of Hendrick
de Keyser, sculptor of the tomb for William the Silent in Delft, with its four bronze
cardinal virtues, echoing those on Primaticcio's monument for Henri II in St.-
Denis. See Chew, 133, and Whinney, *op. cit.*, 25 and Plate 18A, for the Stone
monuments. The tomb of Helena Sneckenburg and her husband in Salisbury
Cathedral (1635) is adorned with cardinal virtues, among which Temperance with
bowl and jug follows the Italian tradition.

[116]Comparatively few artists who employ the symbol of the bridle or the bit insist
that Temperantia wear it in her mouth, but, as we have seen, Giotto does so in the
Arena Chapel, and so do some of the artists who adopt the new iconography. On
one of the sixteenth-century stalls of the Church of St. Bertrand de Comminges
near Lourdes is a bridled Temperantia, and in the Chapel of Pius V in the Vatican
a fresco by Iacopo Zucchi (also sixteenth century) shows Temperantia herself with
a bridle and one of her attendants gagged. A red sandstone Temperance (1695)
now in the Historischen Museum, Frankfurt am Main, formerly at the
Reineck'sche Haus, Hasengasse 4, wears a gag. The most graceful adaptation of
the motive of the bridle is that by Raphael in the Stanza della Segnatura (1509–
1511). Soon thereafter Giulio Romano gave Moderatio a bridle in the Sala di
Constantino in the Vatican (1520). It was used again for Temperantia by Caracci
in the Camerino Farnese in 1595, following Marcantonio's engraving after the
design by Raphael, and by Domenichino in the Galleria Farnese in 1607–1608
(John Rupert Martin, *The Farnese Gallery* [Princeton, 1965] 37, 128). Ripa's first
design for Temperantia includes a bridle; thereafter it becomes commonplace.
The illustrators of emblem books do not shrink from the grotesqueness of representing allegorical figures with the bit between their teeth, but they are more likely
to bridle the vices than the virtues (cf. Veronese's Virtue subduing Vice, in the
Villa Maser, Van Marle, II, Fig. 7). Consult Chew, "The Allegorical Chariot in

mon of the three symbols. Evidently the relation of Temperantia
to *temperare* made a greater impression on the minds of artists
than did her kinship with *tempus*. It is probable, moreover, that
the association of the figure of Time (or even Death) with the
hourglass discouraged artists from representing Temperantia
with this device.[117] Only in France was the clock really popular.

HISTORICAL EXEMPLARS

Two further devices in the iconography of Temperance—
historical representatives and symbolic animals—remain to be
mentioned before we consider the last of the great innovations,
the emblem books of the sixteenth century, which dominate
baroque art. It will be recalled that illustrations of *Somme le Roi*
and other books of devotion in the thirteenth century were wont
to portray the consequences of vice by showing appropriate
scenes from the Old Testament. Thus Judith decapitating
Holophernes could represent the triumph of either Castitas or
Temperantia. Now, with greater conciseness, Holophernes himself, or Epicurus, or Tarquin, stood for Luxuria, the vice most
often opposed to Temperantia. This innovation originates in Italy
before the middle of the fourteenth century.[118] In France the

English Literature of the Renaissance," Meiss, 39, and Fig. 5, for an engraving by
Johannes Galles of the Chariot of Virtue, drawn by Venus, Ceres, Cupid, and
Bacchus, all of whom have bits in their mouths. The Angel of Temperance, iden-
tified by the two vessels that she carries, hovers in the air above Virtue.

[117]For the ways of representing Time (beginning with the confusion of Chronus
and Cronus in late antiquity) consult Panofsky, *Studies*, 69–93. Death holds the
hourglass on Bernini's tomb for Pope Alexander VII in St. Peter's. Another symbol shared by Tempus and Temperantia was the compass, an attribute of Time in
the allegory of Prudence, S. Carlo ai Catinari, Rome, and of Temperantia on the
tabernacle of Or S. Michele and in Caccini's statue (note 91, above).

[118]The basic study is that by Julius von Schlosser, *Jahrbuch der künsthistorischen
Sammlungen des allerhöchsten Kaiserhauses* 17 (1896) 13–100, which discusses the
relation between the lost frescoes by Giusto Menabuoi in the Church of the Eremitani in Padua (before 1397) and two Italian MSS of the second half of the fourteenth century (now in Vienna and Florence), showing personified virtues with
exempla horribilia underfoot (Temperantia thus triumphs over Epicurus), and Liberal Arts with their historical representatives. Slightly earlier are Niccolò da
Bologna's miniature of the Virtues and the Arts from Giovanni Andrea's *Novella
super libros Decretalium* (Milan, 1354) (See Appendix) and the Chantilly MS by
Bartolommeo de' Bartoli, dated by Von Schlosser 1353–1356. The Chantilly MS
opposes Holophernes to Temperantia; see Leon Dorez, *La Canzone delle Virtù e*

earliest example seems to be the *Heures* of Simon Vostre in the late fifteenth century, where Temperantia is depicted with Tarquin underfoot (Mâle, III, Fig. 188). In this instance Holophernes is at the foot of Fortitudo (Fig. 187). Books of Hours popularized this iconography, which appears with considerable frequency in tapestries as well and is known to have adorned at least one famous tomb (since destroyed), that of Bishop Erard de la Marck of Liège (1535), on which the personified cardinal virtues were shown trampling historical representatives of the vices. Temperantia thus triumphed over the figure of Tarquin, and an inscription explained, *Temperantia Tarquinium immoderatum extinguit* ("Temperance crushes the licentious Tarquin"). A Flemish tapestry in the Madrid collection also shows Temperantia (here identified by her clock and spectacles) with Tarquin underfoot (Mâle, III, Fig. 193).

Oddly enough, the converse of this iconography (the personified virtues in the company of representative heroes) is rare, although it is common in pictures of the liberal arts and the *Triumphs* of Petrarch. As is well known and amply documented, the late Middle Ages and early Renaissance, throughout Europe, but especially in Italy, witnessed a prodigious revival of interest in the biographies of ancient heroes and heroines, both mythical and historical, an interest reflected in cycles of *uomini famosi* in palaces and public buildings. The influence of Petrarch's *De Viris Illustribus* on the Sala Virorum Illustrium of the Carrara Palace in Padua is but the best-known instance. Yet few of these pictorial cycles connected the heroes with personified virtues. Evidently the tradition of the *psychomachia* was so strong that even in iconographic patterns like that of Giusto in the Church of the Eremitani in Padua the appearance of the liberal arts with their representatives could not induce the painter to depict the virtues with

delle Scienze di Bartolomeo di Bartolo da Bologna (Bergamo, 1904). Early fifteenth-century sketches in the Stamperia in Rome employ the same theme (Van Marle, II, 16 and Fig. 12). A pageant held in Edinburgh in 1503 to celebrate the wedding of James IV included a tableau of the cardinal virtues treading on four exemplars of the vices: Temperantia on Epicurus, Fortitudo on Holophernes, Justitia on Nero, and Prudentia on Sardanapalus (Chew, 123). Sardanapalus is trampled by Temperantia in a tapestry once belonging to the Countess of Shrewsbury (1520–1607), according to M. Jourdain, *Burlington Magazine* 16 (1909–1910), 97 ff.

theirs. Instead, they trampled on figures representing the opposed vices. Among the relatively few portrayals of personified virtues with *exempla bona*,[119] rather than *horribilia*, Perugino's cycle in the Collegio del Cambio in Perugia at the end of the fifteenth century is the most elaborate. Each virtue is accompanied by three heroes (two Roman, one Greek), those with Temperantia being Scipio Africanus, Cincinnatus, and Pericles. The choice of heroes was determined by the philosopher Francesco Maturanzio, who provided the program for the cycle and supplied the explanatory verses beneath each picture.[120] Although it has been suggested that the heroes derive ultimately

[119]A very early forerunner of this motive may be found in the Bamberg Apocalypse (1001–1002), which associates Moses with purity (*munditia*), Abraham with obedience, Job with patience, David with penitence (Katzenellenbogen, 15 and Fig. 14). A few Renaissance examples: Vasari's design for the Compagnia della Calza in Venice; Francesco Pesellino's *Seven Virtues and Liberal Arts* (see Chapter 1, note 156, and Plate III), the Cassone in the Spiridon Collection, Paris, cited at the end of Chapter 1, and the painted ceiling by Girolamo Mocetto in the Musée Jacquemart-André, Paris, where Lucretia is the heroine of *Temperantia*. The frescoes of the antechapel in the Palazzo Pubblico in Siena by Taddeo di Bartolo combine personified virtues with heroes of the Roman republic (Nicolai Rubinstein, *art. cit.*, 179–207). The virtues include three of the cardinal four, but omit Temperantia, putting in her place Magnanimitas (who sits at the right hand of Temperantia in Lorenzetti's fresco next door). In certain respects Magnanimitas resembles Temperantia; for example, her motto (*Nec successibus extollitur nec infortunis deicitur/ Opus eius parcere subiectis et debellare superbos:* "She is not uplifted by success nor cast down by misfortune: Her task is to spare the conquered and fight down the proud") first recalls a passage in the *Ethics* of Aristotle about the highminded man (1123a 34 ff), but then quotes *Aeneid* 6. 853, a line often taken as an allusion to *temperantia*. The heroes linked with Magnanimitas include Scipio Africanus, a type of *temperantia* in Perugino's fresco in the Collegio del Cambio. See above, note 94.

[120]Consult Fiorenzo Canuti, *Il Perugino* (Siena, 1931) I, 138. The Temperantia inscription reads as follows:

> Dic, dea, quae tibi vis. Mores rego,
> pectoris aestus tempero et his alios
> cum volo, reddo pares.
> Me sequere; et qua te superes
> ratione docebo.
> Quid tu quod valeas
> vincere maius erit.

> Tell, goddess, what is your wish. Morals I guide,
> The heart's passions I moderate and when I wish
> I make others equal to these.
> Follow me; and I will teach you how to conquer yourself.
> What greater thing will there be which you could overcome?

from Cicero's *De Officiis,* a copy of which belonged to the communal library in Perugia, these particular exemplars do not in fact appear in Cicero's treatise. One ancient source who does name all these heroes as models for the various aspects of *temperantia* *(moderatio, abstinentia, continentia,* and *disciplina militaris)* is Valerius Maximus,[121] whose compilation of moral anecdotes in nine books not only served as the greatest storehouse of *exempla* available to the Middle Ages, but in the fourteenth century inspired equally influential imitators, of whom it is necessary to mention only Petrarch and Boccaccio.

SYMBOLIC ANIMALS

The use of symbolic animals in connection with both virtue and vice goes back, of course, to the *Physiologus* and the *Bestiary* and beyond, into pagan antiquity, but it becomes an important motive in iconography only in the fourteenth and fifteenth centuries.[122] In France, to be sure, the thirteenth-century manuscript of *Somme le Roi* referred to above already shows personified virtues standing on animals representative of vices (Castitas on a pig),[123] and the heraldic animals on the shields held by the Gothic virtues

---

[121]Lionello Venturi, *Il Perugino: Gli affreschi del Collegio del Cambio* (Turin, 1955) 101–102, discusses the *De Officiis* theory, but rejects it, suggesting that the frescoes of famous men by Ghirlandaio in the Palazzo Vecchio in Florence exercised a more powerful influence on Perugino. For the exemplars in Valerius Maximus, see, for example, *De moderatione* 4. 1. 4 (Cincinnatus), 4. 1. 6 (the Elder Scipio), 4. 1. 10 (the Younger Scipio), *De abstinentia et continentia* 4. 3. 1 (the Elder Scipio), 4. 3. 13 (the Younger Scipio); Ext. 1 (Pericles); *De disciplina militari* 2. 7. 12 (the Elder Scipio), 2. 7. 1 (the Younger Scipio), 2. 7. 7 (Cincinnatus). Cicero, *De Off.* 2. 76, praises the Younger Scipio for his *abstinentia.*

[122]In ancient literature the principal sources are Aristotle, *History of Animals,* Plutarch, *Gryllus,* Pliny the Elder, *Natural History,* Aelian, *On the Nature of Animals,* Ps.-Plutarch, *On Animals,* Solinus, *Collectanea Rerum Memorabilium.* Patristic writers dealt with this theme in connection with the Hexaemeron; they include Origen, Basil, Gregory of Nyssa, and Ambrose. Melito's *Clavis Scripturae Sacrae* was an important source for the Middle Ages, as were Isidore, *Etym.* 12, and the *Physiologus* itself. On this work and its sources consult Max Wellmann, *Philologus, Supp.* 22.1 (1930) 1–116; see also Réau, I, 138–140, and George Boas, *The Hieroglyphics of Horapollo* (New York, 1950).

[123]Mâle, III, 328 ff., traces the development of this motive and suggests likely sources in French literature. See Katzenellenbogen, 61 and notes 4 and 5, on some important forerunners of this theme: Herrad of Landsberg's chariots of Avaritia and Misericordia, drawn by symbolic animals (see Fig. 60), and a twelfth-century liturgical bowl in Xanten, which relates the Gift-Virtues to Old Testament figures and symbolic animals (consult Tuve, "Virtues," II, 61, note 96).

obviously serve as means of identification. But the principal impetus for the fourteenth-century fashion came from a popular book, the *Pélerinage de vie humaine*, by Guillaume de Deguilleville (ca. 1330-1335), in which the vices were personified as women and two of them were mounted on symbolic beasts: Gluttony on a pig and Lust on a horse.[124] An important fourteenth-century manuscript of a treatise on the deadly sins (Bib. nat. franç. 400, dated ca. 1390)[125] is illustrated with personifications of the sins (some male, some female), each one assigned to a specific social position, riding on a symbolic beast, and holding a bird which is in some way connected with the sin in question. Gluttony here is a young knight riding on a wolf and holding in his hand a kite (Mâle, III, Fig. 183). Luxuria is a woman riding a goat and carrying a dove (Mâle, III, Fig. 184). The significance of the birds is explained, as Mâle points out,[126] in the *Dieta Salutis* erroneously ascribed to St. Bonaventure, which compares gluttony to a bird of prey and lust to a voluptuous bird, such as a dove. The choice of a wolf to represent Gula needs no explanation, and as far as the

[124]Mâle, III, 329. The persistent mediaeval association of the horse with wantonness finds a precedent not only in Jeremiah 5:8, but also in the imagery of passion common in Greek literature (for example, the death of Hippolytus in Euripides' tragedy, with the interpretation of the myth by Ambrose, *De Virginibus* 3. 2, the charioteer's struggle with the wanton horse in Plato's *Phaedrus*, the significance of the centaur in mythology and art). See Virgil, *Aeneid* 11. 493-497 (*equus luxurians*). Aelian 4. 11 comments on the wantonness of mares, already a commonplace in Horace, *Odes* 1. 25. 13-14 (*flagrans amor et libido / quae solet matres furiare equorum*). In Petrarch's *Triumphs*, the chariot of Amore is drawn by horses (the corresponding chariot in Ovid, *Amores* 1. 2. 23-42 is drawn by doves). For other implications of the horse in mediaeval art, consult Rowley, *art. cit.*, 82, and for the horse as a symbol of *superbia* (as in the medallion worn by Holophernes in the Judith of Donatello) see Pope-Hennessy, II, 286. See Panofsky, *Titian*, 118 and note 22, on the significance of the unbridled horse in Renaissance art and the importance of Valeriano in popularizing it.

[125]See also (on this MS and its relation to the procession of sins in the *Mirour de l'omme* of Gower, vv. 241-300, 757-9720, and in Spenser's *Faerie Queene* 1. 4) Chew, 88-89, and Chew, "Spenser's Pageant of the Seven Deadly Sins," *Studies in Art and Literature for Belle da Costa Greene* (Princeton, 1954) 37-54. Although Mâle, III, 330-332 regarded this MS as the oldest illustrated French treatise on the deadly sins, Saxl (*art. cit.*, above, note 30, 104, note 2) cites an illustrated edition of the *Lumen animae* by Godfridus Canonicus, dated 1332, which shows virtues and vices as knights riding on animals.

[126]III, 331-332.

goat is concerned, we need only recall that Scopas depicted the Pandemian Aphrodite at Elis riding on a bronze goat (Pausanias 6. 25. 1) and that in Romanesque sculpture Luxuria (or Voluptas) often takes the form of a naked woman riding a goat or a ram, as in a relief at the Cathedral of Auxerre.[127] This mode of depicting the vices gained wide popularity and is seen, not only in illustrated moral treatises, but in tapestries and mural painting, especially in country churches in France, from the late fifteenth century well into the sixteenth.[128]

A further complication in the iconography of the virtues was introduced when it became customary to give not only the vices but also the virtues symbolic mounts. The revival of the theme of the *psychomachia* in the fifteenth century produced a new crop of illustrations of the two groups in battle. At first the virtues rode on war horses, the vices alone having symbolic beasts, as in the miniatures from the *Chasteau de Labour* by Pierre Gringoire (1499) reproduced by Mâle (III, Fig. 190, where Chastity on a horse is opposed by Lechery on a goat, and Fig. 191, where Sobriety on a horse meets Gluttony on a pig), but in time the virtues became more venturesome. A sixteenth-century manuscript in the Cluny Museum shows Sobrietas on a donkey and Castitas on a turtledove (Mâle, III, 338). Flemish tapestries adopt this kind of symbolism, but substitute fantastic and exotic animals, such as the unicorn, the dragon, and the camel, taken from German bestiaries and inspired by such books as the Augsburg edition of the *Buch von*

---

[127]Consult the commentary on Pausanias by J. G. Frazer (London, 1898) IV, 105–106, for ancient representations of Aphrodite riding on a he-goat and for theories about the origin of this type. Richard Hamann, *Burlington Magazine* 60 (1932) 91 ff., discusses the Auxerre relief and its relations. See note 33, above.

[128]See Mâle, III, 333–334, for lists of French rural churches where the vices are so depicted and for some of the many variations in the correspondences between animals and vices (for example, gluttony sometimes rides a bear and lust a monkey; the pig is assigned now to gluttony, now to lust, appropriately enough, since both are opposed to the same virtue, *temperantia*). On tapestries, especially those in England, see Chew, 88–89, 266–269. In the procession of sins in the *Faerie Queene*, Pride rides in a coach drawn by the symbolic beasts of the other six deadly sins, but elsewhere she sometimes rides a lion. Sloth rides an ass (which Chew, 101, calls "the most nearly consistent of all the emblematic animals"), Gluttony a pig, Lechery a goat, Avarice a camel, Envy a wolf, Wrath a lion. See Chew, 95–113, for a full discussion of parallels in literature and art.

den sieben Todsünden und den sieben Tugenden (1474), which has woodcuts of the virtues and vices in combat mounted on such animals.[129]

The unicorn, of all the animals linked in any way with sophrosyne/*temperantia*, has appealed most strongly to the imagination of artists of several periods. Pliny and Aelian record its marvelous powers: that it can purify poisonous liquids, so that a cup made of its horn is an antidote to poison contained therein, and that it is the most difficult of all animals to capture,[130] but it was the story told in the *Physiologus* that made the most profound impression. Here it was said that the unicorn can be captured only by a virgin, and this account, repeated by Isidore of Seville, Honorius Augustodunensis, and other authors influential in the Middle Ages, was popularized by the *Bestiary*.[131] The *Physiologus* was compiled in Alexandria in the second century after Christ and, in all probability, translated into Latin by the fifth. The oldest extant illustrated manuscript of the work (the Berne codex 318 of the ninth century, which goes back, it has been suggested, to an Alexandrian archetype)[132] contains a picture of the unicorn; it is a familiar figure in Byzantine miniatures and mosaics and in Romanesque and Gothic churches, but the period of its greatest vogue does not come until the fourteenth century and thereafter.[133] Only when the unicorn is depicted in a context that links it

[129]See Mâle, III, 339–340, and consult Chew, 336, note 10, for tapestries representing the sins and the virtues in combat, the sins mounted on symbolic beasts; see also notes 8 and 9.

[130]Pliny, *Hist. Nat.* 8. 31. 76 (*asperrimam . . . feram monocerotam*); Aelian, 3. 41 (on the drinking cup made of the horn).

[131]For a comprehensive account of this subject, consult Shepard, *op. cit.* (above, note 54), and Tuve, "Virtues," II, 60–64.

[132]On the Berne MS consult Helen Woodruff, *Art Bulletin* 12 (1930) 226 ff.; see Fig. 20 for the unicorn.

[133]Consult J. Ebersolt, *La miniature byzantine* (Paris, 1926) Plate XIII.2, for a ninth-century scene of the capture of the unicorn, illustrating Psalm 92:11. Van Marle, I, 180–183, lists unicorns in Lombard and Romanesque art and on German coffrets of the fourteenth and fifteenth centuries. See Van Marle, II, 445–457, for an expanded list from the twelfth century onward. For the unicorn as a symbol of pride (to be overcome by humility or purity) consult Tuve, "Virtues," II, 62–63. The unicorn symbolizes the vice of lechery in the fourteenth-century relief in the choir of the church of Hol in Brabant (cited by Réau, I, 92), where, like the more usual ram, it is ridden by a naked woman. Leonardo da Vinci considered the

with the legend of the *Physiologus* can it be associated with *temperantia* or *castitas*. The hunting of the unicorn, the emblematic use of the unicorn with a lady as a symbol of chastity, and the presence of unicorns drawing the triumphal chariot of Pudicizia in the illustrations of Petrarch's *Trionfi* are the three categories in which this link is certainly found. The legend that the unicorn's horn has medicinal or purifying powers results in still further iconographical developments, only distantly related to sophrosyne.

The capture of the unicorn became an allegory of the Annunciation or the Incarnation, with the Virgin representing Mary, the unicorn Christ, and the hunter the Angel Gabriel. It is popular in France, Germany, and Switzerland, especially as a theme for tapestries and ivory caskets,[134] but it evidently held less appeal for Italian artists. They instead employed the unicorn, usually in conjunction with a lady, as an emblem of chastity in a great variety of contexts, of which marriage cassoni, miniatures, and medallions are perhaps the most characteristic. The emblem may serve to compliment the virtue of a specific woman, as in the medallion by Pisanello for Cecilia Gonzaga (1447), which shows a young girl sitting in the moonlight with a great shaggy unicorn at her side.[135] Or it may allude to heraldry, since the unicorn appears in many coats of arms. An example is the lavish use of unicorns in the decoration by Pierin del Vaga for the ceiling of the Camera del

unicorn a symbol of unrestrained passion because of its love for maidens (*The Literary Works of Leonardo da Vinci,* ed. Jean Paul Richter and Irma A. Richter [London, 1939] II, 265). In the *Fior di Virtù,* ch. 34, the unicorn is an emblem of intemperance.

[134]Van Marle, II, Figs. 469, 470, reproduces two fourteenth-century scenes of the hunting of the unicorn (a miniature and an ivory); see pages 450–453 on tapestries employing this theme.

[135]See G. F. Hill, *Medals of the Renaissance* (Oxford, 1920) Plate III.5. Since St. Cecilia is a virgin-martyr, hence a type of virginity, the choice of the unicorn is particularly apt. The moon suggests Diana. Hill, Plate III.9, shows a medallion by Lixignolo (for Borso d'Este) on which a unicorn purifies a stream by plunging his horn into the water. See Réau, I, 92, for an engraving (ca. 1560) which shows a similar scene, part of a series celebrating the virtue of Diane de Poitiers. On the *deutera physis* of the unicorn (its power to purify water), mentioned only in the Greek text of the *Physiologus*, see Liliane Châtelet-Lange, *Art Bulletin* 50 (1968) 51–58. See Van Marle, I, Fig. 506, for a portrait of Gabrielle d'Estrées at the bath (Musée Condé) which includes in the background a tiny framed picture of a unicorn, on the back of a chair. Cf. Tervarent, *s.v. Licorne,* 239.

Perseo in the Castel Sant' Angelo (Van Marle, II, Fig. 475), a
compliment to the commandant of the fortress at the time when
the paintings were done. Mâle has noted the double significance
of the unicorn in the picture of Temperantia by Domenichino in
one of the pendentives of the cupola of San Carlo ai Catinari in
Rome; it represents chastity, a virtue subordinate to *temperantia*,
but it also alludes to the coat of arms of the Borromeo family to
which St. Charles belonged (Plate IX).[136]

The unicorn was the inevitable choice for the chariot of
Pudicizia in illustrations of Petrarch's *Trionfi*. The motive of the
triumph constitutes one of the chief legacies of Rome to Renaissance iconography, and in the *Amores* of Ovid there is a memorable description of the triumph of Amor (1. 2. 23–42) which clearly
inspired Petrarch. In the Ovidian account Amor's triumphal procession includes two captives, Pudor and Bona Mens, who are
closely akin to Sophrosyne (Bona Mens may, in fact, represent an
attempt to translate the Greek word). Only in the case of Amore
does Petrarch himself specify a triumphal car, but artists supplied
this detail for all six Triumphators, Love, Chastity, Death, Fame,
Time, and Eternity. Petrarch describes the personified Chastity in
terms reminiscent of descriptions of Sophrosyne in late Greek
literature, both Patristic and Byzantine, still further enriched by
mediaeval bestiary and lapidary lore. Chastity (Pudicizia) wears a
robe more white than snow and in her hand carries a shield like
that of Perseus, who slew Medusa. Her attributes include a pillar
of jasper and a chain of diamond and topaz, with which she has
fettered Amore and leads him captive. In her train are many
personified abstractions (Prudence, Modesty, Glory, Persever-
ance, Purity, Honor, and Maiden Shame), but also included are
the mythical and historical exemplars of chastity, enumerated in

[136]Mâle, IV, 393, note 1. The Borromeos included on their coat of arms the
bridle, the camel, and the unicorn, all emblems of temperance or chastity. Allegories of chastity employing the unicorn and the lady and dating from the
sixteenth century or thereafter include those of Domenichino (the one just mentioned and the one in the Galleria Farnese, see note 149 below), the stucco by
Niccolo Menghini above the second arch on the left side of the nave of St. Peter's
Basilica (see Robert Endgass, *Art Bulletin* 60 [1978] 96–108), and the group by
Francavilla in the Niccolini chapel in Sta. Croce, Florence.

Plate IX. Allegory of Temperance by Domenico Zampiero (Domenichino), detail of pendentive of cupola, San Carlo ai Catinari, Rome (1628). Alinari/Editorial Photocolor Archives.

Chapter 1, most of whom derive from Valerius Maximus' *exempla pudicitiae* (see Plate I).[137]

The procession goes first to Liternum, where Scipio the Elder had his retreat, and then to Rome, to the shrines of Venus Verticordia and Pudicitia Patricia. In the temple of Pudicitia, says Petrarch, are Hippolytus and his biblical counterpart, Joseph. The emblem on the banner carried in the procession is a white, unspotted ermine in a field of green, about whose neck is a golden chain, set with topaz.[138] The ermine symbolizes purity because it was reputed to surrender to its pursuers in preference to soiling its white fur by taking refuge in the earth.[139] The topaz, the diamond, and the column of jasper are all related, in the mediaeval moral synthesis, to various aspects of chastity and purity.[140]

[137]See the section *De pudicitia:* 6. 1. 1 (*Lucretia . . . dux Romanae pudicitiae*); 6. 1. 2 (Verginia and her father); 6. 1 Ext. 3 (*Teutones coniuges*), etc. For Tuccia, see Valerius Maximus 8. 1. 5 and Pliny *Hist. Nat.* 28. 2. 12. Boccaccio's *De Claris Mulieribus* includes as models of chastity most of Petrarch's exemplars.

[138]See Van Marle, II, 111-151, for a discussion of the illustrations to the Triumphs and for pictures of many tapestries, cassoni, and miniatures that employ the theme. Fig. 134 (Pencz) is especially good for the individual attendants of Chastity: Judith with the head of Holophernes, Verginia with her father, Tuccia with the sieve. The throne of Chastity is supported by a sphinx, and the procession approaches a round temple like that of Vesta, representing the shrine of Pudicitia Patricia. For earlier uses of the theme of the chariot of virtue or vice, see Katzenellenbogen, 61, Chew, passim, and Chew's two articles cited in notes 116 and 125 above. There is a tradition of an allegorical chariot whose wheels are moved by the cardinal virtues; see Katzenellenbogen, 61, note 4, for an example dated 1216-1223, and cf. Dante, *Purgatorio* 29.

[139]For the symbolic value of the ermine consult *The Literary Works of Leonardo da Vinci* (above, note 133) II, 266 and 276. Leonardo lists the ermine under moderation in his notes for a bestiary. The breastplate of Minerva on the Fregoso monument by Cattaneo in Sta. Anastasia, Verona, has an ermine with the motto *Potius mori [quam foedari]* ("Better to die than be defiled"); see Mario Praz, *Studies in Seventeenth-Century Imagery* (Rome, 1964) 51-52. Carpaccio's *Portrait of a Young Knight* (Thyssen Collection, Lugano) includes several emblems signifying purity, including an ermine and the motto *Malo mori quam foedari* (1510-1520). In Lorenzo Lotto's *Triumph of Chastity* in the Palazzo Rospigliosi-Pallavicini, Rome, Chastity is identified by the ermine that creeps across her chest (Bernhard Berenson, *Lorenzo Lotto* [London, 1956] Plate 230). Consult Tervarent, *s.v. Hermine*. On the *Ermine Portrait* of Elizabeth I, see Frances A. Yates, *J.W.C.I.* 10 (1947) 27 ff.

[140]The principal mediaeval source for allegorical or mystical significance in gems is Marbod of Rennes, *De Lapidibus (P.L.* 171, 1737 ff.). See 1 (*De adamanti*), 4 (*De jaspide*), 13 (*De topazio*), 16 (*De amethysto*). Cf. also the poem of Meliteniotes, *To*

The *Trionfi* of Petrarch formed an enormously popular subject for tapestries, caskets, and paintings. Probably the most famous adaptation of the theme, apart from the total cycle, is the diptych by Piero della Francesca in the Uffizi (ca. 1465), representing Battista Sforza, Duchess of Urbino, in a triumphal car drawn by unicorns. She is accompanied by the theological virtues. The Duke, in the corresponding portrait, rides on a car pulled by horses, which should represent the Triumph of Love, according to the usual system, but since he is being crowned by a winged figure, standing behind him in the chariot, the picture serves also as a triumph of Fame. Before him in the car sit the four cardinal virtues.[141]

Equally unusual is an exquisite miniature representing the Triumph of Chastity in a manuscript of the *Trionfi* belonging to the Walters Art Gallery and dated ca. 1477–1480. It lacks the familiar chariot and procession, but is faithful in many other de-

---

Sophrosyne (above, note 4), which constitutes almost a dictionary of mineralogy. Réau, I, 135–136, lists the principal gems and their significance. On the emerald as a symbol of chastity and its appearance in Dante, see Vincenzo Cioffari, *Speculum* 19 (1944) 360–363.

[141]The legend beneath the *Triumph of the Duchess* includes an allusion to the Mean (cf. Horace, *Serm.* 1. 1. 106) as well as an echo of the famous epitaph of the poet Ennius (*ap.* Cicero, *Tusc. Disp.* 1. 15. 34). Another famous series of Triumphs from the fifteenth century in Italy is that in the Palazzo Schifanoia in Ferrara (1467–1470), where the labors of the seasons and the signs of the zodiac are combined to present a picture of the virtues of the Prince (for this interpretation, see Eberhard Ruhmer, *Tura, Paintings and Drawings* [London, 1958] 27 ff.). Although no procession among those surviving from the series has been identified as a Triumph of Chastity, the chariot of Minerva is drawn by unicorns, and there were also Triumphs of Diana and Vesta, which doubtless included some elements of the iconography of chastity. The chariot of Luxuria (for December) is drawn by monkeys, which symbolize the passions. Correlations between the virtues and the signs of the zodiac or the planets are not lacking in late antiquity, the Middle Ages, and the Renaissance. In Hermetic literature, for example, Mercury was reputed to confer on mankind Sophia, Sophrosyne, Peithô (Persuasion), and Alêtheia (Truth); consult Th. Zielinski, *Archiv für Religionswissenschaft* 8 (1905) 365. In Dante's Paradise the sphere of Saturn, where the souls of the great ascetics dwell, was identified with the cardinal virtue of *temperantia* (*Paradiso*, Canto 21). Vasari describes his design for the exterior walls of a Florentine house, showing the Ages of Man and linking each Age with a planet, a virtue, an art, and a sin. The Age of Youth is pictured with the planet Venus and the virtue of temperance (personifed and holding a bridle). The corresponding art is rhetoric, and the sin is fraud (Chew, 164).

tails to the text of the Triumphs of Chastity and Death. Chastity, or Laura, standing near a column of jasper, wards off with a shield Cupid's darts, while three of her four attendant maidens hold spears with green pennants charged with ermines. The landscape in the foreground suggests the coast near Baiae, but in the background is the shrine of Pudicitia in Rome. Above this scene is a smaller picture of Dido committing suicide, and below is Judith leaving the tent of Holophernes, whose head she displays (Plate X). The opening page of the text (fol. 23) shows Cupid bound to the initial Q of the first word (*Quando*) with his arms behind his back. He is blindfolded, and his bow and quiver lie useless at his feet. At the bottom of the page is a lady with a unicorn. The text rests against an elaborate architectural frame, hung with a backdrop whose border shows the rape of the Sabine women. The frame itself is supported by two golden sphinxes, traditional symbols of silence and other forms of restraint (Plate XI). Two more sphinxes adorn the framework of the frontispiece, below the miniature of Judith.

This manuscript appears to be unique among fifteenth-century illustrations of the *Triumph of Chastity* in replacing the conventional unicorn-chariot and procession with Laura's defense against Cupid's darts. The substitution places a special emphasis on the lady herself—Petrarch's *bella donna*—and her triumphant virtue. The artist has been identified with the Master of the Vatican Homer, a Paduan influenced by Mantegna, probably working in Rome after 1466.[142]

THE EMBLEM BOOKS

The great vogue for emblem books, beginning in the sixteenth century, but reaching its peak in the two following centuries, introduced certain novelties into the representation of the virtues allied with *temperantia*. We shall confine our attention to the *Iconologia* of Cesare Ripa, probably the most influential of the emblem books, which drew upon the symbols published by Alciati and Valeriano, as well as the great manuals of mythology by Car-

[142]Consult Dorothy Miner, *Journal of the Walters Art Gallery* 32 (1969) 41–115, for a full description of the six frontispieces to the *Trionfi* and the historiated initials beginning the text of each. Figures 43–57 reproduce all twelve folios.

Plate X. Illustration from Petrarch's *Triumph of Chastity,* by Master of the Vatican Homer (ca. 1480). Walters Art Gallery, Baltimore, MS 755, fol. 22ᵛ.

PVDICICIAE TRIVM
PHVS SECVNDVS
VANDO ADVN
GIOGO ET IN
VN TEMPO
QVIVI
DOMITA LAL
TEREZA DE GLI DEI
E de gli huomini uidi al mondo oui.
I presi exempio de lor stati tri
Facendomi profitto l'altrui male
In consolar i casi, e dolor mei.
C he si ueggio dun arco, e duno strale
Pheto percosso, el giouine dabido,
Lun detto Deo, e l'altro huom parmi tale.
E e ueggio ad un baccio, giusnon solido
Ch'mor pio del suo sposo li moue amor
Non quel denar, come il publico gride

Plate XI. Initial page, Petrarch's *Triumph of Chastity*, by Master of the Vatican Homer (ca. 1480). Walters Art Gallery, Baltimore, MS 755, fol. 23.

tari, Giraldi, and Natalis Conti.[143] Ripa prescribes the proper
methods of depicting Modestia, Castitas, Pudicitia, Abstinentia,
Continentia, Mediocritas, and Temperantia, using certain motives
familiar from antiquity and others that are genuine innovations in
this context. Modestia holding a scepter surmounted by an eye is
derived from hieroglyphics and is explained as a symbol of power
guided by reason. Castitas holds a scourge in one hand, a sieve in
the other, while at her feet is a blindfolded Cupid. The scourge is
a generalized symbol of mortification of the flesh, the sieve comes
from Roman legend (the Vestal Tuccia, accused of incest, proved
her chastity by carrying water in a sieve from the Tiber to the
Temple of Vesta),[144] and the blind Cupid is linked with Chastity
from the fourteenth century onward.[145] Pudicitia holds a lily, sets

[143]The earliest true emblem book was the *Hieroglyphics* of Horapollo, emanating
from Alexandria (perhaps in the fourth century after Christ) and printed by
Aldus in 1505. Several of the emblems allude to some aspect of sophrosyne, and in
the history of the iconography of this virtue it holds an early and important place.
See George Boas, *The Hieroglyphics of Horapollo* (New York, 1950), for a translation
of this work and an account of its history and influence. For a discussion of the
impact of the *Hieroglyphics* on Italian artists and Dürer, consult Panofsky, *Albrecht
Dürer* (London, 1948) I, 173 ff. The triumphal arch of Maximilian I carried
symbols from the *Hieroglyphics* including the bull (representing discretion) as well
as heraldic motives, such as the insignia and motto (HALT MASS!) of the Order of
Temperance (I, 178; II, Fig. 227). The first edition of the *Emblemata* of Alciati
appeared in 1531, followed by Piero Valeriano's *Hieroglyphica* in 1556 and Ripa's
Iconologia in 1593. The first edition of the *Iconologia* was not illustrated, but
beginning with the edition of 1603 illustrations proliferated. For a bibliography of these and other emblem books, consult Praz, *op. cit.* (note 140, above),
241–576. A helpful account of Alciati's debt to the Greek Anthology may be found
in James Hutton, *The Greek Anthology in Italy to the Year 1800* (Ithaca, N.Y., 1935)
195–208. The extensive influence of the emblem books in English literature and
art is traced by Henry Green, *Shakespeare and the Emblem Writers* (London, 1870),
Rosemary Freeman, *English Emblem Books* (London, 1948), and Chew, 279–298,
and the article cited in note 116, above. See also Panofsky, *The Iconography of
Coreggio's Camera di San Paolo* (London, 1951) 33 ff. For a partial catalogue of
known works of art from the sixteenth to the mid-eighteenth centuries derived
from Ripa, consult Erna Mandowsky, *Untersuchungen zur Iconologie des Cesare Ripa*
(Hamburg, 1934) 70–83.

[144]Valerius Maximus, 8. 1. 5; Pliny, *Hist. Nat.* 28. 2. 12.

[145]Panofsky, *Studies*, 126, note 79, observes that not until Petrarch used the
motive of the fettered Cupid in his *Triumphus Pudicitiae* (vv. 94 ff.) did this figure
symbolize chastity. Illustrators of the *Triumphs* used the blindfolded Cupid as well
(Van Marle, II, Fig. 132), but, as Panofsky points out (112–121), the blindfold
originally signified irrationality and evil, rather than defeat. The blindfold appears in the allegory of Chastity in S. Francesco, Assisi, where Amor is driven away

one foot on a tortoise, and wears a veil. Ripa explains the lily as a
traditional symbol of virginity (citing Jerome, *Against Jovinian* 1.
285 as his authority, as well as the Song of Songs, 2. 6) and for the
veil refers to the Roman imperial coins in honor of Sabina and
Otacilia Severa, the veils worn by Penelope and Helen in the
Homeric poems, and the treatise of Tertullian, *De Virginibus
Velandis.* The tortoise derives from Phidias' statue of Aphrodite
at Elis.[146]

Abstinentia touches her lips with her right hand and in her left
holds a delicate morsel of food. She displays a motto: *Non utor ne
abutar* ("I do not use, lest I abuse"). Continentia holds an ermine,
which eats only once a day and prefers to be captured rather than
soil its fur. Mediocritas with her right hand holds a lion on a chain
and with her left a lamb, or holds in one hand the earth, in the
other the sky. Her motto is *Medio tutissimus ibis* ("You will go most
safely by the middle course," from the advice of Sol to Phaethon
in Ovid, *Metamorphoses* 2. 137).

Temperantia has several possible modes of representation. One
portrays her as a woman holding a bridle in one hand and a clock
in the other, while behind her looms an elephant. The bridle and
the clock, familiar from earlier iconography, are explained in
conventional terms, but the elephant is not, as one might expect
from the *Bestiary,* a symbol of chastity. Rather, his presence is
accounted for by a story going back to Plutarch (and already cited
by Piero Valeriano in his emblem book), in which the elephant
figures as a symbol of moderation. A Syrian elephant was fed a
certain measure of grain each day by his master's servant. For
several days the servant neglected his duty and then gave the
elephant the entire amount all at once. The elephant divided it

---

from the Tower of Chastity by Death and Penance (ca. 1320–1325). For Triumphs
of Chastity having Cupid without the blindfold, see Plate I and Van Marle, II,
Figs. 139, 140, 146. An elaboration of the theme of the fettered Cupid may be seen
in Signorelli's painting of Chastity binding Amor, in the National Gallery, London; in the background is a triumphal procession (Van Marle, II, Fig. 116).

[146]See the article by Heckscher referred to in note 12, above. One of the most
celebrated statues of Pudicitia designed to meet Ripa's specifications is that by
Antonio Corradini in the Chapel of San Severo in Naples (the tomb of the Sangro
family, ca. 1755–1766), where the treatment of the veil is of paramount interest
and the tortoise is omitted.

into portions, one for each day, and ate them in the presence of his master, who thus learned of the servant's dereliction. The elephant had won fame as a symbol of chastity from stories in the *Bestiary* about the mandrake root and other evidences of secrecy and modesty in begetting and giving birth to young. Hence it sometimes appears embroidered on priestly vestments, especially chasubles, as an emblem of sacerdotal chastity, but it could also be employed, like the unicorn, in complimentary allusions to a lady's virtue. A famous example is the medallion in honor of Isotta of Rimini by Matteo de' Pasti (1446).[147] Now, however, the elephant enjoys renewed popularity as a type of moderation, although its connection with chastity can hardly have been forgotten. An elaborate instance of the complete Temperantia type, according to Ripa, may be seen on the ceiling of the Medici-Riccardi Palace in Florence, where the *Apotheosis of the Medici* by Luca Giordano (1670–1683) includes the cardinal virtues, among which Temperantia is portrayed with elephant, clock, and bridle (Plate XII).[148]

[147]Considered by W. S. Heckscher (*Art Bulletin* 29 [1947] 155–182) an emblem of chastity in marriage. Consult this useful article on Bernini's elephant and obelisk in the Piazza Minerva for the ancient sources (Pliny, Aelian, the *Physiologus*) and for mediaeval and Renaissance interpretations of the moral significance of the elephant (pages 171–177 especially). Tervarent, 155, *s.v. Eléphant,* cites an engraving in which Pudicia (*sic*) rides an elephant, Libido a boar. See also Edwin and Dora Panofsky, *Gazette des Beaux Arts* 52, no. 2 (1958) 131–135, on the *éléphant fleurdelysé* in the Gallery of Francis II at Fontainbleau, with note 48 on the elephant as a symbol of chastity complimenting Diane de Poitiers (a parallel to the unicorn referred to in note 135 above). Horapollo makes the elephant fleeing from a ram and a pig the emblem of a king retreating from folly and intemperance. For the elephant embroidered on priestly vestments see E. P. Evans, *Animal Symbolism in Ecclesiastical Architecture* (New York, 1896) 113 f.

[148]Other figures include a Sobrietas, mixing water with wine, and allegories of Luxuria, Avaritia, and Paupertas. The death of Adonis occurs in the neighborhood. The figures of Continentia and Castitas in the Camera degli Sposi of the Palazzo Zuccari in Rome combine several elements soon to be included in Ripa's *Iconologies* (and possibly serve among his sources). Continentia holds a key (attributed by Ripa to Sobrietas) and a bridle, while Castitas with head veiled wears white and has a dove at her right hand, a boar underfoot. See Werner Körte, *Der Palazzo Zuccari in Rom* (Leipzig, 1935) Plates 27, 28. Obviously inspired by Ripa are the graceful stuccoes with which Giacomo Serpotta (1656–1732) adorned many churches and oratories in Palermo and other Sicilian towns. His three principal achievements, the oratories of Santa Zita (1685), San Lorenzo (1707), and San Domenico (1717) in Palermo, include many allegorical figures derived from the

Plate XII. Allegory of Temperance, detail of ceiling by Luca Giordano. Palazzo Medici Riccardi: Florence.

Other ways of picturing Temperantia are suggested by Ripa, and as his work went through further editions, more were added. One that recalls an ancient conception of sophrosyne/*temperantia* as the force that can extinguish flame requires the personified virtue to hold a pair of tongs, in which is grasped a piece of red-hot iron, while the other hand holds a vase of water, presumably for tempering the iron, an attitude reproduced by Giuseppi Raffaelli in the Temperantia occupying one of the niches of the ambulacrum that connects the atrium of St. Peter's Basilica with the wing holding the statue of Charlemagne. The motive of restraint is expressed by still another image, which shows Temperantia holding in her right hand a silver bridle, in her left a medallion with the motto *Virtutis instrumentum*.

Ripa draws freely on the world of plants for allegorical symbolism. His description of Marital Chastity suggests that the personified virtue carry in her right hand a branch of laurel and wear on her head a garland of rue, while in her left hand she holds a turtledove, emblem of *pudicitia* from the most ancient times. Rue, by the sharpness of its scent, has the power to restrain lust, he explains, while laurel derives its connection with chastity from the myth of Daphne and her metamorphosis in escaping the lust of Apollo. Other plants, flowers, and trees appear among the emblems related to virtues that form a part of the concept of sophrosyne/*temperantia,* the most general in its implications being the palm. This had always symbolized the martyr's triumph in Christian art and during the first four centuries of Christianity had become closely connected with the concept of sophrosyne because of the Christian ideal of the virgin martyr. In Carolingian miniatures all four cardinal virtues are sometimes shown holding branches of palm, and in the Lombard mosaic at S. Benedetto Po the same situation obtains. Now Ripa prescribes as one method of representing Temperantia a woman clothed in purple, holding in her right hand a branch of palm, in her left a bit or bridle. These are, in fact, the attributes of Temperantia in Caracci's painting for

Iconologies, although Serpotta is also capable of great originality. None of the oratories contains a conventional Temperantia, but various facets are present, such as Castitas with a unicorn (San Lorenzo) and Puritas with a lamb and a child in San Domenico.

the Camerino Farnese (1595),[149] in that of the Alberti brothers for the Sala Clementina in the Vatican (1602), and in the cupola painting of San Carlo ai Catinari in Rome (ca. 1628), where Domenichino shows Temperantia (see Plate IX) herself holding the palm and the bridle and leaning on a camel,[150] while two *putti* perform the symbolic action of mingling water with wine, and a young girl with a unicorn sits at the feet of the central figure. Another of the images prescribed by Ripa for Chastity involves a woman holding a branch of cinnamon, which, being aromatic and costly, teaches that this virtue is not easy to attain. The lily, as we have already seen, is a traditional attribute of Pudicitia, which Ripa retains.[151]

[149]On the allegories of virtue depicted on the ceiling consult John Rupert Martin, *Art Bulletin* 38 (1956) 103, and see Fig. 24 (Temperantia) and Fig. 27 (Castitas with turtledove). The cardinal virtues, with Caritas in place of Prudentia, also appear in medallions by Caracci on the walls of the Galleria Farnese, where Temperantia holds only a bridle. Above the door is Domenichino's Lady with a unicorn. For the unicorn as a device of the Farnese family, ubiquitous at the Roman palazzo and at Caprarola, see Tervarent, *s.v. Licorne.*

[150]The camel, which like the unicorn forms part of the arms of the Borromeo family, owes its reputation for *temperantia* to two characteristics: its ability to go for long periods without drinking and its power to judge accurately the exact burden it can carry. It therefore represents two different facets of *temperantia: sobrietas* and *discretio.* Like the unicorn, which symbolizes both chastity and lechery (as well as pride), the camel may be a type of lust, according to Leonardo's notes for a bestiary (see above, notes 133, 140). For the camel as a symbol of avarice, see Chew, 106. The camel represents sobriety in an engraving by Cesare Reverdino, illustrating the definition *Temperantia est moderatio cupiditatum rationi obediens,* which shows the personified virtue holding two vessels and having a camel at her feet (Tervarent, *s.v. Chameau;* cf. Bartsch, Vol. XV 482, no. 31). The figure holding a disk with a camel in the virtue cycles of Notre Dame, Chartres, and elsewhere is sometimes identified as Temperantia (Réau), sometimes as Oboedientia (Mâle, II, 128). Filarete's frieze (1440-1445) on the reverse of one of the bronze doors of St. Peter's, showing the master and his *discipuli* in a dance which moves from intemperance to virtue, represents the former by a man riding on an ass and holding a jug, the latter by a dromedary. See Charles Seymour, Jr., *Sculpture in Italy 1400-1500* (London, 1966), Plate 55B. The design constitutes the artist's signature (Filarete - "Lover of virtue").

[151]Instances could be multiplied in which the lily is linked with the virtues of purity, chastity, and temperance. See note 30, above, and cf. Réau, I, 140-141, for a bibliography of works dealing with the symbolism of flowers. Temperantia in the cupola painting by Gaulli (Baciccio) in Sta. Agnese in Agone, Rome (1666-1672), holds a sheaf of lilies, while a garland of white roses is placed on her head by Fama. This painting, like Domenichino's in San Carlo ai Catinari, employs several motives from Ripa: above Temperantia a *putto* holds a bridle; before her are two

The animals allied with these virtues by Ripa or other authors of emblem books include the elephant, the ermine, the turtledove, the tortoise, the beaver, and the unicorn. The only significant type of sophrosyne/*temperantia* in the animal world omitted by the emblem books is the stag, which according to the *Bestiary* served as a warning against drink, because its horns became entangled in the bushes at the water hole.[152] A new addition to the symbolic animals is the bull, which in the *Hieroglyphics* of Horapollo typifies control of the passions, because it never approaches the cow after she has conceived. A man made temperate by misfortune may be indicated, according to Horapollo, by a picture of a bull girt with wild figs, since a bull when in rut puts wild figs about him and thus becomes calm.[153] One of Ripa's designs for Temperantia in the edition of 1767 involves a lion harnessed to a bull.

The influence of the emblem books on artists from the sixteenth

---

more *putti*, one holding a torch, the other blindfolded and supine; at her feet a gaily dressed woman greedily reaches for coins and jewels scattered on the ground; in the background are the Lady and the unicorn and another *putto* holding a torch. Behind Temperantia still another *putto* holds a lute, emblem of harmony. See North, "Temperance," Fig. 7. Alciati recommends the pennyroyal (*pulegium*) as an emblem of purity; this herb was used in rites of purification in the Eleusinian Mysteries. The vine and the ivy, both associated with Bacchus from antiquity, are linked with sophrosyne / *temperantia* at various times and places. See, for example, the set of thirteenth-century enameled plaques now in the Cathedral treasury of St. Stephen, Vienna, each of which shows, in the upper half, a biblical scene, and in the lower half, a personified virtue. The plaque devoted to *temperantia* has, above the personified virtue (who mingles wine and water), a picture of Joshua and Caleb carrying a huge cluster of grapes into the Promised Land; see Viktor Griessmaier, *Burlington Magazine* 63 (1933) 108–112, Plate D. Ivy crowns Temperantia on the arca of St. Peter Martyr in San Eustorgio, Milan, and is coiled around the arm of this virtue on the tomb of Queen Mary of Hungary in Sta. Maria Donna Regina, Naples. Dioscorides identified rue with moly, symbol of sophrosyne in Homeric allegories (Buffière, 292, note 67).

[152]Hence on some sixteenth-century tapestries (described by Mâle, III, 340), when Chastity rides a unicorn, Temperance rides a stag. In Ripa's *Iconologia* the stag appears in the emblem of Prudence.

[153]See Boas, *op. cit.* (above, note 143). For the beaver as a type of *castitas*, consult Réau, I, 76–132. The dolphin also appears in groups representing some aspect of temperance; for example, the Temperanza of Bartolommeo Ammanati in the courtyard of the Bargello, Florence (a youth with dolphin-entwined anchor, the traditional emblem of the proverb *Festina lente*), the Luca Giordano Apotheosis of the Medici, and the Temperance monument in Washington, D.C. (above, note 11).

century to the end of the eighteenth is so pervasive as to rival the impact of the *Psychomachia* itself in the Middle Ages. Although symbols and allegories of the kind prescribed by Alciati and Ripa are more ubiquitous in Italy than anywhere else, they crossed the Alps in great numbers and left their mark on literature and art in northern countries as well. No attempt can be made here to pursue them in their further travels, but an indication of their appeal and potentiality for still further development may be found in a unique seventeenth-century still life by Jan Simonsz Torrentius, one of the very few surviving works by this mysterious and tormented Dutch artist. It suggests temperance or moderation by an arrangement of symbolic objects in the spirit of the emblem books: a glass tumbler, only partly filled, stands between a water jug and a wine tankard. Two clay pipes on either side of the tumbler, their bowls facing downward, direct attention to a piece of paper with musical notations on which the tumbler stands. But instead of a drinking song, the paper contains a warning to practice moderation. Above the glass hangs a bridle (Plate XIII).[154]

The vogue for representing personified abstractions died with the passing of the taste for allegory and the extinction of the sort of wit that delights in learned and allusive jests. After the close of the eighteenth century we find few examples—even in Rome—of the cardinal virtues (or of Sophrosyne/Temperantia by herself) in painting, sculpture, or the minor arts. A notable exception dating from the middle of the nineteenth century is the Torlonia Chapel in the Lateran Basilica, embellished with statues of the cardinal virtues according to Ripa. Temperantia holds a bridle in her hand, and at her feet is a small and beguiling elephant. The last papal tomb to employ Temperantia is that of Clement XIV by Canova (1787) in Dodici Santi Apostoli, which shows the personified virtue in an attitude of mourning, leaning on the sarcophagus and holding in her hand the reins of an inconspicuous bridle.[155]

[154]It has been suggested that Torrentius modeled this emblem on the device of his mentor, Roemer Visscher, which combined a drinking glass (in Dutch, "roemer") with a tankard and a jug, and that Rosicrucian symbolism determined the arrangement of the objects. Consult A. J. Rehorst, *Torrentius* (Rotterdam, 1939), especially pages 73–80, 166–170, and Figs. 2, 42–43, 45.

[155]See Renzo U. Montini, *Le tombe dei papi* (Rome, 1957) Plate 173. Other papal tombs employing the cardinal virtues are mentioned in North, "Canons and

Plate XIII. Emblem of Temperance by Jan Simonsz Torrentius (1614). Rijksmuseum,
nsterdam, No. 2311, D1.

Church windows of stained or painted glass offer a few modern examples; in the nineteenth and twentieth centuries the virtues return, for the most part, to a religious context.[156] Close to the end of the eighteenth century (1785) Sir Joshua Reynolds designed a window (painted by Thomas Gervais) for the Ante Chapel of New College, Oxford, which contains a sequence of seven personified virtues, the cardinal and theological, with conventional attributes (Temperance mingling water and wine and having a bridle at her feet)—"half-dressed languishing harlots" as they were termed by one critic.[157] An early twentieth-century window in Wells Cathedral employs a once popular motive: Temperance extinguishing a flame by pouring water over it. The chapel of the Cornell United Religious Work in Anabel Taylor Hall at Cornell University presents a cycle of virtues in stained glass, most of them indicated only by name (Temperance is among these), but each having subordinate virtues depicted symbolically. The subdivisions of Temperance, which owe little to tradition, are Health (represented by a tree). Self-respect (a handbell), and Efficiency (a cogwheel).[158] Inscribed on this window is a quotation from Hamlet (3. 2): "For in the whirlwind of passion you must acquire and beget a temperance that may give it smoothness."

The absence in our own time of vigorous new styles of representing the virtues indicates, not only the unpopularity of representational art, but more generally the decline of interest in the

---

Hierarchies of the Cardinal Virtues," in *The Classical Tradition: Literary and Historical Studies in Honor of Harry Caplan,* ed. Luitpold Wallach (Ithaca, N.Y., 1966) 165–183.

[156]Some exceptions, which present the cardinal virtues in a secular environment, include the relief of Temperance (holding a bridle) on the memorial to the temperance advocate, Sir Wilfred Lawson, on the Embankment, London, and the busts of the four virtues above the main portal of the ministry of Grazia e Giustizia on the Via Arenula in Rome. The entrance pavilion to the Library of Congress in Washington, D.C., has murals representing the virtues in the north and south corridors. They include the cardinal four, with traditional attributes (Temperance pouring from pitcher to bowl), plus Patriotism, Concord, and Industry.

[157]See the guidebook by W. G. Hayter, Warden of New College in 1962, for a copy of which I am endebted to Lore Ostwald.

[158]The iconography is ascribed to Edmund Ezra Day, president of Cornell from 1937 to 1949.

traditional Platonic-Stoic approach to ethics, for, as we have seen, each of the important innovations in the iconography of the virtues from late antiquity to the age of baroque has sprung from some fresh idea about the nature of these or closely related moral values, their links with one another, their power over the soul, or their effect on society. Although some of these new ideas are known to us, as Lynn White, Jr., has observed, mainly from nonverbal symbols (taking the place of texts, when the "mutual accommodations between different activities within a culture ... seem ... to be subliminal rather than intentional"[159]), we can for the most part identify with precision the works of literature, whether poetry or prose, religious or secular, that have expressed the important new insights and thus inspired new ways of portraying virtues and vices, from the *Psychomachia* in the early fifth century through the Carolingian *speculum principis* and the thirteenth-century moral and theological tracts, all the way to the emblem books of Alciati and Ripa, which proliferated in the wake of the Council of Trent and guided the artists of the Counter-Reformation.

It is this close connection between the history of ideas and changing fashions in iconography that makes the study of how the virtues appeared in art so useful a clue to their status in philosophy, religion, political or social life at various periods, ever since the day in the seventh century B.C. when Cypselus or his heirs dedicated the famous chest. And few indeed are the tools available to the historian or the philologist that so effectively mingle the *utile* with the *dulce*—like the Horatian Temperantia of the Hildesheim font, *delectando pariterque monendo*—delighting and instructing in equal measure.

[159] *Art. cit.* (above, note 91), 198.

Appendix: Unusual Attributes of Temperantia

An unusual set of attributes appears in a MS of the Decretals (Milan, Ambr. MS B 42 inf., fol. 1) dated 1354, where a miniature by Niccolò da Bologna depicts the seven virtues and the seven liberal arts, the virtues with *exempla horribilia* of the opposed vices at their feet, the arts with their historical representatives. Temperantia holds on her lap a model of a walled town with tall turrets and has in her right hand a key which she is about to put into the lock of the gate. At her feet is Epicurus in a position of abject surrender. (See Pietro Toesca, *Il Trecento* [Turin, 1951] Fig. 693, and E. H. Gombrich, *Symbolic Images* [London, 1972] Fig. 75.) A related miniature in Vienna shows Temperantia holding a model of a church, out of which grows a tree bearing the names of twelve subdivisions of temperance according to the *Summa Theologiae* of St. Thomas; she has no key, but Epicurus crouches underfoot. See Julius von Schlosser, *Jahrbuch der künsthistorischen Sammlungen der allerhöchsten Kaiserhauses* 17 (1896) 13–100, Plate III.1. For the closed door and tower originating in Ezechiel 44:1–4 as symbols of virginity consult Eugene Cantelupe, *Art Bulletin* 46 (1964) 226, note 50. Danae's tower symbolizes chastity according to Fulgentius Metaforalis (Panofsky, *Titian*, 145; cf. Hans Liebeschütz, *Fulgentius Metaforalis* [Leipzig and Berlin, 1926] 56). An entirely different conception of Temperantia leads to the castle-and-key imagery in a Spanish poem of 1396, which describes the seven virtues, and attributes to Temperantia two keys, those of Matt. 16:19, and a castle representing the kingdom of Heaven. See Archer Woodford, *Speculum* 28 (1953) 521–524. An attendant of Temperantia holds a key in the ceiling painting by Luca Giordano, the *Apotheosis of the Medici,* in the Medici-Riccardi Palace, Florence (1682–1683; see Plate XII), as does the Continentia of the Camera degli Sposi in the Palazzo Zuccari in Rome (ca. 1590). In emblem literature the key becomes a symbol of sobriety (Ripa, edition of 1613) or silence, as in the statue representing Secrecy in the series related to Confession in Sta. Maddalena in Rome (ca. 1727). See Chew, 122–124, for Sobriety with a key resting on her shoulder and a fish in her hand, found in John Daye, *A Booke of Christian Prayers* (1578).

It may be useful here to gather references to other uncommon attributes of Temperantia, of whatever date. They include a child (representing innocence?) in the arms of Temperantia in the *Liber Scivias* by St. Hildegard of Bingen, 1141–1150 (Katzenellenbogen, Fig. 48), an incense-boat on the pulpit in the Duomo in Siena, 1268 (Enzo Carli, *Il pulpito di Siena* [Bergamo, 1943] 22–23 and Plate 14), and a skull and mirror in the *Heures* of Simon Vostre, 1502 (Chew, 135). Réau, I, 183, note 4, observes that the confusion between the words *mors* (bridle) and *mort* (death) gave Temperantia a skull on the stalls of the Cathedral of Auch. A sickle designates Temperantia on the ceiling of the Baroncelli Chapel, Sta. Croce, Florence, by Taddeo Gaddi, ca. 1337. Cf. Chew, 126–127, for another instance of a pruning instrument used to symbolize temperance. Among several more familiar attributes, a small coffer appears in the famous miniature of Temperance and the other three cardinal virtues illustrating Jean Mansel's *La fleur des histoires* (Brussels, Bib. roy. 9392, fol. 448ᵛ), ca. 1460. Temperantia is seated, holding the coffer on her left knee, on which rests her hand, grasping a pitcher; in her right hand is a pair of spectacles; see Eugène Bacha, *Les très belles miniatures de la Bibliothèque royale de Belgique* (Brussels and Paris, 1913) Plate 24. The pitcher and the coffer appear in another Brussels MS, that of Christine de Pisan's *Epître d'Othée;* consult J. Van den Gheyn, *Christine de Pisan* (Brussels, 1913) Plate 3.

Rarest of all are the summary figures that seek to represent several virtues simultaneously. The lost keystone figure of the rood-loft in the Cathedral at Mainz was of this type, according to Katzenellenbogen, 54, note 1; it represented a man with arms and legs extended in the form of a cross, holding in his hands a balance and a jug, treading underfoot a lion and a dragon. A scroll explained the meaning: *Quattuor hic posita: mixtura, leo, draco, libra signant temperiem, vim, jus, prudenter habentem.* Molsdorf, no. 1060, describes a similar figure on the roof of the Rittencapelle at Hassfurt am Main, dating from the fifteenth century. Bellini's enigmatic *Summa Virtus* in the Accademia in Venice is sometimes interpreted as a representation of Temperance, Justice, and Fortitude, but while Temperantia might indeed be suggested by the two vessels, the other attributes (the blindfold, the flowing forelock, and the globe underfoot) imply Fortune; see Chew, 35–69, and Figs. 52–68. The tomb of Louis Brézé, husband of Diane de Poitiers, in the cathedral of Rouen (attributed to Jean Goujon, ca. 1540) is adorned with a composite figure representing all four cardinal virtues, plus Endurance: a woman who has a bridle in her mouth, a serpent twined around her right arm, a dragon's head clutched in her right hand, and a sword in her left is seated in a bramble bush. Consult Chew, 85, for composite figures representing several of the deadly sins, and for a composite allegory depicting Francis I of France with the attributes (hence the qualities) of Mars, Minerva, Mercury, and Cupid, see *The Age of the Renaissance*, ed. Denys Hay (London, 1967) 178.

Index

Achilles, 32, 41, 69, 75, 90
Actaeon, 50
Adkins, A. W. H., 100 n.26
Adonis, 67
Aelian, *On the Nature of Animals,* 241
n.122; 1.13: 182 n.11; 2.31: 182
n.11; 3.41: 244 n.130; 3.44, 3.5: 182
n.11; 4.11: 242 n.124; 8.17: 182 n.11;
10.33: 182 n.11
Aeschines, 1. 7–12, 20, 137: 123; 21:
124; 25: 126; 25–26: 165; 141–150:
41; 180–181: 94 n.11; 180–181: 167;
182: 127; 184: 128; 195: 167; 2. 4–5:
166; 176: 101 n.28; 3. 168: 102 n.30,
137 n.2
Aeschylus, 39, 66
—*Agamemnon* 176–183: 60
—*Choephoroe* 585–652: 51
—*Eumenides,* 69; 516–537: 99 n.23;
614–618: 148; 681–706: 99 n.23;
1000: 97, 99 n.23; 1019: 97
—*Oresteia,* 97, 99
—*Persians,* 99; 648, 680–842: 147
—*Prometheus Bound,* 32, 60; 216ff,
442ff: 147; 240–241, 939–941, 970:
99 n.22
—*Seven against Thebes (Septem),* 150;
375ff: 181 n.9; 568: 39, 175; 571–
586: 175; 591–592: 40, 175; 592:
150; 601: 207; 610: 142, 175
—*Suppliants,* 49; 106: 207; 197–203:
148
Agamemnon, 90
Agathon, 143

Aidôs (modesty), 87–88, 93 n.6, 146
n.21, 177, 179
Akolasia (wantonness), 103, 114, 127
Alain de Lille, *Anticlaudianus* 7.115–
116: 37 n.30; 8.324–333: 181 n.9
Alciati, *Emblemata,* 250, 253 n.143
Alcidamas, *Odysseus* 13–21: 162
Alcuin, 198 and n.44
—*De Animae Ratione, P.L.* 101, 640D:
199 n.45
—*De Virtutibus et Vitiis, P.L.* 101, 613ff:
198 n.45
Alexander the Great, 26, 41–44
Amazonomachy, 28 and n.6
Ambrose
—*De Helia* 9.29: 189 n.28, 215 n.80
—*De Obitu Theodosii* 13, 14, 25: 223
n.93; 34, 40–51: 120, 200 n.47
—*De Obitu Valentiniani Consolatio* 9, 10,
15–17: 225 n.93
—*De Officiis Ministrorum* 1.6.21,
2.22.115: 193 n.34
—*De Paradiso,* 202; 3, *P.L.* 14, 296ff:
203 n.55
—*De Viduis* 7.40: 189 n.28, 215 n.80
—*De Virginibus* 3.2: 242 n.124
—*De Virginitate* 1.17–18: 204 n.60
—*Ep.* 51: 120
—*Ex. in Luc.* 5.64: 210 n.66
Amphiaraus, 39–40, 104, 125, 142,
149–151, 175–176
Anacreon, Frg. 348: 67 n.112
Anderson, A. R., 55 n.72
Anderson, Warren D., 65 n.102

Andocides, 101; *On His Return* 26: 164;
  On the Mysteries 109, 140: 101 n.29;
  124–131: 166 n. 60; 141: 164
Andrea da Firenze, 218 n.86
Andreia (manliness), 44–45 n.3, 107–
  108, 118, 179 n.4, 187
Angiola, Eloise M., 220 n.88
Animals, symbolic of virtue or vice,
  181–182, 228, 241–250, 259
Anonymous Iamblichi, D-K 89, p. 400:
  137 n.2
Anon. Prolegomena 32, 216 Rabe:
  155 n.38
Antelami, Benedetto, 211–212
Anthologia Palatina 5.179: 191 n.31;
  7.81: 98 n.20; 9.132: 191 n.31;
  11.32: 73
Antiphon, *Tetralogies* 158–160; 1.3.3,
  1.3.11: 167; *Herodes* 1–5: 163
Antisthenes, *Ajax, Odysseus,* 161
Antony, Edgar, 194 n.36, 196 n.37
Apeiria (inexperience), *topos* in rhetoric,
  149, 163–164
Aphrodite (Venus), 70–71; of Elis (by
  Phidias), 182–183, 221 n.90
Apollo, 30–32, 61–65; and Coronis, 50;
  and Daphne, 257; and Marsyas, 62
Apragmosynê (aloofness, absence of
  meddling), 95; rhetorical *topos,* 102,
  149, 159–163
Apteker, Jane, 222 n.90
Apuleius, *Metamorphoses* 5.30: 180 n.8,
  191 n.31
Arachne, 30, 68
Arbor bona, 206–212
Areopagus, 100, 124, 129
Aretê (courage, excellence, moral
  virtue), 137–138, 140, 161–162, 177
  n.3
Aretê politikê (political excellence, suc-
  cess), 44, 64, 68, 87, 89–114, 135
Aristophanes
—*Acharnians,* 151
—*Birds* 1540: 99 n.24
—*Clouds* 962, 1067: 103 n.34; 962,
  1024–1027: 125 n.79; 1063ff: 36
—*Frogs* 1043: 51 n.56
—*Thesmophoriazusae* 548: 48 n.52
—*Wasps* 950–958: 151
Artemis (Diana), 49–50, 66–67, 221
  n.90
Atê (infatuation), 90
Athena (Minerva), 28–32, 67–70;
  Chalinitis, 31, 200 n.47

Athenaeus, 6.245: 129 n.93; 13.559C:
  51 n.56
Auctoritas, 136, 146–147, 152, 172
Augustine, *Against the Academics* 2.9.22:
  78 n.137
—*City of God* 4.20: 183
—*De Gen. contr. Man.* 2.10.13–14: 203
  n.55
—*Solil.* 1.14.24–25: 78 n.137
Augustus, *Res Gestae* 34.3: 152
Aulus Gellius 6.14.6–7: 173 n.76;
  6.14.7: 171 n.71; 7.8: 82; 14.4: 178
  n.3
Autarkeia (independence), 114
Axiôma (high repute), 136, 152–154
Axiopistia (*fides,* credibility), 139–141,
  147, 150, 156
Axtell, Harold L., 184 n.14
Aymard, Jacques, 34 n.22
Ayrton, Michael, 221 n.90

Babelon, Jean, 236 n.113
Bacchylides, 64; 13.183–189: 93;
  15.59–63: 28
Bacon, Helen, 39 n.35, 176 n.83
Barrett, W. S., 35 n.24, 149 n.26
diBartolo, Taddeo, 218 n.87, 225 n.94
Basilikos logos (address to a king), 45, 91,
  104
Bassett, Edward L., 86 n.153
Bellerophon, 26, 30–31, 33–37, 69, 200
  n.47
Beltrán, Luis, 120 n.67
Berenson, Bernhard, 218 n.87, 248
  n.139
Bernardo, Aldo, 84 n.151
Bernards, M., 208 n.65
Bestiary, 241, 254–255, 259
del Biondo, Giovanni, 220 n.87
Blunt, Anthony, 231 n.108
Boas, George, 241 n.122, 253 n.143,
  259 n.153
Boccaccio, *De Claris Mulieribus,* 248
  n.137
Born, Lester K., 144 n.53
Botticelli, 70
Braswell, B. K., 30 n.10
Brilliant, Richard, 29 n.7, 185 n.15
Bromberg, Anne Ruggles, 185 n.15
Brown, Norman, 75 n.130
Brunetto Latini, *Tesoretto,* 222
Buchheit, Vinzenz, 144 nn.15, 17
Buchthal, Hugo, 230 n.105

Buckler, W. H., and W. M. Calder, ed., 54 n.70
Buffière, Felix, 41 n.38, 68 n.114, 78 n.136, 259 n.151
Burgess, Theodore C., 143 n.12, 144 n.16
Burn, A. R., 30 n.12
Burton, R. W. B., 50 n.54, 64 n.100, 118 n.65
Bush, Douglas, 79 n.140
Busolt, Georg, and Heinrich Swoboda, 129 n.92

Caccini, Giovanni, 223 *and see* Plate VII
Callahan, John F., 78 n.137, 79 n.138
Callimachus, Frg. 114: 65 n.104
Calza, Raissa, 183 n.13
Cameron, H. D., 39 n.35
Canuti, Fiorenzo, 240 n.120
Caratzos, Aristide D., 79 n.139
Cardinal virtues, canon of, in: Aeschylus, 39; Carolingian times, 198–202; epideictic oratory, 143–144; *epitaphios logos*, 143; fourteenth-century Italy, 223–227; Pindar, 142; Plato, 104–108, 144; tomb sculpture, 227, 238
Carli, Enzo, 220 n.89, 266
Carnicelli, D. D., 24 n.1
Carracci, Annibale, 80
Castitas (chastity), 211, 215, 218–220
Cebes, *Pinax (Tabula)*, 55; 20.207: 178–179
Centauromachy, 28–29 and n.7
Chantraine, Pierre, 59 nn.84, 85
Charites (Graces), 177
Chase, G. H., 39 n.35, 181 n.9
Châtelet-Lange, Liliane, 245 n.135
Chaucer, *Troilus and Criseyde* 2.104–105: 40 n.36
Chesterton, G. K., 190 n.30
Chew, Samuel C., 237 nn.115, 116; 239 n.118; 242 n.125; 243 n.128; 244 n.129; 248 n.138; 249 n.141; 253 n.143; 258 n.150; 266–267
Chiron, 38
Chrēstos (useful), 102, 135
Chrysippus, 178 n.3; *SVF* 3.691, 692, 693: 117
Cicero
—*Ad Atticum* 13.28.3: 42
—*Ad Quintum fratrem* 1.1.22: 83
—*Brutus* 114–115: 168 n.63; 185, 187–188, 197, 276: 169 n.64

—*De Finibus* 5.12.49: 77 n.135
—*De Imperio Cn. Pompei* 10.27–16.48: 170; 14.41: 81 n.144
—*De Inventione* 1.22: 172 n.75; 2.59.117: 174 n.78; 2.164: 185 n.17
—*De Legibus* 3.3.7: 130 n.96
—*De Officiis*, 198 n.44; 1.159: 199; 2.76: 241 n.121
—*De Oratore* 1.87: 157; 2.115, 121, 128: 169 n.64; 2.182: 154; 2.182–184: 170 n.67; 2.183: 170 n.68; 2.184: 170 n.66; 2.211: 170 n.68; 2.229–230: 168 n.63; 2.317: 170; 2.321: 172; 2.343ff: 174 n.78
—*De Republica* 4.6.6: 130
—*De Senectute* 6.20: 94 n.11
—*Hortensius* 2.24: 84 n.150
—*In Verrem* 2.4.33: 81 n.144
—*Orator* 20–22: 171; 69: 169 n.64; 69–70: 171; 102: 170 n.70; 118: 157 n.42; 128: 170
—*Partitiones Oratoriae* 74ff: 174 n.78
—*Philippica* 2.28, 69:130
—*Pro Caelio*, 170 n.70; 172
—*Somnium Scipionis* 9.21: 84
—*Tusc. Disp.* 1.15.34: 249 n.141; 3.10.21: 42
Cioffari, Vincenzo, 249 n.140
Clairmont, Christoph W., 54 n.70, 65 n.101
Clark, Kenneth, 221 n.90
Claudian, *De Con. Stil.* 2.22.6, 100–122: 185 n.19; 2.22.132–133: 189 n.29
Cleanthes, 60 and n.87; *SVF* 1.526: 78
Clementia, 45, 104, 184–185
Commager, Steele, 73 n.126
Connor, W. Robert, 102 n.31
Conrad of Hirzau, *Speculum Virginum*, 208–210
Cope, E. M., 136 n.1, 141 n.9; and J. E. Sandys, 141 n.9, 152 n.34, 169 n.65
Cornford, F. M., 47 n.48, 57 n.77
Coster, Charles H., 121 n.71
Coulter, James, 153 n.36, 159 n.45, 161 n.51
Courcelle, Pierre, 79 n.138
Crates, 177
Crichton, G. H. and E. R., 220 n.88
Critias, Frg. 6: 95 n.13
Cumont, Franz, 78 n.136
Curtius, Ernst Robert, 174 n.79
Cynic diatribe, 114–115
Cyprian, *De zelo et livore* 16: 189 n.27

D'Alverny, M. Th., 212 n.69
Danae, 184 n.14, 265
Dante, *Paradiso* 3.34ff: 133 n.105; 21: 120, 249 n.141
—*Purgatorio* 19.7-33: 77 n.135; 29: 248 n.138
Day, Edmund Ezra, 262 n.158
Daye, John, *A Booke of Christian Prayers,* 266
Decker, Hans, 212 n.70
de Deguilleville, Guillaume, *Pèlerinage de vie humaine,* 242
Delphic maxims, 30, 38, 40, 63
Democritus, Frg. 294: 207
Demosthenes, 19.251ff: 165; 19.285-286: 167; 21: 166 n.60; 21.219-222, 227: 168; 24.75: 102 n.30; 27.2: 149 n.26; 38.26: 164; 47.53-56: 128 n.88; 55.7: 149 n.26; 59.64-71: 128 n.89
Demus, Otto, 210 n.66, 213 n.73
Des Places, Edouard, S. J., 64 n.99
Détienne, Marcel, 31 n.15, 69 n.115, 78 n.137, 127 n.84
Dido, 23-24, 53 n.64
Dikaiosynê (justice), 87-88, 105, 143, 178 n.3, 179 n.4
Dikê (justice), 87-88, 93, 142, 178 n.3, 187 n.24
Dillon, Myles, 33 n.18
Dio Chrysostom, *Or.* 1: 55, 115 n.55; 1-4: 46 n.47; 2.53, 55-56: 114 n.54; 2.54: 114, 115 n.55; 2.70-71: 114; 2.79: 117; 3.67, 10: 114; 32: 115 n.55
Diogenes Laertius, 3.43: 109 n.44; 6.7: 56
Dionysius of Halicarnassus
—*Ant. Rom.* 2.25, 2.26-27: 130 n.95; 2.69: 53 n.65; 4.64.4: 52
—*Lysias* 8: 156 n.40
Dionysus, 71-73
Dittenberger, Wilhelm, 129 n.94
Dodds, E. R., 30 n.12, 53 n.66, 59 n.84
Domenichino, 246, 258 and n.149 *and see* Plate IX
Dorez, Leon, 238 n.118
Dorigo, Wladimiro, 28 n.5, 34 n.22
Douglas, A. E., 170 n.69
Dover, K. J., 126 n.82, 158 n.44
Downey, Glanville, 187 n.24
Drastêrion (the active principle), 95, 100
Drew-Bear, Thomas, and W. D. Lebek, 61 n.88

Dunbabin, J. J., 31 n.15
Durry, Marcel, 113 n.52
Dvornik, Francišek, 120 n.68

Ebersolt, J., 244 n.133
Ehrenberg, Victor, 95 n.14, 159 n.46
Eirênê (Peace), 93, 142, 178 and n.3, 187 n.24
Eisler, Colin, 187 n.22
Else, Gerald, 140 n.8
Emblem books, 250-260
Endgass, Robert, 246 n.136
Enkrateia (self-control), 76
Ennius, 249 n.141
Ennoia (insight), 178 n.3
Ephebia, 124-126
Ephorus, 64
Epicharmus, Frg. 286: 48 n.51
Epieikeia (reasonableness), 102 n.31; 138, 140 n.8, 155, 166, 170, 174 n.77
Epistêmê (wisdom), 38, 45 n.43, 100, 105, 178 n.3, 179
Epitaphios logos, 143 and n.13
Epitaphs, 96-97, 177
Esdaile, K. A., 237 n.115
Êthopoiia (portrayal of character), 139, 147, 158, 160
Êthos (character) as a mode of persuasion, 136-152, 154-158, 168-176
Euboulia (good planning), 99
Eubulus, 51 n.56
Euergesia (benefaction), 143, 145, 148, 159-162, 164
Eukosmia (orderliness), 126
Eunoia (good will), 140-141, 146, 155, 159
Eunomia (good order), 93, 97-98, 142
Euripides, 67
—*Alcestis* 182, 615: 48 n.52
—*Andromache* 235: 48 n.52
—*Autolycus,* Frg. 282.23-28: 137 n.2
—*Bacchae,* 32; 170ff: 73 n.124; 504, 641: 71; 604ff: 72 n.123; 1341-1343: 72
—*Bellerophon,* 32; Frg. 285: 34
—*Electra* 53, 261, 367, 378, 382, 386-387: 99
—*Hecuba* 293-295: 152
—*Heracleidae,* 75 n.131
—*Hercules Furens* 339-347: 58 n.81; 1002-1006: 69
—*Hippolytus,* 35, 71, 148-149, 242 n.124; 1420-1422: 67 n.109

—*Hypsipyle*, 40 n.36, 149–151, 175;
Frg. 22.9–10: 150 n.29; Frg. 60.44–
45, 54, 115–117: 150; 58–59: 61 n.89
—*Iphigeneia in Aulis* 543–545: 31 n.13
—*Ixion*, 32
—*Medea* 214: 128 n.87; 545ff: 148
—*Phaethon*, 32
—*Phoenissae* 177–178: 40 n.36, 175;
523–525, 532, 554: 151 n.31; 541–
544: 26; 1111–1112: 23, 40, 150, 176
—*Stheneboea*, Frg. 672: 34
—*Suppliants*, 45; 423–425: 152
—*Troades* 645–656: 48 n.52, 110
—Fragments, 503: 31 n.13
Eusebeia (piety), 45 n.43, 93, 149, 177
Eustathius, 78; *Commentarii ad Homeri
Odysseam* I.1581: 38 n.31
Eustathius Makrembolites, *Hysminê and
Hysminias* 2.2–6: 179 n.4, 190 n.30;
4.23: 181, 191 n.31
Euteleia (frugality), 177
Evagoras, 45
Evans, E. P., 255 n.147
Evans, Joan, 191 n.33, 194 n.37, 196
n.38, 202 n.53, 203 n.54, 204 n.59

Fantham, Elaine, 139 n.6, 169 n.64,
170 n.66
Farnell, L. R., 69 n.115
Fears, J. Rufus, 41 n.39
Fehrle, E., 35 n.24
Festus, 236, 237, 243: 183 n.13
Filarete, 258 n.150
Finley, J. H., Jr., 152 n.35
Fletcher, Phineas, 223 n.92
Florus, 1.22.40: 81 n.143
Fontenrose, Joseph, 27 n.4
Fonts, baptismal, 193–194, 204; holy
water, 221 n.90
Forrest, W. G., 94 n.9
Fountains, adorned with virtues, 225,
226 n.94
Franciscan iconography, 218 and n.87
de Francovich, Geza, 211 nn.67, 68,
212 n.69
Frazer, Sir James, 133 n.102; 243 n.127
Freeman, Rosemary, 253 n.143
French moral treatises, 215–217
Freyhan, R., 197 n.42
Friedländer, Paul, 96 n.16

Gaisser, Julia H., 30 n.11, 34 n.19
Garvie, A. F., 49 n.53

Gaulli (Baciccio), 190 n.30, 258 n.151
Germanic iconography, 212–214
Gigantomachy, 27–30, 28 n.5
Giordano, Luca, 67, 255, 266 *and see*
Plate XII
Giotto, Arena Chapel, 197, 217; Assisi,
Lower Church, 218
Godfridus Canonicus, *Lumen Animae*,
242 n.125
Godwin, Frances, 189 n.28, 215 n.77,
216 nn.82, 83, 217 n.84
Gogarty, Oliver, 71 n.121
Gombrich, E. H., 179 n.4
Gorgias, 143–144, 160
—*Epitaphios*: 144 n.15
—*Helen* 1: 143
—*Palamedes* 1–3, 29–32: 161; 15, 21:
153
Gower, John, *Mirour de l'omme* 241–
300, 759–9720: 242 n.125
Green, Henry, 253 n.143
Green, Rosalie, 194 n.36
Green, William M., 197 n.43
Greenhill, E. S., 207 n.64, 208 n.65
Gregory, Pope, 198; *Moralia in Job*
31.45: 189 n.29
Gregory of Nazianzus
—*Anth. Pal.* 1.93: 180 n.5
—*Carmina Historica (De Seipso)* 45.
229ff (*P.G.* 37, 1369ff): 84 n.152,
178 n.2, 179 and n.5
—*Carmina Moralia* 2.536–539, 543–
545, 580–582 (*P.G.* 37, 620–624)
—*Oratio* 43 (*P.G.* 36, 524): 182 n.11
Gregory of Nyssa, *De Beatitudinibus*,
P.G. 44, 1213ff, 1241: 210 n.66
Griessmaier, Viktor, 259 n.151
Grimaldi, William M. A., S. J., 145
n.19, 158 n.43
Gringoire, Pierre, *Chasteau de Labour*,
243
Grivot, Denis, and George Zarnecki,
194 n.37
Grube, G. M. A., 173 n.76
Guthrie, W. K. C., 66 n.108, 178 n.2
Gynaikonomoi (superintendents of
women), 129–130

Hagneia (purity), 177–179
Hamann, Richard, 192 n.33, 243 n.127
Hamdorf, F. W., 178 n.2
Hamilton, J. R., 41 n.39

Hanfmann, George M. A., 178 n.3, 187 n.24, 202 n.52
Hanna, Ralph, III, 189 n.27
Hanson, Anne Coffin, 225 n.94
Harrison, A. R. W., 128 n.89
Hasychia (Att. *Hêsychia,* quietness), 98, 102, 177
Hayter, W. G., 262 n.157
Haywood, R. H., 81 n.142
Heckscher, W. S., 182 n.11, 183 n.12, 254 n.146, 255 n.147
Heinze, Richard, 172 n.73
Hellwig, Antje, 141 n.10, 158 n.43
Heracles, 41, 80, 84
Herington, C. J., 28 n.7
Herodotus, 1.31: 63 n.96; 7.10: 148 n.25
Herrad of Landsberg, *Hortus Deliciarum,* 79; 205; 217 n.85; 241 n.123
Hesiod, 59; *Erga* 214ff: 110; 287–292: 55; *Theogony* 27: 38 n.32
Hildegard of Bingen, *Liber Scivias,* 266
Hill, G. F., 245 n.135
Hippolytus, 33–37, 67, 187
Hipponax, 63: 98 n.20
Hoener, Karl, 67 n.112
Höistad, Ragnar, 41 n.38, 77 n.134
Homer
—*Iliad* 1: 69; 1.248–249: 136 n.1; 1.273–274: 146; 2.434–440: 136 n.1; 4.310–316: 136 n.1; 5: 30 n.11; 5.440–443: 32, 63; 9.18: 90; 9.79: 136 n.1; 9.94: 136; 9.103–105: 146; 9.179: 136 n.1; 9.443: 137; 9.506–509, 640: 146 n.21; 10: 74 n.128; 11.784: 146; 16.386: 59 n.84; 19.270–272: 90; 21.462–464: 62; 23: 74 n.128; 24: 30; 24.114: 90; 24.503–504: 146 n.21
—*Odyssey,* 40; 69; 1: 59; 1.334: 184 n.14; 2.230–234: 147 n.22; 6.149–185: 147; 7.60: 28; 7.323ff: 38 n.31; 11.576–600: 30; 13.332: 74 n.128; 14.81ff: 59 n.85; 20.18: 76; 20.23: 74 n.129; 24: 59 n.85; 24.351–352: 59
Homeric Hymns, to Aphrodite 5.20: 67 n.112; to Apollo, 61; to Dionysus 7.49, 54: 72; 7.13–15: 72 n.123; to Hermes 4.368–386: 137
Homoiôsis (likeness) to God, 61 n.88, to man, 58
Homonoia (reconciliation), 101, 103

Honorius Augustodunensis, *P.L.* 172, 443: 182 n.11
Horace
—*Epistles* 1.2.17–18, 23–26: 77; 2.3.343: 204
—*Odes* 1.5.1: 190 n.30; 1.12.13–16: 60 n.87; 1.18.7: 73; 1.25.13–14: 242 n.124; 1.27.3: 73; 1.36.15: 190 n.30; 1.38.3–4: 190 n.30; 2.3.14: 190 n.30; 2.10.17–20: 65; 2.11.14: 190 n.30; 3.4: 119; 3.4.45–48: 60 n.87; 3.4.60: 65 n.105; 3.4.60–64: 64; 3.4.79–80: 37; 3.7.13–20: 34 n.20; 3.19.22, 3.29.3: 190 n.30; 4.6.1–3: 62 n.92; 4.7.25–28: 36; 4.11.25–29: 34 n.20
—*Sermones* 1.1.106: 249 n.141
Horapollo, *Hieroglyphics,* 182 n.11; 253 n.143; 255 n.147; 259
Houvet, Etienne, 198 n.43
Huart, Pierre, 95 n.14
Hugh of St. Victor, *De Bestiis, P.L.* 177, 72–73, 25, 26: 182 n.11; *De Claustro Animae, P.L.* 176,1052–1053: 206 n.62
Hughes, Merritt, 79 n.140
Hulbert, Viola B., 200 n.48
Hutton, James, 253 n.143
Hybris (arrogance, violence), 98, 100, 123; punishment of, in myth, 26–33
Hygieia (health), 177–178
Hyginus, 256: 48 n.52
Hypereides 6.4: 168 n.62; 6.8: 143 n.14

Iamblichus, *Letter to Arete on Sophrosyne:* 29 n.8; *De Vita Pythagorica* 57: 77 n.135
Isaeus, 1.1, 4.28–30: 103 n.33; 8.5, 10.1: 149 n.26; Frg. 30: 164
Isidore of Seville, 198; *Etymologiae* 2.24.6: 200 n.47; 12: 241 n.122
Isocrates, 103–104, 124
—*Antidosis* 67–70: 104; 111: 103; 278: 154
—*Areopagiticus,* 45; 4, 13, 20, 37, 48: 103 n.34
—*De Bigis* 28: 143
—*Evagoras,* 45, 104, 143–144; 8: 142; 22: 165
—*Helen* 31: 45 n.43, 100, 105, 144
—*Nicocles,* 104, 143–144; 29–30: 163
—*On the Peace,* 103–104; 30, 58, 119: 100 n.27, 103 n.36
—*Panegyricus,* 45; 3, 104, 173: 103 n.35; 80–82: 168 n.62

Jacoby, Felix, 143 n.13
Jaeger, Werner, 38 n.33, 58 n.80
Jantzen, Hans, 213 n.72
Jean of Hanville, *Architrenius*, 37 n.30
Jerome, *Adversus Jovinianum* 1.285: 190
n.30, 254
John Cassian, *Conlationes* 2.1–4: 201
n.50
John Chrysostom, *Hom. XV in Matt.*,
210 n.66
John Climacus, *Scala Paradisi*, 188
John of Wales, *Breviloquium de
virtutibus*, 232
Joly, Robert, 179 n.4
Jourdain, M., 239 n.118
Judith, 187 n.28, 215–217
Julian
—*Letter to a Priest* 303D: 40 n.36
—*Misopogon* 342D-364D: 115 n.55
—*Or.* 1.17A: 185 n.19; 32B, 41C,
45C–46D: 46 and n.46; 41C–D: 185
n.19
—2.56D-57A, 75Aff: 46; 95A, 100C:
185 n.19
—3.123B: 185 n.20; 127C–D, 128D: 28
n.6, 51; 127D: 184 n.14
Julius Pomerius, *Vita Contemplativa*
3.19: 201–202 n.51
Juvenal, 6.306-313: 133 n.103; 6.308:
183 n.13; 10.325: 34 n.20, 51 n.56

Kabirsch, Jürgen, 185 n.18
Kahr, Madlyn Millner, 184 n.14
Kaibel, Georg, 125 n.77
Kakia (cowardice, wickedness), 55, 138
Katzenellenbogen, Adolf, 187 n.24,
188 nn.25, 26, 191 nn.32, 33, 196
nn.37, 38, 197 nn.40, 43, 201 nn.49,
51, 202 n.51, 203 n.54, 206 nn.62,
63, 207 n.64, 211 n.67, 212 n.71, 214
n.75, 216 n.81, 240 n.119, 241 n.123,
248 n.138, 267
Kennedy, George, 136 n.1, 139 n.6,
143 n.13, 145 n.20, 153 n.37, 159
n.45, 161 n.152, 162 n.53, 172 n.74
Keuls, Eva, 49 n.53
Kitzinger, Ernst, 187 n.23
Klein, H. Arthur, 236 n.114
Köhler, Wilhelm, 201 n.49
Körte, Werner, 255 n.148
Kosmer, Ellen, 215 n.79
Kosmos (order), 97, 105
Kosmos akosmos (adornment un-
adorned), 55, 179, 186

Kuhn, Helmut, 57 n.77
Künstle, Karl, 187 n.24, 197 n.40, 214
n.74
Kurtz, Donna C., and John Boardman,
54 n.70

Lacey, W. K., 127 nn.83, 85, 128 n.86
Laistner, M. L. W., 201 n.51
Lattimore, Richmond, 48 n.52, 52 n.58,
54 n.68, 118 n.64
Laura, 24, 83, 250
Leonidas of Tarentum, *Anth. Pal.*
7.452: 37 n.29
Levi, Doro, 36 n.27, 187 n.23
Lexis êthikê, 157
Libanius, 1.7: 51 n.57
Liberal Arts, with cardinal virtues, 199,
222, 230 n.107, 265
Liternum, 23, 83, 248
Livy, 1.57.9: 54 n.67; 1.57-59: 52 and
n.61; 8.18: 132; 9.18.1: 42; 10.23.1-
10: 132; 10.23.3-10: 183 n.13;
10.23.4-11: 53 n.63; 26.50: 81 n.143;
29.14.12: 53 n.64; 30.14: 82; 34.1-
8: 131; 38.52: 82; 38.56.10-13: 82
Lloyd-Jones, Hugh, 57 n.79, 59 n.84
Loeffler, Elaine, 184 n.15
Lord, Mary Louise, 53 n.64
Lorenzetti, Ambrogio, Fresco of Good
Government, 226–227
Lucian, *Dialogues of the Gods* 23: 68
n.113; *Piscator* 16: 179 n.4
Lucretia, 23, 52-53, 248 n.137
Luke, 1:29, 1:34: 213–214
Lycophron, *Menedemus*, Frg. 3: 115
n.56
Lycurgus
—of Athens, 109, 124-126; *Against
Leocrates* 11: 126 n.81; 146-150: 168
n.62
—of Sparta, 94, 117, 123
Lydus, Joannes, *De Mensibus* 4.65: 132
n.102
Lysias, 12.3: 149 n.26; 12.21: 164;
14.12: 167 n.61; 14.25-29: 166 n.60;
14.30-40: 162 n.54; 16.11, 18.20: 160
n.50; 19.2: 149 n.26; 21.19: 164;
22.20: 116 n.59; 24.15: 160 n.50;
27.5: 116 n.59

Macrobius, 198; *Saturnalia* 1.17.13: 65
n.104; *In Somnium Scipionis*, 84 and
n.153; 1.8: 199 n.46
de Maffei, Fernanda, 229 n.102

Magnanimitas (greatness of soul), 225 n.94
Mâle, Emile, I, Figs. 264, 265: 192 n.33; II: 196 nn.38, 39, 40, 207 n.64, 258 n.150; III: 215 n.77, 231 nn.108, 109, 236 n.113, 241 n.123, 242 nn.124, 125, 243 n.128, 244 n.129, 259 n.152; IV: 246 n.136
Mandowsky, Erna, 253 n.143
Mantegna, 70, 191 n.31, 193 n.35, 250
Marbod of Rennes, *De Lapidibus*, 248 n.140
Marriage Sarcophagi, 184
Marsyas, 62, 64-65
Martianus Capella, *Marriage of Mercury and Philology*, 198; 2.127-130: 186; 2.128-129: 199; 5.502-503: 174
Martin, Henry, 197 n.41, 215 n.78
Martin, John Rupert, 80 n.141, 188 n.25, 237 n.116, 258 n.149
Martin of Bracara (Ps.-Seneca), *Formula Vitae Honestae*, 231; 4: 200 n.47; 6-9: 199 n.46
Mattingly, Harold, 184 n.14, 185 n.16
Maximus of Tyre, 41.5: 57 n.76
Mayo, M. E., 184 n.14
Megalopsychia (greatness of soul), 44, 187-188
Meiss, Millard, 218 n.87, 230 n.105, 238 n.116
Melisande Psalter, 192-193
Meliteniotes, 179 n.4; 248-249 n.140
Melito, *Clavis Scripturae Sacrae*, 241 n.122
di Mena, Juan, *El Laberinto de Fortuna*, 119
Menander Comicus, *Monostichae* 545: 148 n.24
Menander Rhetor, 3.363: 129 n.94
Mendell, E. L., 194 n.37
Merkelbach, Reinhold, 54 n.67
Mesk, Josef, 113 n.52
Methodius, *Symposium* 8.3.83: 207
Milton, John, *Comus* 452, 636, 766: 80; *Second Defence*, 83
Miner, Dorothy, 250 n.142
Mitchel, Fordyce, 125 nn.76, 78
Mitford, T. B., 178 n.2
Moderatio (moderation), 174, 199-200, 241
Modestia (modesty, self-restraint), 174, 193-194, 196 n.37, *and see* Plate IV
Molsdorf, Wilhelm, 207 n.64
Mommsen, T. E., 55 n.74

Montagu, Jennifer, 35 n.23
de Montault, Barbier, 223 n.91
Montini, Renzo U., 260 n.155
Moria logou (*partes orationis*, parts of the oration), 155-156, 163-168
Morrow, Glenn, 64 n.98, 108 n.42, 117 n.62
Mourelatos, Alexander, 57 n.76
Münz, Ludwig, 236 n.114
Murphy, Charles T., 151 n.32
Murray, Oswyn, 118 n.63
Musurillo, Herbert, S. J., 56 n.75

Nemesis, 178 and n.3
Neopythagoreans, theory of kingship, 112
Nero, as model of *clementia*, 46
Nestor, as exemplar of eloquence, 38, 136, 146, 171; as *sôphronistês*, 46, 116
New (Rouen) Iconography, 200, 231-236
Nisbet, R. G. M., 170 n.70
Nock, A. D., 55 n.74
Nomoi peri sôphrosynês (*leges de pudicitia, de adulteriis*), 131-132
Nonnus, *Dionysiaca* 14.363, 15.80, 33.368: 236 n.114
Nördstrom, Folke, 192 n.33
North, Helen F., 33 n.17, 39 n.35, 44 n.42, 47 n.49, 48 n.50, 53 n.73, 60 n.86, 63 n.96, 73 n.125, 76 n.132, 88 n.1, 95 n.14, 98 n.8, 106 n.39, 107 n.40, 112 nn.48, 49, 119 n.66, 142 n.11, 144 n.15, 171 n.72, 178 n.2, 180 n.7, 188 n.24, 201 n.49, 259 n.151, 260 n.155

Odysseus, 40-41, 74-80
Oehler, J., 125 n.76
Ogilvie, R. M., 52 n.61, 53 n.62
Olympiodorus, *In Phaed.* 45: 181 n.10
Onions, R. B., 90 n.2
Or San Michele, Tabernacle, 211, 222, 238 n.117
Ottò, Walter F., 66 n.107
Ovid
—*Amores* 1.2.23-42: 242 n.124, 246; 1.2.31-32: 184 n.14
—*Fasti* 4.157: 133 n.102; 4.290-348: 53 n.64
—*Metamorphoses* 1.454: 62; 1.510-511: 62 n.91; 2.137: 254; 6.5-145: 29 n.9
—*Remedia Amoris* 135-150: 227 n.97; 139: 191 n.31

Palmer, Robert E. A., 53 n.63, 132
nn.100, 101, 183 n.13
Pan, 62
Panofsky, Erwin, 55 n.74, 67 n.110, 84
n.153, 179 n.4, 184 n.14, 187 n.23,
204 n.60, 228 nn.98, 99, 230 n.106,
231 n.108, 236 n.113, 238 n.117, 242
n.124, 253 nn.143, 145
Panofsky, Erwin and Dora, 255 n.147
Parke, H. W., and D. E. W. Wormell,
63 n.95
Parma, Baptistery of, 211–212
Patterson, Annabel M., 174 n.77
Paul, *Eph.* 6.13ff: 181 n.9; 6.16: 189;
Gal. 5.22: 207
Pausanias, 1.8.2, 1.33.3ff, 5.18.2: 178
n.3; 6.25.1: 243; 9.11.2: 69 n.115
Peek, Werner, 99 n.22
Peleus, 33–36
Pencz, George, 24
Peraldus, *Summa de vitiis et virtutibus*,
215 n.77
Pericles, 44, 103, 240
Perkins, John Ward, 183 n.13
Perseus, 29
Perugino, 225, 240
Pesellino, Francesco, 86 *and see* Plate
III
Petrarch
—*Africa*, 84
—*De Viris Illustribus*, 239
—*Triumph of Chastity (Pudicizia)*, 23–24,
83, 133 and n.104, 183, 246, 249–250
—*Triumphs (Trionfi)*, 242 n.124, 246–
250
Pfeiffer, Rudolf, 65 n.103
Pfohl, Gerhard, 96 nn.17, 18, 97 n.18
Phidias, Athena Parthenos, 28 and n.7;
Elean Aphrodite, 182–183, 221 n.90
Philanthrôpia (clementia), 114, 185
Philodemus, *On the Good King According
to Homer*, 118
Philo Judaeus, *Legg. All.* 1.14.43: 203
n.55; 1.14.43–45, 1.17.56–58: 207
n.64
Phrenes (midriff? lungs? feelings,
mind), 89–90
Phronêsis (prudence), 68, 100, 105, 108,
140
Physiologus, 182 n.11, 241
Pindar
—*Isthmian* 8: 36 n.25, 93; 8.24–29: 142
—*Nemean* 1.67f: 28; 3.53ff: 38; 5.32ff:
36 n.25; 8: 75 n.130

—*Olympian* 1.56: 119; 2.75–76: 38
n.31; 3.43–44: 41 n.38; 13.6–7: 142
—*Paean* 1.10:93
—*Pythian* 1: 27, 60; 1.70: 64; 2.21–48:
31; 2.22: 119; 2.74: 38 n.31; 3.20–
23: 50; 3.61–62: 31 n.14; 3.63: 38;
3.86–103: 35; 4.90–92: 66; 5.64–67:
64; 8: 60, 75 n.130; 8.12–20: 28;
12.10–11, 18–21: 65
de Pisan, Christine, *Épître d'Othée*,
232–233 *and see* Frontispiece
Pisano, Andrea, 218 *and see* Plate VI
—Giovanni, 220–221 and n.90
—Nicola, 220
Pistis (good faith), 93, 177
Pittacus, 30, 122–123; Frg. 10.13: 98
n.20
Plants, allegorical significance of,
257–258 and n.151
Plato
—*Apology*, 104–105, 163 n.58; 36D:
176 n.81; 41B: 76
—*Charmides*, 64; 155D: 56; 164D: 63;
171D–172A: 105
—*Critias* 121C: 116 n.59
—*Epistle* 6, 117
—*Gorgias*, 90, 100 n.27; 478D: 116
n.59; 487A–B: 141; 491B–C, 492Aff:
90 n.3; 491D: 105; 492D1–493D4:
53 n.66; 506C–508C: 27
—*Laches* 188C–D: 157–158
—*Laws*, 64, 73, 122; 1 and 2: 71;
637A–B: 95 n.13, 108; 666A–C: 73
n.124; 691C–E: 94; 710A5ff: 108
n.41; 710A–711E: 38 n.33, 116;
710C–D: 136; 711E: 116,136;
716C–D: 61 and n.88; 730E: 163;
802D–E: 108; 802E: 111 n.46; 806C:
129 n.91; 815D: 108; 854D: 116
n.59; 908E, 963A–966B: 108;
964A4ff: 108 n.41
—*Menexenus* 246D–248A: 143 n.14
—*Meno* 73A6ff: 99 n.25; 74Bff: 110
—*Phaedo* 68C–E: 106; 69A: 116 n.59;
82C: 106
—*Phaedrus*, 56, 73, 120, 180, 242
n.124; 230A: 56, 227 n.97; 246E: 60;
269E–270D: 145
—*Protagoras*, 87–88; 323A: 88
—*Republic*, 104–107; 2 and 3: 48, 107;
4: 198 n.44; 8: 57, 107; 361B, 362A:
176 n.81; 378 E: 58; 390D: 76;
399D–E: 65 n.102; 432A: 106; 471A:
116 n.59; 493Aff: 56; 547E: 107;

Plato (*cont.*)
560B–C: 57 n.78; 588B–C: 56;
588Bff: 227 n.97
—*Statesman* 307E–308A, 307C: 107
—*Symposium* 196B–197A: 143;
209A6–8: 105
—*Theaetetus* 173Cff: 144 n.17; 176A:61
n.88
—*Timaeus*, 57; 29D: 54 n.71; 70Eff:
227 n.97
Pleonexia (overreaching), 27, 98, 100
Pliny the Elder, *Natural History*, 241
n.122; 7.35: 53 n.64; 8.5.13: 182
n.11; 8.31.76: 244 n.130; 10.52.104,
10.86.188: 182 n.11; 28.2.12: 53
n.65, 248 n.137, 253 n.144
Pliny the Younger, *Ep.* 3.18.1–2, 3–4:
113; *Panegyric* 3.2, 9.1, 16.1–3, 17.4,
21.1, 47.6, 54.5, 55.5, 58.2: 113 n.51
Plotinus, *Ennead* 1.6.8: 78, 84 n.150
Plutarch
—*Lives: Alexander* 21.11: 81 n.145; 30:
42 n.41; 30.10: 81 n.145; 42.7–10: 42;
Aristides 3.5: 176 n.81; *Caesar* 17:
42; *Cleomenes* 16: 94 n.10; 11, 13:
117; *Dion* 6: 52 n.58; *Fabius Maximus*
19.4: 181 n.9; *Lycurgus* 12: 95 n.12;
30: 117; 31: 94; *Marcellus* 9.6–7: 181
n.9; *Nicias* 8.6: 126 n.81; *Numa* 20.8:
112 n.48; *Solon* 14.6: 98 n.19; 21:
127; 21.5: 128 n.87; 23.2: 127 n.85;
Sulla (Comparison with Lysander) 3.
2–5: 131 n.97
—*De Fort. Alex.* 2.6: 81 n.145; 326E: 44;
338D: 42 n.41
—*De Fort. Rom.* 5: 184 n.14
—*De Iside et Osiride* 48 (370C): 70
—*Gryllus:* 241 n.122
—*Moralia:* 142D: 183 n.12; 295C: 92
n.5; 381E: 183 n.12; 776D: 117;
789E: 94 n.11; 806F–807A: 102
n.31; 988F–991D: 78; 1126C–D: 117
n.62
Polybius, 6.48.8: 92 n.10; 10.19.3: 82
n.148; 10.19.7: 81 n.143; 31.24–30:
118
Polypragmosynê (meddling), 95 and
nn.14, 15, 100
Pope-Hennessy, John, 86 n.154, 218
n.87, 220 n.88, 221 n.90, 228 n.99,
229 n.102, 237 n.115, 242 n.124
Porphyry, *De Abstin.* 3.11: 182 n.11
Porter, Arthur Kingsley, I: 189 n.28,

203 n.54, 204 n.58; III: 203 n.54,
204 n.57, 211 n.67
Praz, Mario, 248 n.139, 253 n.143
Prior, E. S., and A. Gardner, 194 n.36
Prodicus, 55; 179 n.4
Prometheus, 87–88
Propertius, 2.6 and 7: 133 n.103;
3.19.3: 200 n.47; 3.24.19: 184 n.14;
4.7.55ff: 51 n.56; 4.11.52: 53 n.64
Protagoras, 87–88
Prudentius, *Psychomachia,* 188–198,
263; 40–52, 58–69, 76–88, 98–108:
189; 354–355: 190 n.30; 371–406,
427–431, 433–446: 190; 881–883:
190 n.30
Ps.-Andocides, 4.13–33: 166 n.60;
4.40: 167 n.61
Ps.-Bonaventure, *Dieta Salutis,* 242
Ps.-Demosthenes, 60.3, 6, 17: 143 n.14;
61.30: 41
Ps.-Hugh of St. Victor, *De Fructibus
Carnis et Spiritus,* 206, 215; 1: 206
n.62; 9–10: 189 n.29
Ps.-Plato, *Axiochus* 367A: 125 n.76
Ps.-Plutarch, *On Animals,* 241 n.122
Psychomachia (battle of the soul), 188–
198. *See also* Prudentius
Pudicitia (*Pudicizia,* Chastity), 23–24,
183–184, 189, 246–250
—*Patricia,* 23, 131–133, 248
—*Plebeia,* 232
Puech, Aimé, 186 n.22

Quintilian, 1.9.3: 173; 4.1.6–12, 13:
172 n.75; 6.2.8–10: 170 n.67; 6.2–
20: 173–174

Rabanus Maurus, *P.L.* 109, 539–559:
216 n.83; *P.L.* 110, 1118: 228 n.100
Raby, F. J. E., 37 n.30
Radulphus Glaber, *Historia Sui Temporis, P.L.* 142, 613–615: 202 n.52
Raggio, Olga, 223 n.91
Rambaud, Michel, 45 n.45
Raphael, 84–86, 237 n.116, 255–257,
260
Raubitschek, A. E., 30 n.13
Réau, Louis, I: 190 n.30, 192 n.33, 194
n.34, 196 nn.37, 38, 39, 40, 202 n.52,
203 n.56, 241 n.122, 244 n.133, 245
n.135, 249 n.140, 258 nn.150, 151,
259 n.153; II: 189 n.28, 201 n.49,
215 n.81
Reckford, Kenneth J., 35 n.24, 119
n.66, 128 n.87

Reesor, Margaret, 111 n.47, 117 n.61
Rehorst, A. J., 260 n.154
Reinmuth, O. W., 125 n.76, 126 n.80
Renehan, Robert F., 125 n.78
Rhadamanthys, 38, 41, 92
Rhetorica ad Alexandrum, 3: 166; 11, 22, 32: 156 n.41; 29: 151 n.33, 156 n.39; 35: 165; 36: 151 n.33, 172 n.75; 37: 155; 38: 153; 1442a 7ff: 139 n.6
Rhetorica ad Herennium, 174; 1.8.13: 164 n.59; 3.6.10: 174 n.78
Richter, Jean Paul and Irma A., 245 n.133, 248 n.139
Ripa, Cesare, *Iconologia*, 180, 250-260
Rivers of Paradise, equated with cardinal virtues, 202-204
Robert, Carl, 36 n.26, 187 n.23
Robertson, D. W., 28 n.6
Robinson, D. M., 34 n.22
Robinson, Richard, 122 n.72
Roscher, W. H., 178 n.2
Rosenmeyer, Thomas, 39 n.35
Rosenthal, Earl, 41 n.38
Rowley, George, 226 n.95, 242 n.124
Rubinstein, Nicolai, 225 n.94, 226 n.95, 240 n.119
Ruhmer, Eberhard, 249 n.141
Ryan, Eugene E., 145 n.19
Ryberg, Inez Scott, 113 n.50, 184 n.15

Sacraments, correlated with virtues, 216-217
Sallust, *Catiline* 54: 176 n.81
Salmi, Mario, 191 n.33
Sassetta, 42, 218, *and see* Plate II
Saxl, Fritz, 190 n.30, 207 n.64, 214 nn.75, 76, 242 nn.125, 126
Schiller, Gertrud, 214 nn.74, 75
Schleier, Reinhart, 179 n.4
Schmitt, M. L., 31 n.15
Schubring, Paul, 24 n.1, 82 n.147, 86 nn.155, 156
Scipio Africanus (Elder), 23, 26, 80-86, 240, *and see* Plate III
Scipio Africanus (Younger), 83, 86 n.153
Scullard, H. H., 81 n.142, 82 n.146, 84 n.151
Séchan, Louis, and Pierre Lévêque, 59 n.83, 61 n.90, 64 n.97, 66 n.108
Segal, Charles, 118 n.64, 153 n.36, 159 n.45
del Sellaio, Jacopo, 24 *and see* Plate I

Semonides, 7.108-110: 48 n.51
Seneca
—*De Beata Vita* 15.5: 181 n.9
—*De Beneficiis* 2.16.2: 42 n.40
—*De Clementia* 1.1.3: 181 n.9, 217 n.85; 1.11.12: 185 n.17; 1.25.1, 2.3.3: 46
—*Ep.* 51: 83
—*Ep.* 83.19, 23: 42 n.40
—*Ep.* 86: 83
—*Ep.* 113.29: 42 n.40
Serpotta, Giacomo, 255 n.148
Setton, Kenneth, 121 n.71
Seven Wise Men, 30, 98 and n.20
Seznec, Jean, 193 n.35
Shapiro, Maurice, 227 n.97
Shepard, Odell, 203 n.54, 244 n.131
Shepherd of Hermas, Vis. 38.1-7: 186; *Sim.* 9.15.1-3: 186 n.21
Sheppard, J. T., 30-31 n.13
Silius Italicus, *Punica* 15.18ff: 186 n.21; 15.28ff: 84 n.152; 15.96ff: 191 n.31; 15.274-285: 84; 17.20-47: 53 n.64
Skemp, J. B., 107 n.40
Sobrietas (sobriety), 189-190
Socrates, as type of sophrosyne, 38-39
Solinus, 196; 241 n.122
Solmsen, Friedrich, 57 n.79, 93 n.6, 138 n.4
Solon, 6.3: 110; as model of sophrosyne, 45, 97, 123
Somme le roi, 197, 215-216
Sophia (wisdom, competence), 87, 178 n.3
Sophocles, 32, 63 and n.96, 68 n.114, 75
—*Ajax*, 75-76; 132: 40; 293: 110-111; 670-677: 26
—*Niobe*, 32
—*Oedipus at Colonus*, 75 n.131
—*Oedipus Tyrannus* 161: 67; 583ff: 149
—*Philoctetes* 1259-1260: 40, 76
—*Thamyris*, 32
—Fragments, 61: 111 n.45; 622: 99 n.23, 152 n.35; 718: 207; 762: 179 n.5
Sôphronistêrion (House of Correction), 108-109, 115
Sôphronistês (castigator, prudent counselor), 29, 46, 59, 62, 68, 72, 114-122, 167
Sôphronizein tous allous (to instill sophrosyne in others), 32, 128, 163, 167

Sophrosyne, exemplars of: divine, 57–73; human, 33–54, 74–86, 238–241; animal, 241–250

Sophrosyne, Latin equivalents of, 183–186, 199 and n.46

Sôtêria (safety), 168 and n.62

Speculum Virginum, 208–210, *and see* Plate V

Spenser, Edmund, *Faerie Queene* 1.4: 242 n.125; 1.4.21: 191 n.33; 2.1.51–56; 2.12.30–87; 2.12.32: 79; 5.9.30: 217 n.85; 5.9.31: 79

Spoudaios (serious), 102

Stanford, W. B., 74 nn.127, 128, 129

Statius, *Thebais* 4.222: 40 n.36, 176

Stechow, Wolfgang, 52 n.61, 184 n.14

Stern, Jacob, 36 n.25

Stettiner, Richard, 188 n.26

Stoics, theory of virtue, 111

Strabo, 8.5.5: 94 n.10; 9.3.11: 64 n.98

Stromberg, Rheinhold, 33 n.18

Strong, Roy C., 53 n.66

de Surigny, A., 223 n.91

Susanna, 48, 187 n.24

Susarion, 51

Süss, Wilhelm, 136 n.1

Swarzenski, G., 212 n.69

Swinburne, Algernon, 190 n.30

Symeonides, Sibilla, 225 n.94

Synesius, *Ep.* 58, 72, 90: 121 n.71; *Ep.* 105: 121 n.70; *On Kingship* 2: 121

Synkrisis (rhetorical comparison) 45, 51, 165

Syssition (common mess), 94–95, 124

Tandoi, V., 125 n.78

Teiresias, 68, 73

Telemachus, 47, 74

Temperantia, emblems of: bridle, 199–200, 217, 236, 254; clock, 231–236; compass, 222–223; hourglass, 226; mingling of water and wine, 201, 229, 231, 236; quenching of flame, 201, 257, 262; sheathed sword, 205, 218; sickle, 223; sieve, 253; spectacles, 231; spurs, 231; windmill, 231

Tertullian, *De Spectaculis* 29.5: 186, 191 n.31; *De Virginibus Velandis*: 254

de Tervarent, Guy, 202 n.51, 223 n.91, 245 n.135, 248 n.139, 255 n.147, 258 nn.149, 150

Theagenes of Rhegium, 68 n.114

Theodectes, 155, 169

Theodulf of Orleans, *De Septem*

Liberalibus Artibus, 177, 199–200 and n.47, 202

Theognis, 177; 39–42: 92; 377–380: 60, 92; 704, 713: 38 n.31; 1081–1084: 92 n.5; 1135–1142: 93 n.6; 1325–1326: 47

Theological (Pauline) virtues, combined with cardinal virtues, 205–207, 214–217, 220–223, 225, 228, 237, 242

Theophrastus, 42, 154

Theseus, 28–29, 44–45

Thomas Aquinas, St., 215; *De Sacramentis*, 217; *Summa Theologiae*, 265; 2.2.161, 152, 3 *ad* 2: 223 n.91

Thompson, Stith, 33 n.18

Thomson, George, 98 n.21

Thornton, Agathe, 74 n.129

Thrasymachus, Frg. 1: 101 n.29

Thucydides, 1.78.1–4: 99 n.24; 1.80–86: 148 n.25; 1.84.1: 95; 2.60.5–6: 141; 2.60–64: 148 n.25; 2.65.8–9: 152; 2.65.9, 3.82.8: 100; 3.65.3: 115 n.57; 4.18.4: 99 n.24; 6.87.2: 95; 6.87.3: 95 n.15; 8.24.4–5: 103 n.36

Tietze-Conrat, E., 193 n.35

Tikkanen, J. J., 188 n.25

Titanomachy, 27

Tob. 2.11–14: 216 n.81

Toesca, Pietro, 229 n.101, 265

Tolnai, Karl, 236 n.114

Tomb sculpture employing virtues, 227–238

Torrentius, Jan Simonsz, 260 *and see* Plate XIII

Toynbee, Jocelyn M. C., 183 n.13, 184 n.14, 229 n.101

Treu, Max, 54 n.67

Tria genera causarum (three types of case), 138–139

Tria genera dicendi (three types of style), 145 n.20

Tristram, E. W., 191 n.33

Triumphal processions, Renaissance series, 249 n.141

Tronzo, William L., 204 n.57

Tuccia, 24, 53, 248 n.137

Tuve, Rosemond, I: 196 n.39; II: 189 n.29; 203 n.54; 207 n.64; 215 nn. 77, 79; 217 n.84; 232 n.110; 233 n.111; 241 n.123

Valentiner, W. R., 222 n.90, 230 nn. 103, 104, 105

Valeriano, Piero, *Hieroglyphica*, 250, 253 n.143, 254
Valerius Maximus, 2.7.1; 2.7.7; 2.7.12; 4.1.4; 4.1.6; 4.1.10; 4.3.1; 4.3.13, Ext. 1: 241 n.121; 6:52 n.60; 6.1.1; 6.1.2; 6.1 Ext. 3; 8.1.5: 53 n.65, 248 n.137, 253 n.144; 4.1.6: 82; 4.3.1: 81 n.143
Van Lohuizen-Mulder, Mab, 86 n.156
Van Marle, Raimond, I: 244 n.133, 245 n.135; II: 24 nn.1, 3, 70 n.117, 86 n.155, 187 n.24, 191 n.33, 193 nn.34, 35, 197 n.40, 214 n.74, 221 n.90, 226 n.94, 228 n.98, 239 n.118, 245 n.134, 248 n.138, 253 n.145
Venturi, Adolfo, 221 n.90
Venturi, Lionello, 241 n.121
Venus Cloacina, 53; Pudica, 221 and n.90; Verticordia, 23, 53 n.64, 248
Vesta (Hestia), 49, 221 n.90
Vian, Francis, 28 n.5, 69 n.116, 72 n.122
Vincent of Beauvais, *Speculum Morale*, 214-215
Virgil, *Aeneid* 1:71, 227; 1.57: 217 n.85, 227 n.96; 1.46, 150, 153, 296: 227 n.96; 1.149: 227; 4.130-168: 66 n.108; 6.853: 240 n.19; 7.789ff: 181 n.9; 7.803-817, 11.581-584: 52 n.59; 11.493-497: 242 n.124
Vlastos, Gregory, 98 n.21
von Schlosser, Julius, 238 n.118, 265
Vostre, Simon, *Heures*, 239, 266

Waites, M. C., 55 n.72, 179 n.4
Wallace, M. B., 96 n.18
Wallach, Luitpold, 198 n.45, 200 n.48, 225 n.93
Watson, Arthur, 208 n.65
Webster, T. B. L., 30 n.11, 34 n.21, 149 n.27, 150 n.28
Weigirt, Hans, 196 n.37

Weinberg, Gladys D. and Saul, 29 n.9
Weitzman, Kurt, 36 n.27, 182 n.11
Wellmann, Max, 241 n.122
Wenzel, Siegfried, 203 n.53
West, M. L., 92 n.4
Wethey, Harold E., 236 n.113
Whinney, Margaret, 237 n.115
White, Jr., Lynn, 222 n.91, 226 n.95, 233 n.111, 234 n.112, 236 n.113, 263 n.159
Wilkinson, C. K., 187 n.24
Willcock, M. M., 30 n.10
Williams, Gordon, 54 n.69
Wind, Edgar, 62 n.93, 65 n.101, 70 n.119, 84 n.153, 222 n.90
Winternitz, Emanuel, 65 n.101
Wittkower, Rudolf, 70 n.118, 222 n.90
Wolff, Erwin, 105 n.38, 118 n.64
Woodbury, Leonard, 62 n.91
Woodruff, Helen, 188 n.26, 244 n.132

Xenophanes, 58-59
Xenophon
—*Apology*, 105
—*Cynegeticus* 1.1-16: 38 n.34; 1.11: 36 n.27
—*Cyropaedia* 1.2.8: 110; 1.2.9: 109; 6.1.47: 81 n.145
—*Memorabilia* 1.3.7: 76; 1.6.1-6: 76 n.133
—*Oeconomicus* 7-8: 99 n.25

Yates, Frances A., 53 n.66, 203 n.53, 248 n.139
Yohannan, John D., 33 n.18
Young, David C., 118 n.65

Zeus, 57-61
Zielinski, Th., 249 n.141
Zuntz, Gunther, 143 n.12

Library of Congress Cataloging in Publication Data

North, Helen
    From myth to icon.
    (Cornell studies in classical philology; v. 40)
    Includes index.
    1. Temperance (Virtue) in art.   2. Arts, Greek.   3. Mythology,
Greek.   4. Temperance (Virtue) in literature.   I. Title.   II. Series: Cornell
University. Cornell studies in classical philology; v. 40.
NX650.T45N67   700'.938   79-9205
ISBN 0-8014-1135-1